The Schocken

GUIDE to

JEWISH

BOOKS

The Schocken
GUIDE to
JEWISH
BOOKS

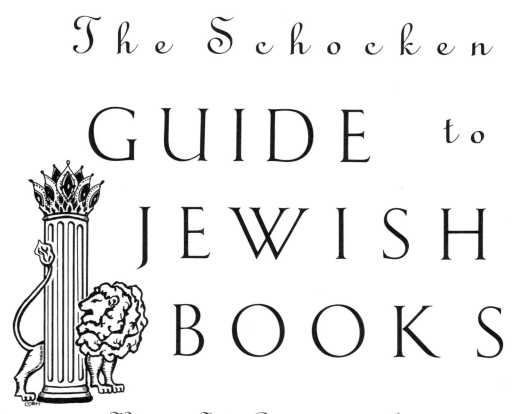

*Where to Start Reading about Jewish
History, Literature, Culture, and Religion*

EDITED BY

BARRY W. HOLTZ

Schocken Books, New York

Library of Congress Cataloging-in-Publication Data
The Schocken Guide to Jewish Books: where to start reading
about Jewish history, literature, culture, and religion
/ edited by Barry W. Holtz.
p.   cm.
Includes index.
1. Jews—Bibliography.   2. Judaism—Bibliography.
3. Jewish literature—Bibliography.   I. Holtz, Barry W.
Z6366.R4 1992
[DS102.95]
016.909′04924—dc20   91-17760

ISBN 0-8052-4108-6
Illustrations copyright © 1992 by Betsy Platkin Teutsch
Manufactured in the United States of America
First Edition

This book is dedicated to the memory of

Baruch Bokser and Wolfe Kelman, two great teachers

who knew Jewish books and loved them

CONTENTS

Acknowledgments

What to read? It is a question that can be asked about many subjects, but certainly the enormous wealth of material dealing with different aspects of Jewish life and culture can be particularly overwhelming for a reader. This book began with an idea: how can people be helped to find their way through the ever-widening maze of Jewish books? How can we devise an approach for discovering appropriate books in the many different areas encompassed by Jewish thought, history, religion, and experience? These questions were first posed to me by André Schiffrin during the time when he was at Pantheon Books. He suggested that I come up with a volume for Schocken Books which would try to deal with these issues and it is through his urging that I first got involved with this project.

It was my particular good fortune that I got to work on this book with an insightful and creative editor at Schocken Books, Bonny Fetterman. She has been my collaborator at every stage of the project: she believed in it, she helped map out its plan, and she worked alongside me in thinking about each chapter in both its formative and final versions. Working together with her in such a collegial fashion has been one of the high points of doing this book.

Two friends helped me think about the concept of the book in its earliest stage and later joined as contributors. My thanks to Alan Mintz and Michael Paley for their counsel and assistance. My friend Nessa Rapoport also helped me think through the original concept. I appreciate her continuing good advice. In similar fashion I was encouraged also by the support of my agent, Pam Bernstein.

Thanks also to Alice Jaffe who helped me track down illustrations for the book. She and I both appreciate the advice and practical suggestions from Sharon Liberman Mintz at the Library of the Jewish Theological Seminary of America.

My colleagues at the Melton Research Center—in particular Edy Rauch, the center's other codirector—offered support, good spirit, and assistance. Pauline Rotmil and Robin Aronson assisted greatly with their administrative support.

It is thanks to the dedication and serious thought that the sixteen other writers gave to this project that this book was able to come to fruition. I appreciate the way that the contributors enthusiastically joined in and took time from their many other activities to participate in this book.

As usual many thanks to my wife, Bethamie Horowitz, for her help, encouragement, and understanding. My daughter, Sophia, was born right around the time that I agreed to do this project. Although right now she doesn't quite get what this is all about, I hope someday that she too will come to love Jewish books.

Finally, I thought it appropriate to dedicate this book to the memory of two friends, both rabbis, both eclectic and wide-ranging intellects, both lovers of Jewish books of all sorts, who died the summer this volume was written.

The Schocken

GUIDE to

JEWISH

BOOKS

INTRODUCTION

Barry W. Holtz

A few years back I was invited to contribute an article to a magazine on the subject of a "lifetime reading plan" for Jewish books. Soon after agreeing, I began to think twice about the assignment. That innocuous little phrase, "lifetime reading plan," suddenly seemed to echo with questions. In what sense was Jewish "reading" reading at all? Was there such a thing as a reading "plan" in the Jewish tradition? And how does reading fit into the "lifetime" of the individual Jew? These are not simple matters and the more I thought about them the more complicated they became.

Take "plan" to begin with. Let us suppose that I have decided to master a particular field, any field. For my own curiosity, I want to learn everything I can possibly learn about, say, computers. I can begin to map out a course of learning for myself. I can consult some basic popular books about computers and begin to get a sense of the dimensions of the field; I can follow those simple books to more complex investigations; I can use the bibliographies that I find in some books to build other bibliographies. I will soon get an idea about the aspects of computers

A Yemenite child in Israel learns to read Torah from his grandfather. (Photograph by Zion M. Ozeri)

that interest me and those that do not—I might want to learn about programming, but not about microchips, about modems, but not disk drives. And with intelligence and diligence I will get as far as my abilities will take me. I create a plan, probably not a lifetime plan, but who knows? I can spend as long on it as I like.

Is this what we mean by a lifetime reading plan in Judaism? Is it mastery? Is it "covering material," as teachers like to say? A reading plan, as I have implied, suggests an important notion: you read one thing, master it, finish it, and then you move on to the next thing. This is not a surprising idea. Most of Western education follows the same approach. But how much does this resemble traditional Jewish ideas about these matters?

Think for a moment: In Judaism we read our key book and then we read it again. And again. The weekly cycle of Torah readings *is* a lifetime reading plan—but it is one text that is endlessly repeated. When the talmudic rabbis say of Torah "turn it and turn it again for everything is contained in it," they are asserting their own version of a lifetime reading plan. Indeed, the daily prayers of the traditional liturgy also include large sections of "study" material in the midst of the morning prayers. This, too, is repeated every day.

Of course there is mastery in the traditional Jewish consciousness as well. We admire the learned sage, the *talmid hakham,* who has "been through" the entire Talmud, and the great scholar possesses a mastery not just of the Torah itself, but of a wide range of different commentaries on the Torah. But in traditional Jewish culture both the competence of the master and the structured routine of Torah study that all Jews participate in can hardly be called part of a "plan," at least in the way that we use the phrase.

Note also that I have been using the word "reading" and that too raises difficulties. In traditional Jewish vocabulary we usually speak about "learning" (*lernen* in Yiddish) or "studying" the classic Jewish works, not reading. Reading suggests a solitary activity—perhaps the model is the quiet contemplation of the monastery—certainly not the frenetic din of the yeshivah's study hall. There learning is a public activity, almost a ritualized event. As scholars have long pointed out, for Judaism, study is a kind of devotional activity which is a communal rite. How does that jibe with our Western notion of the solitary reader? Jewish study seems to work better as group activity. So perhaps we should be considering a lifetime "study" plan, an endeavor of a community.

One way to get around this difficulty of reading versus study (or individual versus group) is to point out that up to now I have been talking about the reading or studying of traditional Jewish texts like Torah and Talmud. What about considering instead those books of history, biography, literature, and scholarship, mainly of this century, that would fit more conventionally with the notion of reading a book? These works often can serve to illuminate the texts of the Jewish past and yet are considerably more accessible than the texts themselves. In this context think, for example, of reading Gershom Scholem's writings about Jewish mysticism in contrast to the difficult kabbalistic texts themselves.

But we should not let ourselves off the hook too easily. For even reading books of this more conventional "modern" sort can be intimidating. First, because one of the most difficult experiences for an adult learner to face, in any endeavor, is the sense of incompetence that comes with learning something new. True, there is something exciting about that which is novel, but that feeling can easily be offset by the frustrations, perhaps even the shame, involved in being ignorant. I use "shame" quite deliberately. For many adult Jewish readers there are old negative stereotypes to overcome—bad childhood experiences in Hebrew School perhaps. But, more importantly, there is also the shame of admitting that one does not know what others may assume one knows.

How do people who are used to being successful in their regular lives—in demanding professions perhaps—deal with not knowing the rudiments of Jewish history and culture? Experts in adult education refer to this issue as the question of "empowering" the learner. That is, the student must feel that he or she is more than the passive recipient of knowledge imparted from above.

But empowerment is not the only issue that must be confronted. A lifetime of Jewish learning involves something else as well. The beginning student is often overwhelmed by the sheer immensity of the library of Jewish reading.

"Of making many books there is no end." So we read in the Bible. That these words are found in Ecclesiastes, a biblical book filled with cynicism and despair, offers us little comfort. For at one time or another who has not felt that overwhelming sense of inadequacy when confronted with a bookstore's stacks and shelves? Who has not felt a bit like a sailor venturing into uncharted seas?

For the reader of Jewish books navigating these waters may be even more daunting. Excepting an Elie Wiesel here or an I. B. Singer there, the names of authors are likely to be less familiar, the subjects more obscure, and the selection even narrower. What help can someone looking to learn about Judaism, Jewish history, or Jewish culture seek out?

The purpose of this book is to help answer that question. Our hope is to offer the general reader a way to find his or her path through the maze of Jewish books that we might find in a bookstore or library. For anyone who has ever taken an adult education course, listened to a lecture at the local synagogue or community center, or whose curiosity has been piqued by an article about an area of Jewish knowledge, this guide will offer direction for further reading.

The mission of this book is to take a wide-ranging view of many different subject matters and to provide a kind of "talking bibliography" for each area. By "talking bibliography" I mean that rather than being presented with a list of books in the subject area, readers should hear the voice of an expert in the field at hand guiding them through that subject.

Picture the following: You have just heard a lecture by an expert in some area of Jewish culture at a local college, Jewish community center, synagogue. After-

The Hebrew writer
S. Y. Agnon in his library
(Schocken Books)

wards, you've managed to corner the speaker in the library and you ask, "What should I read to learn more about your topic? I'd like to spend some time reading about the Holocaust or the Jews in the Middle Ages or the Talmud" or whatever the lecturer's topic was. And there, with the library around you, the expert offers you a kind of guided tour through the available books in the field.

The various experts who have written the chapters in this book have tried to do that task. Their assignment was not only to list the books in their field and describe them, but to write their recommendations in the form of an essay which would give a sense of context for each book and in some cases a sequential order to the books suggested. These essays, then, try to outline what are the big issues in each field and what are the questions that the books in the field try to explore.

The chapters in this book assume that the reader is *not* another scholar or a student in a graduate seminar, but is a serious adult who, without reading specialized studies of an academic sort, wishes to further his or her knowledge in the field. The experts were asked to construct a course of study for that kind of audience. Thus in the chapters of this book we are not looking to footnote every scholarly debate. The technical points of scholarship are not the point here, unless they are meaningful to the general reader. What matters is the big picture and the books and issues that such a general reader might find of interest.

This book begins with a chapter entitled "Ports of Entry." Here the author tries to address those books which, in his view, offer the best introduction to various aspects of Jewish life and experience, particularly those dimensions that are religious at heart: study, celebration, spirituality, and theology. From there the volume turns to books about the Bible and its world and, proceeding more or less chronologically, subsequent chapters look in detail at books about the world of the Talmud, the Jews in the Middle Ages, the experience of modernity in Europe, Jewish life in America from colonial times to the present, the Holocaust, and books about Zionism and Israel.

From there, we devote chapters to specific themes or areas of interest. The story of Jewish mysticism from its origins to the twentieth century is covered in one chapter. A chapter on Jewish philosophy looks at the key questions that motivated the thinkers and theologians of the past and the present. A chapter on Jewish women's studies maps out this new and emerging field.

Three chapters on literature follow. The first is devoted to Hebrew literary works available in English translation; the second looks at Yiddish literature translated into English; the third traces the remarkable story of Jewish fiction in America.

The concluding chapter of this book offers suggestions about books appropriate for young adults. What books would make a good *bar* or *bat mitzvah* present? What, this chapter explores, are the books that we'd like young people to have as they start a Jewish library?

Please note that in general we have tried to focus on books that are currently in print, but, sad to say, books nowadays go out of print quickly and some real classics or key books are no longer available. The writers of the chapters have taken as a rule of thumb that books currently not in print which are mentioned in the essays are limited to those likely to be found in a good public library. Some of these titles have been reprinted many times. We have tried to cite the most recent edition of the works mentioned, preferably in paperback.

In his *Shirat Yisrael*, Moses Ibn Ezra, the great twelfth-century Spanish poet, had the following thing to say about the reading of Jewish books: "A wise teacher and skilled instructor should be more dear to you than books. Turn to the books only if you can find no teacher." Even today, in an age of rapid communication and numerous publications, these words may have something to say to us. No book can replace the human communication we find in conversations with a good teacher, but by placing within the pages of this volume the advice and good counsel of a number of attentive teachers we hope we can begin to open up pathways for a lifetime of reading.

PORTS OF ENTRY: INTRODUCTORY JEWISH BOOKS

Lawrence Square Kushner

Many beginning students of Judaism are deterred by the mistaken notion that there is some kind of official or even logical curriculum they should follow. This is simply not the case. Unlike perhaps any other discipline, there is no one proper place to begin. The elements in the network of Jewish literacy are so intricately and interdependently connected to one another, and, even more important, require such personal involvement, that there are as many paths as there are students.

It is said that just as there were 600,000 Jews who received the Torah at Sinai, there must be 600,000 Torahs, 600,000 paths leading to God, unique to each individual. But do not be disappointed or frustrated with the apparent direction of your path, for sooner or later, each one leads to every other one and each one requires that you know every other in order to properly understand it. A great Hebrew novelist and a student who has just learned the letter *aleph* are the same; a great scholar of Talmud and a student who has just read that "In the beginning God created the heavens and the earth," are the same; a virtuoso of performing commandments and one who has just decided to light *Shabbos* candles are the same; they are all travelers on the way without end.

To make matters more confusing, Judaism is a literary tradition. This is to say that its commencement and subsequent expression have taken predominantly literary forms. Judaism commences with God giving the Jews a book and saying something like, take this home and read it. It is hardly surprising therefore that with a book for a central symbol, we Jews have produced such a disproportionately large number of them.

Furthermore, because Judaism is a spiritual tradition—that is, a tradition designed to help people discover who they are and what they should do about it—much of Judaism cannot be mastered dispassionately or objectively the way one might learn "about" French civilization, American literature, or Japanese gardens. Ultimately, Judaism must be lived personally. Reading about dwelling in a *sukkah* can never be a substitute for dwelling in one, learning about *Shabbos* can never be a substitute for making one.

The same is true for the very act of study itself. In Judaism, you can study a holy text or you can "fulfill the commandment" to study a holy text, that is, to commence your reading with a blessing and read the words of the text as if they originated from God and were addressed to you personally! In Judaism, study itself can be an act of prayer.

One final introductory point: there is no fixed path, no step-by-step curriculum for learning, or entering Judaism. You can begin anywhere and move in any direction you like. And, no matter where you begin, you will discover there is something you should have learned first. Ultimately, you may even wind up back at the Bible stories you learned in the third grade and discover they are more profound than you had ever thought.

Torah

As I mentioned above, the touchstone, not only of Jewish literacy but of Judaism as well, is God's revelation to humanity. More than a book or even a book of ultimate wisdom, the Torah (or Five Books of Moses, or Pentateuch, or Humash) is the blueprint for creation, the DNA of being itself. In one way or another, every Jewish book is only a commentary on the Torah. In a revealed religion there can be no novelty for everything is already known. Creativity must therefore masquerade as commentary.

Now there are two ways to open the Torah and, depending on your answer to the following question, you should consider either beginning or ending your search with it. If you are convinced that the Torah has nothing more to do with God (Who or Whatever that is) than any other great book, then wait a while before reading it. If, on the other hand, you are prepared to consider the preposterous and mysterious possibility that the Holy One of Being can somehow "get through" to people and that the Torah just may be a memento of a time when that happened, then the Torah is already a potentially holy text for you. And you should probably begin your learning there.

The best way to read Torah is with a *Hevra*, a small group which meets weekly specially for this purpose—usually on the Sabbath. Most synagogues have one. The program of reading usually follows the weekly lection, or *Parashat Ha-Shavuah*, according to which the Five Books are divided into fifty-four portions. Through an ancient (and complicated) system, portions are arranged so that on

A woman cantor leads the Sabbath morning service. (Photograph by Lori Grinker/Contact Press Images)

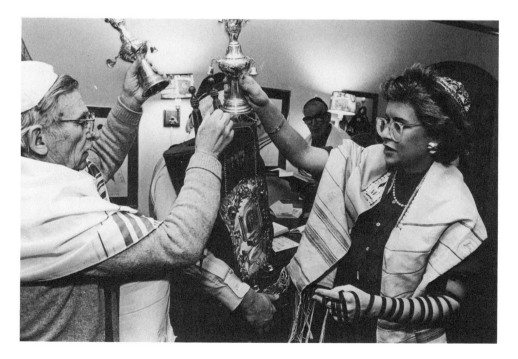

each non-holiday Sabbath a section is read. Each Sabbath is in turn named after the portion read on it and a vast amount of traditional religious writing assumes that the reader is studying the Torah, weekly portion by weekly portion. Often participants are encouraged to read the half dozen or so biblical chapters of the weekly *parasha* in advance of each Sabbath's discussion. Each section has its own classic themes and unresolvable arguments with an annual rhythm all their own. If you will, they constitute the "root directory" for traditional Jewish learning.

Obviously, the best way to read the Torah is in Hebrew. For most beginners, English is the only option. There are two translations available. One was commissioned by the Jewish Publication Society in 1917 and reads like the Jewish equivalent of the King James Version. It is biblical and even holy sounding but for sustained reading it is also cumbersome and opaque. In 1962 the Jewish Publication Society (JPS) commissioned a new translation which has received universal acclaim and is the best option for the serious reader.

The New JPS Translation is available simply as The Torah [1962], the first five books of the Hebrew Bible or, TANAKH: A New Translation of the Holy Scriptures According to the Traditional Hebrew Text published subsequently by JPS in 1985. In 1981, the Union of American Hebrew Congregations (Reform movement) offered *The Torah: A Modern Commentary* (1981) which, in addition to the new JPS translation, features the vocalized Hebrew text, copious commentaries by Rabbis Bernard Bamberger and W. Gunther Plaut, and gleanings from a wide range of classical and secular sources. It is available in both English opening (left to right) and Hebrew (right to left) formats and provides the beginning and intermediate student with the promise of many years of challenging study. My chief complaint is that it replaces the centuries-old weekly Torah portion divisions with ones that its editors apparently find more appropriate and then introduces each "new" section with an introductory page—set in larger type than the text of the Torah itself. Despite this hubris, the "Plaut commentary" as it is widely known, is a work of exceptional erudition and elegance and properly the first book in any Jewish library.

Companions to Torah Study

For more traditional companions to the weekly Torah reading cycle, consider the classic works of Jacobson and Leibowitz. Originally written in Hebrew, these take a theme or themes traditionally associated with each *parasha* and develop them through the lenses of classical sources. B. S. Jacobson's *Meditations on the Torah: Topical Discourses on the Weekly Portions in the Light of the Commentaries* (Tel Aviv: Sinai Publishing, 1969) is an anthology of fifty-four essays touching on a wide array of the themes of Jewish thought, each one refracted through classical rabbinic sources.

Almost thirty years ago, the World Zionist Organization commissioned Professor Nehamah Leibowitz to write a series of articles, each treating one theme of each weekly *parasha*. These short essays were mailed out to the membership of the World Zionist Organization and quickly became the stuff of millions of sermons. They were so popular that Leibowitz was invited to keep writing them for several years. Happily, they have been collected, translated, and published in six volumes (the Book of Exodus takes two) as *Studies in the Weekly Parasha* (Jerusalem: World Zionist Organization, 1962–80). For any student seeking an entrance into traditional Jewish modes of understanding the Torah text, Leibowitz is indispensable. Indeed, simply reading the titles of each chapter's theme provides a bird's-eye view of traditional Torah thought.

Bible

More contemporary approaches to the Torah text obviously abound. The biblical scholarship of Martin Buber combines the master's spiritual power and religious reverence with critical scholarship. Perhaps the best example is *Moses: The Revelation and the Covenant* (Atlantic Highlands, N.J.: Humanities Press International, 1988), in which Buber attempts to reconstruct the biblical reality without compromising historical accuracy. We are offered what remains one of the most compelling explanations of what really happened during the going out from Egypt (see especially chapters "The Burning Bush," "Moses and Pharaoh," and "The Wonder at the Sea") in a way which does not injure the sanctity of the sacred text. I know of many families who read selections at their Passover *seders*.

The great mystic and social activist, Abraham Joshua Heschel's *The Prophets*, 2 vols. (Harper & Row, 1969 and 1971), attempts to similarly understand an experience—unique to classical Hebrew civilization—wherein human beings "feel" for God. We often speak of God as being anthropomorphic but rarely, reminds Heschel, do we consider the Holy One to be anthropopathic. Like Buber's Moses, we frequently encounter doses of easy and even exciting theology and are rewarded with a modern way of feeling reverence for the Bible without compromising our contemporary intellectual integrity.

Almost seventy-five years ago, a Danish, Christian Bible scholar, Johannes Pedersen, set out to reconstruct biblical culture. The result was a four-volume (usually published in two large ones) set, *Israel: Its Life and Culture* (Oxford University Press, 1926). And, while four-volume works are not usually recommended to beginners, this one reads with such insight and ease that it is easily within the reach of any novice. Furthermore, it is as much about the religious life of Jews as it is about the Bible. One example, Pedersen notices that there is a lot of blessing going on in the Bible and attempts to figure out what it means. "The act of blessing another, *berekh*," observes Pedersen, "means to communicate to him strength of soul, but one can communicate to him only of the strength one has in oneself. He who blesses another gives him something of his own soul. . . . By means of the word something is laid into the soul of the other, but behind the word stands the soul which created it."

For those wishing more dispassionate companions to the first books of the Bible, the volumes by Nahum Sarna, *Understanding Genesis* (Schocken Books, 1970) and *Exploring Exodus* (Schocken Books, 1986), are excellent. Sarna takes the main problems raised by the text and explains them in the light of contemporary scholarship. Sometimes we are disappointed that what we thought was an extraordinary religious idea, in the light of comparative anthropological research is not only not unique, but probably misunderstood as well. Other times we are astonished to understand the Bible in its real historical context. My chief frustration as a spiritual teacher with these fine books is that they often answer more questions than they ask.

Barry Holtz's excellent anthology, *Back to the Sources: Reading the Classic Jewish Texts* (Summit Books, 1986) continues to provide the beginning student with a superb collection of essays walking the reader back into the classical Jewish books. Holtz has invited some of the most thoughtful and respected young teachers of our generation to introduce Judaism's great books and provide the reader with a program for how to open them.

Finally, Stephen Mitchell's introduction to and translation of *The Book of Job* (North Point Press, 1987) may provide encouragement and even comfort to those who remain convinced that Job must have some great teaching and solace for them but cannot figure out what it is. (Do not confuse this with Doubleday's earlier edition of Mitchell's translation, *Into the Whirlwind* (1979), which unfortunately lacks his extraordinary introduction.) Mitchell is obviously fluent also in Eastern religious thought and brings this to his work. The result is high poetry; the mystery and awe of the sacred text are made alive again.

Spiritual Awareness

It could be a life crisis, a worship service, or a walk on the seashore, but sooner or later, most people are touched spiritually. They come to this rabbi and ask in 600,000 different ways, "What does Judaism have to say about such moments?" While they often do not realize it, they are asking about the intersection of core religious tradition and the innermost essence of their selves. One little anthology, for several decades now, remains the volume of choice: Martin Buber's *Hasidism and Modern Man* (Atlantic Highlands, N.J.: Humanities Press International, 1988). Properly criticized by scholars of Hasidism as being more Buber than Hasidism, and more poetry than history, this book evocatively touches on all the great themes of Jewish spirituality, from ecstasy to community, from integrity to the presence of God. Especially sections 2, "The Life of the Hasidim," and 4, "The Way of Man According to the Teaching of Hasidism," published independently as: *The Way of Man* (Secaucus, N.J.: Citadel Press, 1966), are accessible to serious students of all ages and backgrounds.

Equally enriching is Abraham Joshua Heschel's classic essay, *The Sabbath: Its Meaning for Modern Man* (Farrar, Straus and Giroux, 1975). Heschel claims to teach about the observance and sanctity of the seventh day but instead describes the principal dichotomy between sacred and secular. In the introduction, he writes: "There is a realm of time where the goal is not to have but to be, not to own but to give, not to control but to share, not to subdue but to be in accord." *The Jewish Sabbath: A Renewed Encounter* (Schocken Books, 1991) by Heschel's student, Pinchas H. Peli, is an inspiring appreciation of the spiritual dimensions of the Sabbath.

The teachings of Rabbi Nahman of Bratslav, the eighteenth-century Hasidic master, have yet to find a contemporary equal. Nahman, a brilliant and creative genius, was in all probability afflicted with bouts of severe depression. His followers continue to release little rearrangements of his writings under various titles.

His *Restore My Soul, Meshivat Nefesh,* translated by Avraham Greenbaum (Jerusalem: Breslov Research Institute, 1980), remains a treasury of insight and comfort.

Martin Buber's two-volume collection, *Tales of the Hasidim,* now available in one volume (Schocken Books, 1991), remains a classic. Buber retells the stories often in an almost Zen-like manner and lays open before us one of the last great flowerings of the Jewish spiritual impulse.

For those who want to start at the very beginning, I offer my own: *The Book of Miracles: A Young Person's Guide to Jewish Spiritual Awareness* (Union of American Hebrew Congregations, 1987), written for children and parents to read to one another; and *The Book of Letters: A Mystical Hebrew Alef-Bait* (Woodstock, Vt.: Jewish Lights Publishing, 1990), a spiritual, meditative guide to the letters of the Hebrew alphabet. Finally, I would like to recommend my book, *God Was in This Place and I, i Did Not Know: Finding My Self, Spirituality, and Ultimate Meaning* (So. Woodstock, Vt.: Jewish Lights, 1991). In it, I imagine seven conversations Jacob had with classical Jewish teachers who tried to instruct him about the meaning of his dream and the search for ultimate meaning.

Prayer

Somewhere between personal spiritual search, poetry, and prayer is Arthur Green and Barry Holtz's wonderful little anthology of translations, *Your Word Is Fire: The Hasidic Masters on Contemplative Prayer* (Schocken Books, 1987). The editors assemble and arrange the teachings of key hasidic *rebbes* on prayer and, in so doing, offer us not only a perceptive insight into the classical hasidic soul, but also implicitly recommend a model for our own prayer life. Abraham Joshua Heschel's slender book on the meaning of Jewish prayer, *Quest for God* (formerly, before feminism, *Man's* Quest for God) (Crossroad, 1982), beautifully blends theology with inspiration.

Much more academic, but also rewarding, is Louis Jacobs's *Hasidic Prayer* (Schocken Books, 1973). Replete with primary source quotations, Jacobs systematically examines the style and uniqueness of communal and personal hasidic liturgy. Likewise, B. S. Jacobson's *Meditations on the Siddur: Studies in the Essential Problems and Ideas of Jewish Worship* (Tel Aviv: Sinai Publishing, 1966) is an excellent collection of challenging essays on the major elements of Jewish prayer from a traditional perspective. Also, Max Arzt's *Justice and Mercy: Commentary on the Liturgy of the New Year and the Day of Atonement* (Holt, Rinehart & Winston, 1963) is an instructive, albeit occasionally too thorough, companion to the traditional high holyday liturgy. For those seeking a genuflection-by-genuflection guide to orthodox prayer, Hayim Halevy Donin's *To Pray As a Jew* (Basic Books, 1980) is very helpful. Aryeh Kaplan's *Jewish Meditation* (Schocken Books, 1985) offers a sensitive blend of traditional form with contemporary eclectic spiritual practices.

The choice of a prayer book is obviously a very personal business, yet no beginning shelf of Jewish books could be complete without one. I am not speaking here about prayer books (or, *siddurim*) which you will find in synagogue prayer halls and which have been designed primarily for congregational worship. I am speaking instead about personal prayer books—ones you keep at home, consult before festive meals, take with you on trips, or use as a script for your morning meditations. The most complete Hebrew-English prayer book, without cumbersome commentary, yet sadly burdened with an archaic, sexist translation, is Philip Birnbaum's *Daily Prayer Book: Ha-Siddur Ha-Shalem* (Hebrew Publishing Co., 1977) available both in hard and soft cover, regular and small (4 × 6 inches!) format.

The new Reconstructionist prayer book, *Kol Haneshamah: Shabbat Eve* (Reconstructionist Press, 1989), has so much new commentary, innovative graphics, and so many new prayers that it transcends its narrower movement parentage and enters the category of personal prayer book. The poetry and meditations are fresh and moving, the insights and layout are engaging and challenging. *Kol Haneshamah* unlocks doors we did not know were even there.

With thousands of years and hundreds of cultures' worth of data, we can safely conclude that the more Hebrew a Jew knows, the more he or she will prefer to pray in Hebrew. This is not to say, of course, that God doesn't understand all languages but rather that the idiom, sound, and even the graphics of Hebrew seem to work best for Jewish prayer. Or, to put it another way, if you know Hebrew—even just a little bit, you'll pray in Hebrew. For those just making their way into Hebrew literacy, *The Complete Metsudah Siddur*, edited by Avrohom Davis (New York: Metsudah Publications, 1990), provides a Hebrew-English line-by-line translation in parallel columns.

Religious Thought

For a systematic, bird's-eye view of Jewish religious thought, Jacob Neusner's *The Way of Torah: An Introduction to Judaism* (Belmont, Calif.: Wadsworth Publishing, 1988) is very accessible. Written as "the Jewish volume" in a series of texts for a college-level world religion course, the book concisely introduces all of Judaism's major themes. Neusner is one of this country's most prolific and controversial academics and consistently presents the old material in creative ways. For this reason, even students who have a solid Jewish background will be challenged to rearrange many of their ideas.

More technical, but in no way representative of theology's otherwise well-deserved reputation for boredom and opacity, Abraham Heschel's *God in Search of Man: A Philosophy of Judaism* (Farrar, Straus and Giroux, 1976), remains the most elegant Jewish theology available. Heschel was not only a brilliant theologian but a gifted wordsmith as well. His ideas come in two or three paragraph-long blocks which are set off by subtitles. These, in turn, are bundled into dozens of short chapters, each followed with extensive scholarly apparatus for the more academically inclined. All of this results in a volume able to be opened and read at random on almost any page. The theology itself is strong on God, religious experience, history, and Torah, but weak on Israel. Skip the first few chapters; they do read like theology.

Neil Gillman's recently published *Sacred Fragments: Recovering Theology for the Modern Jew* (Jewish Publication Society, 1990) is the result of teaching Jewish theology to Conservative rabbinic students. As the title suggests, it makes theology accessible again. Without oversimplification or the density that has given theology a bad name, the author neatly arrays all the basic "moves" and leaves us with a post-theist, post-humanist Jewish theology. Gershom Scholem, the master historian of Jewish mysticism's collection of essays *On the Kabbalah and Its Symbolism* (Schocken Books, 1969) captures much of the great scholar's intellectual creativity. The second essay, "The Meaning of the Torah in Jewish Mysticism," is an exciting doorway into Judaism's other worlds.

The Israeli Talmud scholar and kabbalist Adin Steinsaltz has written a very easy introduction to mystical thought, *The Thirteen-Petaled Rose* (Basic Books,

1985). Steinsaltz is without question one of the generation's most respected religious writers. He has managed to maintain credibility within the academic, liberal, and orthodox communities. Many readers, including myself, simply cannot swallow much of the first chapter's discussion of angels and regret that it was chosen to commence the book. Just skip it and get on with Steinsaltz's easy and brief summary of Jewish mystical thinking. Novelist Herman Wouk's *This Is My God* (Touchstone, 1986), remains a coherent, Orthodox introduction to Judaism.

While certainly not in the same category with the work of Scholem and Steinsaltz, I still like my own introduction to mystical thinking, *Honey from the Rock: Visions of Jewish Mystical Renewal* (Woodstock, Vt.: Jewish Lights Publishing, 1990). It is an attempt to synthesize the worldview of the kabbalah with some of my own ordinary life experiences. It is not so much a kabbalistic primer or a personal diary but a model for helping the reader to imagine how kabbalah might inform his or her own ordinary life experiences. One can be, if not a kabbalist, then at least their legitimate and reverent heir; the ancient mysteries still instruct.

Holidays and Life Cycle: General Introductions

Almost forty years ago, anthropologists Mark Zborowski and Elizabeth Herzog realized that those little eastern European villages or *shtetls* that everyone's parents (it was forty years ago) seemed to come from nurtured a highly complex and vanishing culture. Like Eskimos or Polynesians, eastern European Jewish villagers also had their own unique patterns of behavior, institutions, and meaning systems. Employing the emerging tools of cultural anthropology, Zborowski and Herzog set about interviewing representatives of this culture. The result is *Life Is with People: The Culture of the Shtetl* (Schocken Books, 1962), the most comprehensive and paradigmatic presentation of *shtetl* culture produced. Because its authors are not peddling Judaism, the book is refreshingly unhomiletical. One person interviewed said, "If God lived in this *shtetl*, all His windows would be broken!" And, because the vast majority of American Jews trace their cultural ancestry back to eastern Europe, to learn what was the "Mama's job," or what did it mean to go "off to school," is to understand the cultural base of American Judaism.

If such a prospect feels too ambitious, or you are convinced that you must begin even before the beginning, then, from the plethora of competing excellent "introductions," two stand high. The first is a Harry Gersh's fourth grade text, *When a Jew Celebrates* (Behrman House, 1971). Gersh explains all the basic words in simple yet even poetic language. Such a book should not be limited to children. Another introduction, recently completed by Anita Diamant and Howard Cooper, is *Living a Jewish Life: Jewish Customs, Traditions, and Values for Today's Family* (HarperCollins, 1991). Cooper runs a big religious school, Diamant writes for the *Boston Globe;* they are "a perfect match" for this assignment. Just as its title promises, Cooper and Diamant provide a comprehensive primer for setting up a Jewish home.

Holidays

Under the general rubric of holidays and life cycle is a category of books that are meant to be consulted but not read from beginning to end. Because of the amount of detailed information they provide, the theological biases of their respective authors cannot be concealed. This is in no way a shortcoming, nor should it deter the more serious student with a differing religious bent from paying them careful attention. Indeed, not only is our tolerance for varieties of religious experience besides our own a precise barometer of our own spiritual security, it is also a prerequisite for genuine religious growth. So, if you're a Classical Reform Jew, read the Orthodox one and if you're a Torah Jew, read how the Reformers respond to the tradition.

Of the Jewish living reference books, Isaac Klein's *Guide to Jewish Religious Practice* (Jewish Theological Seminary/Ktav Publishing House, 1979) is the most accessible. Klein was a professor at the Jewish Theological Seminary, the Conservative rabbinical seminary, and this book seems to be an exhaustive presentation of his courses to rabbinic students on normative Jewish practice. While the text is presented in numbered paragraphs, the author embellishes the material with frequent citations from the Bible and Talmud which place each legal section in its larger literary context. Meticulous notes, bibliography, and index, together

On the first day of Rosh Hashanah, the Jewish New Year, Jews gather by a running stream for *tashlich*—the symbolic casting off of sins. (Photograph by Bill Aron)

with pertinent phrases in original Hebrew, make this guide a treasury for more sustained inquiry. Yet there is no reason why any serious student with little or no background cannot consult this book from the outset.

From the Reform movement come two excellent summaries of mainstream liberal Jewish practice: Peter Knobel's *Gates of the Seasons: A Guide to the Jewish Year* (New York: Central Conference of American Rabbis, 1983) and Simeon Maslin's *Gates of Mitzvah: A Guide to the Jewish Life Cycle* (New York: Central Conference of American Rabbis, 1979). Each book succinctly outlines what Jews do, why they do it, and offers transliterated guides to the appropriate blessings for each occasion. For the past several decades, the Reform movement has grown increasingly touchy about claims that it countenanced any behavior, or lack thereof, as religiously acceptable. This is, of course, not only egregious but historically inaccurate as well. Knobel's and Maslin's books are examples of the Reform's deliberate attempt to define itself in terms of what liberal Jews do instead of what they don't do. These books are well written, well reasoned, instructive, and beautiful.

Almost two decades ago, three graduate students, Richard Siegel, Michael Strassfeld, and Sharon Strassfeld, following the model of the enormously popular *Whole Earth Catalog,* compiled a compendium of information designed to guide a new generation of Jews back into Jewish practice. They called their book *The Jewish Catalog: A Do-It Yourself Kit* (vol. 1, Jewish Publication Society, 1973). Not only was it a great idea, several hundred thousand Jews apparently thought so too and bought the book, thus making Jewish publishing history. *The Jewish Catalog,* and its subsequent sister volumes 2 and 3, became the principal guidebook for a new generation of Jews, for the *havurah* movement, and for the modest Jewish spiritual renewal that has blessed the final decades of this century. Volume 1 remains an excellent, though now dated, treasury.

Michael Strassfeld went on to write the even more useful *The Jewish Holidays: A Guide and Commentary* (Harper & Row, 1985). This is easily the most thorough, popular introduction to the festival year on the shelf. While its focus easily reveals Strassfeld's strong Conservative background, the book is a natural first choice for any liberal Jew. Furthermore, by inviting five of the most innovative teachers in the country to offer their own marginal comments to the text, Strassfeld successfully evokes the intra-page conversation of the Talmud and other rabbinic sources.

Hayim Halevy Donin's *To Be a Jew: A Guide to Jewish Observance in Contemporary Life* (Basic Books, 1972) is a solid home reference book for times when the table is all set for a holiday meal and you're not sure what to say or when to say it, a kind of Jewish Emily Post. The author is a traditionally observant Jew and occasionally comes off sounding judgmental. Nevertheless what it may lack in flexibility or creativity, it makes up for in ease of use.

Finally, the Orthodox Israeli writer Eliyahu Kitov, in *The Book of Our Heritage* (Feldheim, 1978), offers us a month-by-month, three-volume banquet table of customs, insights, laws, and homilies, as well as a synopsis of Orthodox praxis on the entire annual cycle of holy days, festivals, and fast days. That he seems to be writing from a time long ago is both this work's problem and its charm. It is especially valuable for those who seek some access into the richness of traditional Judaism but do not have Orthodox friends to eavesdrop on. Irving Greenberg, one of America's most respected liberal Orthodox teachers, wrote *The Jewish Way: Living the Holidays* (Summit Books, 1988) which offers probably the most concise and readable introduction to traditional observance. Likewise, Blu Greenberg, a feminist and an Orthodox Jew, is the author of *How to Run a Traditional Jewish Household* (Simon & Schuster, 1985) which smartly fulfills the promise of its title. *Jewish Literacy* by Joseph Telushkin (Morrow, 1991) is a one-volume encyclopedic guide to Jewish concepts, history, and rituals.

In addition to being one of this generation's great political activists, Arthur Waskow is also probably the most well known and eloquent spokesperson for New Age Judaism. His *Seasons of Our Joy: A Celebration of Modern Jewish Renewal* (Beacon Press, 1990) takes the reader through the holiday and festival calendar but, in addition to the standard fare of what Jews do, he also adds to each holiday his own political-activist twist. The result is clearly the most contemporary and "relevant" of all the "introduction" books. We are constantly amazed by the scope of his religious creativity and prophetic zeal. This lovely volume is further enhanced by papercuts done specially for it by Martin and Joanne Farren.

Life Cycle

Anita Diamant writes for Jews who are otherwise well-read but who are Jewishly illiterate. Her style is neither juvenile nor condescending. Indeed, it assumes the reader is eager to get caught up on matters Jewish. With her *Jewish Baby Book* (Summit Books, 1988) and her *The New Jewish Wedding* (Summit Books, 1986)

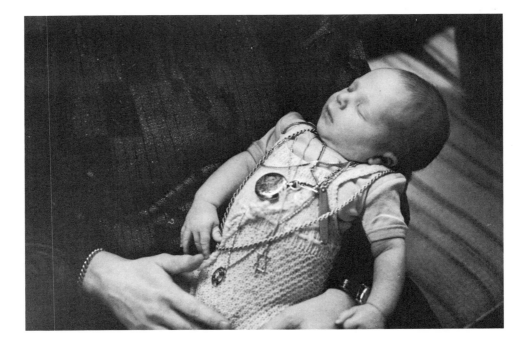

Pidyon Ha-Ben. With this ritual, a mother's first son is "redeemed" from service in the Temple. Traditionally, the child is adorned with ornaments to mark the occasion. (Photograph by Dan Lencher)

she has created a new genre of "introductions." In addition to covering all the pertinent topics, she treats the reader to a feast of ancient and cutting-edge contemporary customs and suggestions. While she faithfully represents the full range of contemporary religious observance, her sympathies are clearly left of center. If you are about to have a baby or about to get married (preferably in the reverse order), Diamant's books are such an easy and rewarding place to begin that many rabbis wisely request couples read them in advance of showing up for the appointment.

There is sadly very little written of much help on *bar* and *bat mitzvahs*. This is especially painful, since in America today, owing to upward mobility, the geographic dispersion of extended families, later marriages, and older grandparents, this event has taken on even greater significance than it once did. Virtually every celebratory practice, once reserved for weddings, is now commonplace at most *bar* and *bat mitzvahs*. (For suggestions of books for young people about the *bar* and *bat mitzvah*, see the last chapter of this volume.)

And then alas, there are funerals. The most thorough, popular presentation of Judaism's laws and customs can be found in Maurice Lamm's *The Jewish Way in Death and Mourning* (New York: Jonathan David, 1972). Lamm is an Orthodox rabbi, and his book is a kind of contemporary synopsis of traditional Jewish law.

After the funeral, Jack Riemer's anthology, *Jewish Reflections on Death* (Schocken Books, 1976), will be of great comfort. Riemer has brought together a diverse sampling of traditions and meditations which remind us that others have walked this dark valley before us. From the death-bed stories of hasidic *rebbes* to contemporary ethical wills, we are reminded to consider our own three score years and ten. For this reason, this slim volume makes excellent reading in preparation for the High Holy Days as well.

Experiencing History

Perhaps the most eloquent expression of the meaning of Jewish history can be found in Martin Buber's collection of essays, *Israel and the World: Essays in a Time of Crisis* (Schocken Books, 1963). Buber is never easy reading but in this case well worth the extra effort. The essays "The Faith of Judaism," "The Man of Today and the Jewish Bible," "The Spirit of Israel and the World of Today," and "The Land and its Possessors" are thrilling examples of how one of the greatest teachers Judaism has ever produced understands Jewish purpose in history. Buber is an ardent Zionist and pacifist.. He believes that there is a reason why Israel must be the center of the Jewish people and a light to the nations of the world.

Yosef Hayim Yerushalmi's *Zakhor: Jewish History and Jewish Memory* (Schocken Books, 1989) is a little book that was originally delivered at the University of Washington as four lectures. The essays are very readable and introduce us to the complexities of historical reconstruction. Many students are surprised, for instance, to learn that what we know as Jewish history literally did not exist until a few hundred years ago. Prior to that time, our people preserved memories in profoundly different ways.

Two classic novels of the Holocaust have become required introductions to the Jewish historical experience. The first, by a French Jew, André Schwarz-Bart, is *The Last of the Just* (Atheneum, 1973). Winner of numerous literary prizes, Schwarz-Bart chronicles a family line through centuries of European anti-Semitism. According to legend, God would have long ago given up on the world were it not for the righteousness of thirty-six just souls, or *Lamed-vovniks*. Often they are not known to others of their generation, or to even themselves, yet they are the real pillars of the universe. And according to Schwarz-Bart, his friend,

Ernie, who perished in the gas chambers, was the last of the just men. The second novel, of course, is Nobel laureate Elie Wiesel's *Night* (Bantam, 1982), an autobiographical novel based on his own life experience as a teenager in Auschwitz. Be sure to give yourself enough time for a long walk alone after completing either of these heartrending, riveting, and chastening novels.

In *Where We Are: The Inner Life of America's Jews* (Harper & Row, 1988) Leonard Fein, one of American Jewry's leading sociologists, founder of *Moment* magazine, and liberal politico, explains the dynamics, predicaments, and secular psyche of American Jews. For Fein, the primary reality is the Jewish people, how they see themselves, and who they really are. His book is as good a mirror as we have. If Fein is the *mavin* of Jewish politics, Eugene B. Borowitz is the expert on the Jewish soul. Borowitz teaches religious thought at the Hebrew Union College, the Reform rabbinical school; he is Reform Judaism's most respected theologian, and founder of *Sh'ma*, a journal of Jewish social ethics. *The Mask Jews Wear: The Self-deceptions of American Jewry* (Port Washington, N.Y.: Sh'ma, 1980) shows this gifted observer of Jewish religious life at his best. The book is properly classified somewhere between social commentary and theology and, as such, can serve as a natural bridge for students moving cautiously from one discipline to the other. Paul Cowan's *An Orphan in History* (Doubleday Anchor, 1990) provides a spiritual autobiography which sets much of the above in the human context of one man's life. Cowan shares with the reader his search for Jewish identity and his "own way home." Finally, in *Mixed Blessings: Overcoming the Stumbling Blocks in an Interfaith Marriage,* Paul Cowan and his wife, Rabbi Rachael Cowan (Viking Penguin, 1988), share the wisdom they learned from their own experience about coming to terms with religious differences in marriage.

Life and Text

Before concluding with three little anthologies of classical rabbinic thought, I want to recommend Barry Holtz's *Finding Our Way: Jewish Texts and the Lives We Lead Today* (Schocken Books, 1990). Holtz gives the reader textual access to all the major concerns of Jewish life, from Israel to interpersonal relations. Like so much of the other work of this master teacher, Holtz's book empowers the reader.

For six or seven centuries, the rabbis of the Talmud and the Midrash produced the largest corpus of religious literature in human history. They wrote, fantasized about, and commented on everything, especially the Bible. Without the literary lenses they created, Judaism as we know it would be unrecognizable. Indeed, with the possible exception of the books on Jewish history and politics discussed above, all the books in this essay are, in one way or another, only further refractions of rabbinic thought.

Professor Nahum N. Glatzer, a product of Buber and Rosenzweig's *Lehrhaus* in pre-war Germany, translated and edited a slender anthology of midrash entitled, *Hammer on the Rock: A Short Midrash Reader* (Schocken Books, 1962). The title itself is an allusion to a passage in Jeremiah suggesting how the word of God, like a hammer striking stone, fires sparks in all directions. Midrash is the unique Jewish literary art form which comments on the biblical text, adding to it undreamed-of dimensions. The translations are rendered in poetic form, forcing us into a slow read. Through Glatzer's masterful use of language, the English reader is rewarded with the flavor of classical Hebrew study.

Shmuel Yosef Agnon, Israel's greatest author, collected and arranged legends, laws, and homilies surrounding the ten days from Rosh Hashanah to Yom Kippur, or as Jewish tradition names them, *Days of Awe* (Schocken Books, 1965). There is no commentary, no secondary interpretation; the primary texts are simply allowed to speak for themselves. The average selection is only a page long. The beginning student, especially one seeking preparation for the High Holy Days, could find no better doorway.

Finally, I want to recommend Shalom Spiegel's *The Last Trial: On the Legends and Lore of the Command to Abraham to Offer Isaac as a Sacrifice: The* Akedah (Schocken Books, 1969). Spiegel, in what can only be called an intellectual *tour de force*, takes a medieval poem of Jewish martyrdom and uses it as a device for closely reading the twenty-second chapter of Genesis, which depicts the binding of Isaac on Mount Moriah. Drawing on a diverse range of religious, historical, and literary traditions, raising questions we were convinced were heretical, considering possibilities we find horrifying and exalting, Professor Spiegel demonstrates what it might mean to truly study the Bible. And this at last, and of course, brings us back to the sacred text of the Torah, from whence everything begins. . . .

CHAPTER 2

THE BIBLE AND ITS WORLD

Everett Fox

The Hebrew Bible is the cornerstone of Judaism. Throughout the ages it has been the garment in which the Jewish people has clothed itself in its wanderings. It has served as the springboard for rabbinic law and wisdom, for medieval philosophy, poetry, and mysticism, and occasionally as the inspiration for modern religious and political thought.

The uses to which Jews have put the Bible over the ages form a fascinating chapter in cultural history; but what do they mean for a reader who is struggling to find a way to understand the text in our time, when so often we feel the huge distance between ourselves and what was once viewed as Holy Scripture? Ever since the early nineteenth century, when they began to attain civil rights in Europe, the vast majority of Jews have abandoned the traditional practice of committing religious literature to memory in childhood for the purpose of being able to draw on and be molded by it throughout life. The Bible, which once served as a frame of reference into which the Jew fit his or her own experiences, has in modern times often been consigned to the realm of the past.

Present-day Jews thus find themselves in a bind. Estranged from a way of life that taught familiarity with the Bible, they may want to encounter the text anew; but can this really be done without a knowledge of the Hebrew language or the experience of growing up with the Bible? Moreover, can it be done within a larger culture that essentially sees the Hebrew Bible as the "Old Testament"—that is, as something outmoded and superseded by the "New"?

In this brief essay I would like to sketch out a positive answer to these questions. I will begin by considering some important aspects of the Bible; then I will turn to a list of books that I hope will provide for in-depth learning.

The Bible is an anthology. Ta biblia, the Greek word from which the English *Bible* is derived, means "books," and that is what we have here: a thirty-nine-volume library from various periods and points of view. This is crucial for understanding the Bible, for it means that it is not easy to find a consistent "biblical" view on any one topic. To be sure, there are key concepts such as covenant (the pact between God and Israel), the redemption of the Israelites from Egypt, and reward and punishment in this life; but throughout the text, there are also clear indications of strong disagreements about many other issues—for instance, where to worship God, whether or not children are punished for their parents' sins, and whether monarchy is a good thing. This multifaceted aspect of the Bible left the door open for many centuries of interpretation, and was quite significant, for it became a characteristic of later Judaism to tolerate or at least debate different points of view. Rabbinic Judaism's central collection of literature, the Talmud, is in fact the record of ancient disagreements on major and minor points of law, thought, and practice.

Historical reporting is not the central goal of the text. We commonly understand history as *how things happened;* most people view it through dates, names, and places, with economic, political, and social factors—or sometimes great individuals—"causing" events to occur in the way that they do.

The Bible does not fit this definition. Although the first large part of its text, Genesis through Kings, *does* recount a kind of history of the Israelite people, from its origins down to the sixth century B.C.E., it is history with a purpose: an account of the dealings of Israel with its God. The text itself admits this; it often omits background information that a modern historian would find crucial. The book of Exodus, for instance, does not bother to tell us *which* king of Egypt is the famous Pharaoh—because he is more important to the writer as a type than as a particular historical figure. The Bible's history writing resembles a psychological portrait more than it does a newspaper account; just as we make choices in what we consciously remember about our own lives, so the Bible selects what bears most directly on the self-understanding of the people of Israel. In the end, the

Bible is primarily concerned with who Israel is and what its obligations are. Some history *can* be gleaned from the text, but the historian must do his/her work with great care.

The Bible reflects ancient Jewish beliefs, but is not the sole source of Judaism as we know it. Despite the strong influence of the Bible on later Jewish thinking, it does not contain detailed prescriptions for change; these were added by subsequent generations, speaking in what they felt was the true spirit of the text. Thus, the complex laws and life-style of Judaism as we know it stem from the rabbinic and not from the biblical period. A person who attends a Jewish wedding or funeral today, or goes to a Rosh Hashanah service, or watches Orthodox Jews study, is a witness to rituals that would have been unfamiliar in biblical times. Therefore, anyone wanting to learn Judaism through reading the Bible will be disappointed. As a way of life and thought, Judaism is better grasped through the study of post-biblical materials such as Talmud and Midrash (see the essays later in this volume).

The Bible, as understood by Judaism, exists in two major sections. In a sense, for Jews there are two Bibles to consider: the Torah (Five Books of Moses or "Pentateuch") and everything else, the thirty-four remaining books in what Christians call the "Old Testament."[1] The Torah, which covers less than a quarter of the text proper, was the first part of the Hebrew Bible to be canonized (recognized as sacred and authoritative), perhaps in the fifth century B.C.E. From then on, Jews searched the Torah not only for moral instruction and inspiration, but also looked to it as a practical document which could serve as their constitution. Along with the process of extrapolating law from the Torah may have come the important custom, still practiced, of reading a portion of the Torah weekly on the Sabbath. This undoubtedly solidified the position of eminence that the Torah occupied, and helps to explain Judaism's great emphasis on these five books as opposed to the rest of the Bible.

As for the rest, biblical books fall into two categories: the first includes material read in the synagogue, such as the prophetic excerpts from such books as Isaiah, Jeremiah, and Ezekiel. These are attached to the weekly Torah readings, and, since they conclude the biblical readings in the service, are called *haftarot* (sing. *haftarah*,[2] "conclusion"). Also read in synagogue are the so-called Five

---

[1] Jews dislike using the term "Old Testament" since it implies that the Hebrew Bible has been surpassed or superseded by the "New Testament."

[2] This word, which in its older, central European pronunciation comes out as *haftorah*, bears no actual connection with the word *Torah*, despite its sound.

Scrolls: Ecclesiastes, Esther, Song of Songs, Ruth, and Lamentations; and also the book of Jonah—all on different holidays during the Jewish year. And finally, many of the 150 poems in the book of Psalms found their way into daily, weekly, and festival prayers.

The second category of "everything else" includes such books as Joshua, Judges, Samuel, and Kings (from which *haftarot* are occasionally taken as well), much of the prophets, and "wisdom" books such as Proverbs and Job. These have received rather less attention in Jewish tradition, as they were not read publicly.

The Bible is best studied with others. Traditional Judaism recommends the acquiring of both a teacher and a fellow student, and this is still good advice. Learning the Bible is a process of dialogue with the text, but it is facilitated when others are involved, no matter what their level. And there is an additional benefit: learning a common text creates community. Jews today rarely agree among themselves about religion or politics; gathering around a text may preserve and even create bonds that have been difficult to forge in other contexts. In any event, I would urge the reader to find a person or group of people with whom to study Bible.

With the above said, I would like now to recommend a journey through the Bible, via a selection of books. The choice is of course mine; but I have tried to glean from many hours of both teaching and conversation some of the common threads of concern expressed by people who are serious about approaching the Bible. Naturally a selection was necessary; there is literally no end of books on the Bible. So I have tried to choose those which are most directly of use to a person seeking to engage in study.

Reading the Bible
Introductions to the Text

As you set out to read the text, you should consult an introductory work to put the Bible in perspective. As in any field, there exist many such introductions, and not unexpectedly, they vary widely in their readability and helpfulness. A good place to start might be Samuel Sandmel's *The Hebrew Scriptures* (Oxford University Press, 1978), which goes book by book through the text. It quotes biblical passages at length, thus doing away with the common practice of throwing chapter and verse numbers at the reader. Sandmel provides a good deal of information about the text and the world behind it. He is also sensitive to the Bible's literary qualities, which he explores in another worthwhile book, *The Enjoyment of Scripture* (Oxford University Press, 1972). The latter will serve equally as a fine introduction to the Bible, particularly for those who are interested in its artistry.

A thematic entry-point into the Bible can be found in the opening articles of *Back to the Sources: Reading the Classic Jewish Texts*, edited by Barry Holtz (Summit Books, 1986). The three pieces, "Biblical Narrative," "Biblical Law," and "Biblical Poetry," do a good job of describing major characteristics of biblical literature, giving the reader a sense of what he or she will find in the text and supplying some high-level bibliography.

Articles in the *Encyclopaedia Judaica* (Keter Publishing Co., 1972) and *Harper's Bible Dictionary* (Harper & Row, 1985), which I will describe shortly, may also serve the purpose of introducing the material for serious reading.

An issue peripheral to study but important in Jewish practice is the rules for reading the Bible in synagogue. A book that tells you "everything you ever wanted to know" about this topic—including how Torah scrolls are written and read, and the procedures for being called up to the synagogue reading—is Alfred J. Kolatch's *This Is the Torah* (Jonathan David, 1988). Its question-and-answer format makes this work extremely accessible.

The Text

Which English text should you use? Given the large number of translations on the market, many of them quite recent, this is an important question; but it is even more so when one takes into account that the precise wording and mode of expression in the Bible has always been of very great concern to Jews. In a culture that has based much of its law and thought on evolving interpretation of a sacred text, the exact way in which the Bible speaks has always been crucial. This area is of particular concern to me as a translator of these texts.

Biblical Hebrew, as we have it, is a language of relatively small vocabulary (spoken, and perhaps even written, biblical Hebrew undoubtedly included much more); at the same time, its power in narrative, poetic, and even legal settings is often overwhelming. The biblical writers were master rhetoricians, that is, they knew how to compress strong emotions and exhortations into pregnant words and phrases. Even within long stretches of the text, individual units retain a brevity and power of expression. In addition, there are various stylistic devices in the text that convey its message, such as puns, plays on words, repetition of key words, and allusions to other characters/situations. In short, the Hebrew Bible uses language, especially spoken language, with great force and artistry to make its mostly non-artistic points.

But the text of the Bible is not always clear or fully understandable. Over the course of the centuries, meanings and usages of words became obscure; errors in copying the text were made even by devoted scribes; and gaps appeared in the text, whether by conscious design or by the loss of words or phrases in the process of transmission. These problems have given rise to centuries of educated guesswork, often over passages of central importance for Judaism and Christianity. They, and the desire to bring the Bible to a variety of peoples and a variety of historical situations, have led to numerous attempts to render the text into other languages.

The most famous translation of the Bible into English is the 1611 King James or "Authorized" Version (referring to its official commissioning by James I of England). It created what we think of in English as "biblical language," and its echoes are still with us. While the King James Bible caught some of the original's grandeur, it also created its own; while it used the best scholarship of its day, it could not have anticipated the striking developments of modern scholarship. The last century has witnessed an explosion of new knowledge about the ancient Near East and its languages and cultures, with the result that we now know astronomically more about the Bible's setting—and specific language—than was possible for the last two millennia. For these reasons, I would not recommend use of the King James Bible, or its Jewish revision, the 1917 JPS (Jewish Publication Society) version. In their place I would suggest three recent translations.

First, in increasing use in a variety of Jewish settings, is *Tanakh*,[3] the so-called *New JPS* version (one-volume edition of the entire Bible, Jewish Publication Society, 1985). It is unmatched for accuracy and honesty (notes at the bottom of the page include "meaning of Hebrew uncertain"), and reflects great erudition in both Semitics (the ancient languages of the Near East) and traditional Jewish commentaries, which displayed an intuitive grasp of linguistic problems. This translation serves as the text for both the Plaut and New JPS commentaries (see

---

[3] "*Tanakh*" is a common Hebrew term for the Bible. It is an acronym for *Torah, Neviim* (Prophets) and *Ketuvim* (Writings).

below), and is increasingly finding its way into synagogues and homes. Its short-comings lie mainly in the realm of art: it is sometimes rather colloquial, and often lacks the rhetorical force of the Hebrew. For this reason, it comes across as almost a commentary to the Hebrew, albeit one of the best available. In any event, the New JPS translation is an absolutely indispensable tool for anyone who has a serious interest in the Bible.

Second, and most recent as of this printing, is the *New Revised Standard Version* (Oxford University Press, 1989). This is a clear and rather literal render-ing of the Hebrew based on recent Bible scholarship. It manages to reflect some of the elegance of the Hebrew, and can be very profitably used in personal study, providing a useful contrast to other translations. The *NRSV* does include the New Testament, but its "Old Testament" text does not have marginal references to the coming of Jesus as some Christian Bibles do.

Third and last, covering the first two books of the Torah at present, with the rest on the way, is my own work, *Genesis and Exodus* (Schocken Books, 1990). This stands at the other end of the spectrum from standard Bible translations in English, including the two just mentioned; it focuses on the style and rhetoric of the Hebrew, and is geared for reading aloud. It tries to reproduce some of the stylistic features of the text that I mentioned above—repetition and plays on words, to name two—in order to help the English reader sense inner meanings and connections that are usually lost in translation. A system of notes and com-mentary accompanies the text, to help the process along. This translation can be used as an entry into biblical language, and as a vehicle for studying the Bible in a traditional way—by paying close attention to the particular modes of expression used in the text.

People tend to be attracted to one kind of translation or the other, but I want to suggest here that you might consider studying the Bible with several. Transla-tion, after all, is best seen as a tool for study. To use a musical analogy: a favorite recording might serve well for inspiration or entertainment; but if you really want to appreciate the original and its richness, you should own or at least listen to a number of recordings. Doing the same with translations of the Bible will prepare you well for the next step: interpretation.

Commentaries

Since ancient times, Jews have studied the Bible with two fingers—one on the text and one on commentaries. Following the invention of movable type in the fifteenth century, Hebrew Bibles have almost always been printed with a few lines of text in the middle of the page, and several medieval commentaries (in different typefaces) surrounding them. This practice is an important adjunct to Bible study. Let me again begin with the Torah.

There are two contemporary commentaries which have the great merit of combining meticulous recent scholarship with insights from the long Jewish tradition of Bible interpretation. The first, done under the auspices of the Reform movement, is *The Torah: A Modern Commentary*, edited by W. Gunther Plaut (Union of American Hebrew Congregations, 1981). Arranged for synagogue use (that is, by weekly readings), this large volume has comprehensive contents: line-by-line comments clarifying the text; introductions to sections and books; "Gleanings" from later Jewish tradition (ideas and practices); and valuable extended discussions on important biblical concepts and institutions, as well as on the Bible's ancient Near Eastern background.

In the process of appearing at this writing is the JPS *Torah Commentary* (Jewish Publication Society, 1989–), with individual volumes by distinguished Bible scholars Nahum Sarna (*Genesis; Exodus*), Baruch Levine (*Leviticus*), Jacob Milgrom (*Numbers*), and Jeffrey Tigay (*Deuteronomy*). In its volume-by-volume form, it is a majestic piece of scholarship, with its clear commentary, its constant comparison with what we know about the cultures and languages of the ancient Near East, and its use of the medieval commentators' insightful observations on biblical language. Particularly valuable are the excurses at the end of each volume (*Numbers* contains seventy-seven of them!), which deal with specific issues and problems (for example: "The Name 'Israel,'" "The Meaning of the Dietary Laws," "Family Structures in Biblical Israel," "Prophecy in Israel and the Ancient Near East"). Using these volumes for the study of the Torah will put you current with the best in Bible scholarship. It will not necessarily guide you in religious matters, for that aspect of the Bible, while present, is somewhat in the background here. It should also be mentioned that a one-volume synagogue version of this work, which cuts down on technical matters, edited by series editor Chaim Potok, is slated to appear. It will include the weekly *haftarot*, with commentary by Michael Fishbane, whose *Text and Texture* (Schocken Books, 1979), can also be recommended as a fine close reading of some important biblical texts.

Another scholarly series, not yet complete, covers most "Old Testament" books, one per volume. *The Anchor Bible* (Doubleday, 1964) offers translated text, with exhaustive introduction, notes, and commentary. While as a whole the series is not really aimed at lay people, there is much to be learned from these books for those willing to make the effort; the introductions alone are quite informative and useful. Finally, there are numerous commentaries on specific books of the Bible, usually referred to in bibliographies of fuller works.

Thus far, the modern commentaries. But it is a long-standing Jewish tradition to study the Bible with the medieval commentators (mostly from France and Spain) as teachers who are there to answer one's questions and to point out problems. These commentators, whose concerns range from the "simple" meaning of the text to their own observations on ethics, historiography, and mysticism, have become available to the English reader in increasing measure. Though their work is treated elsewhere in this volume, it will be appropriate to cite a few books here. A wonderful introduction to the commentaries is Edward Greenstein's article in *Back to the Sources* (cited earlier); he not only lays out general principles but also gives you a good idea of the various personalities, even constructing a semifictional dialogue between them on a few specific biblical texts.

Thus armed, you can proceed to M. Rosenbaum and A. M. Silbermann, *The Pentateuch with Rashi,* 5 vols. (Feldheim, 1973), if you want to concentrate on the eleventh-century master who was (and still is) the most celebrated of the medieval commentators, or to the *Soncino Chumash* (Soncino Press, 1947), for a digest of several of them. A stunning work is *Studies in the Book of Genesis . . . Deuteronomy,* 6 vols. (Jerusalem: World Zionist Organization, 1981), by Nehama Leibowitz, a renowned and much-loved teacher of Bible in Israel for the last several decades. She weaves a stimulating set of questions on the text through comments by centuries of classical commentators, making relatively inaccessible sources available to the general reader. Leibowitz is sensitive to language and message; her work constitutes a mini-course in how Jewish tradition has read the Bible—and its layout facilitates weekly study, keyed as it is to the individual Torah readings.

In that vein, I should mention a series written from an Orthodox viewpoint that makes extensive use of classical traditions on the texts. The *ArtScroll Tanach,* edited by Meir Zlotowitz and Nosson Scherman (Mesorah Publications, 1976–85), showcases individual biblical books with its own translation (based closely on traditional readings of the text), and excerpts liberally from the medieval sources. It is wholly oriented toward an Orthodox view of Jewish thinking and observance, to the exclusion of modern "critical" scholarship, and so is less interested in the ancient Near East and the evolution of the text than in how the Bible supports classical Jewish religious thought and practice.

A final note on a book that has been conspicuously absent so far. Joseph

Hertz's *The Pentateuch and the Haftorahs* (New York: Soncino Press, 1960) has been a staple in American (and British) synagogues for several generations. It has often been the main contact that present-day Jews have had with the Bible. The Hertz *Chumash* (five books) has served well as a one-volume edition, presenting text, scholarly observations, and insights from Jewish tradition in a usable format—and demonstrating that the text is best studied with some kind of commentary. On the other hand, its tone is pompous, its translation (the 1917 JPS version) outmoded, and much of its message seems to stem from an apologetic thrust, such as harping on the spiritual superiority of ancient Judaism and the Jewish contributions to civilization over the ages, and vehemently rejecting the "Documentary Hypothesis" current among the Bible scholars of his time (described below). In the end, Hertz's edition is best left to rest in peace. It has been superseded by Plaut and JPS, whose scholarship and general thrust will be more appealing to contemporary Jews.

Once we get beyond the Torah, there are many single volumes, usually on individual books of the Bible, that both beginners and more advanced students will find rewarding. A particularly lovely edition of *The Five Scrolls* has been put out by the Central Conference of American Rabbis (1984). It offers brief but suggestive introductions, a reworked nineteenth-century English translation which has a lot of charm, festival prayers at the end of the book, and a short "Guide to Further Reading."

The Soncino Bible, ArtScroll series, and Anchor Bible, which we mentioned above in reference to the Torah, encompass most of the remaining books of the Bible as well, and are quite useful for study, each with its distinctive contribution. We should also mention some treatments of specific books: Robert Gordis's *Koheleth: The Man and His World* (Schocken Books, 1967), a thorough study of Ecclesiastes; Marcia Falk's *The Song of Songs* (Harper & Row, 1990), a beautifully translated, explicated, and printed version of a unique biblical book; Nahum N. Glatzer's *The Dimensions of Job* (Schocken Books, 1969), which looks at Job in both biblical terms and through the eyes of later interpreters; and Elias Bickerman's *Four Strange Books of the Bible* (Schocken Books, 1967), on Jonah, Daniel, Ecclesiastes, and Esther. For the prophetic books as a whole, one might consult Abraham Joshua Heschel's monumental *The Prophets*, 2 vols. (Harper & Row, 1969 and 1971). Here is scholarship combined with appropriate passion (Heschel was a key Jewish religious figure in the civil rights and anti-war movements). In addition to discussing individual figures, the author focuses on important characteristics of prophetic thinking and experience.

Dictionaries/Encyclopedias

A serious reader of the Bible should have a solid reference tool at his or her disposal, for looking up names, concepts, and other information as it is encountered in reading the text. If you have access to it in a library, or happen to own one already, the sixteen-volume *Encyclopaedia Judaica* (Keter Publishing Co., 1972) contains a large number of articles on all aspects of the Bible by leading scholars. While much new research has taken place since 1972, the *E.J.* is still a powerful tool for the study of the Bible. For those who prize portability, the recent *Harper's Bible Dictionary* (Harper & Row, 1985) is also of excellent quality. The articles are by scholars from a range of backgrounds, and deal with broad topics as well as with details. Some striking ones that readers might find helpful include: "Source Criticism," "Archaeology, History, and the Bible," "Sociology of the Old Testament," "Women," and "The Temple." The volume is lavishly illustrated with plates and photos, and has excellent maps. It should be mentioned that the New Testament is fully represented in it, in contrast to the *E.J.*

Reading about the Bible: Some Questions
Who Wrote the Bible?

For several centuries, scholars have been seeking to reconstruct the process through which the Bible came into being. Once one moves beyond the Orthodox view that the Torah is of divine origin, one encounters a debate that is still raging. Nineteenth-century Bible critics identified four "documents" or strands, which they named J, E, D, and P, from different periods and schools of thought, that they believed were woven together by a "redactor" (possibly in the plural) in the sixth or fifth century B.C.E.; this view, usually called the Documentary Hypothesis (the approach is called Source Criticism), has been modified again and again, and the process of the Bible's creation is still not agreed upon. What *is* certain is that the final editing process created a new work that is a mixture of previous ideas and events, and which is the Bible that has been familiar to us for the last two millennia.

The most accessible presentation of the issues of the Bible's authorship, with a new solution thrown in, is Richard Friedman's *Who Wrote the Bible?* (Harper &

The first page of the Book of Exodus, from the Prague Bible of 1525. (Library of The Jewish Theological Seminary of America)

Row, 1989). Friedman makes the tracing of biblical origins sound like a detective story (which it certainly is to Bible scholars); whether or not you agree with his conclusions, you will find yourself drawn into the hunt. There is the added plus that in order to make his case, Friedman brings in a good deal of information and analysis of Israel's history, making this book an excellent introduction to a number of important biblical issues.

What Is the History behind What the Bible Reports?

I suggested above that the Bible is not straight history, but rather an *interpretation*, and a later one at that, of Israel's historical experience. Despite this, or perhaps because of it, many attempts have been made to reconstruct—secularly, as it were—the events narrated in the Bible, and to examine biblical data with the tools of archaeology, textual analysis, and comparative sociology. Many books on this topic exist in the field. A brief, popular study that presents the issues clearly is Harry Orlinsky's *Understanding the Bible Through History and Archaeology* (Ktav Publishing House, 1969). A recent useful work is *Ancient Israel*, edited by Hershel Shanks (Prentice Hall, 1988). Written by several experts in the field, it is concise and authoritative, presenting current theories about the events of biblical times. Finally, *The Bible's First History*, by Robert Coote and David Robert Ord (Philadelphia: Fortress Press, 1988), presents the theoretical core of the stories in the Torah, through the lens of a period later than that of Moses: the court of King David. This work raises fascinating questions about the nature and origin of the Bible, and is ultimately more valuable than the much-publicized *Book of J* by Harold Bloom (Grove Weidenfeld, 1990) which makes use of a misleading translation by David Rosenberg.

What Does Archaeology Tell Us about What the Bible Says?

This question flows naturally from the previous one. Archaeology is one of the primary tools used to look back into the biblical period. For over a century, scholars have been digging up the Middle East, finding everything from pieces of broken pottery to remains of large palaces and temples. In rediscovering the ancient Near East, they have also uncovered much of the biblical world, especially the daily world of farming, commerce, war and, to an extent, religion. While an archaeological dig cannot hope to reveal everything we would like to know, it can tell us a good deal about the general circumstances of life, and politics, in the time of the Bible. An entertaining and informative way to follow developments in this field is through the popular journal *Biblical Archaeology Review*. It contains well-written, well-illustrated articles on the topic, along with new theories and lively arguments about them (its sister publication, *Bible Review*, is also highly recommended; it expands the field of vision to art and literature, with crystal-clear nontechnical articles by experts). A comprehensive book that will introduce you to the methods and some of the results of modern biblical archaeology is *Biblical Archaeology in Focus*, by Keith Schoville (Baker Book House, 1978), which includes discussion of specific archaeological sites and gives a helpful bibliography. A more popular approach, with plenty of illustrations, can be found in Gaalyah Cornfeld's *Archaeology of the Bible: Book by Book* (Harper & Row, 1982).

Where Can I Find Out about the Bible's Wider World—the Ancient Near East?

Israelite society emerged against the background of older cultures: Mesopotamia, Egypt, and Canaan. Thanks to developments in archaeology, we now know a great deal about those societies independently of what the Bible reports. Thousands of texts, on walls, pottery, and clay tablets have taught us much about the languages, concerns, life-styles, and religions of this region, over the course of several thousand years. Much of biblical scholarship is engaged in the study of such materials; the basic idea is that you cannot properly understand the Bible if you are not familiar with the background against which it emerged.

Two thought-provoking books may serve as a solid introduction to an appreciation of ancient Near Eastern thought, culture, and history. Sabatino Moscati's *The Face of the Ancient Orient* (Doubleday, 1962) compares virtually all of the important ancient Near Eastern civilizations (Israelite among them), their history, literature, and religion, in a manner that makes for stimulating reading. *The Intellectual Adventure of Ancient Man* (at one time titled *Before Philosophy*), edited by H. and H. A. Frankfort (University of Chicago Press, 1977), narrows the comparison to the worldviews of two major players, Mesopotamia and Egypt, with final essays on Israelite and Greek thought. Both these books give the reader the flavor of vanished times and places, and a perspective on the emergence of Israel's culture.

More focused on the biblical text itself are two fine books by Nahum Sarna, *Understanding Genesis* (Schocken Books, 1970) and *Exploring Exodus* (Schocken Books, 1986). Here a mine of scholarly information has been presented in detail but engagingly, and one comes to understand these biblical books fully against the background of other cultures and institutions. A much briefer but quite fruitful look at how biblical texts relate to other ancient literature can be found in William Hallo's introductions to each of the Five Books of Moses in the Plaut volume cited above under "Commentaries." D. Winton Thomas's *Documents from Old Testament Times* (Harper & Row, 1961) will give the interested reader firsthand contact with some of the ancient Near Eastern documents that parallel biblical stories and laws. The texts are accompanied by helpful introductions and notes, as well as a bibliography for each section.

What Are Some Specific Approaches to the Bible?

If you are interested in recent scholarly theories about how the Bible came into being, and how the Israelite people progressed through its early history, you will get a good deal of stimulation from Norman Gottwald's *The Hebrew Bible: A Socio-Literary Introduction* (Philadelphia: Fortress Press, 1985). The author, who has pioneered the sociological study of the Bible, thoroughly discusses various approaches to historical and textual problems; the book is arranged in "tracks," demonstrating the multifaceted nature of current Bible studies. Gottwald is challenging but rewarding, and will give people with an analytical bent a lot to think about. In addition, this book contributes greatly to the discussion of Israel's history.

A British entry with the interesting title of *Creating the Old Testament*, edited by Stephen Bigger (Basil Blackwell, 1989), contains useful and thought-provoking essays about the Bible and the way scholars think about it. Also of British origin is Dan Jacobson's *The Story of the Stories* (Harper & Row, 1982), a highly suggestive work by a novelist, which concentrates on the dramatic tensions inherent in the Bible's concept of chosenness. Jacobson's approach is psychological more than religious, and he probes what he sees as the fears and concerns behind the Bible's dynamic.

Anthropology has a great deal to contribute to the understanding of biblical religion, specifically in the area of ritual. Here, although it is not written for a beginner, I would recommend Howard Eilberg-Schwartz's *The Savage in Judaism* (Indiana University Press, 1990). It provides a provocative look at such practices as circumcision and dietary laws, and deals comprehensively with central ideas of purity and holiness, utilizing both past research and Eilberg-Schwartz's own insights.

Finally, the "literary approach" I briefly described in discussing translations is best served by Robert Alter's two celebrated books, *The Art of Biblical Narrative* (Basic Books, 1983) and *The Art of Biblical Poetry* (Basic Books, 1987). These works, which make use of the insights of general literary criticism and are very well written, will sensitize a reader to a host of things to look for even before he or she opens the Bible. Although Alter takes a stance at odds with historically oriented Bible scholarship, the student may also use his work to provide a balance to that approach, rather than as an exclusive point of view. A reader who is interested in viewing specific biblical books in this light will find useful essays in another contribution of Alter's, *The Literary Guide to the Bible*, co-edited with Frank Kermode (Belknap Press/Harvard University Press, 1990).

What about the Place of Women in the Text and the Biblical World?

Since the seventies, spurred on by the rise of women's consciousness and the entry of women into the field, biblical scholars have increasingly turned their attention to how women are portrayed in the text, and how this reflects the social reality of ancient Israel. Many excellent studies of varying length have by now appeared; let me mention just a few that are representative of critical writing on the topic. A famous early work of this type is Phyllis Trible's *God and the Rhetoric of Sexuality* (Philadelphia: Fortress Press, 1978), a close reading of texts that will give the reader pause in thinking about some well-known stories. A wider study that carefully delineates the restricted role of women in the patriarchal texts and society of the Bible is Athalya Brenner's *The Israelite Woman* (Sheffield: JSOT, 1985). Sharon Pace Jeansonne's *The Women of Genesis* (Philadelphia: Fortress Press, 1990), on the other hand, concentrates on the important part that women play in the biblical narrative, at least in Genesis. Finally, Carol Meyers's *Discovering Eve* (Oxford University Press, 1991) is a detailed and fascinating study, combining textual analysis with insights from several disciplines (archaeology and anthropology among them) to paint a picture of early Israelite society and women's role in it.

A Final Question

What Does the Bible Say to Our Situation Today?

Although this is the last question posed here, it is the first one that many people ask when they approach the Bible. The finding of personal meaning in the text has been, after all, the primary goal for many generations of Jews. It is also one of the main reasons that the Bible has survived for so long. The depth of its human situations and characterizations has always made it ideally suited for a search for self.

This illustration of Adam and Eve is from the *Tsene u-Rena*, a sixteenth-century Yiddish translation of the Pentateuch and *haftarot*, which was extremely popular among Ashkenazi Jews, particularly women, for Sabbath reading.

Several modern studies lead the way in this area. The great twentieth-century Jewish thinker, Martin Buber, translated and wrote extensively on the Bible. Some of his more accessible essays on biblical thought are collected in *On the Bible* (Schocken Books, 1982); they are notable examples of a powerful reading of the text that intersperses scholarly objectivity with personal concerns. A more recent and American model of an encounter with the Bible can be found in the work of Arthur Waskow, who has combined political activism with a rediscovery of the biblical text. His *Godwrestling* (Schocken Books, 1978) is a striking modern midrash that weaves text and life together, extrapolating from the troubling Jacob–Esau stories in Genesis insights about struggle in his own life and on the current Israeli-Palestinian scene.

Three highly individual readings of the Bible will round out the picture. The late essayist Maurice Samuel, writing with humor and an obvious love for the text, looks at some favorite biblical characters in *Certain People of the Book* (Union of American Hebrew Congregations, 1977). Since Samuel makes extensive use of later Jewish tradition's views of the Bible, this entertaining book serves a number of purposes wonderfully. David Blumenthal has recently published *God at the Center* (Harper & Row, 1988), a series of meditations on the Torah, keyed to the weekly readings, that are based on interpretations by the great eighteenth-century hasidic master Levi Yitzhak of Berditchev. In this work one can see how many levels of Bible reading can operate simultaneously: the simple text combines with later mystical reflections and the musings of a contemporary scholar, in a search for spiritual meaning. Finally, there is the intriguing *The Bible and Us*, by rabbinic scholar Jacob Neusner and priest-novelist Andrew Greeley (Warner Books, 1990). This book is a series of conversations on many important biblical stories, and how Jews and Catholics have read them. Although it is not, strictly speaking, an introduction to the Bible, it does provide a fascinating look into the worlds of classical Jewish and Catholic tradition as they are read and experienced by two brilliant and articulate readers. Along the way you will learn much about the two religions.

Our brief journey through Bible bibliography has led us to encounter a wide variety of views. The literature that I have cited can point you in vastly different directions, from religious inspiration to historical insights, and from archaeological digging to observations about language and literature. Is there, then, any authentic Jewish approach to the Bible?

The answer, of course, is yes. In the end, the Jewish study of the Bible is not so much a matter of ideology as it is of attitude. One should above all be prepared to become involved with the text. Jewish Bible reading is an active process; it requires attentiveness and a willingness to enter into dialogue with the text. This can encompass everything from reverence—being moved by the encounter with what one perceives to be the divine word, or by the experience of a deeply human moment in the text—to grappling with outrage—being disturbed by God's demand on a character within the text, or on the people of Israel as a whole. But what matters most is that the Bible be read with involvement, and that the text be allowed to become the vehicle of our own ongoing search. In that way, even a modern reader may become one with the many generations of Jews who have seen in the Bible the mirror of their own journey as individuals and as a people.

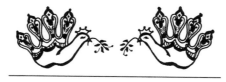

THE WORLD OF THE TALMUD

Eliezer Diamond

In the history of the Jewish people, the period of Rabbinic Judaism was one of incredible transformation. If an Israelite of the First Temple period (c. 1000–586 B.C.E.) were to be transported to the late second century C.E., he would find a form of Judaism almost unrecognizable to him. In place of the Temple, he would find the court and studyhouse of Rabbi Judah the Patriarch, editor of the Mishnah; he would find scholars rather than priests assuming leadership roles in the community; instead of sacrifices, he would find a religious life centered around prayer and study; he would find a focus on the obligations of the individual, as opposed to the First Temple emphasis on the collective fate of the community; and he would learn, to his surprise, that the revelation to Moses at Sinai comprised an Oral Torah as well as a written one. How and why did these fundamental changes take place? The study of the Rabbinic period is essentially an extended effort to answer these questions.

Only a hundred years ago a prospective student of Rabbinic Judaism whose only language was English would have found himself severely hampered by his lack of Hebrew and Aramaic (and, for that matter, Greek, as well as the early languages of Rabbinic scholarship, French and German). Today, almost all major rabbinic texts, as well as numerous scholarly works in Hebrew, French, and German, have been translated into English; moreover, much of the most recent scholarship on the Rabbinic period is being written in English. In contrast to the dearth of material one hundred years ago, today one is confronted with an embarrassment of riches. For the purposes of this essay, this blessing is also a curse; it makes necessary the exclusion not only of many fine works but of whole areas of inquiry as well. Since an exhaustive survey is impossible, I will concentrate on four areas: historical surveys, summaries and analyses of Rabbinic thought, introductions to and translations of the literature of the period, and works on the relationship between Second Temple and Rabbinic Judaism and early Christianity.

Historical Surveys

When we speak of the Rabbinic period, we usually mean an era beginning with the destruction of the Second Temple in 70 C.E. and ending with the Arab conquest of Jerusalem (634 C.E.) and Persia (640 C.E.). Rabbinic Judaism, however, cannot be understood in a vacuum. Rabbinic sources themselves make reference to figures who lived hundreds of years before the Destruction and identify them—whether or not the identification is historically accurate is irrelevant for our present purposes—as links in the chain of rabbinic tradition. Second, although Rabbinic Judaism flourished after the destruction of the Temple, its central images and concerns are adaptations or transformations of the institutions and beliefs of Second Temple Judaism. Therefore, any serious study of the Rabbinic period must begin with a basic familiarity with Second Temple Judaism; I will mention historical works dealing with the Second Temple and then move on to survey works addressing the Rabbinic period.

Second Temple Period

This period itself can be divided roughly into four eras: the Persian period (539–334 B.C.E.), beginning with the return of the Babylonian exiles to Zion and ending with Alexander's conquests; the Hellenistic period (334–164 B.C.E.), the period of Ptolemaic and Seleucid rule culminating with the Maccabean revolt; the Maccabean era (164–63 B.C.E.), a period of Jewish self-rule under the leadership of the Hasmonean family clan; and the Roman period (63 B.C.E.–70 C.E.), initiated by Pompey's intervention in a struggle between two Hasmonean claimants to the Judaean throne and ending with the Great Revolt against Rome and the destruction of the Second Temple. These chronological divisions are frequently employed by historians of the Second Temple period and will be referred to often below.

Two relatively brief works which are highly accessible, and which together provide an excellent introduction to the Second Temple period are Elias Bickerman, *From Ezra to the Last of the Maccabees* (Schocken Books, 1962), and Shaye J. D. Cohen, *From the Maccabees to the Mishnah* (Philadelphia: Westminster Press, 1987). It should be noted that Bickerman's work, which covers the Persian and Hellenistic periods, was first published in the 1940s and should therefore be supplemented by more recent studies. These include Bickerman's own excellent *The Greek Age* (Harvard University Press, 1988), and W. D. Davies and L. Finkelstein, eds., *The Cambridge History of Judaism* (Cambridge University Press, 1984 and 1990), vol. 1 (*The Persian Period*) and vol. 2 (*The Hellenistic Period*). A useful overall survey of the entire Second Temple period—which does not, however, provide as much information about the Diaspora as does Bickerman—is M. Stern, "The Period of the Second Temple," in H. H. Ben-Sasson, ed., *A History of the Jewish People* (Harvard University Press, 1985). Note that Stern does not discuss the Persian period; it is dealt with in the same work by Hayim Tadmor, in "The Babylonian Exile and the Restoration."

One cannot speak of histories of the Second Temple period without mentioning the works of Josephus, a general of the Jewish forces in the Galilee during the Great Revolt against Rome which began in 66 C.E. Josephus surrendered to the Roman forces and eventually, under Roman patronage, wrote two important histories: *The Jewish War*, recording events from the persecutions of Antiochus Epiphanes to the end of the Great Revolt, and *Antiquities*. The latter is Josephus's grand chronicle of Jewish history, beginning with Creation and ending with the onset of the war against Rome; it was written to illustrate the antiquity of the Jewish nation and religion and thereby enhance their prestige in the eyes of Josephus's Gentile readership. Because Josephus lived close to the time of many of the events which he describes and actually took part in others, his work is an invaluable, though not entirely objective, source of information and makes for fascinating reading. The classic translation of his works is the Loeb Classical Library Edition (Harvard University Press, 1978). Volumes 2 and 3 contain *The Jewish*

War and volumes 4–9 comprise *Antiquities. The Jewish War* is also available as a one-volume Penguin Classics paperback (Josephus, *The Jewish War*, [Penguin Books, 1984]): this edition includes a brief but incisive essay by E. Mary Small-wood, a scholar of Roman and Jewish history in Late Antiquity, that introduces us to Josephus, the man and the author.

Each of the four eras of the Second Temple period is important not only for its political and military history. Equally significant for the subsequent develop-ment of Judaism are the socioreligious implications of subjugation by foreign em-pires and consequent contact with new and different cultures. In particular, three phenomena of the Second Temple era should be considered carefully for their impact on the formation of Rabbinic Judaism: the confrontation between Hellen-ism and Judaism, the struggle for political sovereignty which arose from the Mac-cabean revolt, and the formation of various parties and sects, especially the Pharisaic party, among Palestinian Jewry during the Maccabean period.

Hellenism and Judaism

Hellenization of the East, which began with, or rather was accelerated by, Alex-ander the Great's conquests, presented at least two fundamental challenges to Judaism. First, it espoused ideas, such as the supreme value of human thought and skepticism concerning divine involvement in human affairs, that were foreign to the Judaism of the Hellenistic period. Second, it promoted a form of religious syncretism totally incompatible with the exclusive monotheism of Judaism. De-fining what one means by Hellenistic culture is no easy matter; a useful beginning is the chapter entitled "Hellenization," in Morton Smith, *Palestinian Parties and Politics that Shaped the Old Testament* (London: SCM Press, 1971). Smith makes it clear that Hellenism was distinct from both oriental and classical Greek cul-ture, at the same time that it borrowed elements from each.

Two other important discussions of Hellenism as it affected the Jews are Victor Tcherikover, *Hellenistic Civilization and the Jews* (Atheneum, 1970), and Martin Hengel, *Jews, Greeks and Barbarians* (Philadelphia: Fortress Press, 1980). Tcherikover argues that the Greek cities founded in the East by Alexander and his successors were the main agents for the spread of Hellenistic culture, and he analyzes the conflict at the time of Antiochus Epiphanes between Hellenizing Jews and traditionalists, and between moderates and radicals within the Hellen-izing camp, in light of this assumption. Hengel's work shows how the Greek sense of superiority expressed through Hellenistic culture was adapted, ironically enough, by Jewish traditionalists and applied to Jewish self-definition precisely as a means of resisting the attraction of Hellenism.

Those interested in learning how archaeological evidence from Palestinian and Diaspora synagogues and sarcophagi of the Greco-Roman period has been used to postulate the existence of a Hellenistic Judaism quite different from Rabbinic Judaism and its forerunners should read Erwin R. Goodenough, *Jewish Symbols in the Greco-Roman Period,* edited and abridged by Jacob Neusner (Princeton University Press, 1988). Neusner has done a fine job of making Goodenough's voluminous work accessible to the general reader, and his introduction provides a valuable summation both of Goodenough's methods and conclusions and of the arguments set forth by his detractors.

The Maccabean Revolt

The revolt of the Maccabees, which began with uprisings in Jerusalem in 168 B.C.E., and led to the rededication of the Temple, which Hanukkah celebrates, ended with the Seleucid king Demetrius II granting the Jews of Judaea autonomy in 142 B.C.E. The events around the revolt led to the subsequent factionalization of Judaism in at least three ways. First, it brought into sharp focus the intense debate as to whether, and how much, Judaism should be Hellenized, a debate that continues among Jews to our own day (if we substitute "Westernized" for "Hellenized").

Second, the perceived betrayal of tradition by the high priest Jason and by his rival and successor Menelaus, coupled with the passing of the high priesthood to the Hasmonean clan, which had not held that position before, shook popular faith in the priestly leadership and laid the foundation for new religious communities and ideologies which would compete with the priests and the Temple. Finally, the victories against the Seleucids gave Jews the first taste of autonomy since the destruction of the First Temple, raising for the Maccabees and their successors the importance of that autonomy for Jewish self-definition. What would or would not Jews be willing to do for the sake of political sovereignty? At the time of the Great Revolt (66 C.E.) and the Bar Kokhba uprising (132 C.E.) some Jews staked their personal and collective existence on the struggle for independence, while others, for practical or ideological reasons, counseled compromise and accommodation with Rome.

The classic analysis of the Maccabean revolt is that of Elias Bickerman, which appears in popular form in his *From Ezra to the Last of the Maccabees* (previously mentioned). Bickerman argues convincingly that, rather than a revolt against

Antiochus Epiphanes, the uprising was primarily a civil war between those Jews who welcomed and encouraged the introduction of Hellenism into Jewish religious and cultural life and those who opposed it. An equally thoughtful study which complements Bickerman's work both because it takes issue with some of his conclusions and because it shows how Hasmonean attitudes toward Hellenization and sovereignty developed and changed is Tcherikover's *Hellenistic Civilization and the Jews* (mentioned earlier).

Parties and Sects

As mentioned above, the Hasmonean era is one that witnessed the rise of a number of competing religious parties. One of these parties, the Pharisees, is generally assumed to have been the forerunner of Rabbinic Judaism and has therefore been the focus of much scholarly attention. Unfortunately, because of the lack of contemporaneous sources, we know very little for certain about the Pharisees. Were they primarily a political party or rather a religious fellowship that established for itself purity rules similar to those followed by the priests in the Temple? Did the Pharisees in fact shift from being political to pietistic? How much of a popular following, and how much political power, did they have? Two well-known works which address these questions are R. Travers Herford, *The Pharisees* (Macmillan, 1924), and Louis Finkelstein's two-volume work of the same name (Jewish Publication Society, 1938). Herford describes the Pharisees as the creators of the Oral Law; Finkelstein sees them as advocates of the plebeian class of Jewry in their socioeconomic and political struggles with the patrician Sadducees. Both of these works have been largely discredited by subsequent scholarship. We turn, therefore, to more recent and sophisticated treatments of the Pharisees.

One such work is Ellis Rivkin, *A Hidden Revolution: The Pharisees' Search for the Kingdom Within* (Nashville: Abingdon Press, 1978). Aware of the uncritical use of sources by his predecessors, Rivkin constructs a model for isolating historically reliable statements by the rabbis, the New Testament, and Josephus about the Pharisees. He concludes that the Pharisees were a scholarly class that seized the reins of power in the aftermath of the Maccabean revolt. This class incorporated Hellenistic beliefs and practices into its vision of Judaism in order to ameliorate the tension between traditional "biblical" Judaism and Hellenism that led to the Maccabean crisis in the first place. It should be noted that both Rivkin's methods and conclusions have been widely criticized by his colleagues.

Perhaps the most important contribution to the study of Pharisaism has been made by Jacob Neusner. By establishing a scrupulously critical method of isolating rabbinic traditions that can be presumed to predate the destruction of the Second Temple, Neusner has shown that the rabbis of this period, who may or may not be identical with the Pharisees, were primarily concerned with ritual purity. Combining this information with Josephus's accounts of Pharisaic political involvement from the time of John Hyrcanus until that of Salome Alexandra, Neusner hypothesizes that the Pharisees were originally a political party which, upon finding the corridors of power closed to them in the period of Herod's rule (the late first century B.C.E.), transformed itself into a pietistic community. Neusner has written many works about the Pharisees; the best summary of his findings is *From Politics to Piety: The Emergence of Pharasaic Judaism* (Ktav Publishing House, 1979).

The most recent, and arguably the best, study of Pharisaism is Anthony J. Saldarini, *Pharisees, Scribes and Sadducees* (Wilmington: Michael Glazier, 1988). On the one hand, Saldarini, whose work includes a critique of the studies by Rivkin and Neusner, is careful in spelling out what we do and do not know about the Pharisees. On the other hand, operating from the assumption that in the Greco-Roman world of Late Antiquity politics and religion were inseparable, Saldarini attempts to reconstruct the social hierarchy of Jewish Palestine in the late Second Temple period and to locate the Pharisees within it.

Rabbinic Period

We now can turn to historical studies of the Rabbinic period. We should note that Christian scholars, who often see Judaism mainly as the herald of Christianity, are particularly interested in the *early* Rabbinic period, that is, until the defeat of Bar Kokhba in 135 C.E.; they hope to understand Christianity better by studying the Jewish milieu in which it was born. This is one of the reasons that there are many more studies of this period than of the later Rabbinic era. A second reason is that from 135 C.E. on we have few historical sources for the Palestinian and Babylonian Jewish communities other than rabbinic literature. Rabbinic works are extremely problematic sources of historical information, both because the rabbis were not particularly interested in studying and recording history and because these writings obviously reflect events only as the rabbis remember them (or would like them to be remembered). Furthermore, rabbinic writings often are not easily understood and analyzed by historians who have had limited training in studying and interpreting rabbinic literature. Nonetheless, there are a number of fine studies of the Rabbinic period.

The classic study of the earlier Rabbinic era is that of Emil Schurer. Schurer wrote in German; his work was later translated into English and is available in abridged form: Nahum N. Glatzer, ed., *A History of the Jewish People in the Time of Jesus* (Schocken Books, 1961). Although there have been many discoveries and much written since Schurer published his work in the late nineteenth century—indeed, Geza Vermes, Fergus Millar, and Matthew Black have recently issued a revised edition of Schurer's study, *The History of the Jewish People in the Age of Jesus Christ* (Edinburgh: T. & T. Clark, 1973–86)—the one-volume Schocken edition is still a valuable introduction to the early Rabbinic period.

Recently, in an attempt to produce a work that would examine the common roots of Judaism and Christianity, a group of Christians and Jews in the Netherlands commissioned an extensive study of the relationship between Judaism and Christianity in the first two centuries of the Common Era, the *Compendia Rerum Iudaicarum ad Novum Testamentum*. The first two volumes that appeared in this series, S. Safrai and M. Stern, eds., *The Jewish People in the First Century*, vol. 1 (Assen/Philadelphia: Van Gorcum and Fortress Press, 1974) and *The Jewish People in the First Century*, vol. 2 (Assen/Philadelphia: Van Gorcum and Fortress Press, 1987), are a wide-ranging study of the political, social, cultural, and religious history of first- and second-century Jewry.

Lee Levine, in *The Rabbinic Class of Roman Palestine in Late Antiquity* (New York/Jerusalem: Jewish Theological Seminary of America and Yad Izhak Ben-Zvi, 1989), has written a penetrating social history of the rabbinic class in Palestine in the third and fourth centuries. Beginning with the assumption that the rabbis were a relatively small group with limited power, Levine examines how they viewed themselves and interacted with each other, and how they related to other members of the leadership class (i.e., the Patriarch and the wealthy class). Levine's work also represents an important milestone in rabbinic historiography in its extensive use of archaeological evidence.

Works that cover the entire Rabbinic period include Gedaliah Alon, *The Jews in Their Land in the Talmudic Age* (Harvard University Press, 1989), and M. Avi-Yonah, *The Jews under Roman and Byzantine Rule* (Schocken Books, 1984). Perhaps what is most important in Alon's work is his adept use of halakhic (legal) material as a tool for understanding the spiritual, political, and economic life of the rabbis. Avi-Yonah's work pays little attention to religious and cultural issues, but it is a comprehensive political history of the Rabbinic period. We should also mention here two classic essays which, although somewhat outdated in their scholarly method, are vivid evocations of the Talmudic period: Judah Goldin, "The Period of the Talmud," in Louis Finkelstein, ed., *The Jews: Their History,*

Culture, and Religion (Jewish Publication Society, 1960), and Gerson Cohen, "The Talmudic Age," in Leo Schwarz, ed., *Great Ages and Ideas of the Jewish People* (Modern Library, 1977).

All of the works mentioned so far deal almost entirely with Palestinian Jewry; what of the Babylonian Jewish community? It has received less attention from historians for several reasons. To the extent that the interest of at least some Christian scholars in Judaism is fueled by their interest in the origins of Christianity, they are bound to be far less curious about a Jewish community that flourished in an essentially non-Christian environment. Secondly, in contrast to that of Palestinian Jewry, the cultural development of the Babylonian Jewish community seems to have taken place in relative cultural isolation; there seems to have been relatively little cross-pollination between Judaism and the Iranian faiths. The history of Babylonian Jewry therefore becomes, as it were, a purely Jewish affair, one neglected, with some notable exceptions, by the non-Jewish scholarly world.

There are nonetheless two scholars in particular who have done important pioneering work on the history of Babylonian Jewry: Jacob Neusner and Isaiah Gafni. Neusner's five-volume *History of the Jews of Babylonia* (Leiden: E. J. Brill, 1966–70) is an ambitious and wide-ranging work, touching on many aspects of Persian as well as Jewish history. Fortunately, Neusner has made some of his principal conclusions available in a popular condensation entitled *There We Sat Down* (Ktav Publishing House, 1978). In this slim volume Neusner summarizes what the rabbis perceived their importance to be as well as the actual extent of their power and influence in the wider community.

Isaiah Gafni has excelled in mining rabbinic material judiciously for the historical insights it can yield; unfortunately for the English reader most of his work—including a recently published history of Babylonian Jewry—has appeared only in Hebrew. Those interested in a brief summary of some of his major findings concerning the rabbinic community in Babylonia should consult his historical introduction to *The Literature of the Sages: First Part* (Assen/Philadelphia: Van Gorcum and Fortress Press, 1988).

Finally, we should note that another pathway, less historically precise but perhaps more vivid, into the world of the rabbis is that of biographies of key rabbinic figures. Such works include Jacob Neusner's *First Century Judaism in Crisis* (Ktav Publishing House, 1982), a popular version of his biography of Yohanan ben Zakkai, who played an important role in enabling Jews and Judaism to survive the trauma of the Second Temple's destruction; Louis Finkelstein's *Akiba: Scholar, Saint and Martyr* (Northvale, N.J.: Jason Aronson, 1990); and Milton

Steinberg's *As a Driven Leaf* (Northvale, N.J.: Jason Aronson, 1987), a historical novel built around the life of Elisha ben Abuyah, a brilliant rabbi of second-century Palestine who became a heretic. Steinberg's novel is particularly successful in imparting the flavor of rabbinic life and thought.

Rabbinic Thought

Studying rabbinic thought is a particularly formidable task for at least two reasons. The rabbis did not arrange their views according to Western canons of organization, nor did they often abstract broad principles from their detailed legal discourse. It was therefore left to others—medieval Jewish philosophers and modern scholars of Judaica—to make rabbinic thought accessible to the Western reader. We should note further that "rabbinic thought" is somewhat of a misnomer. The rabbinic community included individuals of widely varying viewpoints who did not feel constrained, for the most part, to reach a consensus on matters of theology. Moreover, the Rabbinic period spans six centuries; it is hard to imagine that even those views which did gain general acceptance did not undergo some change over time. Keeping these caveats in mind, let us examine some of the attempts to present rabbinic thought systematically.

As in the case of the socioeconomic and political history of the Rabbinic period, its intellectual history is best understood against the background of the preceding era. An excellent guide to the beliefs of the numerous sects of the Second Temple period is George W. E. Nickelsburg and Michael Stone, *Faith and Piety in Early Judaism: Texts and Documents* (Philadelphia: Fortress Press, 1983). Drawing material from the Bible, the Apocrypha, Josephus, Philo, the Qumran documents, rabbinic literature, and the New Testament, Nickelsburg and Stone present thematically the major theological beliefs and concerns of the Jewish sects of the late Second Temple period.

Turning to studies of rabbinic theology, we begin with the classic work of George Foot Moore, *Judaism in the First Century of the Christian Era: The Age of the Tannaim* (Harvard University Press, 1962). Moore, along with R. Travers Herford, was one of the first Christian scholars of Judaica to attempt to understand Judaism in its own terms, rather than simply as a precursor of Christianity. He explained that this meant paying less attention to the apocalyptic writings of the late Second Temple period—which interested Christian scholars because their messianism seemed to them to prefigure the coming of Christ—and more attention to rabbinic sources. Unfortunately, in at least one important regard Moore ignores his own strictures; although it is clear that the primary interest of the early rabbis was Halakhah (Jewish law), Moore devotes only one section out of seven to a discussion of religious observance. The above and other criticisms notwithstanding, Moore's work was instrumental in putting the study of Rabbinic Judaism on the scholarly agenda.

Another early attempt at presenting rabbinic theology is Solomon Schechter's *Aspects of Rabbinic Theology* (Schocken Books, 1961). This work and Moore's are two sides of the same coin; Schechter's protestations in his introduction notwithstanding, this work is above all an impassioned defense of the nobility of Jewish belief. His choice of topics, as well as the titles he gives them, is a more faithful rendition of the rabbi's theological agenda than is Moore's. Once again, however, the actual details of religious observance get short shrift.

A recent attempt to systematize rabbinic theology is E. E. Urbach, *The Sages* (Harvard University Press, 1987). This work is truly monumental in its scope and is an orderly and sensitive rendering of rabbinic thinking. Like the works above, it too concentrates on the narratives and explicitly theological statements of the rabbis rather than on the implicit theology of the legal rabbinic material.

The most provocative and promising approach to understanding rabbinic thought is that of Jacob Neusner. He understands that rabbinic religion is best understood by means of a thorough analysis of its primary, mainly halakhic, documents. This means differentiating chronologically the strata of each text and examining the agenda of each stratum. This also means that understanding rabbinic thought involves identifying the questions implicitly raised and answered by rabbinic writings rather than superimposing our own questions upon them. A prime example of Neusner's work in this area is his *Judaism: The Evidence of the Mishnah* (Scholars Press, 1988). This book is not an easy one to read, but it is important for anyone seeking to understand the present and future direction of the study of rabbinic thought.

We cannot leave the arena of rabbinic thought without reflecting more upon Halakhah, often translated as "Jewish law" but perhaps better defined as "the Jewish way." Halakhah encompasses every aspect of daily life, both personal and public, and includes aspirations as well as obligations. The study of Halakhah involves tracing its Second Temple origins, understanding its methodology, organizing and conceptualizing its particulars, and investigating the influence of socioeconomic and other factors on its development.

Unfortunately, most of the works available in English are too technical to recommend to the general reader. That having been said, the essays "Oral Torah" and "Halakhah," which appear in Gafni's *The Literature of the Sages: First Part* (mentioned earlier) are fairly readable discussions of Halakhah's origins, development, and methods. Louis Ginzberg's essay "On the Significance of Jewish Law," in his *On Jewish Law and Lore* (Atheneum, 1977), although reductionist in its explanation of halakhic legislation in exclusively economic terms, is an instructive illustration of the way in which Halakhah can be understood as reflecting the socioeconomic concerns of its formulators. A good general survey of the contents and concerns of Halakhah can be found in Adin Steinsaltz's *The Essential Talmud* (Basic Books, 1982).

Rabbinic Literature

Because of the vastness of rabbinic literature it would be foolhardy and counterproductive to discuss the introductions, studies, and translations available for each work in the rabbinic corpus. The rabbis themselves said: "If you take hold of too much you take hold of nothing at all." The following survey therefore looks at representative works from each genre—mishnaic, talmudic, midrashic—of rabbinic writing. For each I have recommended, where possible: an introduction to the cultural and historical context and the concerns and methods of that work; an anthology containing topically arranged excerpts; a study guide; and a reliable, well-annotated translation.

In addition I should point out that there are two other major types of rabbinic literature—mystical writings and liturgical texts—which I will not explore in my discussion here. (Rabbinic mystical sources are discussed in chapter 9, "Jewish Mysticism"; liturgy and its development are explored in chapter 4, "The Jewish Middle Ages.")

Those interested in a concise introduction to the whole of rabbinic literature should read Hermann L. Strack, *Introduction to the Talmud and Midrash* (Atheneum, 1970). This work can be supplemented by the more recent *The Literature of the Sages: First Part* (mentioned earlier). Unfortunately, this volume covers only Mishnah, Tosefta, the Talmuds, and the minor tractates. The projected second volume will cover Midrash, Aggadah, the Targums (Aramaic translations/expositions of the Bible), and liturgy.

Mishnaic literature   This genre includes the Mishnah, the Tosefta—a collection of traditions from the period of the Mishnah which sometimes explain or supplement the Mishnah and sometimes differ with it—and the various *beraitot*—that is, early traditions not incorporated into the Mishnah—found in the two Talmuds. For the most part the style of mishnaic literature is casuistic: Mishnah and Tosefta usually set forth a series of cases illustrating principles of law rather than enunciating those principles explicitly. Another striking feature of Mishnah is the relative paucity of biblical citations. Though many of the rulings and principles in Mishnah and Tosefta are based on scriptural interpretation, one would never know it, based on the evidence provided by the works themselves.

An excellent introduction to Mishnah is Dov Zlotnick, *The Iron Pillar—Mishnah: Redaction, Form, and Content* (Ktav Publishing House, 1988). As the subtitle indicates, Zlotnick deals mainly with the history of the Mishnah's composition—in particular, the role of Rabbi Judah the Patriarch in editing the traditions of earlier generations—and the formal characteristics of Mishnah, particularly those related to its having been originally an oral work that was meant to be memorized. Zlotnick also discusses to what extent Rabbi Judah the Patriarch intended the Mishnah to be an authoritative code of law. A much briefer but still helpful introduction is Herbert Danby's introduction to his translation of Mishnah (see below). Zlotnick's introduction is nicely complemented by Jacob Neusner, *The Mishnah: An Introduction* (Northvale, N.J.: Jason Aronson, 1989), which focuses more on the Mishnah as an articulation of a particular socioreligious vision. Two valuable introductions to the Tosefta are Avraham Goldberg's chapter on the Tosefta, in *The Literature of the Sages: First Part*, and Boaz Cohen's introduction to his *Mishnah and Tosefta Shabbat* (Jewish Theological Seminary, 1935).

There are a number of good Mishnah anthologies. The best is Eugene Lipman, *The Mishnah* (Schocken Books, 1974). This work possesses the dual virtues of brevity and comprehensiveness. It covers all of the tractates, summarizing the subject matter and providing a representative excerpt for each. Another useful anthology, though less comprehensive, is Isidore Fishman, *Gateway to the Mishnah* (Bridgeport, Conn.: Hartmore House, 1976).

When considering a study guide for Mishnah or for any rabbinic text, one should be seeking guidance both in understanding the meaning and implications of the individual words, phrases, and sentences and in gaining insight into the document's organization and broad conceptions. Taken together, two works by Jacob Neusner fulfill these two functions for Mishnah. *Learn Mishnah* (Behrman House, 1978), although written for junior high school students, is a wonderful introduction for students of all ages to the methods and concerns of the Mishnah because its style is lively, it takes nothing for granted, and it is written with an eye to Mishnah's application to contemporary society. The second work, *Invita-*

tion to the Talmud, revised and expanded edition (Harper & Row, 1984), admirably addresses all of the aforementioned agendas. Using the relatively brief and somewhat arcane eighth chapter of Tractate Berakhot as a model, Neusner introduces the reader to Mishnah, Tosefta, the Palestinian Talmud, and the Babylonian Talmud. Neusner is not only adept at shuttling back and forth from the general to the specific, he also enables us to see the relationships and differences among the Mishnah, Tosefta, and the two Talmuds.

When we turn to translations, pride of place with regard to Mishnah belongs to Herbert Danby, *The Mishnah* (Oxford University Press, 1985). This fine translation manages to combine precision and clarity with an impressive fidelity to the style and syntax of the Hebrew original. Its only drawback is the relatively meager number of explanatory footnotes. Another popular translation is Phillip Blackman, *The Mishnah* (New York: Judaica Press, 1962). This seven-volume work includes the pointed and punctuated Hebrew text, extensive explanatory notes, and a reference volume including a general index which can be used to find what Mishnah has to say about a broad range of subjects. For Tosefta one can consult Jacob Neusner's multivolume translation, *The Tosefta* (Ktav Publishing House, 1977–81). Neusner's strength as a translator is that he breaks down long passages into more digestible units in a way that helps one follow the ebb and flow of rabbinic discourse. On the other hand, his translations are at times not as precise as one would wish.

Talmudic literature   When one speaks of rabbinic literature one means, as often as not, the Talmud, particularly the Babylonian Talmud. Ostensibly written as commentaries to the Mishnah, both the Palestinian and Babylonian Talmuds are much more: repositories of legend and lore, theological speculation, and the parry and thrust of legal and logical argumentation. For centuries the hallmark of Jewish erudition was knowledge of these most difficult texts. The Talmud often looms before the beginner as an insurmountable Everest. By setting realistic goals and using the right tools, however, one can find a way to scale this peak.

Introductions to the Babylonian Talmud are legion, but of wildly varying scope and quality. It is difficult to recommend wholeheartedly any of the introductions presently available because few of them take into account the more recent advances in our understanding of the Babylonian Talmud as a literary work—thanks to studies by Avraham Weiss, David Halivni, Shamma Friedman and others—and as a comprehensive religious statement, as has been shown in the works of Jacob Neusner. (Neusner's ideas on this subject appear in accessible form in chapter 1 of his *Invitation to the Talmud,* previously cited.) A notable exception

Using the tools of modern technology for Talmud study. Professor Judith Hauptman, shown here, teaches Talmud at the Jewish Theological Seminary. (Photograph by Lori Grinker/Contact Press Images)

is David Kraemer's recent *The Mind of the Talmud* (Oxford University Press, 1990). This work is, in the words of its subtitle, an intellectual history of the Babylonian Talmud, charting the changing forms of expression and argumentation in the era of the Talmud and using these findings to draw conclusions about the religious concerns and assumptions of the various generations of talmudic rabbis. A popular introduction to the Babylonian Talmud is Adin Steinsaltz, *The Essential Talmud* (previously mentioned). The strengths of this introduction are its articulate, well-organized presentation of the content and methodology of the Talmud and its attempt to explain the Talmud's importance for the contemporary Jew.

In contrast to the Babylonian Talmud, introductions to the Palestinian Talmud are practically nonexistent. The classic introduction is Louis Ginzberg's "The Palestinian Talmud," in his *On Jewish Law and Lore* (mentioned earlier). Much progress has been made in the study of the Palestinian Talmud since Ginzberg's essay was first published in 1941, most of all because of the inestimable contribution of Saul Lieberman and his disciples; Ginzberg's essay should therefore be supplemented by the recent "The Palestinian Talmud," in *The Literature of the Sages: First Part* (previously mentioned).

There are three standard anthologies available for the Babylonian Talmud.

(Actually, although they draw most of their material from the Babylonian Talmud, all three include excerpts from other rabbinic writings as well.) The best of these is C. G. Montefiore and H. Loewe, *A Rabbinic Anthology* (Schocken Books, 1974). The anthology itself is broad in scope and rich in content. The choice of subjects and passages reflects the close attention paid to the views and concerns of the rabbis—rather than, as is sometimes the case, those of the anthologist. The work is further enhanced by Montefiore's introduction, in which he writes thoughtfully about his labors as an anthologist, and by Loewe's learned notes. Finally, because of the work's dialogical and highly personal elements, one has the feeling that the anthology is the product not simply of historical curiosity but of a desire on the part of Loewe and, particularly, Montefiore to define—and thereby reconsider—their own views on life and faith in the light of those of the rabbis. This aspect of the anthology invites the reader to approach rabbinic thinking in a similarly personal way.

A work of similar quality, though more limited in scope, is A. Cohen, *Everyman's Talmud* (Schocken Books, 1975), which was produced at about the same time as *A Rabbinic Anthology*. (In his introduction Montefiore claims that he would not have composed his anthology had Cohen's work appeared earlier; he suggests that his readers may want to purchase Cohen's work as well and even lists its price!) Cohen's work is somewhat less comprehensive—although he does touch on a few areas of Halakhah, a realm neglected almost entirely by Montefiore and Loewe. The weakest of the three anthologies is Louis I. Newman, *The Talmudic Anthology* (Behrman House, 1978). Its method of organization is peculiar and the subjects covered seem to reflect the interests of the editor more than those of the rabbis. As in the case of introductions, the Palestinian Talmud is the poor relation with regard to anthologies as well. One available anthology is Jacob Neusner, *Our Sages, God and Israel: An Anthology of the Talmud of the Land of Israel* (Rossel Books, 1985).

The best introductory study guide for both Talmuds for the reader with no knowledge of Hebrew and Aramaic is probably Neusner's *Invitation to the Talmud* (mentioned above). Also useful as an introduction to the Babylonian Talmud is Neusner's *Learn Talmud* (Behrman House, 1979), a companion volume to his *Learn Mishnah*, mentioned above (in fact, the talmudic passages analyzed in *Learn Talmud* are commentaries to passages of Mishnah studied in *Learn Mishnah*). One should also read Robert Goldenberg's chapter on Talmud, in Barry Holtz, ed., *Back to the Sources: Reading the Classic Jewish Texts* (Summit Books, 1986). It should be said, however—as Goldenberg notes—that the traditional study of Talmud has been with a study partner and/or mentor, and for good reason. Both the complexity of the Talmud and the value of thinking through its implications "out loud" make study with a friend or mentor a *desideratum* of the first order.

The best-known, and only complete English translation of the Babylonian Talmud is that published by the Soncino Press under the editorship of Isidore Epstein (London, 1961). It is available both in a multivolume set which contains only the translation and, for many tractates, in a bilingual edition in which the translation faces the original Talmud text. This translation, though meticulous, is not particularly useful for the beginner; one might say it is *too* faithful to the original in its terse and elliptical style. There are also few notes to help the novice make sense of technical terms and opaque passages. Two new translations-in-progress should prove to be of better help to beginners. One is Adin Steinsaltz, *The Talmud: The Steinsaltz Edition*, vols. 1–3 (Random House, 1989–90). Thus far Steinsaltz has translated the first few chapters of Bava Metzia, one of the tractates with which one traditionally begins study of the Talmud. His edition includes, besides a literal translation and extensive notes, an expanded translation which in effect weaves together translation and basic commentary. A second

Yeshiva students engage in talmudic argumentation. (Photograph by David H. Wells/J. B. Pictures)

translation is now being produced as part of the ArtScroll series by Mesorah Publications (Brooklyn, N.Y.). Thus far the series has produced editions of the tractates Makkot and Eruvin (both were published in 1990). This edition contains an
introduction to each tractate as well as to each of its chapters which gives the
reader basic terms and concepts, extensive notes, and (particularly in the case of
Eruvin) extremely helpful diagrams, and a generally lucid and felicitous English
translation. The Palestinian Talmud is presently being translated into English
under the editorship of Jacob Neusner (*The Talmud of the Land of Israel*, translated by Jacob Neusner, vols. 26–35 [University of Chicago Press, 1982–1990]);
the volumes that have appeared thus far, however, are of uneven quality.

Midrashic literature   Although the rabbis developed a branch of law, the
Oral Torah, that went far beyond the parameters of the Bible, they regarded all
law and theology as being ultimately grounded in the biblical text. The term
"midrash" refers to the rabbinic enterprise of interpreting and, at times, reading
their own ideas into passages of the Bible. Halakhic midrash is devoted to interpreting the legal portions of the Torah, either to generate new laws or to find
biblical support for already existing ones, while aggadic midrash supplies a running commentary to the narrative portions of the Torah; in this form aggadic
midrash is referred to as exegetical midrash. At times aggadic midrash consists of
sermonic exploration of a theme which is suggested by a verse or verses which
serve as a springboard for the sermon; this form of midrash is sometimes referred
to as homiletical midrash. A third form of aggadic midrash is narrative midrash,
a retelling of a biblical narrative with the incorporation of new legends and em-
bellishments.

A good introduction to the genesis and cultural context of midrash is James
Kugel's essay, in James Kugel and Rowan A. Greer, *Early Biblical Interpretation*
(Philadelphia: Westminster Press, 1988). Kugel's essay "Two Introductions to
Midrash," in Geoffrey H. Hartman and Sanford Budick, eds., *Midrash and Literature* (Yale University Press, 1986), helps us understand midrash as the rabbinic
successor to biblical prophecy and also explains the theological assumptions
underlying the midrash's seemingly atomistic treatment of the biblical text. A
fine theoretical and practical introduction to midrash in all its forms is Barry
Holtz's chapter on midrash in *Back to the Sources* (mentioned above).

The classic multivolume midrashic anthology is Louis Ginzberg, *Legends of
the Jews* (Jewish Publication Society, 1956). Ginzberg has in effect written a narrative midrash of his own; he has woven together a myriad of midrashic traditions

and produced a rabbinic retelling of sacred history from Creation to the time of Esther. This seven-volume work includes two volumes of notes which trace each of the traditions incorporated into the text. The greatness of Ginzberg's work, besides its monumental erudition, is that it allows us to see biblical history through the eyes of a midrashist—the terse and often enigmatic biblical text embroidered by lush and sometimes fantastic tales. Its major shortcoming is that, precisely because of the seamless joining of divergent tradition with a total elimination of the exegesis that is their basis, we get little sense of the style and form of the original midrashim. Another valuable addition to the midrashic anthologies available in English is due to appear this year from Schocken Books: William G. Braude's translation of the *Sefer Ha-Aggadah* (entitled in English *The Book of Legends*), a wonderful topically arranged anthology of rabbinic tales and parables compiled by the Hebrew poet Hayim Nahman Bialik and his colleague Yehoshua Hana Ravnitzky. Much briefer than Ginzberg's work but infinitely more successful in evoking the poetic style of midrash is Nahum N. Glatzer, ed., *Hammer on the Rock: A Short Midrash Reader* (Schocken Books, 1962). Like Ginzberg, Glatzer follows the chronology of the Bible. However, the midrashim he chooses tend to be rabbinic attempts to apply the wisdom of the Torah to their own lives and the lives of others. Thus, midrash truly appears in the guise of Torah—a guide for everyday living.

Two works that function both as anthologies of midrash and guides to the study of its various genres are Gary G. Porton, *Understanding Rabbinic Midrash* (Ktav Publishing House, 1985), and Jacob Neusner, *The Midrash: An Introduction* (Northvale, N.J.: Jason Aronson, 1990). Porton translates and analyzes long excerpts from the major halakhic midrashim (Mekhilta, Sifra, and Sifre), the earliest exegetical midrash (Genesis Rabbah), and an early homiletical midrash (Leviticus Rabbah). Though one may quibble with some of his interpretations, the way in which he leads the reader through the complexities of midrashic discourse and his care in pulling together the details of each excerpt to provide a coherent picture of the passage as a whole makes his work a fine introduction for the beginner. Neusner, in contrast to Porton, does not concern himself with close readings of particular passages. He cites midrashim mainly in order to illustrate the stylistic characteristics and thematic concerns of the various midrashic compilations. In short, Porton's book is more useful for becoming familiar with the details of midrashic method; Neusner provides an excellent introduction to the broad characteristics and concerns of a number of early midrash collections.

The most comprehensive translation of aggadic midrash is H. Freedman and Maurice Simon, eds., *The Midrash Rabbah* (New York: Soncino Press, 1977).

This is a translation of those midrash collections for the Pentateuch and the Five Scrolls known as Midrash Rabbah. Unfortunately, as in the Soncino translation of the Babylonian Talmud, fidelity to the original is stressed at the expense of clarity. Two fine, more recent translations of aggadic midrash are Jacob Neusner, *Genesis Rabbah: A New American Translation* (Scholars Press, 1985) and *Pesikta de Rav Kahana*, translated by William G. Braude and Israel J. Kapstein (Jewish Publication Society, 1975). Genesis Rabbah should be read by any student of midrash because it is the earliest compilation of exegetical midrash; Pesikta de Rav Kahana, a collection of occasional sermons compiled some time before 650 c.e., should be read for the sheer pleasure of "hearing" masterfully constructed sermons from the Rabbinic period. Jacob Neusner has translated other aggadic midrashim; a complete bibliography can be found at the end of *The Midrash: An Introduction.*

All of the major halakhic midrashim have been translated into English. The translations include *Mekhilta de Rabbi Ishmael,* translated and edited by Jacob Z. Lauterbach (Jewish Publication Society, 1976); Jacob Neusner, *Sifra: An Analytical Translation* (Scholars Press, 1988); Jacob Neusner and William Scott Green, *Sifre to Numbers: An American Translation* (Atlanta: Scholars Press, 1986); and *Sifre: A Tannaitic Commentary on the Book of Deuteronomy,* translated by Reuven Hammer (Yale University Press, 1986). Last but not least, mention should be made of Judah Goldin, *The Song at the Sea* (Jewish Publication Society, 1990). In this work, a translation of Mekhilta's commentary to Exodus 15, the song which Israel sang at the sea after being redeemed from the pursuing Egyptians, Goldin provides excellent notes and explanations, and the translation itself is unusually and felicitously poetic. This volume can serve as an excellent introduction both to exegetical midrash and to the aggadic form of tannaitic midrash.

Judaism and Christianity

There are good historical as well as contemporary reasons for Jews to be interested in the history of early Christianity: the founders and most of the early adherents of Christianity were Jews; the individual most responsible for the early reform of Christianity was a Jew, Saul of Tarsus, later to be known as Paul; and Christians came to see themselves as the New Israel, that is, as continuators of, and successors to, the covenant God made with the Jewish people. As far as the present is concerned, most Jews live in predominantly Christian societies and are therefore curious about Christianity and its relationship to Judaism. Moreover, Jews are often the objects of their Christian neighbors' curiosity and therefore feel called upon to define, for themselves and for Christians, the similarities and differences between Judaism and Christianity.

A study of early Christianity from a Jewish perspective involves understanding how early Christianity both drew from and reacted against its Jewish roots and how Rabbinic Judaism reacted to the phenomenon of Jewish Christians and Christianity generally. Ideally one should begin by reading those books of Christian scriptures which are most intimately connected with Judaism: the Synoptic Gospels (Mark, Matthew, and Luke), Acts, and Hebrews. A helpful summary of these, and indeed, all the writings in the Christian scriptures from a Jewish perspective is Samuel Sandmel, *A Jewish Understanding of the New Testament* (Ktav Publishing House, 1974). A more technical commentary on the Synoptic Gospels which provides the Jewish background for many of the verses in these gospels is Samuel Tobias Lachs, *A Rabbinic Commentary on the New Testament* (Anti-Defamation League and Ktav Publishing House, 1987). Lach's brief but informative preface surveys previous rabbinic commentaries on Christian scriptures and enumerates the strengths and weaknesses of each.

The extensive citation and interpretation of the Hebrew Bible in Christian writings raises the question of the extent to which Christian interpretation of the Bible was influenced by Jewish exegesis and in what ways it differed. Early Jewish Christians shared with their fellow Jews, after all, a belief in the Hebrew Bible as God's word, and certain exegetical modes of interpreting that word. At the same time, they wished to find in the Bible evidence for a faith that, particularly after the Pauline reforms, was strikingly different from Judaism of their time. A helpful guide to these issues is Rowan Greer's essay, in James Kugel and Rowan A. Greer, *Early Biblical Interpretation* (previously mentioned). Greer defines the different methods of scriptural interpretation used in the early Church and summarizes the debates among early Christians about the degree and nature of the authority of the Hebrew Bible. Another valuable work in this realm is Michael Hilton and Gordian Marshall, *The Gospels and Rabbinic Judaism: A Study Guide* (Ktav Publishing House, 1988). This book grew out of Bible study groups, run jointly by the authors, comprising both Christians and Jews. The work compares the views of Rabbinic Judaism and early Christianity on a number of topics and shows how Jewish and Christian texts are mutually illuminated when read in light of each other.

The two principal figures in early Christianity are Jesus himself and Paul.

Both were steeped in the Judaism of their time and their teachings are therefore heavily colored by Jewish concerns and modes of expression. Geza Vermes, in a scholarly and provocative work, *Jesus the Jew: A Historian's Reading of the Gospels* (Philadelphia: Fortress Press, 1981), claims that the portrait of Jesus painted in the Synoptic Gospels is that of a Galilean holy man, a type familiar to us from contemporary rabbinic sources. Through a study of the titles applied to Jesus in the Gospels, moreover, Vermes argues that the theological claims they represent were both familiar and, at least in theory, acceptable to Palestinian Jews of Jesus' time.

The relationship of Paul to Rabbinic Judaism is more complex. Paul, by concluding that observance of the law (i.e., Jewish law, Halakhah) is unnecessary for one's spiritual salvation, clearly separates himself from the Judaism of his youth, yet he feels compelled to use the methods and sacred texts of Rabbinic Judaism in order to explain and justify this conclusion. A full discussion and analysis of Paul's statements about the law is E. P. Sanders, *Paul, the Law, and the Jewish People* (Philadelphia: Fortress Press, 1983). Sanders shows that although Paul's statements about law cannot be melded into a systematic theology, they all share a common assumption: belief in Christ, rather than observance of the law, is the road to salvation. In the last section of his book, Sanders discusses how Paul, who altered radically what was essentially a Jewish sect so that it became a religious community unto itself, reconciled his apostleship for Christ with his membership in the people of Israel.

Before leaving the discussion of the Jewish roots of Christianity, we should mention the work of Alan F. Segal, *Rebecca's Children: Judaism and Christianity in the Roman World* (Harvard University Press, 1989). Segal reminds us that although Judaism was in existence well before the rise of Christianity, *Rabbinic* Judaism and Christianity developed more or less at the same time. Christianity should not be seen, therefore, merely as an offshoot of Judaism; rather, Rabbinic Judaism and Christianity constitute differing responses—although these responses use similar concepts and terminology—to the political, social, and religious crises of first-century Palestine.

We must finally consider the other side of the coin, that is, Jewish attitudes toward Christianity. There are few explicit references to Christianity in rabbinic sources, making it difficult to assess rabbinic attitudes toward Christianity. Ironically, this task has been made even more difficult because of efforts by medieval Church censors to excise or modify any talmudic references to Christianity. R. Travers Herford, in his *Christianity in Talmud and Midrash* (Ktav Publishing

House, n.d.), collects and analyzes all references in the Babylonian Talmud—including those that were expurgated by Christian censors and therefore do not appear in standard editions of the Talmud—to Jesus and to *minim* (sectarians). Although much of what Herford writes is outdated (the work was first published in 1903), some of his analysis still stands; in any case, many of the talmudic passages themselves, which Herford translates in full, make for fascinating reading.

While Herford deals mainly with aggadic passages, Lawrence H. Schiffman's *Who Was a Jew?* (Ktav Publishing House, 1985) treats rabbinic halakhic texts which discuss definitions of Jewish identity and the implications of these texts for rabbinic acceptance, or non-acceptance, of Jewish Christians as Jews. Schiffman argues that although the rabbis altered their liturgy in a way designed to make Jewish Christians feel uncomfortable in the synagogue, the true break between Rabbinic Judaism and Christianity came only with the admission of gentiles, whom the rabbis could not consider Jews, into the Christian fold.

The period of the rabbis was a crucial and dramatic one for the history of Judaism. The rabbis set for themselves the gargantuan task of constructing a spiritual edifice that could transcend the physical destruction of the Second Temple. The world they created, though it may seem foreign and faraway to many readers, has proven to be one of the most important forces in shaping Judaism to this very day. It is my hope that the works we have reviewed will provide readers with an opportunity to enter that world and reflect on its relevance for their own spiritual and cultural identity.

CHAPTER 4

THE JEWISH MIDDLE AGES

Ivan G. Marcus

The Middle Ages have had a bad press since the fifteenth century when printing was invented. We dismiss it as a time of prejudice, violence, and intolerance, and we take for granted that Jews in the Middle Ages lived worse than most, huddled together in squalid ghettos, deprived of rights, constantly persecuted. But this impression is misleading. Western Civilization as we know it was created in the Middle Ages. For Christians, Muslims, and Jews, it was a time of great creativity which had a lasting influence. In Europe, parliamentary representative government was invented and nurtured; the towns in which most Europeans live today were founded and expanded, magnificent Gothic cathedrals built; universities, too, were invented in medieval Paris, Oxford, and Cambridge; stories about King Arthur's court expressed a new conception of romantic love which only modern feminism has challenged. In the Muslim East, scholars studied and translated Plato and Aristotle and scientific and mathematical texts temporarily "lost" to the West; Muslim Arabs—and Italian Christians—developed instruments of banking and credit for the international commerce which tied them together across the Mediterranean.

Because we live today in a time of renewed religious agitation that traces its origins to medieval beginnings, it is especially urgent that we appreciate how all three Western religious civilizations transformed ancient legacies into the religious cultures that became the new world order of Western Civilization. The Jewish Middle Ages flourished in both Christian and Muslim cultural worlds during this thousand-year period—roughly from the fifth through fifteenth centuries—and were no less protean. Judaism always was a religious civilization or culture, centered on organized communities with leaders, laws, factions, rivalries. Religious interpretation was undertaken not only to fathom God's will but also to govern better in accordance with that will. Politics and religion were complementary, not antithetical, forces. In this respect, medieval Judaism was no different from the other Western religious civilizations of Christianity and Islam.

We can think of defining features of medieval Jewish history externally, in relation to the cultures among which Jews lived, and also internally, in light of how Judaism itself changed between antiquity and modernity. In antiquity, Jews lived as a legally constituted, self-governing religious corporation or polity. The host cultures of Persia, Greece, and Rome were polytheistic and were not committed to a single divine power who monopolized all truth and power over the world. In such an environment, the Jewish community was permitted to practice its ancestral customs—which the Jews called Torah—on a par with other ethnic minorities and with members of the ruling culture of the empire.

This general policy of "corporate equality" changed when the more exclusivistic religious ideologies of Christianity or Islam became world political forces. For different reasons and to varying degrees, Jews in Christian lands and Christians and Jews under Islam were now treated as members of religious corporations that were supposed to be politically, economically, and socially subordinated to the members of the faithful majority. It is this standing of "corporate subordination" under Christian and Muslim rule that defines the Jewish Middle Ages as far as external or non-Jewish social and political power and culture are concerned.

Based on this operational definition, conditions of the Jewish Middle Ages can be said to prevail wherever and whenever Jews were tolerated as a self-governing religious polity under Muslim and Christian regimes and required to be subordinate to the majority culture and society. Viewed this way, medieval Jewish conditions yielded to modernity whenever and wherever corporate subordination was replaced by individual equality, the promise or reality of Jewish individuals living on an equal footing with other citizens or subjects of a particular national state.

Complementing this external framework is an internal one. The Jewish

Middle Ages are also that time when the modes of Jewish religious culture and community typical of ancient or "classical" Judaism were refashioned into "traditional" Jewish civilization. To appreciate this fundamental historical shift, we may compare Judaism in the early seventh century, when the classical phase reached its maturity, with newer expressions of Jewish culture and self-government that emerged in Muslim and Christian lands in the Middle Ages. In the seventh century, Judaism consisted of only a few authoritative books of Jewish wisdom, starting with the rabbis' canonization of the Hebrew Bible, and complemented by the first documents of rabbinic law and lore, such as the Mishnah and Tosefta, the earliest homiletical Bible commentaries on Genesis and Leviticus, some of the obligatory and optional prayers and benedictions, the Palestinian and Babylonian Talmuds, and many customs and practices that the early rabbis included in what they called the "Oral Torah." Despite the rabbis' confidence that they were properly interpreting God's will for their time, it is unlikely that they actually had much influence over the religious lives of most Jews in the classical age.

They achieved this during the next thousand years when Jewish communal life was refashioned and Judaism was transformed. From the new Muslim capital of Baghdad, central Jewish rabbinic authorities called Geonim imposed their interpretation of Jewish law on world Jewry. Aided by the centralized Muslim authority that ruled over ninety-five percent of world Jewry, they made it stick. The Geonim accomplished this by making new legal instruments with which they shaped world Jewry in their own image. They invented the prayer book and thereby standardized the liturgy. They invented the legal code and included in it only their interpretation of the Babylonian, not the Palestinian, Talmud and this provided local judges with legal standards for their communities. And to settle anything left unclear in the codes, the Geonim invented *teshuvot* or answers to questions which religious judges sent to them from every community around the Mediterranean. These legal opinions, also called responsa, became authoritative precedents for centuries. By inventing the prayer book, law codes, and responsa, the Geonim created "halakhic" or religiously binding Judaism for nearly all of the Jewish world, and it remained the constitution of Jewish communal life until the modern age.

A Jew living in the seventh century knew of none of these Gaonic achievements. Nor would he have heard of other medieval Jewish innovations such as liturgical poetry or Jewish religious philosophy. Other refashionings of Judaism that were not part of classical Judaism include the varieties of Jewish mystical lore or kabbalah, Hebrew grammar, manuscript illuminations, Hebrew secular poetry, and Jewish versions of internationally known stories about world figures such as Alexander the Great, King Arthur, as well as original Jewish fantasies. By the twelfth century, side by side with the many forms of traditional Judaism we find in Christian Europe new forms of local Jewish self-government and communal organization. All of these innovative religious and political expressions of the Jewish imagination transformed or reimagined many of the sacred writings of classical Judaism and persisted as central features of traditional Judaism until modernity.

To introduce the reader to these trends at work during the long period when Jews lived in Muslim and Christian lands as a self-governing traditional religious culture, I have selected books with two primary criteria in mind. They offer original and conceptually challenging interpretations of an important aspect of medieval Jewish history or provide the reader access to significant sources from the period. Guidance to further and more specialized work may be found elsewhere, and I want to mention these before proceeding. Several years ago, a few colleagues and I contributed to a book that was devoted entirely to essays about books and articles written on the Jewish Middle Ages. *Bibliographical Essays in Medieval Jewish Studies* (Ktav Publishing House, 1976) is a guide to scholarly works on medieval Jewish civilization that goes into more detail than is possible here. Two other places to find well-crafted short introductory essays on many topics that will be discussed here are the articles on the Jews and Judaism included in Joseph Strayer, ed., *The Dictionary of the Middle Ages* (Scribners, 1982–87) and in the *Encyclopaedia Judaica* (Keter Publishing Co., 1972).

General Surveys

I wish that I could start by recommending books that offer a comprehensive introduction to the entire subject. I cannot because they do not exist. One book that appears to do this, Israel Abrahams's, *Jewish Life in the Middle Ages* (Atheneum, 1969) contains an odd assortment of facts, but is not a coherent narrative history. Obviously, we need just such a book, but at the moment we must settle for a different approach.

Two types of books that are available deal with the medieval period as a whole but do so as part of a larger agenda. We have collections of essays written by several authors on the sweep of Jewish history, and there are one-volume histories of the

Jews written by a single author. Both kinds of books necessarily seek to make sense of some version of the Jewish Middle Ages.

I suggest beginning with a book that has stood the test of time and for which Hadassah, its original sponsor, has every reason to be proud. Although Leo Schwarz's *Great Ages and Ideas of the Jewish People* (Modern Library, 1977) has a relatively weak chapter by Cecil Roth on the medieval period in Christian Europe, the other essays are classics, including Abraham Halkin's essay on the Jews in medieval Muslim culture and society. Among the most valuable chapters is the last one on the modern period written by the master of Jewish history writing in the last two generations, the late Salo Baron. His multivolume *A Social and Religious History of the Jews*, 18 vols. (Columbia University Press, 1952–83) is difficult going for the uninitiated, and Baron never wrote a one-volume history of the Jews. His vision of Jewish history, as a whole, may be understood from reading the first chapters of volume 1 of his *History* and his concluding chapter to *Great Ages*.

Three of Baron's cardinal assumptions underlie my understanding of the Jewish Middle Ages, and they are reflected in the direction I have followed in selecting books for this essay. Baron insisted that (1) Jewish life in the Diaspora was always a legitimate part of Jewish experience, not a footnote to the events in the Land of Israel; (2) the Jews especially in the Middle Ages were politically active makers of their own history, self-governing in their cohesive and richly textured communities, not passive victims; and (3) to understand the history of the Jews requires appreciating the contexts within which the Jews lived, be they the pagan world empires of antiquity, the Muslim or Christian civilizations of the Middle Ages, or the modern nation states.

Schwarz's *Great Ages* is an excellent first book for anyone interested in tasting the conceptual vigor that can be applied to interpreting Jewish history while reading about the entire sweep in sequence. This book still ranks among the all-time best works of Jewish scholarly popularization ever written.

After devouring *Great Ages*, consider two other collections of historical essays. The first is written on a grand scale as a comprehensive history of the Jews, but it is written from a particular point of view. I am referring to the Israeli team history published in English in one volume as *A History of the Jewish People* (Harvard University Press, 1985), edited by H. H. Ben-Sasson, and based on a three-volume Hebrew original. The chapters on the Middle Ages were written by Ben-Sasson and are the equivalent of a one-volume history of the Jews in the Middle Ages. However, it is published as part of a collective work on the entire history of the Jews and is not a separate volume.

Ben-Sasson's account is nuanced and informed by a vast amount of erudition. Of special importance is his interest in Jewish social history and institutions, how the Jewish community actually governed itself and dealt with Christian and Muslim power. He also gives some attention to Jewish economic activities in Muslim and Christian lands. International traders figure no less prominently than money-lenders in this narrative. The comparative approach underlies his presentation of different parts of the Jewish world, and illustrative passages are introduced throughout. And yet, this book does not do justice to the complexity of the story. Little space is devoted to ideas and religious experience except as they relate to social theories and practice. The result is a flattening of the landscape; we see clearly the social institutions but the richness of medieval Judaism as a civilization remains obscure.

Before discussing several one-volume histories written by a single author, one other book should be noted. *Studies in the Variety of Rabbinic Cultures* (Jewish Publication Society, 1991), despite its misleading title, contains historical essays by Gerson D. Cohen, nearly all of which deal with aspects of medieval Jewish cultural history. They provide exciting explorations of Jewish intellectual history on such themes as Jewish interpretations of the Song of Songs; on Esau as the image of the gentile; on Jewish messianic movements, and much more.

Several short histories of the Jews commend our attention, and each presents a clear picture of the Jewish Middle Ages. Some of these books are more outdated than others; some are more biased than others. But they all deserve mention, and I will make recommendations as I go.

One scholar used to say that Max L. Margolis and Alexander Marx, *A History of the Jewish People* (Atheneum, 1969) is as dry as a telephone book, but we all need accurate telephone books. Despite its age, it is remarkably reliable, since it is grounded in the research of Alexander Marx who, with Salo Baron, was one of the two most learned Jewish historians writing in North America in the twentieth century. One may use it profitably as a reference book in place of a one-volume encyclopedia of Jewish history which we still do not have.

But it is also a curiosity. This early-twentieth-century history, written in the shadow of World War I, tells us how some Jewish thinkers then understood that wrenching experience as a disaster well before the Second World War colored the entire century retrospectively. Significantly, Marx and Margolis preserve the fundamental picture of Jewish history that Heinrich Graetz, the nineteenth-century pioneer of Jewish historical scholarship and popularization, bequeathed to the twentieth century. Graetz's legacy was the creative gesture of envisioning all of Jewish history as the story of a single people held together by a collective consciousness shaped by two major factors: Jewish persecution, suffering, and martyrdom, on the one hand, which made Jews feel part of a single heroic people; and, on the other hand, great thinkers and writers who forged religious and cultural bonds that transcended time and place. To Graetz, ideas and martyr-consciousness mattered; communal structures, economic roles, political activities, demographic shifts did not. Marx and Margolis devote most of their chapters on the Middle Ages, half of the book, to these Graetzian themes of Jewish vulnerability and intellectual life.

More than a reference book is Cecil Roth's short, *History of the Jews* (Schocken Books, 1970). It is more somber in tone, partly in response to times of growing hostility of the 1930s. Roth made a living as a professional writer throughout much of his career, and this short version of Jewish history races along from biblical times to the middle of the present century. Its treatment of the Jewish Middle Ages, however, is superficial and adheres to the Graetzian model of persecutions in Christian lands and great books in Muslim ones. It reads well enough, but it has not aged that well.

The church historian Solomon Grayzel wrote A *History of the Jews* (Jewish Publication Society, 1968), and it remains the most commonly used text. Omitting the biblical centuries, it begins with the return to the Land of Israel of some of the Babylonian Exiles of Judea, but it is much longer than Roth's. The first Jewish historian to write after World War II, Grayzel writes to console as well as to enlighten his mainly American Jewish readers. And so he stresses not only Graetz's themes of Jewish suffering and intellectual achievements but also emphasizes Judaism the religion as the binding force in Jewish survival. He ends the original edition, not with the brief summary of the Nazi devastation of the Jews of Europe, but on a remarkably optimistic note about American Jewry and the future. Despite its length and good intentions, Grayzel's book no longer satisfies the modern reader who simply wants a balanced understanding of the history of the Jews in broad historical and cultural contexts.

Robert M. Seltzer's *Jewish People, Jewish Thought: The Jewish Experience in History* (Macmillan, 1980) is a comprehensive one-volume history written by a member of the first generation of American Jewish historians to write for an American university audience—Jew, Christian, and Muslim alike. Although Seltzer correctly states that the Holocaust and the State of Israel are the two great events of recent Jewish history, he wisely does not shape his narrative based on either or both. Jewish social and political activism and Jewish religious diversity in the Diaspora and the Land of Israel remain central assumptions. This breadth and resistance to facile reductionism make his book appropriate for an American reader who wishes to avoid the extreme, ideological colorings of other interpretations.

Seltzer's view of the Jewish Middle Ages, however, is more conventional than his overall plan. It begins with Islam and sketches Jewish communal life in Muslim and Christian lands. Despite attention to economic and social patterns, the briefness of the presentation ends up giving extra weight to anti-Semitism and expulsions, followed by chapters on Jewish intellectuals. A Graetzian paradigm persists: in the Middle Ages the Jews are described mainly as martyrs and authors.

One drawback of this book—and it is not enough to keep me from recommending it as the best one-volume history to date—is its artificial and somewhat misleading separation of Jewish political and religious history, each assigned to separate chapters throughout. This strategy gives the impression that the political and communal history of the Jews is separate from the intellectual and religious story. In some cases this is true, but in many it is not.

The most recent one-volume synthesis is Paul Johnson's *A History of the Jews* (Harper & Row, 1988), and it is deservedly controversial. Written by a Christian historian, it is the most thought-provoking of the one-volume histories. But the short section on the medieval centuries, like Seltzer's, is a condensation of the Graetzian perspective on Jewish collective suffering and intellectual achievements. In the lengthy modern section, some fifty percent of the book, we see for the first time the accepted wisdom that the Holocaust and Zion (Israel) are centrally defining features of modern times; in contrast, there is no significant discussion of American Jewish life.

Despite being grounded in the research of many scholars, Johnson's history also has a distinctive denominational coloring. Unlike Grayzel's it is not a Jewish bias but a Christian one. Johnson makes two fundamental claims about Judaism and the Jews and they underlie the entire narrative. Both are rooted in Pauline Christianity. The first is that "Countless Jews, in all ages, have groaned under the burden" of God's "impossible law," the Torah. The second, complementary claim is that the world and the Jews have not been able to live up to this perfectionism, and in fact this has resulted in the Jews, among others, suffering from evil directed at them in resentment and hostility. Johnson's reading of Jewish history appears to be enthusiastically complimentary of Jewish culture and fortitude. In fact, it is a theological reading of Jewish history grounded in classical Christian premises. Readers who want to have a well-written and stimulating version of the sweep of Jewish history but who also wish to avoid an explicitly Christian perspective would do well to bear this in mind when thinking of reading Johnson's alluring history as a balanced scholarly synthesis.

The Jews in the Muslim and Christian Worlds

Jewish religious culture existed within a Muslim or Christian domain. Three books introduce the reader to Jews and Muslims. These are S. D. Goitein's little text, *Jews and Arabs* (Schocken Books, 1964), which some may find dated, but the insights and humanity of the author defy time and remain relevant. The historical first part of Norman A. Stillman's anthology of source material, *The Jews of Arab Lands* (Jewish Publication Society, 1979) is a more recent narrative and provides a balance of social, political, and cultural themes. Still more ambitious is Bernard Lewis's *Jews of Islam* (Princeton University Press, 1984), which is a **provocative** look at how the Muslim world viewed and treated the Jewish minority in the Middle Ages and how a shared culture developed that broke down in modern times.

For those interested in the communal and everyday social life of the Jews of Muslim societies, we are fortunate to have S. D. Goitein's five-volume study, *A Mediterranean Society* (University of California Press, 1968–88). It is one of the great works of historical research on medieval studies written in this century. This work is based on documents found in the Cairo Geniza, an attic storeroom of a synagogue in Old Cairo. Volume 1 is concerned with economic life, and volume 2 is devoted to the Jewish community in Muslim lands. We get a sense here of the dynamics of the central leaders in Baghdad, the Geonim at the heads of the courts and academies there, and the Exilarch, a Jew claiming descent from King David whose appointment was ratified by the Muslim authorities. Goitein also gives us a nuanced picture of regional Jewish governance, as in Spain, and even of local communal life. Volume 3 portrays the family, volume 4, daily life, and volume 5, the individual.

On the Muslim age in Spain, the distractingly colorful prose of Eliyahu Ashtor's *The Jews of Moslem Spain*, 3 vols. (Jewish Publication Society, 1973–84) may be read with an eye to the cultural and social features there, but another way to appreciate the culture of the Jewish courtiers in Muslim Spain is in Gerson D. Cohen's historical essays and the introduction to his edition and translation of

Abraham Ibn Daud, *Book of Tradition* (Oxford University Press, 1967). For Muslim North Africa, the standard history is H. Z. Hirschberg, *A History of the Jews of North Africa*, 2 vols. (Leiden: E. J. Brill, 1974–81). The Jewish community of medieval Egypt is discussed in Mark R. Cohen's sophisticated political study *Jewish Self-Government in Medieval Egypt* (Princeton University Press, 1981). There is no history in English of the Jews of the Ottoman Empire, although Stillman does touch on them.

There is much less to suggest for comprehensive historical narratives about the Jews in Christian Europe. There is no general book on the Jews of Christian Europe, no history of the Jewish community and its internal workings there, no available histories of major Jewish communities in medieval England, Germany, Italy, or southern France.

William Chester Jordan's *The French Monarchy and the Jews* (University of Pennsylvania Press, 1989) is centered in political history but is actually much

A disputation between Christian and Jewish scholars, from a woodcut by Johann von Armssheim, 1483.

more. For he has succeeded in using pertinent Latin, French, and Hebrew sources of all kinds—official documents, tombstone inscriptions, liturgical dirges, popular moralistic tales (*exempla*)—to probe in detail how Christians came to perceive Jews and eventually interact with them to their harm. And Jordan also has picked up the equally significant and often suppressed story of how medieval Jews looked down on and even wrote mockingly to each other about Christians. In this movingly written study, Jordan has written the best social history of any medieval Jewish minority in Christian Europe, and I recommend it highly as a successful effort to get into the living relationships of medieval Christian society and the Jews.

Jordan's study is also an example of how intelligence, industry, and the imaginative use of a variety of sources can lead to the reconstruction of another cultural world as part of political history. If one were to buy one book on the Jews of medieval Europe, this is it. The title makes the book sound narrow; it is anything but.

The Jews in Christian Spain can be divided into an early medieval Christian or Visigothic phase, preceding the Muslim invasion in 711, and a concluding Christian era leading to the expulsion of 1492. There is no recent study on the first period, about which we know the least. For the later Christian age in Spain, Yitzhak Baer, *History of the Jews of Christian Spain,* 2 vols. (Jewish Publication Society, 1966), is still the standard work. Culturally related to Spain is the Jewish world of southern France whose intellectual picture is developed in Isadore Twersky's rabbinic biography, *Rabad of Posquières* (Harvard University Press, 1962).

Apart from the social and territorial histories, the economic picture may be rounded out by comparing Goitein's volume 1, on economic life in the Mediterranean, and the less diversified and more pernicious story of one of the most troublesome aspects of Jewish economic life in Latin Christendom—moneylending. A recent study of a fascinating case history of medieval French Christians defending a Jewish moneylender they believed was honest and wrongly accused of cheating is Joseph Shatzmiller, *Shylock Reconsidered: Jews, Moneylending, and Medieval Society* (University of California, 1989). Despite the existence of such honest Jewish creditors and appreciative Christian debtors, the generally pervasive negative Jewish stereotype rarely gave way to such exceptions.

Among those who have made cogent cases connecting medieval and modern anti-Semitism, without defining either, is Joshua Trachtenberg, whose *The Devil and the Jews* (Jewish Publication Society, 1983) is a pioneering study of official and popular attitudes toward Jews and draws on literary, representational, as well as institutional sources. Among the expressions of anti-Jewish behavior in Christian Europe was the belief that Jews murdered Christians and used their blood in Jewish rituals. R. Po-chia Hsia's *The Myth of Ritual Murder* (Yale University Press, 1990) is a recent study of this phenomenon in late medieval Germany.

The learned and popular dimensions of Christian anti-Jewish sentiment can sometimes be studied separately. Jeremy Cohen's *The Friars and the Jews* (Cornell University Press, 1984) argues that the new mendicant orders in particular developed the most hostile theological views toward the Jews which eventually led the kings to expel them from Christian society. Learned Jews and Christians occasionally found themselves in public debate about the truth of Judaism in such a way that Jews were increasingly put on the defensive. A study of this problem is Robert Chazan, *Daggers of Faith* (University of California Press, 1988); Cohen's book may also be consulted regarding this.

Other studies explore how ecclesiastical reform often meant hostility toward Jews. Essays by Kenneth Stow, Robert Bonfil, and Zefira Rokeah in Shmuel Almog's anthology *Antisemitism Through the Ages* (Pergamon Press, 1988) and *History and Hate* (Jewish Publication Society, 1986), edited by David Berger, are very stimulating collections. Also of interest to those concerned with Jews and the Church is Kenneth Stow's study, *The '1007 Anonymous' and Papal Sovereignty* (Hebrew Union College Press, 1985). He discusses in detail aspects of Jewish security and their political sophistication in the eleventh to thirteenth centuries, especially in relation to developments in Papal theory and power.

A systematic effort to deal with definitions and the historical applicability of "anti-Judaism" in contrast to "anti-Semitism" is found in Gavin Langmuir's work. Two books are *History, Religion, and Antisemitism* (University of California Press, 1990), devoted to working out a theoretical understanding of the phenomenon, and *Toward a Definition of Antisemitism* (University of California Press, 1990), a collection of historical case studies informed by his approach. Both combine historical research and an appeal to theories of social psychology to interpret anti-Jewish sentiment and behavior from antiquity through the twentieth century. While some readers may find the analysis demanding, the investment is worth making. What remains unclear from Langmuir's sophisticated studies is whether his distinction between historically understandable Christian anti-Judaism, based on rational and observable religious differences, and irrational Jew hatred, based on fantastic or "chimerical" notions of what Christians imagined but never saw Jews do, is sustainable. These studies, and a third on the way, deserve careful attention.

Communal Self-Government

The community was the locus of medieval Jewish civilization. Its self-government, leadership, and the many social services it provided such as care for the poor, the ill, the aged, conducting relations with Christian and Muslim authorities who levied taxes on the community, among many other issues, demonstrate the organized body of traditional Judaism at work.

No one was as fascinated with the Jewish community and its self-governance as Salo Baron. His three-volume study *The Jewish Community* (Westport, Conn.: Greenwood Press, 1972) is still the most comprehensive treatment of the subject. The first part studies each period of Jewish communal life sequentially; the second volume deals with different Jewish institutions such as the school, the family, and types of leadership. Only Ben-Sasson's survey, mentioned earlier, comes close to the scope of Baron's treatment.

Within the framework of the Jewish community, religious courts dealt with the application and interpretation of Jewish law. These courts were empowered by Jewish tradition and by the Christian or Muslim authorities to deal with matters that included family law (marriage, divorce), economic obligations (damages, monopolies), ritual law (Sabbath, holidays, dietary regulations, family purity rules), and a host of other religio-legal matters that most Jews today no longer have to solve in Jewish courts. There are still some areas in which Jews may choose to do so, but in most of the world, this is optional. In the Jewish Middle Ages, it was not optional, and was the keystone of Jewish self-government enjoyed by Jewish communities in Christian and Muslim lands.

One result of these centuries of judicial experience is an accumulation of cases and precedents, legal theories and philosophies that deal with religious governance. It is unfortunate that most of the research and monographs written on the history of Jewish legal traditions is not accessible to the general reader, but there are a few exceptions. The systematic or jurisprudential approach to Jewish legal history is a relatively new field of investigation, and it has benefited from the scholarly and juridical mind of Menahem Elon whose *Principles of Jewish Law* (New Brunswick, N.J.: Transaction Books, 1987) deals with such topics as property, torts, family law and inheritance, and criminal law. His multivolume work on this subject is being translated and will appear in the near future.

In addition to the legal history approach, we also have some collections of texts derived from social settings. Louis Jacobs's anthology *Jewish Law* (Behrman House, 1968) offers selections of Jewish classical legal texts followed by passages from Jewish codes and legal answers (responsa) to issues that arose in the course of living in a medieval Jewish community. It is enough to whet the appetite. A broader range of responsa is available in Solomon Freehof, *A Treasury of Responsa* (Ktav Publishing House, 1973).

For an in-depth encounter with one of the greatest Jewish legal minds, Rabbi Moses ben Maimon's (Maimonides) *Code* is available in English in several volumes from the Yale Judaica Series edition published by Yale University Press and is nearly complete. A sophisticated historical and cultural analysis of this work is Isadore Twersky, *Introduction to the Code of Maimonides (Mishneh Torah)* (Yale University Press, 1980). Twersky's selection from the *Code* is also available with some of Maimonides's other important writings, including some of his letters, and a superb introduction in *A Maimonides Reader* (Behrman House, 1972). However much Maimonides inspires with his intellectual and religious depth, readers should remember that the most authoritative code of Jewish law, Rabbi Joseph Caro's (d. 1575) *Shulhan Arukh* (Prepared Table) remains untranslated.

Most of the Talmudic commentary literature is also inaccessible, but Jacob Katz has pioneered a kind of Jewish sociological history that pays attention to persisting social types and makes use of legal sources in teasing out the social and religious dynamics of Jewish life in Christian Europe. Three of his books on medieval Jewish history are *Exclusiveness and Tolerance* (Behrman House, 1983) on Jewish perceptions of and relations with Christians in the central Middle Ages; *Tradition and Crisis: Jewish Society at the End of the Middle Ages* (Schocken Books, 1971), which will be reissued in a new and fully annotated translation by Bernard Cooperman in 1993; and *The "Shabbes Goy": A Study in Halakhic Flexibility* (Jewish Publication Society, 1989). They are challenging studies that enable us to appreciate how religious law was the living constitution of medieval Jewish communities, and how it responded to ever-changing historical circumstances.

Synagogue Life

Although sermons were not always preached in synagogues on a weekly basis, there is a vast literature of written versions of Jewish sermons that gives us some idea about religious mentalities and world views outside the judicial system. A book of great learning and grace is Marc Saperstein's *Jewish Preaching* (Yale University Press, 1989). It offers a historical survey and interpretation of the genre of Jewish preaching, translates a selection of sermons—the earliest mostly from Spain and Italy—and concludes with additional texts that are not themselves sermons but which he refers to as "Sources for the History and Theory of Jewish Preaching." This book is beautifully edited and highly recommended.

When preached, the sermon was part of the larger cultural fixture of the Jewish liturgy, a subject once studied in depth but more recently almost ignored. Among the exceptions is Lawrence Hoffman's *The Canonization of the Synagogue Service* (University of Notre Dame Press, 1986) which deals with the Gaonic achievement mentioned earlier of fashioning the fixed liturgy or Siddur. It is carefully researched and demonstrates how Jewish prayer developed between classical and early traditional Judaism. The most comprehensive history of the liturgy is Ismar Elbogan's study first written in German (1913), next translated into Hebrew (1973), and now being translated into English by Raymond P. Scheindlin (Jewish Publication Society). In the meantime, one may consult the more popular *Jewish Worship* (Jewish Publication Society, 1971) by Abraham Millgram. For the traditional Jewish prayer book, with a complete English translation, Philip Birnbaum's, *Daily Prayer Book* (Hebrew Publishing Co., 1977) is handy, but any comprehensive denominational prayer book will be interesting.

Although we need an anthology of Hebrew religious poetry from early Palestinian beginnings to today, three books contain a sampling. Least satisfying, because of the few examples of liturgical poetry it contains, and its poor indices, is T. Carmi's *Penguin Book of Hebrew Verse* (Penguin Books, 1981). It is more valuable as a broad introduction to Hebrew poetry in general. Some liturgical poems are translated in Jakob J. Petuchowski, *Theology and Poetry* (Oxford University Press, 1978). A third book, this time devoted to the religious poetry of Spain, is Raymond P. Scheindlin's *The Gazelle: Medieval Hebrew Poems on God, Israel, and the Soul* (Jewish Publication Society, 1991). It features thirty short religious lyrics, with verse translations, which Scheindlin places in the historical and aesthetic contexts of earlier Jewish religious poetry and Spanish secular court poetry. His earlier anthology and study of the latter, *Wine, Women and Death* (Jewish Publication Society, 1986), is the best book on medieval Hebrew court poetry. Both are highly recommended.

In addition to the required and optional prayers and occasional sermons, another feature of most Jewish worship is the public reading from the Bible. Medie-

A detail from the opening of the Song of Songs, from the Rothschild Mahzor (Festival Prayer Book) of 1492. (Library of The Jewish Theological Seminary of America)

val Jewish authorities pioneered yet another genre of Jewish culture in the running Bible commentary. While most of these remain untranslated, two are of special significance and are available in complete English translations. The first, from late-eleventh-century France, is *The Pentateuch with Rashi*, 5 vols. (Feldheim, 1973), translated and annotated by M. Rosenbaum and A. M. Silbermann. Rashi's was and remains the most widely studied Jewish commentary on the Torah. It combines a selection of classical rabbinic comments with attention to the text's peculiarities and ambiguities. It also reflects Jewish life in Christian Europe because Rashi viewed the world as a Jew who lived among Christians.

A clear presentation of Rashi and the entire school of Bible interpretation that focused on the *peshat*, or historical contextual reading of Scripture, is Edward L. Greenstein, "Medieval Bible Commentaries" in *Back to the Sources* (Summit Books, 1986). Most helpfully, Greenstein presents passages from the Hebrew Bible and from Rashi's comments side by side so that the reader can compare them and consider their relationship.

A very different author, who lived in a different Christian society, was Rabbi Moses ben Nahman (Nahmanides), who wrote his commentary on the Pentateuch in Christian Spain in the thirteenth century. A renowned legal scholar and kabbalist, Nahmanides's commentary is available in Charles Chavel's complete translation, *Ramban (Nahmanides) Commentary on the Torah*, 5 vols. (New York: Shilo Publishing Co., 1971). Although he was a mystic, Nahmanides's commentary is mainly devoted to the overt meaning of the biblical narrative.

But Jewish, and Christian, biblical commentary should not be thought of simply as one kind of writing on the periphery of the main fabric of medieval Jewish and Christian culture. Both European medieval civilizations were committed to being biblical cultures, each in its own way continuously interpreting and applying accumulated meanings of the sacred text. A brilliant history of a single biblical verse which has recently aroused much controversy in debates over fertility, birth control, and environmental conservation is Jeremy Cohen, *"Be Fertile and Increase, Fill the Earth and Master It"* (Cornell University Press, 1989). Cohen shows that ancient and medieval Jews and Christians never interpreted Genesis 1:28 to justify the exploitation of the earth's natural resources.

The Inner World of Individuals

After reading about various aspects of Jewish political, social, and public religious life, it is time to consider ways to get at the more private world of individuals and how they perceived the world in which they lived. One way to do this is through original or primary sources and pictorial representations that survive from the Middle Ages. There are few books that provide an introduction to Jewish representational art and material culture, but an excellent one is Thérèse and Mendel Metzger's *Jewish Life in the Middle Ages* (Alpine, 1982). Here, illuminated manuscript representations of Jewish life are collected and arranged according to aspects of daily life, life-cycle events, and holiday celebrations. Although this book relies exclusively on pictorial sources and does not pay enough attention to written texts when the authors interpret the scenes, the reader can visually enter the cultural world of Jewish medieval times in this beautifully presented volume. Another standard presentation of Hebrew manuscript art is Bezalel Narkiss's *Hebrew Illuminated Manuscripts* (Leon Amiel, 1969); many of the plates can also be found in the *Encyclopaedia Judaica*.

A book that is still available and which introduces the genre of Hebrew manuscript illumination and discusses the development of the stylistic and historical features is Joseph Gutmann, *Hebrew Manuscript Painting* (George Braziller, 1978). It shows that Jews were not averse to the representational arts in the centuries of classical and of traditional Jewish culture, even though it is often thought that the second commandment (Exodus 20:4) prohibits it. We still do not have a good study of "visual and verbal" emphases in Jewish civilization, but it is clear that the story is a complex one and will take us to the very heart of Jewish cultural adaptation, selection, and self-definition. Another work that illustrates medieval Jewish manuscript illumination and features stimulating and informed essays on the history of the Jewish book is *A Sign and a Witness: 2,000 Years of Hebrew Books and Illuminated Manuscripts* (Oxford University Press, 1988), edited by Leonard Singer Gold. It was published to accompany a grand exibition of the Hebrew book at the New York Public Library. A magnificent new study of Jewish marriage contracts (*ketubot*) is Shalom Sabar, *Ketubbah* (Jewish Publication Society, 1990), lavishly illustrated with many color and black-and-white reproductions.

The statues of *Ecclesia* (Church) and *Synagoga* (Synagogue) from the West Facade of Notre Dame Cathedral in Paris. The Church is shown triumphant, with scepter, orb, and crown; the Synagogue is blindfolded, with a broken staff and a fallen crown. (Photograph by Ivan G. Marcus)

A different aspect of representational art in the Middle Ages is the stylized symbolic forms that Christian artists used to depict Jews and Christians in the Middle Ages. They represented both faith communities symbolically in the form of two women: the downcast *Synagoga* stood for the Jew and the triumphant *Ecclesia* represented the Christian Church. The theme is explored, with copious illustrations, in Wolfgang S. Seiferth's *Synagogue and Church in the Middle Ages* (Frederick Ungar, 1970).

Apart from visual representations we may get closer to the Jews who lived in the Middle Ages by reading some of the written sources that they produced. A few anthologies are worth mentioning, and because they have introductions and headnotes, one will not get lost. Still the only omnibus reader on the Jewish Middle Ages is Jacob Rader Marcus, *The Jew in the Medieval World* (Westport,

Conn.: Greenwood Press, 1975). In it one will find public documents on political and ecclesiastical policies and acts toward the Jews, sources about individuals of great influence in Jewish life, and occasionally an opportunity to glimpse snapshots of ordinary Jews, Christians, and Muslims living ordinary lives.

More specialized, but still dealing with major aspects of the subject are Norman A. Stillman's *Jews of Arab Lands* and Robert Chazan's *Church, State and Jew in the Middle Ages* (Behrman House, 1979). Both contain introductions that set into a historical framework the documents that are selected. Stillman's book begins with a short history of the Jews under Islam and is an extensive and interesting social, political, and cultural treatment. Chazan focuses on the theme of Jewish security in Christian Europe and the relative roles played by Church and State in enhancing or diminishing it.

Other collections enable us to enter the private world of certain individuals who wrote about their world. Franz Kobler's *Letters of Jews through the Ages* (Hebrew Publishing Co., 1978) contains a variety of letters that individuals sent to someone, but often in an official, not a personal, capacity. Based on documents preserved for centuries in the Cairo Geniza, S. D. Goitein's *Letters of Medieval Jewish Traders* (Princeton University Press, 1973) gives us detailed correspondence between Jewish merchant family members actually engaged in business activities. Many open up to us the world of everyday life, such as this correspondent who writes from Alexandria, Egypt, to a great merchant prince: "I have written you a letter before, but have seen no answer. Happy preoccupations—I hope." A third and entirely different type of "letter" is the ethical will, a moralistic letter written by a father to his children. A collection is available in Israel Abrahams's *Hebrew Ethical Wills* (Jewish Publication Society, 1976). From a later time, *The Memoirs of Glückel of Hameln* (Schocken Books, 1977) describes a mother's world view for her children. Still another type of source that sheds light on individuals and communities is the travel diary. Several are translated in Elkan N. Adler's *Jewish Travellers in the Middle Ages* (Dover, 1987).

Another way to approach the inner world of individuals is by focusing on the shared cultural values reflected in literary sources and in rituals and celebrations. By using literary and anthropological approaches, historians may be able to "get inside the heads," so to speak, of medieval Jews and catch them in the act of being themselves. A good way to begin is with literary narratives. The best anthology of Hebrew narrative is David Stern and Mark Mirsky, *Rabbinic Fantasies* (Jewish Publication Society, 1990). It contains anonymous and authored compositions that deal with religious struggle, sex and love, death and "collective memory," the way a culture selectively preserves what it finds significant about its past and about itself. Two lengthy Hebrew narratives from medieval Germany preserve Jewish collective memories about Crusade riots there in 1096. Under attack, Jews acted out their ancient self-image as righteous and pious Temple Priests and sacrifices. They ritually killed their own families and then committed suicide, actions which the Jewish narrators—and later European Jewish legal opinion—considered praiseworthy. For these pure Holy Ones had avoided being polluted by Christianity which they despised and to which they preferred the promise of eternal life. The texts are translated with notes and commentary in Robert Chazan, *European Jewry and the First Crusade* (University of California Press, 1987).

A collection of stories retold in late medieval central Europe about ancient rabbinic sages and Jewish Hasidim (Pietists) from medieval Germany is the *Ma'aseh Book* (Jewish Publication Society, 1981), edited by Moses Gaster. Another collection, this time of texts written by Karaites—those Jews in the Muslim world who had refused to become part of the mainstream rabbinic Jewish culture—is Leon Nemoy, ed., *Karaite Anthology* (Yale University Press, 1952). These writings are not story cycles, but they preserve local Babylonian Jewish customs and life patterns despite the attempt of the Geonim in Baghdad to make them conform to their authoritarian norms and practices.

Two books that catalog diverse Jewish customs about the festivals and life-cycle events or rites of passage are Hayyim Schauss, *The Jewish Festivals* (Schocken Books, 1973), and *The Lifetime of a Jew*, rev. ed. (Union of American Hebrew Congregations, 1976). There is much information in these two books, and historians are beginning to appreciate the richness of Jewish collective celebration and memory as important historical sources.

Yet another and very important aspect of Jewish culture—high as well as low, elite as well as popular—is what is still called Jewish "magic." Joshua Trachtenberg's *Jewish Magic and Superstition* (Atheneum, 1970) provides an intelligent catalog of many practices that are preserved in Jewish texts. They include making use of special formulas, such as different versions of the Name of God, spells, charms, and incantations, and they include different gestures and actions accompanied by words. Historians of religious cultures, including medieval Judaism, no longer can dismiss or bracket such practices as "magic" in contrast to "religion" because this distinction is evaluative, not descriptive. Often as not, a consideration of a culture's gestures and ceremonies discloses fundamental assumptions in its world view, and historians of Jewish culture must pay attention to them, not only to learned books written by philosophers or rabbinic jurists. A collection of such texts is T. Schrire, *Hebrew Magic Amulets* (Behrman House, 1982).

Implications

An anthropological, as well as an historical, perspective reminds us that the Jews in the Middle Ages were a total culture. Whether we look at the political dynamics of Jewish leaders dealing with Muslim or Christian authorities or consider Jewish lay and rabbinic governance of a Jewish community, Jews developed a rich political tradition and exercised power despite their vulnerable standing in the larger society. Within the communal setting, Jewish thinkers transformed the ancient biblical and rabbinic sources into the living constitution of everyday life. Wherever Jews lived, they shared a world civilization based on some common norms that made one Jewish community recognizable to members of another.

And yet, within this newly standardized world of traditional Judaism, local nuance developed and individual experimentation prevailed. In Europe, self-government was local, not regional, and anticipated the congregational and local communal autonomy in much of Jewish life today. Individual religious expression was fostered, not stifled, in spontaneously composed synagogue poetry, and in mystical exercises designed to give cosmic meaning to the religious commandments or to transport the mystic toward the divine. And circles of religious philosophers grappled for the first time with the twin attractions of Athens and Jerusalem.

Above all, the Jews in the Middle Ages—men, women, and children—lived rich public and private lives filled with rituals, ceremonies, and other symbolic acts that linked each individual's experience to the collective memory of the Jewish past. Daily routines of prayer, work, and study; festivals throughout the year; life-cycle events from birth to death, were as much a part of the medieval Jewish world as were the political realities of Muslim or Christian power, or the influence exerted within the Jewish community by the learned, wealthy, and influential families. To understand the medieval world we have lost is to reimagine Jewish life as a complete, dynamic, if vulnerable, culture, which along with Christian Europe and Islam, constitute Western Civilization.

CHAPTER 5

THE EUROPEAN EXPERIENCE: JEWS CONFRONT MODERNITY

Michael Stanislawski

The history of the Jews in modern times is a dramatic and exciting tale, filled with unprecedented successes and unparalleled horrors. At virtually one and the same time, Jews experienced the greatest liberation in their history—political, social, intellectual, artistic, economic—and the greatest disaster ever to afflict the Jewish people, the Holocaust. In this period, Jews were able to create and invent rich and inspiring new expressions of their religious and national identities, while at the same time they paid the price of their unprecedented freedom, the loss of large numbers of Jews to indifference and assimilation. New Jewish communities were established and grew to astonishing size and importance, while other Jewish centers, often centuries old, witnessed decline, stagnation, and even destruction.

The complex story of the intermingling of grand hope and utter despair, of spectacular accomplishment and astonishing failure, is the core of the Jewish experience in modern times.

When that period actually began is the subject of specialized, and oftentimes arcane, dispute among professional historians, and need not delay us too much here. It is clear that, on the one hand, a new period of Jewish history began in the wake of the Spanish Expulsion of 1492 and the transformation of European Jewry in the sixteenth century. It is equally apparent, on the other hand, that something radically new and of revolutionary import to the meaning of Judaism and the life of the Jews began to occur in the early decades of the eighteenth century—that constellation of forces, ideas, and events that we generally define as modernity. This essay will, therefore, begin with a brief guide to the historical literature on the so-called early modern period of Jewish history, from the early 1500s to the early 1700s, and then plunge in detail into the literature on the last three centuries of Jewish life in the European lands.

Before doing so, however, it might be helpful to discuss in brief the major textbooks and histories of the entire early modern and modern period, for readers who would like an overview of the whole journey before embarking on its first leg.

General Histories

Perhaps surprisingly, there is still no excellent overall survey of Jewish history that satisfies the needs and expectations of either lay readers or academic experts. Whether the problem is that Jewish history in these centuries is simply too large a topic for one author to cover adequately, or only that the right book has yet to be written, we are left with a handful of first-rate (and a huge number of second- and third-rate) textbooks and surveys that can be of great use to many readers.

An essential tool in the study of this period is Paul Mendes-Flohr and Jehuda Reinharz, *The Jew in the Modern World: A Documentary History* (Oxford University Press, 1980), a fascinating collection of primary sources relating to Jewish history from 1649 to the present, with some good introductions and explanatory notes. Highly useful, too, are the relevant chapters in Robert M. Seltzer, *Jewish People, Jewish Thought: The Jewish Experience in History* (Macmillan, 1980), which seeks to integrate religious, intellectual, and political history. A very readable and coherent summary of early modern and modern Jewish history is S. Ettinger, "The Modern Period," in H. H. Ben-Sasson, ed., *A History of the Jewish People* (Harvard University Press, 1985); readers should understand, however, that Ettinger's view of Jewish history is informed by a very heavy ideological slant, resulting from his deeply held Zionist view that essentially dismissed the struggle

for emancipation and a vibrant Jewish life in the Diaspora as naive, and ultimately futile and counterproductive, goals.

A very different position on the nature and meaning of modern Jewish history
was taken by the dean of Jewish historians in America, Salo Wittmayer Baron,
whose multivolume *Social and Religious History of the Jews,* 18 vols. (Columbia
University Press, 1952–83) unfortunately did not reach this period. Baron's vastly
influential views on this subject, however, can be gleaned from his beautiful essay
on the modern period in Leo Schwarz's *Great Ages and Ideas of the Jewish People*
(Modern Library, 1977)—perhaps the most eloquent and informative short, in-
terpretative, summary of the subject yet written. For a much longer, detailed, and
far less sophisticated narrative history, readers might peruse with profit Howard
Sachar, *The Course of Modern Jewish History* (Vintage Books, 1990). Finally,
many readers, especially those interested in the way Jewish history was written in
the past, would benefit from reviewing the last two volumes of the first professional history of the Jews, written in Germany in the nineteenth century by the
great historian Heinrich Graetz, translated into English under the title *History of
the Jews* (Jewish Publication Society, 1894). Graetz's accomplishments were truly
magnificent, but his highly polemical, old-fashioned style and viewpoint are foreign to most readers today. Nonetheless, no serious student of Jewish history of
any period, including this one, should miss Graetz's lively, and vastly influential,
reconstruction of the history of the Jews.

The Jews in Europe, 1500–1750

The centuries between the Expulsion from Spain in 1492 and the dawn of the
modern age in the mid-eighteenth century witnessed crucial and fascinating
transformations in the lives of European Jewry. Most obvious, of course, was the
elimination of one of the main centers of Jewish life and civilization in the world,
the Jewish community in the Iberian peninsula, and the consequent dispersal of
Spanish and Portugese Jews to various parts of the world. This new "Sephardic
Diaspora" was continually reinforced by subsequent waves of Jews from Spain and
Portugal who had converted to Christianity but retained, to one extent or another, their Jewish memories and traditions, if not a dramatic, secret, adherence
to their ancestral faith. This migration served not only to fructify and expand

already existing Jewish communities in various parts of Europe, but also to extend Jewish presence to areas legally closed to Jews. Thus, for example, the Jewish communities of Italy and the European parts of the Ottoman Empire were radically transformed and enriched by the arrival of thousands of Jewish refugees from Spain and Portugal into their midst, while, at the same time, "Portugese merchants" nominally professing Christianity would move to an area formally forbidden to Jews, establish themselves there, and gradually emerge into the open as Jews. In this way, much of western Europe—long barren of Jewish life, due to expulsions and legal impediments—was slowly but inexorably reclaimed for Jewish settlement, life, and culture; Jewish communities such as those in London and Amsterdam grew at a steady pace from these modest beginnings.

This remarkable story can be followed in detail in the classic, if somewhat hyperbolic, works of the great Anglo-Jewish historian, Cecil Roth, especially his *History of the Marranos* (Sepher-Hermon Press, 1992) and *The Jews in the Renaissance* (Jewish Publication Society, 1978). A more modern and sophisticated analysis of the history of the Marranos and the Sephardic Diaspora can be found in Yosef Hayim Yerushalmi, *From Spanish Court to Italian Ghetto* (University of Washington Press, 1981). The most engaging entree into the world of Italian Jewry in the seventeenth century, in which Jews enjoyed possibly the greatest degree of integration into non-Jewish society until the modern period, is the autobiography of Rabbi Leon (Judah Aryeh) Modena, one of the most intriguing and controversial figures of Italian Jewry, published as *The Autobiography of a Seventeenth-Century Venetian Rabbi: Leon Modena's Life of Judah*, edited by Mark R. Cohen (Princeton University Press, 1988).

At the same time that the Sephardic communities of western and southern Europe were expanding, the Ashkenazic Jewries of central and eastern Europe were undergoing their own unprecedented growth and development, vying for importance and centrality in the Jewish world. Although plagued by frequent persecutions and local expulsions, the Jews of the German-speaking lands continued to flourish, and especially in the late seventeenth and early eighteenth centuries, to come into greater and more intensive contact with their non-Jewish neighbors. The most poignant and moving testimony of this Jewish culture is *The Memoirs of Glückel of Hameln* (Schocken Books, 1977), a captivating account of the life and times of a wealthy, proud, and pious Jewish woman of the period.

For all the importance of the experience of Jews in central Europe in this period, it was the Jewry of eastern Europe that emerged, in the sixteenth and seventeenth centuries, as the dominant force in Ashkenazic Jewish life, and in many ways, as the intellectual and biological center of world Jewry in the early modern period. (The centrality of east European Jewry was matched only by the Jews of the Ottoman Empire, outside the purview of this essay.) The Jewish communities of Poland, Lithuania, and the Ukraine had been growing since the late thirteenth century, but it was in the sixteenth century that they reached their own "Golden Age," both quantitatively and qualitatively.

Perhaps the most remarkable characteristic of east European Jewry in this period was its success in creating in its midst a Jewish society based almost exclusively on the culture, law, and dictates of Talmudic Judaism. In sharp contrast to Spanish Jewry in its Golden Age, Polish-Lithuanian Jews were essentially cut off from and not interested in non-Jewish literature, philosophy, or science, preferring instead to concentrate on the inner core of Jewish life and faith—the study and practice of Halakhah (Jewish law), and other facets of the internal Jewish dispensation. This religious orientation was, of course, made possible by the very idiosyncratic nature of Polish society itself, as well as the general political and economic context in which east European Jews lived. But however self-evident the importance of this context is to contemporary scholars of east European Jewry, the Jews of this civilization truly regarded themselves as living in a virtually self-contained Jewish universe, closer in beliefs and way of life to the farmers of ancient Palestine than to the peasants of the surrounding villages.

The most important survey of the history of the Jews in eastern Europe in these centuries is still the first such work: Simon Dubnow, *History of the Jews in Russia and Poland* (Jewish Publication Society, 1920), written by one of the most important Jewish historians, and a central force in modern Jewish politics as well. Dubnow's view of Jewish history in eastern Europe was vastly influential, and though its basic premises, approach, and conclusions seem dated and somewhat ethnocentric to many contemporary historians, his work is the essential starting point for all explorations of this field. A more modern, but far less successful work on this Jewry is Bernard D. Weinryb, *The Jews of Poland* (Jewish Publication Society, 1976)—an attempt to provide a social and economic history of the Jewish community in Poland until 1800; in the process, unfortunately, the grandeur and accomplishments of Polish-Jewish civilization are generally ignored, or given short shrift.

Possibly the best introduction to Jewish life in the early modern period as a whole is Jacob Katz, *Tradition and Crisis: Jewish Society at the End of the Middle Ages* (Schocken Books, 1971; a new translation is scheduled for publication in 1993 by Schocken Books). This is a brilliant attempt by a leading historian and sociologist of the Jews to describe the foundations of Jewish life in central and eastern Europe before the modern age: subjects treated include the relations between Jews and non-Jews, Jewish economic activity, community organization and structure, intercommunal relations, the nature of the Jewish family, kinship system, and religious and education institutions. Although this work has, to be sure, been criticized as presenting a too static and undifferentiated portrait of Ashkenazic Jewish society, it stands out as the one peerless guide to what Jewish life was like in the autonomous Jewish communities of pre-modern Europe.

That life was ineluctably affected by the great messianic crisis of the mid-seventeenth century, occasioned by the rise of the false messiah, Sabbetai Zevi. Although the precise extent to which Jews around the world believed in Sabbetai Zevi as the messiah is still unclear, there is no question that every segment of world Jewry was engulfed viscerally, emotionally, and spiritually in the passions, debates, and drama of this messianic episode, as well as by the enormous cover-up that followed in the wake of Sabbetai Zevi's conversion to Islam in 1666. The most detailed, influential, and controversial work on this pseudo-messiah and his movement is Gershom Scholem, *Sabbatai Sevi: The Mystical Messiah* (Princeton University Press, 1973), undeniably one of the most important works of Jewish historical scholarship in the twentieth century. Readers wishing a shorter guide to Scholem's views on this subject may read the chapter "Sabbatianism and Mystical Heresy" in his *Major Trends in Jewish Mysticism* (Schocken Books, 1961); those wishing to pursue this topic, especially in regard to the emergence of an underground movement maintaining belief in Sabbetai Zevi as the messiah even after his apostasy, ought to read Scholem's magnificent, if very difficult, essay "Redemption through Sin," reproduced (along with other studies on this issue) in his *The Messianic Idea in Judaism* (Schocken Books, 1971).

The Emergence of Modernity

Most scholars of Jewish history now agree that the eighteenth century heralded a revolution in Jewish life that is still continuing to this day, the revolution of modernity. First and foremost, the spread of the new Enlightenment movement affected Jews deeply, both as participants in its creation and as objects of its analysis. The Enlightenment, which preached the primacy and equality of every

Men in top hats waving
lulav (palm branches) at
the North London
Synagogue for *Sukkot*, the
Feast of Tabernacles.
(*The Graphic*, 1872)

individual, regardless of faith, class, or origin, also broadcast the supremacy of rationalism over superstition, the ability of every human being to reach the truths about human (and Divine) existence through rational cogitation alone, and the consequent equality of all religious traditions based on pure faith. Formal religion, in other words, was now deemed to be a matter of individual conscience, relegated to the private domain where it could not perpetuate restrictions on individual liberty. This novel and revolutionary idea required the Jews, for the first time, to define themselves in the terms of the Enlightenment's debate: were the Jews a nation, or simply adherents of a faith, parallel to other communities of faith?

This question was closely intertwined with the political revolution of the eighteenth century, in which the ideas of the Enlightenment about individual liberty led ultimately—in quite a complex manner—to the French Revolution and the overall transmutation of European states from traditional monarchies to modern nation-states, often assuming a democratic and republican character. Where would the Jews fit in this new kind of political entity? Would they—could they—be equal citizens of the French state, and later the other new nation-states that emerged in Europe? In other words, the quandary of Jewish legal emancipation rose to prominence in Jewish life from the 1780s on, as well as the corollary dilemma of how Jewish communal life was to be organized in the new, modern society in which the old, autonomous, Jewish community was now deemed anachronistic.

Intimately connected with these intellectual, ideological, and political struggles was the social and economic transformation of Europe, and hence European Jewry, in this period: the spread of the Industrial Revolution, the abandonment of agriculture by the mass of the population, the emergence of the new middle class, the vast movement to the cities and towns of Europe, the development of the new liberal professions and the industrial proletariat. All of these phenomena affected the lives of European Jews in direct and profound ways.

There is no simple guide to how Jews reacted to these challenges and played a crucial role in the emergence of modern civilization. In addition to the excellent studies of separate facets of this complex story discussed below, readers are advised to turn to Jacob Katz, *Out of the Ghetto: The Social Background of Jewish Emancipation, 1770–1870* (Schocken Books, 1973), for a brilliant introduction to many aspects of this subject. A more detailed discussion of the effect of the Enlightenment on Jewish thought and action, as well as the role that individual Jews played in developing Enlightenment thought, can be found in Michael A. Meyer, *The Origins of the Modern Jew: Jewish Identity and European Culture in Germany, 1749–1824* (Wayne State University Press, 1972). In addition, Alexander Altmann, *Moses Mendelssohn: A Biographical Study* (University of Alabama Press, 1973)—a dense but fascinating biography of Moses Mendelssohn, one of the leading philosophers of the Enlightenment and by far the most important Jewish Enlightenment figure—is highly recommended. An entirely different, and highly disputed, view of the effect of the Enlightenment on the Jews is presented in Arthur Hertzberg's *The French Enlightenment and the Jews: The Origins of Modern Antisemitism* (Columbia University Press, 1990).

The transformation of Judaism that followed in the wake of the Enlightenment's redefinition of religion can be seen most clearly in the emergence of the three new forms of Jewish religious life in Germany in the nineteenth century: Reform Judaism, Modern Orthodoxy, and Positive-Historical Judaism, the forerunner of Conservative Judaism. The best study of this fascinating phenomenon is Michael A. Meyer, *Response to Modernity: A History of the Reform Movement in Judaism* (Oxford University Press, 1990). Readers would also gain a great deal from reading one of the works of the founder of Modern Orthodoxy in Germany, Samson Raphael Hirsch, *The Nineteen Letters on Judaism* (Feldheim, 1969). Closely allied with this denominational and spiritual development was the emergence of new literary and scholarly traditions and movements in European Jewry, closely chronicled in volumes 9 through 12 of Israel Zinberg, *A History of Jewish Literature* (Hebrew Union College Press/Ktav Publishing House, 1978).

The struggle for Jewish emancipation in western and central Europe can best be surveyed in the textbooks listed at the beginning of this essay, as well as in Jacob Katz's already mentioned *Out of the Ghetto,* and the relevant documents in the Mendes-Flohr/Reinharz reader (mentioned earlier), *The Jew in the Modern World.* The social and economic transformations in Jewish society, more difficult to follow without having access to rather technical studies, are also summarized in Katz's *Out of the Ghetto.* Readers may also read with profit Cecil Roth, *History of the Jews of England* (Oxford University Press, 1964), which chronicles, among other things, the rise of the wealthy Anglo-Jewish elite, including the Rothschild family.

Jews in Eastern Europe

At the same time as west European Jews were experiencing the radical changes associated with the Enlightenment and emancipation, the Jews of eastern Europe were facing a very different set of both internal and external challenges. First and foremost, from the middle of the eighteenth century on, east European Jewry was ineluctably transformed by the emergence, growth, and dramatic spread of Hasidism. This revolutionary new form of Judaism was based on the mystical teachings of Lurianic Kabbalah, which spread from Safed to Italy to Poland in the late seventeenth and early eighteenth centuries and here underwent a thoroughgoing transmutation, under the auspices of a remarkable group of spiritual teachers and leaders led by Rabbi Israel Baal Shem Tov. From a rather isolated revivalist sect in the backwaters of the Ukraine, Hasidism quickly spread to all parts of eastern Europe, soon winning the allegiance of the vast majority of the Jews of Russia, Poland, and the Ukraine. These Jews were attracted at once by its novel theology of personal communion with the Divine, its compelling rituals and embrace of song, dance, and other means of celebrating the commandments with joy, and especially by the charisma and religious magnetism of its leaders. Violently opposed by the rabbinic establishment, particularly in Lithuania, Hasidism nonetheless succeeded in overwhelming its opposition, and ultimately forged an alliance with the other traditional forces in eastern European Jewish society against the onslaught of modernity.

The literature on Hasidism is truly immense, ranging from numberless renditions of hasidic tales to highly technical scholarly explications of its mystical and theological secrets. The most important first work to read is the collection of legends about the founder of the movement, the Baal Shem Tov, translated into English as *In Praise of the Baal Shem Tov,* edited by D. Ben-Amos and J. Mintz (Schocken Books, 1984). Next, the reader should turn to Martin Buber, *The Origin and Meaning of Hasidism* (Humanities Press International, 1988) for a very readable summary of the understanding of the movement by its most prominent Western student and proponent. Buber's interpretation of Hasidism has, however, been seriously challenged by many scholars, including Gershom Scholem, whose chapter on Hasidism in his *Major Trends in Jewish Mysticism* (Schocken Books, 1961) is an invaluable guide to many aspects of the movement's religious stance. (For more on Hasidism, see the chapter on Jewish mysticism in this book.)

In the decades following the emergence and spread of Hasidism, the ideas and cultural positions of the Enlightenment began to enter into eastern European Jewry as well, leading slowly but surely to the emergence in Russia and Poland of modernist Jewish politics, culture, and religious sensibility. This phenomenon can be followed in great detail in Israel Zinberg's *History of Jewish Literature,* mentioned earlier, and in a delightful anthology of memoirs of east European Jews—which includes some useful hasidic material as well—Lucy Dawidowicz, *The Golden Tradition* (Schocken Books, 1984).

This intellectual and literary development was connected in many complicated ways to the political revolution that overwhelmed east European Jewry from the end of the eighteenth century, when the Polish-Lithuanian Commonwealth was destroyed, its territories annexed by its giant neighbors Russia, Prussia, and Austria. The vast bulk of the Jewish population of former Poland was now under the sway of czarist Russia and its infamous legal and social systems. The classic guide to the subsequent history of the Jews in Russia and Poland is Simon Dubnow's above-cited *History of the Jews in Russia and Poland;* more modern and concise is Salo W. Baron, *The Russian Jew under Tsars and Soviets* (Schocken Books, 1987). For a taste of contemporary scholarship that departs from the classic historians' view by attempting to present Russian-Jewish history within the context of modern Russian history, see my own book, *Tsar Nicholas I and the Jews: The Transformation of Jewish Society in Russia, 1825–1855* (Jewish Publication Society, 1983).

An excellent way to enter into the inner workings of east European Jewry in this period is through literature, particularly translations of classics of Yiddish fiction. Irving Howe and Eliezer Greenberg, A *Treasury of Yiddish Stories*, rev. ed. (Viking Penguin, 1989) is one such, as is the most recent rendition into English of Sholem Aleichem's great Tevye stories—*Tevye the Dairyman and the Railroad Stories*, translated and with an introduction by Hillel Halkin (Schocken Books, 1987).

Modern Jewish Society, Culture, and Politics, 1881–1939

The early 1880s marked a watershed in Jewish history, both in western and eastern Europe. In France, Germany, Austria, and Hungary, the gains of Jewish emancipation and the consequent social and economic success of the Jews began to be questioned and opposed by new anti-Semitic forces, parties, and ideologies, often tied to the current pseudo-science of racism. Modern anti-Semitism differed from the traditional variety in that it appeared to be based not on religious differences and prejudices—which could in theory evaporate after the conversion of the Jews—but upon biology and blood, from which there was no escape. Intimately tied with the new nationalist forces sweeping through European society, anti-Semitism began to pose a serious, and unexpected, challenge to the Jews. There are countless works on the history of modern anti-Semitism; one of the most successful and best-informed recent attempts at an overall study of the problem is *From Prejudice to Destruction: Anti-Semitism, 1700–1933* by Jacob Katz (Harvard University Press, 1982). Undoubtedly the most unexpected and influential outbreak of anti-Semitism occurred in France after the arrest and trial of Captain Alfred Dreyfus, whose conviction on charges of treason split French society in two, and thrust anti-Semitism to the center of political discourse in the very home of Jewish emancipation and equal rights. An absolutely first-rate guide to this crucial chapter in modern Jewish history can be found in Norman Kleeblatt, ed., *The Dreyfus Affair: Art, Truth and Justice* (University of California Press, 1987)—a lavishly illustrated catalog to an excellent museum exhibit on the subject, supplemented by informative articles by noted scholars.

Virtually simultaneous with the rise of political anti-Semitism in western Europe was the outbreak of a series of armed attacks against the Jewish communities of the Russian Empire. The story of these pogroms is amply documented in Simon

Dubnow's *History of the Jews in Russia and Poland,* cited previously, though once more, professional historians are now beginning to question the accuracy of the standard account, which held the Russian government to blame for the planning and execution of these anti-Jewish massacres; scholars now argue that the pogroms were unplanned, spontaneous outbursts caused by serious social and economic rifts within Ukrainian society.

Be that as it may, the shock and horror felt by Jews both within and outside the Russian Empire in response to these pogroms was connected with two other fundamental features of Jewish life in these decades. The emigration of Jews from Russia, Poland, and other parts of eastern Europe had started long before the pogroms and was often motivated by quite different factors, such as overpopulation and economic necessity. But soon the political despair that spread through Russian Jewry after the pogroms acted as a spur to emigration, and the movement of Jews from eastern Europe to other parts of the world, most notably the United States, Palestine, and parts of western Europe, took on truly mass proportions. The most dramatic consequence of this emigration of millions of Russian Jews was the rise of American Jewry to a position of prominence and power within World Jewry, and the fascinating transformation of American Jewish life and culture that ensued—subjects covered in chapter 6 of this book.

Covered, too, in chapter 8 of this book, is the story of the rise of Zionism in these years, about which, therefore, only a few words need be said here. The new Zionist movement held that the only solution to the plight of the Jews in modern society was the self-emancipation of the Jewish people—the creation of a Jewish polity in their ancestral home. This idea emerged both in reaction to the new forms of anti-Semitism, and to the spread of the concepts and categories of modern nationalism to the Jews. This application to the Jews of the new notions of nationality, nation-state, and national liberation led not only to Zionism, but also to other ideologies of modern Jewish nationalism, some of which—such as the Bundist movement—also attempted to apply the doctrines of socialism to the Jewish case. The best survey of the fascinating ideological and political permutations and combinations that ensued is Jonathan Frankel, *Prophecy and Politics: Socialism, Nationalism, and the Russian Jews, 1862–1917* (Cambridge University Press, 1981)—a rather densely written but extremely rewarding study. Of the vast number of political tracts and platforms that were published in this period perhaps the most beautifully written are the essays of Ahad Haam, the creator of Cultural Zionism, translated into English and with an introduction by Leon Simon, *Selected Essays of Ahad Haam* (Atheneum, 1981).

The outbreak of World War I in the summer of 1914 launched another crucial

Students in a vocational training workshop in the U.S.S.R. pose beneath a portrait of Stalin. (Credit: Joseph Rosen. YIVO Institute for Jewish Research)

era in modern Jewish history. The "war to end all wars" pitted hundreds of thousands of Jews against one another in the uniforms of all the combatant powers, and then transformed the map, social structure, and culture of Europe for decades to come. Perhaps the most obvious outcome of the First World War was the destruction of the three main empires of Europe: the Russian, German, and Austro-Hungarian. East European Jewry, still the largest in the world, now found itself divided between the Soviet Union and newly independent Poland. The best survey of Soviet Jewish history is Salo W. Baron, *The Russian Jew under Tsars and Soviets*, cited earlier; useful too is the collaborative study edited by Lionel Kochan, *The Jews in Soviet Russia Since 1917* (Oxford University Press, 1970). Zvi Gitelman, *A Century of Ambivalence: Jews in Russia and the Soviet Union, 1881 to the Present* (Schocken Books, 1988), is an excellent history with photographs and text.

For a concise and informative summary of the history of the Jews of Poland in the interwar period, see Ezra Mendelsohn, *The Jews of East Central Europe Between the World Wars* (Indiana University Press, 1983), which also has chapters on the Jewish communities of Hungary, Czechoslovakia, Rumania, and the Baltic states. Lucjan Dobroszycki and Barbara Kirshenblatt-Gimblett, *Image Before My Eyes* (Schocken Books, 1977), is a first-class photographic study of Polish Jewry in this period. A wonderful insider's view of Polish-Jewish society and culture is provided by the many works of Isaac Bashevis Singer translated into English; his *In My Father's Court* (Fawcett, 1980) is especially recommended for this purpose.

The fall of the German and Austrian empires led, as well, to a fundamental realignment of both the context and the content of Jewish life in the German-speaking lands. The Jews of Weimar Germany, for example, emerged as the quintessential case study of both the possibilities—and the pathology—of Jewish integration in modern Western society. For just over a decade, German Jewry experienced the greatest amount of social, economic, and intellectual success, before the Weimar Republic succumbed to the Nazi horror.

In this period, a fascinating phenomenon occurred among a small, but highly influential group of German-Jewish youth: a rejection of their parents' middle-class life, coupled with a condemnation of the comfortable but largely placid form of Judaism practiced by many German Jews. Young intellectuals such as Martin Buber, Franz Rosenzweig, Gershom Scholem, and in a different place and manner, Franz Kafka, began to seek out the meaning of their Jewishness and to explore new forms of Jewish spirituality, identity, and consciousness that would have lasting implications for decades to come. One of the best guides to this renascence of Jewish life in Germany is Nahum N. Glatzer, *Franz Rosenzweig: His Life and Thought* (Schocken Books, 1961), which reconstructs from letters and other documents both Rosenzweig's life and thought and the cultural milieu out of which he emerged. Another excellent memoir that illustrates many aspects of Weimar German society is Gershom Scholem's lively autobiography, *From Berlin to Jerusalem* (Schocken Books, 1988). Finally, Franz Kafka's "Letter to My Father" in *The Sons* (Schocken Books, 1989)—a searing, angry, and passionate denunciation of his father's way of life, including his brand of Judaism—presents to the reader an unparalleled example of the "generation gap" that pervaded central European Jewry in the interwar years.

While German-speaking Jewry was descending into its morass, and eastern European Jews were struggling with their own blend of crisis and creativity, the Jews in other parts of Europe—Italy, France, Great Britain—were developing their own unique and fascinating histories. Two memoirs from very different parts of Europe and very different Jewish communities can help the reader understand the spectrum of Jewish life and experience in the interwar years: Dan Vittorio Segre, *Memoirs of a Fortunate Jew: An Italian Story* (Dell, 1988), is a beautifully wrought account of an assimilated Jewish youth in Fascist Italy; David Dalin, *Between Two Worlds* (University of Alabama Press, 1989), is a loving but unsentimental portrayal of growing up Jewish in Edinburgh in the 1920s and 1930s.

The Rise of Nazism and the Holocaust

The literature on the destruction of European Jewry during World War II is enormous, and growing every day, due to the sheer horror of the story, the unfathomable cruelty and suffering, and the imponderable lessons of the Holocaust. This subject is treated extensively in chapter 7 of this volume.

The following is but a small list of crucial works on the subject, which can serve the reader both as general introductions and as guides to further reading: Lucy Dawidowicz, *The War Against the Jews: 1933–1945* (Free Press, 1986); Michael R. Marrus, *The Holocaust in History* (University Press of New England, 1987); and Raul Hilberg, *The Destruction of the European Jews* (rev. ed., 3 vols., Holmes & Meier, 1985). Hilberg's work is by far the most detailed and exhaustive history of the Holocaust, and as such serves as an unparalleled resource; his views on Jewish passivity in the face of persecution, however, have been widely criticized and debated.

Three further works can serve as excellent examples of case studies of the fate of individual Jewries during the war: Michael R. Marrus and Robert O. Paxton, *Vichy France and the Jews* (Schocken Books, 1983); Yisrael Gutman, *The Jews of Warsaw, 1939–1943: Ghetto, Underground, Revolt* (Indiana University Press, 1982); and Leonard Baker, *Days of Sorrow and Pain: Leo Baeck and the Berlin Jews* (Oxford University Press, 1980). Finally, two fictionalized memoirs can be highlighted from among the thousands of first-person accounts and literary reworkings of the horrors of the Holocaust: Elie Wiesel, *Night* (Bantam, 1982)— still perhaps the most captivating and disturbing work of this sort; and Primo Levi, *Survival in Auschwitz: The Nazi Assault on Humanity* (Collier/Macmillan, 1988).

Reconstruction and Renewal

In the aftermath of the Holocaust, the most pressing goal of Jews the world over was finding a safe haven for the survivors of the tragedy. That story is intimately intertwined with the battle for the establishment of the State of Israel, chronicled elsewhere in this volume, as is the second most compelling phenomenon of post–World War II Jewish history, the rise of American Jewry to a position of power and prominence within the Jewish world.

In Europe itself, the surviving Jews were divided into essentially three groups: In western Europe and the British Isles, large Jewish communities continued to flourish, reinvigorated both by the establishment of the State of Israel and by the immigration to these countries of Jews from other parts of the world. In central and east central Europe, Jews struggled to reconstitute their destroyed communities, but to little avail, especially after the onslaught of Stalinism added yet another formidable obstacle to Jewish life; the vast majority of the Jews of these lands emigrated to Israel or America. Finally, the largest Jewish community in Europe remained that of the Soviet Union, whose struggles and fate continue to occupy a central place in contemporary Jewish life. The best guides to the post–1945 history of Soviet Jewry are the Baron, Kochan, and Gitelman volumes listed above. The most useful survey of the Jewish communities in western and eastern Europe in this period can be found in Howard Sachar, *Diaspora: An Inquiry into the Contemporary Jewish World* (Harper & Row, 1986).

The future of European Jewry is, of course, impossible to predict. Indeed, perhaps the only clear lesson of European Jewish history in the centuries surveyed in this essay is precisely the unpredictability of history in general, and Jewish history in particular. But it seems safe to conclude that whatever the future may hold, Jews will continue to form a crucial part of European society, and European Jewish history will remain at the forefront of the collective experience and the collective memory of the Jews, for better and for worse.

C H A P T E R 6

THE AMERICAN JEWISH EXPERIENCE

Jonathan D. Sarna

A book tour through the American Jewish experience can proceed along three parallel routes. The quickest but least scenic route follows the trail blazed by the one-volume overview. Here one can journey through more than three centuries of American Jewish history—religion, society, economics, politics, and culture—all in a few hours or less. More time-consuming but infinitely more satisfying and memorable is the route that starts off with the colonial period, when American Jewry was young, and moves chronologically era by era, stopping off along the way for both primary and secondary source readings on each period in American Jewish history down to the present. Finally, there is the meandering route that proceeds thematically. Here one may linger over a single aspect of American Jewish life, study it in depth and over time, and then move on to another theme, and then another, until the entire terrain becomes familiar.

This guide offers suggestions for those reading their way along any of these paths—or all three of them at once. The first part surveys recent textbooks; the second part, the longest section, reviews key books covering the major chronological periods in American Jewish history; and the third part looks at books on selected specific themes of the American Jewish experience, from anti-Semitism to Zionism, with stops in-between. Happy reading!

Overviews

The classic overview, read by more students of American Jewish history and life than any other and still in print more than three decades after it first appeared, is Nathan Glazer's *American Judaism* [1957] (University of Chicago Press, 1988), the finest brief (214 pp.) introduction to the subject in print. Glazer focuses on religious history, assumes no previous knowledge or background, and writes en-

American Jews greeting new immigrants. A decorative illustration reprinted by the Hebrew Publishing Company in 1909. The Hebrew quotation held aloft by the eagle reads: "Hide us in the shadow of your wings." (Library of The Jewish Theological Seminary of America)

gagingly, interspersing wise sociological observations into his narrative. To be sure, some of his interpretations are by now dated and several chapters should be substantially revised to take account of recent scholarship. But as a quick overview and ready reference, the book remains unsurpassed.

Other one-volume histories are longer, more recent, and more comprehensive than Glazer's. They attempt to survey not just religious history, but the social, economic, political, and cultural aspects of the American Jewish experience as well. The most respected of these are Henry L. Feingold's *Zion in America* (Hippocrene, 1981) and Abraham J. Karp's *Haven and Home: A History of the Jews in America* (Schocken Books, 1985). Feingold's reads better and is particularly strong on twentieth-century developments and on the larger American setting, while Karp is stronger on pre-twentieth-century developments and on religious and cultural history; he also includes a fine selection of primary sources. Arthur Hertzberg's widely publicized *The Jews in America: Four Centuries of an Uneasy Encounter* (Simon & Schuster, 1990) is more an interpretation of American Jewish history than a narrative history, and "uneasy" is the key to the interpretation. While a useful corrective to more celebratory interpretations of American Jewish life, the book is seriously marred by tendentiousness, overgeneralization, and an embarrassingly large number of factual errors. For a brief and more balanced interpretation, originally published in the *Harvard Encyclopedia of American Ethnic Groups* (Harvard University Press, 1980), see Arthur A. Goren, *The American Jews* (Harvard University Press, 1982). Finally, I must admit to having myself published a textbook in American Jewish history entitled *The American Jewish Experience* (Holmes & Meier, 1986). Unlike the narrative histories described above, mine is a reader: a collection of articles, written by the leading historians of American Jewish life and supplemented by introductions, notes, and bibliographies. Since all of these volumes, mine included, are poorly illustrated, they may be read in conjunction with Allon Schoener's *The American Jewish Album: 1654 to the Present* (Rizzoli, 1985), the most scrumptious picture book history of American Jews ever produced.

Period Pieces

Practically everything that one could possibly want to know about America's earliest Jews, from their arrival in the New World to the American Revolution, is found in Jacob R. Marcus's three-volume magisterial study entitled *The Colonial American Jew* (Wayne State University Press, 1970). Marcus devoted over two decades to the study of this subject, and this is his magnum opus, three volumes and more than 1650 pages long. If that seems like more than one needs to know, read the last chapter (chapter 77), entitled "Summary," and then dip into any other chapters that appear to be of interest. See also Marcus's earlier two-volume work, *Early American Jewry* (Jewish Publication Society, 1951, 1953; two volumes in one, Ktav Publishing House, 1974), which is organized geographically by region and includes fascinating personal letters and petitions written in the colonial period.

Aaron Lopez of Newport, Rhode Island, is the only colonial American Jew who has received a full-scale biography, Stanley F. Chyet's *Lopez of Newport: Colonial American Merchant Prince* (Wayne State University Press, 1970). A great deal about the lives and activities of other colonial Jews, however, can be gleaned from published primary sources collected in Jacob R. Marcus's *American Jewry, Documents, Eighteenth Century* (Hebrew Union College Press, 1959). Other significant documents, particularly of a political nature, may be found in Morris U. Schappes's *A Documentary History of the Jews in the United States 1654–1875* (Schocken Books, 1971), a book that no serious student of American Jewish history can be without. Readers should be warned, however, that some of Schappes's headnotes reflect his political bias and are tendentious in the extreme.

The American Revolution was in many respects a turning point in American Jewish history. Jews participated in the Revolution; one Jew, Haym Salomon, achieved modest fame as a merchant and broker in Philadelphia; and all Jews benefited from the new Federal Constitution (1787), as well as the Bill of Rights (1791) that was soon added to it. The most comprehensive one-volume study of Jews in this period is Samuel Reznick's *Unrecognized Patriots: The Jews in the American Revolution* (Westport, Conn.: Greenwood Press, 1975). It not only examines the military and economic contributions that Jews made, but also devotes chapters to such formerly taboo subjects as Jewish loyalists during the Revolution and the postwar quest for pensions, compensation, and honorific recognition. *Jews and the Founding of the Republic*, edited by Jonathan D. Sarna, Benny Kraut, and Samuel K. Joseph (Markus Wiener, 1985) covers some of this same ground, but in a different format. Geared more to teachers and students, it contains primary sources, secondary articles, maps, illustrations, bibliographies, and a guide to available resource materials.

The years between independence and the beginning of large-scale central European Jewish immigration to the United States in the 1840s are now considered to have been a formative period in American Jewish history, an era when many of the basic characteristics of the community took shape. One can get a fine sense of the period as a whole by perusing the magnificent three-volume documentary history edited by Joseph L. Blau and Salo W. Baron entitled *The Jews of the United States 1790–1840: A Documentary History* (Columbia University Press, 1964). This was part of a project to document all of American Jewish history, and one can only lament that it was not carried forward. The first narrative history of this era has appeared only recently as volume 1 of Jacob R. Marcus's massive *United States Jewry, 1776–1985* (Wayne State University Press, 1989). As usual, the erudition is awesome, but the volume's length and style make it ill-suited for novices. One of the era's central themes, the Jewish struggle for political and religious equality, is examined in Morton Borden's *Jews, Turks and Infidels* (University of North Carolina Press, 1984). It surveys the major state battles, as well as subsequent controversies down to the end of the nineteenth century, which pit Jews against those seeking to "Christianize" the country. My own biography of Mordecai M. Noah, the foremost Jewish leader of this period and a significant Jacksonian-era journalist and politician, is more broadly concerned

A New Year's card, with a Yiddish greeting. (Library of The Jewish Theological Seminary of America)

with Jewish-Christian relations, particularly as they affected native-born Jews, like Noah, who sought to participate as equals in American society. The book is entitled *Jacksonian Jew: The Two Worlds of Mordecai Noah* (Holmes & Meier, 1981).

The influx of Jews from Germany and Poland transformed the American Jewish community and inaugurated a new era known as the "German period" in American Jewish history. Naomi W. Cohen's *Encounter With Emancipation: The German Jews in the United States 1830–1914* (Jewish Publication Society, 1984) is the first synthetic treatment of this subject, and it convincingly argues that it was the German Jews who "set the institutional framework and the codes of behavior that, with relatively few important qualifications, obtain today." There is no better book for a reader's tour of the period to start with. Earlier articles by Rudolf Glanz, who pioneered the study of this period, remain valuable, and many of them are collected in his *Studies in Judaica Americana* (Ktav Publishing House, 1970).

The Civil War divided the American Jewish community, as it did the nation as a whole. It also forms the subject of two of the best books ever written in American Jewish history, Bertram W. Korn's *American Jewry and the Civil War*, rev. ed. (Atheneum, 1971) and Eli N. Evans's *Judah P. Benjamin: The Jewish Confederate* (Free Press, 1989). Korn traces Jewish involvement in slavery and in the nationwide debate over whether it should be abolished, as well as the experiences of Jews on the battlefield, the campaign to win Jews the right to serve as chaplains in the Northern army, the controversy over General Grant's infamous order expelling Jews from his war zone, and the problem of anti-Semitism in both the North and the South. Evans details the fascinating life of the Confederate vice president, Judah P. Benjamin, "the brains of the Confederacy," emphasizing Jewish aspects of his career, as well as the prejudice that he faced as a Jew.

The best known and certainly the best selling book on elite Jewish life in this period is Stephen Birmingham's *Our Crowd* (Berkley Books, 1985), a mixture of fact, anecdote, and titillating gossip that recounts the story of New York's German-Jewish financial moguls. Leon Harris's *Merchant Princes* (Harper & Row, 1979) employs the same formula in presenting the story of America's leading German-Jewish department store magnates. Even if good reading, neither book substitutes for a rigorous historical treatment. Unfortunately, the book that comprehensively explains how the mass of immigrant Jews in this period earned their living, moved up the economic ladder, and in a few cases achieved legendary financial success has not yet been written. In the meanwhile, for a highly suggestive case study, see Elliot Ashkenazi, *The Business of Jews in Louisiana, 1840–1875* (University of Alabama Press, 1988). A great deal of economic (as well as social) data is also contained in Malcolm Stern's *First American Jewish Families: 600 Genealogies, 1654–1977* (American Jewish Archives & American Jewish Historical Society, 1977). This is the basic genealogical history of early American Jews, and it discloses the intricate web of family ties that played so significant a role in promoting Jewish upward mobility.

Religiously, the German period in American Jewish history witnessed what Leon Jick, in the title of his book, describes as *The Americanization of the Synagogue, 1820–1870* (University Press of New England, 1976). The best available synthetic treatment of Jewish religious life during this era, Jick's survey focuses on the changes wrought by America on Jewish religious life. The remarkable rise and development of the Reform movement in Judaism is explored in the appropriate chapters of Michael A. Meyer's award-winning *Response to Modernity: A History of the Reform Movement in Judaism* (Oxford University Press, 1990). The volume places American developments within the context of Reform's development throughout the world, and is particularly strong on the movement's intellectual history. It might be read in conjunction with the lively *Reminiscences* of Rabbi Isaac Mayer Wise (Salem, N.H.: Ayer, 1975), the most important of American Reform Judaism's founding fathers, who offers a first-person account of the key nineteenth-century developments in which he participated. In *The Emergence of Conservative Judaism: The Historical School in 19th Century America* (Jewish Publication Society, 1965), Moshe Davis analyzes the other powerful stream within American Jewish religious life of this period, the effort to forge a modernized traditional Judaism for American Jews. While the "Historical school," as Davis describes it, is something of a historical construct, the communal developments that he traces are essential to understanding the subsequent development of both Conservative Judaism and Modern Orthodoxy.

The interior world of America's nineteenth-century central European Jews—their home life, social life, manners, and mores—are best explored through primary sources. Much can be learned from the fascinating and well-rounded collection of *Memoirs of American Jews 1775–1865*, 3 vols. (Jewish Publication Society, 1955), edited by Jacob R. Marcus. These memoirs were written by women as well as men, and reflect the experiences of Jews in different regions of the country. From 1859 to 1862 a Jewish traveler named I. J. Benjamin toured America, and he subsequently issued a book in German recounting his travels and describing Jewish life in the New World as he had experienced it. Translated into English by Charles Reznikoff, the work appeared in two volumes under the title *Three Years in America,* with an introduction by Oscar Handlin (Salem, N.H.: Ayer, 1975), and makes for fascinating reading.

A wonderful but unfortunately long out of print autobiographical novel by Harriet Lane Levy entitled *920 O'Farrell Street* (Salem, N.H.: Ayer, 1975) depicts the home life of a well-to-do Jewish family in turn-of-the-century San Francisco. The author re-creates the people, the rooms, and even the prejudices that characterized the world of her youth, and she sets them forth in an engaging, winsome manner. A similarly revealing volume by Alexandra Lee Levin probes the rich family life of *The Szolds of Lombard Street* (Jewish Publication Society, 1960). Using surviving correspondence, she describes a half-century in the development of one of Baltimore's most cultured Jewish families, whose eldest daughter, Henrietta, went on to a remarkable career in Jewish communal life, and is best remembered as the founder of Hadassah. The most recent full-scale biography of Henrietta Szold is Joan Dash's *Summoned to Jerusalem: The Life of Henrietta Szold* (Harper & Row, 1979).

The mass immigration of east European Jews to the United States, beginning in 1881, transformed the American Jewish community and changed the course of American Jewish history. The great themes of this era—the arduous trek from old world to new, the long process of Americanization, and the slow climb up the economic ladder to success—are the stuff of great literature. Small wonder, then, that books dealing with the immigration story could fill a large bookcase. The best single book on the subject is Irving Howe's *World of Our Fathers* (Schocken Books, 1989), a magnificent, highly readable synthesis that covers the entire sweep of the immigration story from east European *shtetl* to postwar suburb in 700 pages of memorable text. The focus here is on New York, to the exclusion of other communities where immigrants settled, and Howe is noticeably weak on such subjects as women immigrants and immigrant religion. But the strengths of the book far outweigh its deficiencies. A separately published documentary consisting of primary sources and illustrations is well worth reading in conjunction with the book; see Irving Howe and Kenneth Libo, *How We Lived* (New York: Richard Marek, 1979).

A second brilliant introduction to the major themes of the immigration story is Moses Rischin's *The Promised City: New York's Jews, 1870–1914* (Harvard University Press, 1977), a classic in the field. Unlike *World of Our Fathers,* it is a model of compression, just 265 pages of text. It places the immigration story firmly within the context of New York urban history, and examines "the search

Child refugees of the Holocaust arrive in New York Harbor. (American Jewish Joint Distribution Committee Archives)

for community in New York . . . the story of the encounter between New York and the great Jewish migration." The chapter "Germans versus Russians," a fair-minded perspective on intracommunal tensions among New York Jews, is particularly significant.

Other key works basically fill out the immigration story, exploring in detail themes that Howe and Rischin touch on only in passing. Susan A. Glenn, *Daughters of the Shtetl* (Cornell University Press, 1990), Sydney Stahl Weinberg's *The World of Our Mothers* (Schocken Books, 1990), and Elizabeth Ewen's *Immigrant Women in the Land of Dollars* (Monthly Review Press, 1985) all focus on Jewish immigrant women; Ewen's book also covers Italian women. Thomas Kessner, likewise interested in the comparison of Italians and Jews, explores immigrant mobility. His conclusion in *The Golden Door* (Oxford University Press, 1977) is that at least for New York's immigrant Jews (1880–1915) America *was* the land of opportunity—more so, indeed, than for other immigrant groups. In *Going to America, Going to School* (Westport, Conn.: Greenwood Press, 1986), Stephan F. Brumberg helps explain why. This sensitive analysis of the Jewish immigrant encounter with the New York public schools illuminates the strengths and weaknesses of "Americanization" programs, and shows how public schools did ultimately succeed in providing children with the tools they needed to advance themselves. Arthur A. Goren's *New York Jews and the Quest for Community* (Columbia University Press, 1982), a classic in the field, explores yet another dimension of Americanization, the early-twentieth-century effort by leading New York Jews to forge an organized and united Jewish community, or *kehillah*, by wedding traditional Jewish forms to contemporary American ideals. The experiment failed; in Goren's capable hands, however, the story of the *kehillah* becomes a valuable case study illuminating wide areas of the immigrant experience as a whole. Finally, and in a class by itself, stands Hutchins Hapgood's *The Spirit of the Ghetto*, first published in 1902 and now reprinted with an excellent introduction by Moses Rischin (Belknap Press/Harvard University Press, 1983). Hapgood's is, in Rischin's words, "the first authentic study by an outsider of the inner life of an American immigrant community" and a "superb portrait of the emergent golden age of the Lower East Side." Enriched by more than fifty drawings by Jacob Epstein, it is still a fine introduction to the cultural life of the immigrant ghetto.

Besides these secondary sources, anyone seriously interested in east European Jewish immigration to the United States should be sure to read plenty of primary sources, the writings of the immigrants themselves. Mary Antin's *From Plotzk to Boston* (Markus Wiener, 1986), written when she was twelve, describing her journey to America, as well as her more mature work, *The Promised Land* (Princeton University Press, 1985), written when she was thirty, are particularly well known. Her sensitivity and keen powers of observation, as well as the light her books shed on what immigration meant to women and children help explain why both volumes are back in print. But readers must remember that Antin had a hidden agenda: to counter those who sought to restrict immigration believing that newcomers could never be assimilated. Other memoirs, written at different times and with different agendas, may be found in Uri Herscher's *The East European Jewish Experience in America: A Century of Memories* (Cincinnati: American Jewish Archives, 1983); Stanley F. Chyet's *Lives and Voices: A Collection of American Jewish Memoirs* (Jewish Publication Society, 1972); and Harold U. Ribalow's *Autobiographies of American Jews* (Jewish Publication Society, 1965).

Literary accounts offer even more compelling depictions of what the immigrant experience was like. The most important of these by far—arguably, indeed, the greatest of all immigrant novels—is Abraham Cahan's *The Rise of David Levinsky* (Harper & Row, 1960). Written in the first person by the renowned editor of the *Jewish Daily Forward,* the novel explores the life and mind of a prototypical Jewish immigrant who escaped Russian poverty, worked his way through the immigrant sweatshops, and emerged, outwardly successful but inwardly lonely and unfulfilled, as a major cloak manufacturer in New York City. As a psychological portrait of immigration the story is without peer. Cahan's earlier writings about Jewish immigrants, fictional and nonfictional alike, may be found in his collection of short stories, *Yekl and The Imported Bridegroom and Other Stories of the New York Ghetto* (Dover, 1978), and in Moses Rischin's brilliant anthology, *Grandma Never Lived in America: The New Journalism of Abraham Cahan* (Indiana University Press, 1985). A quite different but no less powerful fictional portrayal of the Jewish immigrant experience, from a woman's point of view, may be found in the writings of Anzia Yezierska, particularly *Bread Givers* (Persea Books, 1975), "a struggle between a father of the Old World and a daughter of the new," as well as her selected writings reprinted in *The Open Cage: An Anzia Yezierska Collection* (Persea Books, 1979). Henry Roth's *Call It Sleep* (Avon Books, 1976), rediscovered in 1960 and now considered to be a classic of modern American fiction, presents a darker picture of immigrant life, as seen through the eyes of a child growing up in the tenements of New York City. The darkest picture of all, penned by an avowed Communist with a pronounced ideological agenda, is Michael Gold's *Jews Without Money* (Carroll & Graf, 1984) a novel of protest written in the depths of the Depression.

Two other primary sources, originally written for immigrants in their own language, are now available in translation. The first, my *People Walk on Their Heads: Moses Weinberger's Jews and Judaism in New York* (Holmes & Meier, 1982) renders into English an 1887 volume in Hebrew by a Hungarian immigrant rabbi describing—and deploring—the state of Orthodox Judaism in America. It offers an unusual and highly negative portrayal of immigrant life from the perspective of a religious traditionalist who found America to be an amoral, materialistic land, "a world turned upside down." The second primary source, *A Bintel Brief,* edited and with an introduction by Isaac Metzker (Schocken Books, 1990), makes available in English a remarkable collection of letters, originally published in the famous *bintel brief* ("bundle of letters") daily advice column of the Yiddish-language *Jewish Daily Forward.* The letters were addressed to the editor and cover a wide range of immigrant problems: political, romantic, generational, and religious. Abraham Cahan's clever answers and Harry Golden's chatty, retrospective notes make the volume as enjoyable as it is informative.

World War I and the introduction of strict immigration restrictions, in 1924, marked the beginning of a new era in American Jewish history, one which saw American Jewry rise to a position of wealth, power, and influence on the national and international scenes. No survey does full justice to this theme, but three books are well worth reading: Ronald Sanders's *Shores of Refuge* (Schocken Books, 1989), a sensitively written history of worldwide Jewish emigration, with much information on the interwar years; Judd Teller's *Strangers and Natives* (Delacorte Press, 1968), a perceptive and well-written journalistic account of "the evolution of the American Jew from 1921 to the present"; and Lucy S. Dawidowicz's *On Equal Terms: Jews in America, 1881–1981* (Holt, Rinehart & Winston, 1982), a brief overview that is especially strong on the Holocaust period. Focused monographs have only just begun to consider this period, and most concentrate on New York, where the bulk of Jewish immigrants and their children lived. Jeffrey S. Gurock's *When Harlem Was Jewish* (Columbia University Press, 1979) chronicles sixty years in the history of one community of New York Jews, including an important chapter on the emergence of synagogue-centers in Harlem during the 1920s and 1930s, and valuable background on black-Jewish relations. *At Home in America* by Deborah Dash Moore (Columbia University Press, 1981) examines the children of New York's east European Jewish immigrants and the world that they created. It traces the emergence of middle-class Jewish ethnicity during this period, and shows how Jews "established the limits of their assimilation into American society." Gurock's social history of Yeshiva University, *The Men and Women of Yeshiva* (Columbia University Press, 1988), and Jenna Weissman Joselit's lively portrayal of *New York's Jewish Jews: The Orthodox Community in the Interwar Years* (Indiana University Press, 1990) carry forward these themes, dealing in different ways with the efforts of second-generation Jews to reconcile Jewish tradition and American life. Joselit's earlier book, *Our Gang: Jewish Crime and the New York Jewish Community* (Indiana University Press, 1983), looks at the darker side of this story, the Jews who sought to advance in American society through criminal means.

The greatest expression of Jewish ethnicity during this era was, of course, the Zionist movement, the effort to create a Jewish homeland in Palestine for the Jewish people. Melvin I. Urofsky's *American Zionism from Herzl to the Holocaust* (Doubleday, 1976) is the best-known and best-written history; for more on the

Zionist movement, see "Themes" below. Mordecai Kaplan's writings also gave voice to these questions of peoplehood and alienation. Kaplan's *Judaism As a Civilization: Toward a Reconstruction of American-Jewish Life* (Jewish Publication Society, 1981), a classic of contemporary American Jewish religious thought, was published during this period and reflects Kaplan's sense of "the present crisis in Judaism." The solutions he proposes in the book, including Zionism, became the basis for the Reconstructionist movement in Judaism. For Kaplan's subsequent writings, see *Dynamic Judaism: The Essential Writings of Mordecai M. Kaplan*, edited by Emanuel S. Goldsmith and Mel Scult (Schocken Books and Reconstructionist Press, 1985).

A disproportionate number of books dealing with the post-immigration decades of the twentieth century concern themselves in one way or another way with American Jewry's role in the Holocaust. David S. Wyman's brilliantly researched and sensitively written *The Abandonment of the Jews: America and the Holocaust, 1941–1945* (Pantheon Books, 1986) is the standard account of this tragic episode, and should be read first. Leonard Dinnerstein's *America and the Survivors of the Holocaust* (Columbia University Press, 1982) takes up where Wyman leaves off and recounts the appalling history of the immediate post-Holocaust years when anti-Semites and restrictionists combined in an effort to bar Jewish refugees from America's shores. For other works on America and the Holocaust, see chapter 7 in this volume.

Studies of American Jewry in the postwar period—often called the "contemporary era" though it is now approaching its half-century mark—are too numerous even to list. Moreover, much of the literature is highly technical, full of difficult-to-read tables and obscure jargon. The place to begin reading, then, is with Chaim I. Waxman's *America's Jews in Transition* (Temple University Press, 1983) a fine survey textbook. It both clarifies the major questions posed by students of contemporary Jewish life and synthesizes available data. See also Marshall Sklare's somewhat dated but still valuable textbook, *America's Jews* (McGraw-Hill, 1971). Sklare, the "founding father" of American Jewish sociology, has also edited a series of pathbreaking readers in the field: *The Jews: Social Patterns of an American Group* (Free Press, 1958); *The Jewish Community in America* (Behrman House, 1974); and *The Jew in American Society* (Behrman House, 1974). (The two Behrman House volumes were abridged into one entitled *American Jews* [Behrman House, 1983]). These bring together diverse articles on a wide range of sociological issues concerning American Jews, illuminated by Sklare's introductory comments.

Besides these volumes, readers should acquaint themselves with some of the major monographs that have helped to define our understanding of contemporary American Jewish life and the challenges it confronts. Marshall Sklare's Lakeville studies, particularly *Jewish Identity on the Suburban Frontier* (University of Chicago Press, 1979), is a good one place to begin, for it introduces many of the themes, questions, and analyses that influenced a whole generation of Jewish social scientists. This was one of the first studies-in-depth of a Jewish community—a suburb of Chicago—and it serves as something of a benchmark, a standard of comparison against which subsequent community studies may be measured. Charles Liebman's *The Ambivalent American Jew: Politics, Religion and Family in American Jewish Life* (Jewish Publication Society, 1973) moves beyond the focused study of one community in an ambitious effort to interpret American Jewish life as a whole. "The American Jew is torn between two sets of values—those of integration and acceptance into American society and those of Jewish group survival," according to Liebman, and to his mind the two values are incompatible. The volume's ambivalent stance reflects, in part, Liebman's Zionist sympathies and echoes several themes explored years earlier in Ben Halpern's *The American Jew: A Zionist Analysis* (Markus Wiener, 1988). See also Liebman's detailed studies of American Jewish religious life, originally published in the *American Jewish Year Book* (1965, 1968, 1970) and reprinted with a new introduction in *Aspects of the Religious Behavior of American Jews* (Ktav Publishing House, 1974).

Charles Silberman's *A Certain People: American Jews and Their Lives Today* (Summit Books, 1986) presents a much more upbeat vision of American Jewish life. Celebrating the many positive changes that transformed the American Jewish community during his own lifetime, Silberman's readable and well-researched volume summarizes reams of data on the economic condition of American Jewry, the growth of philanthropy, the decline of anti-Semitism, the renewal of Jewish religious life, and most controversial of all, the demographic changes that he interprets in a characteristically optimistic vein. Calvin Goldscheider's *Jewish Continuity and Change: Emerging Patterns in America* (Indiana University Press, 1986), while much more scholarly and theoretical, makes a parallel case for the claim that American Jewry is being transformed, not weakened, by the forces of modernization. For an illuminating analysis of the issues behind the resulting clamorous debate over the character of American Jewish life today and the changes shaping the community of tomorrow, see Steven M. Cohen, *American Assimilation or Jewish Revival?* (Indiana University Press, 1988).

Two other highly significant volumes are enormously helpful in the quest to understand the contemporary American Jewish community. Daniel J. Elazar's *Community and Polity: The Organizational Dynamics of American Jewry* (Jewish Publication Society, 1976) analyzes American Jewish organizational life from a political science perspective. It makes available a wealth of data on the community's various components and functions, and shows how the polity has changed over time, in response to new problems and circumstances. No finer study of the inner workings of the American Jewish community exists. Jonathan Woocher's *Sacred Survival: The Civil Religion of American Jews* (Indiana University Press, 1986) examines these same community organizations from the perspective of a student of religion. His analysis of American Jewish civil religion, the myths, symbols, and rituals that bind the organizational leaders of American Jewish life together, explains a great deal, not only about the leadership of American Jewry but about contemporary American Judaism as a whole. See also Jacob Neusner's essays on the central religious myths of contemporary American Judaism, collected in his *Stranger at Home: "The Holocaust," Zionism, and American Judaism* (University of Chicago Press, 1985).

Themes

While many of the central themes of American Jewish history have been dealt with in the chronological section above, certain topics have an integrity, a literature, and a reading public all their own. The section that follows covers only selected areas where notable books have appeared recently.

Anti-Semitism

Anti-Semitism in American History, edited by David A. Gerber (University of Illinois Press, 1987), with contributions from fourteen different scholars, is the best single volume on the subject and includes a brilliant introductory essay by the editor. Earlier, pioneering essays by John Higham have not been superseded, however, and are reprinted in updated form in Higham's *Send These to Me: Immigrants in Urban America* (Johns Hopkins University Press, 1984). Atlanta's sensational Leo Frank case of 1913, in which Frank, a Jew, was wrongly accused of murdering thirteen-year-old Mary Phagan and then lynched in an atmosphere of anti-Semitic hysteria, has formed the subject of many books. The best and most insightful by far is Leonard Dinnerstein's *The Leo Frank Case* (University of Georgia Press, 1987), a model study which places the incident in its proper historical context. Dinnerstein has also written a valuable book of essays on American anti-Semitism, *Uneasy At Home* (Columbia University Press, 1987).

Black-Jewish Relations

Bittersweet Encounter: The Afro-American and the American Jew by Robert G. Weisbord and Arthur Stein (Westport, Conn.: Greenwood Press, 1970) is a comprehensive survey that covers the history of black-Jewish relations with special emphasis on flashpoints, such as the Arab-Israeli conflict and the 1968 New York public school crisis. The volume, however, needs updating. Today, it is best read in conjunction with Jonathan Kaufman's powerful journalistic account, *Broken Alliance: The Turbulent Times Between Blacks and Jews in America* (New American Library, 1989).

Culture

Stephen J. Whitfield's sparkling essays collected in two volumes, *Voices of Jacob, Hands of Esau: Jews in American Life and Thought* (Hamden, Conn.: Archon Books, 1984) and *American Space, Jewish Time* (Hamden, Conn.: Archon Books, 1988), probe a wide range of cultural themes, including liberalism, popular culture, and the Holocaust. As the titles of his books imply, he is especially interested in the interrelationship between the American and Jewish traditions, the "dual legacy of the modern American Jew." For the effects of this same interrelationship on the domestic culture of American Jews, see *Getting Comfortable in New York: The American Jewish Home, 1880–1950*, edited by Susan L. Braunstein and Jenna Weissman Joselit (New York: Jewish Museum, 1990), a lavishly illustrated volume based on an exhibit at the Jewish Museum. The radical young Jews who emerged in the 1930s and eventually became known as the New York Intellectuals form the subject of numerous recent books; see especially Alexander Bloom's *Prodigal Sons: The New York Intellectuals and Their World* (Oxford University Press, 1986). For those on the other side, concerned about the perpetuation of Jewish culture in America, see my history of the Jewish Publication

Society, *JPS: The Americanization of Jewish Culture, 1888–1988* (Jewish Publication Society, 1989).

Local History

The best history of an American Jewish community, for most readers, will be the history of their own community, a history that celebrates the community that they know and love. Objectively, however, some community histories *are* better than others: they are better researched, better conceptualized, and better able to relate local concerns to national ones. Hyman B. Grinstein's *The Rise of the Jewish Community of New York* (Jewish Publication Society, 1945) and Edwin Wolf 2d and Maxwell Whiteman's *The History of the Jews of Philadelphia from Colonial Times to the Age of Jackson* (Jewish Publication Society, 1975) are recognized classics; both fill important gaps in our understanding of early American Jewish life. Of the more recent local histories, Lloyd Gartner's *History of the Jews of Cleveland* (Cleveland: Western Reserve Historical Society, 1978) gets top honors as a work of scholarship. In a class by itself stands Eli Evans's intimate and highly readable *The Provincials: A Personal History of the Jews in the South* (Atheneum, 1973), a volume that captures the feel and texture of southern Jewish life. To find out if the Jewish history of the place you call home has yet been written, see the bibliography of local community and synagogue histories in Alexandra Shecket Korros and Jonathan D. Sarna, *American Synagogue History: A Bibliography and State-of-the-Field Survey* (Markus Wiener, 1988).

Religious Movements

The classic study of an American Jewish religious movement is Marshall Sklare's *Conservative Judaism* (Lanham, Mich.: University Press of America, 1985), a brilliant combination of sociology and history that analyzes the movement in its American setting from the perspective of both lay and professional members. No comparable volume explores the Reform movement, but its history has been magnificently detailed in the appropriate chapters of Michael A. Meyer's, *Response to Modernity: A History of the Reform Movement in Judaism* (Oxford University Press, 1990.) Orthodoxy, until recently, has not been nearly so well served by sociologists and historians. The best one-volume works are Reuven P. Bulka's *Dimensions of Orthodox Judaism* (Ktav Publishing House, 1983), a collection of previously published articles that stresses the theme of diversity and examines the movement's contemporary challenges, and Samuel C. Heilman and Steven M. Cohen's *Cosmopolitans and Parochials* (University of Chicago Press, 1989), a sociological study of "what Jewish Orthodoxy has become in America today." Much can also be learned from Aaron Rakeffet-Rothkoff's biographies of two great American Orthodox leaders: *Bernard Revel: Builder of American Jewish Orthodoxy*, 2d ed. (Feldheim, 1980) and *The Silver Era in American Jewish Orthodoxy: Rabbi Eliezer Silver and His Generation* (Feldheim, 1981). To date, only one book-length study of the contemporary Reconstructionist movement has appeared: *Exploring Judaism: A Reconstructionist Approach* by Rebecca T. Alpert and Jacob J. Staub (Reconstructionist Press, 1985). A brief, popular volume written for members of the movement and potential recruits, it does nevertheless express the movement's basic tenets and outlook. See also Marc Lee Raphael's *Profiles in American Judaism: The Reform, Conservative, Orthodox, and Reconstructionist Traditions in Historical Perspective* (Harper & Row, 1988) for a textbook survey of all four movements.

Sephardim

The twentieth century witnessed a small but important migration to America of Sephardic Jews, mostly from the Ottoman Empire. Overshadowed by the much larger number of east European immigrants, these Jews, who spoke Ladino (Judeo-Spanish) rather than Yiddish and often lived and worked apart from the east Europeans, are only now being rediscovered. The most comprehensive introduction to the subject is Joseph M. Papo's *Sephardim in Twentieth Century America: In Search of Unity* (San Jose: Pele Yoetz Books, 1987), a synoptic history containing a great deal of useful information, important biographical sketches, and other invaluable appendices. Marc D. Angel's *La America: The Sephardic Experience in the United States* (Jewish Publication Society, 1982) focuses more narrowly on the period 1910–25. It tells the story of New York's Sephardim as seen through the eyes of journalist Moise Gadol and his Judeo-Spanish newspaper, *La America*.

Synagogues and Temples

By far the best general book on the American synagogue, the oldest and most significant institutional expression of American Jewish life, is *The American Synagogue: A Sanctuary Transformed*, edited by Jack Wertheimer (Cambridge University Press, 1988). Its fourteen chapters, all by leading scholars in the field, include a historical overview, three denominational perspectives, and ten thematic articles on subjects that range from synagogue music to the development of mixed seating. The volume is best read in conjunction with two other recent books of enviable quality: *The American Rabbinate: A Century of Continuity and Change, 1883–1983*, edited by Jacob R. Marcus and Abraham J. Peck (Ktav Publishing House, 1985), and *Chosen Voices: The Story of the American Cantorate*, by Mark Slobin (University of Illinois, 1989). Samuel Heilman's remarkable ethnographic study of an American Orthodox synagogue, *Synagogue Life: A Study in Symbolic Interaction* (University of Chicago, 1979), offers a different perspective on the synagogue, focusing on how individuals interact while in its midst, and what these "performances" mean. The book may be read in conjunction with Riv-Ellen Prell's *Prayer and Community: The Havurah in American Judaism* (Wayne State University Press, 1989), an insightful participant-observer study of a Los Angeles countercultural *havurah*, and what it reveals about the way Jews pray.

Thought

Arnold Eisen's *The Chosen People in America* (Indiana University Press, 1983) can be considered the first serious study of American Jewish thought. It traces the efforts on the part of American Jewry's best minds to reconcile the Jewish idea of chosenness with America's sense of egalitarianism. Along the way, the volume brims over with insights concerning a wide range of American Jewish thinkers, many of whom have been ignored for far too long. For more recent developments in Jewish religious thought, see Robert G. Goldy, *The Emergence of Jewish Theology in America* (Indiana University Press, 1990), which focuses on the decades since World War II.

Women

The Jewish Woman in America by Charlotte Baum, Paula Hyman, and Sonya Michel (New American Library, 1975) was in its day a pathbreaking volume that posed new questions, utilized long-forgotten sources, and inspired untold numbers of Jewish women to reclaim their own past. Ideally, the volume should be read in conjunction with Jacob R. Marcus's *The American Jewish Woman: A Documentary History* (Ktav Publishing House, 1981), a mammoth compendium of 177 well-chosen primary sources (1047 pp.) that traces, through documents, the experience of Jewish women from colonial times to 1980. See also, Marcus's own fact-filled narrative history, *The American Jewish Woman, 1654–1980* (Ktav Publishing House, 1981), as well as chapter 11 in this volume, which lists other works.

Zionism

Besides Melvin I. Urofsky in his well-written volume, mentioned above, and its sequel *We Are One: American Jewry and Israel* (Doubleday, 1978), only Naomi Cohen has attempted a full-scale survey. Her *American Jews and the Zionist Idea* (Ktav Publishing House, 1975) focuses on the Zionist idea and the differences between American Zionism and its European counterparts. Much can also be learned from the biographies of Zionist leaders, notably Lewis J. Paper, *Brandeis* (Seacaucus, N.J.: Citadel Press, 1983), and Philippa Strum, *Louis D. Brandeis: Justice for the People* (Schocken Books, 1989), on Supreme Court Justice Louis D. Brandeis; Melvin I. Urofsky, *A Voice That Spoke for Justice: The Life and Times of Stephen S. Wise* (SUNY Press, 1981) on Rabbi Stephen S. Wise; and Marc Lee Raphael, *Abba Hillel Silver: A Profile in American Judaism* (Holmes & Meier, 1989), on Rabbi Abba Hillel Silver.

Zionism marks the concluding stop on our book tour through the multifaceted world of the American Jewish experience. Of course, extensions are possible. Those interested should consult Jeffrey Gurock's *American Jewish History: A Bibliographical Guide* (Anti-Defamation League of B'nai B'rith, 1983), the best one-volume inventory of the field. For up-to-the-minute information on new books and articles in the field, see Nathan Kaganoff's semiannual listing of "Judaica Americana," in *American Jewish History,* the quarterly journal of the American Jewish Historical Society.

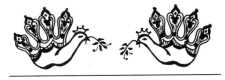

CHAPTER 7

THE HOLOCAUST

Deborah E. Lipstadt

No area of Jewish studies has experienced as significant a spurt of interest in recent years among scholars, students, and the population at large—Jewish and non-Jewish—as the Holocaust. The most cursory examination of any bibliography on topics in Jewish history and literature will quickly reveal that for close to twenty-five years after the end of World War II books on and interest in the Holocaust was minimal. Even the Eichmann trial did not arouse much interest on the part of historians or readers. Hannah Arendt's *Eichmann in Jerusalem* (Penguin, 1977), which addressed the question of the banality of evil, prompted some discussion among American intellectuals but it did not penetrate the fog or break the silence which seemed to surround this topic. Survivors rarely spoke about what happened to them and no one seemed interested enough to ask. With the exception of Yad Vashem in Jerusalem and a number of other museums in Israel, there were virtually no museums, research centers, memorials, or courses on the topic. Textbooks and curricula in Jewish and non-Jewish schools studiously avoided this subject.

Today, as is obvious to all, the situation has changed dramatically. The

United States Holocaust Memorial Council recently published a list of over one hundred Holocaust memorial organizations in the United States and Canada. And that list is far from complete. On over one thousand different American campuses courses on the Holocaust are offered.

The growth of interest in this topic evolved in the late 1960s. The Six-Day War and the rise in ethnicity in America contributed to it. A post-Holocaust generation of "baby boomers," were then on college campuses and in the process of revolting against the "establishment." They used the Holocaust as a means of differentiating between themselves and their parents' quiescent generation. During the 1970s the Holocaust was increasingly made part of the Jewish communal agenda. As the survivors achieved both the age and the material security to feel at ease in America, they began to support the building of museums and memorials.

In the late 1970s NBC's miniseries, "Holocaust," while trivializing the event in many respects, also generated interest in the topic. Now the Holocaust was something worthy of prime time. Also by the late 1970s books, articles, memoirs, novels, and psychological, sociological, and philosophical studies began to appear in incredible numbers. The growth of interest was staggering. It is probably safe to say that no other limited era in history—twelve years—has had as many volumes devoted to it as has the Holocaust.

Consequently, those who are anxious to probe this material face both a rich selection from which to choose and a challenge. The proliferation of material has been so intense that the uninitiated reader can easily be overwhelmed.

The reader's excursion into this topic is further complicated by the fact that the Holocaust is not one but a series of stories, each focusing on a different set of characters who can be broadly subsumed under the headings: perpetrators, victims, and bystanders. But within each group there are a variety of actors each of whom played dramatically different roles. The perpetrators include high-ranking Nazis who conceived of this horrendous act as well as bureaucrats who sat in railway offices devising the schedules for the trains which carried victims eastward; SS guards who volunteered for service in places such as Auschwitz and Treblinka as well as government clerks who registered Jewish property and stamped a "J" in Jewish passports; and members of the Einsatzgruppen who shot millions of Jews on the Russian front and those who in 1933 devised the regulations which legally excluded Jews from jobs as judges, teachers, and lawyers. Each contributed in a different degree and fashion to this event we have come to call the Holocaust.

The victims are an equally diverse group and any discussion of their behavior must take those different attributes and experiences into consideration. They were old and young, rich and poor, highly assimilated and extremely traditional Jews. There were those who lived in countries where Jews were barely distinguishable from the majority population and those who lived in virtual isolation from their non-Jewish neighbors. There were those who fought and those who did not; those who tried to escape and those who followed orders; and those who maintained their religious faith and those who lost it.

The bystanders include individuals, groups, and institutions with vastly different characteristics. The most notable difference was between those who had the actual power to rescue, e.g., the American and British governments, and those who only had the power of persuasion to try to convince others to act, e.g., world Jewry. There were bystanders who witnessed what was happening in front of their eyes and those who heard about it from afar. There were those who hid Jews and those who stood idly by. Particular attention has been focused on those bystander institutions such as the International Red Cross and the Vatican whose response to this tragedy was at odds with their own moral mandate.

Where does one begin? How should one make sense of this material? One way may be to isolate some of the most frequently asked and perplexing questions about this event. These queries can be grouped into a number of broad categories.

Uniqueness—Was the Holocaust unique? Was Hitler any worse than myriad other reprehensible historical figures including Stalin and Pol Pot? Other than their use of modern means of destruction—gas chambers—are the crimes of the Nazis fundamentally different from other genocidal outrages, such as the Armenian massacres? How do they differ from other acts of anti-Semitism? If the Crusaders or Chmielnicki had had the "benefit" of twentieth-century technology, would their actions have been the equivalent of the Final Solution?

Resistance—How did the Jews respond? Is there any truth to the charge that they went "like sheep to the slaughter"? How do we define resistance? Do resisters include only those who physically resisted or can we adopt a broader definition of resistance without diluting its meaning? Why did some non-Jews resist Nazi orders and hide Jews while others turned them in?

Knowledge—Who knew what and when did they know it? Was the existence of Auschwitz and the other death camps a secret until the end of the war? Were Jews aware of the true meaning of "relocation" and "resettlement" in the East? When people, both victims and bystanders, say they did not know, was their ignorance a result of a lack of information or an inability to make the leap of the imagination necessary to grasp the implications of what they were hearing? If so much information was available—as it was—during the war, why do so many people claim to have been so utterly shocked by what they saw once the war was over?

World Response—How did the rest of the world respond? What did the Allies *do* and what *could* they have done to prevent the Holocaust from happening? Was there military action that they could have taken which would have stopped the killings?

How did Jewish communities, particularly those in Allied lands, respond? What *could* they have done? Were they indifferent to the suffering of their fellow Jews or are post-Holocaust generations applying a contemporary standard of action to previous generations? Did they have the political clout to effect any real changes in Allied policy?

There are also an array of questions regarding the post-Holocaust era. Some are theological, while others are psychological and sociological. How can one reconcile a compassionate and just God with the Holocaust? Is religious faith possible after the Holocaust? What about the survivors, how did they fare? How were they able to resume their lives? What about their children: What impact has this event had on them? Why were so many perpetrators able to elude punishment? Finally, how has the Jewish community incorporated the Holocaust into the contemporary communal agenda? Is there such a thing as "too" much emphasis on this topic or are such fears without basis?

The books discussed in the following pages were chosen because they address themselves to these questions to one degree or another. We begin our excursion through this field with two caveats. There are many works on the Holocaust which are not included here. Many will peruse this essay and notice that volumes they admire are missing. This is probably the result of the limits of space and the need to select books which will be of interest to the non-specialized reader. It is certainly not a reflection on the intrinsic value of a particular book.

The second caveat is that there is no one mandated entry point into this complex field. Some will choose to begin with a memoir, such as Elie Wiesel's *Night* (Bantam, 1982) or Primo Levi's *Survival in Auschwitz* (Collier/Macmillan, 1988), while others may choose a more straightforward historical overview. The order in which I present these books tends to adhere to a historical unfolding of events. Some readers will choose to follow this order, while others will create their own sequence.

Given the complexity of this topic a comprehensive history of the Holocaust is extremely important. This is particularly so because many people have been exposed to disparate parts of this history but have never really grasped how the various pieces fit together. What connection is there between the Versailles Treaty and the rise of Nazism? What relationship, for instance, is there between the course of the war on the Russian front and the pace of the killings?

The best known of any of these overviews is Lucy Dawidowicz's *The War Against the Jews: 1933–1945* (Free Press, 1986). It generated a great deal of attention partly because it appeared just when interest in the Holocaust was growing. Well written and of a manageable length, it will probably not overwhelm the reader. The major shortcoming of the book is that it fails to address certain crucial topics. There is virtually no attention paid to the fate of Jews in Western Europe. More importantly, there is little description of how the death camps functioned and what life and death were like in them. The book places an unduly heavy emphasis on ghetto life, particularly in the Warsaw ghetto. Dawidowicz, who had a long commitment to the Jewish Labor Bund and Yiddishist movement, focuses on the role the Bundists played while virtually ignoring the contributions of other organizations, including the Zionists. Dawidowicz, anxious to demonstrate that the Jews did not meekly submit to their fate, devotes a significant portion of the book to the important cultural and social organizations that existed in the ghetto. In so doing she makes an important point about the role of spiritual resistance but she inadvertently makes the ghetto sometimes sound like a Jewish cultural center rather than the inferno it was. Nonetheless the book is valuable and a good place to gain a general overview of the event.

A less compellingly written but more comprehensive portrait is provided by Yehuda Bauer in *A History of the Holocaust* (Franklin Watts, 1982). One of the strengths of the book is that it devotes a significant amount of space to the history of emancipation, anti-Semitism, and Weimar Germany. Consequently the reader is helped to understand that the Holocaust did not spring *de novo* but had its roots in European history. Bauer's discussion of life in the ghettoes as well as that of the death camps is far more complete than Dawidowicz's and he includes a number of maps which allow the reader to place the event in a geographic context.

Readers who wish to broaden their grasp of the geographic context in which the Holocaust occurred would be well advised to peruse Martin Gilbert's *The Macmillan Atlas of the Holocaust* (Da Capo Press, 1984). With over three hundred maps it serves as an important reference tool which helps place the Holocaust in the broader picture of World War II.

The most recent and most comprehensive of any of these volumes is Leni Yahil's *The Holocaust: The Fate of European Jewry, 1941–45* (Oxford University

Press, 1990). Because of its comprehensive nature it will probably eventually become the text of choice in classes and seminars on the Holocaust. In contrast to Raul Hilberg's classic three-volume work, *The Destruction of the European Jews*, rev. ed. (Holmes & Meier, 1985), Yahil is not attempting to break new ground in this book but to synthesize much of what has already been written. It addresses many of the questions that have been raised by scholars during the past forty-five years. Her audience is the non-specialist who is interested in more than a cursory overview. Hilberg's *magnum opus* may be too dense a work for the general reader. Moreover, its focus is on the German bureaucracy which carried out the Final Solution and not on the victims or any of the ancillary issues.

Among the questions that often arise in the course of an exploration of this topic are: How did the nation which was considered to be the seat of culture and intellectual accomplishment, the home of Beethoven and Schiller, become the place where the most odious event in human history was launched? How were Hitler and his Nazi followers able to win control of the nation? What were the German public's reactions to Nazi ideology in general and Nazi anti-Semitism in particular? Did they enthusiastically go along with all aspects of his preaching? Was this something forced on them?

One of the studies that helps us begin to answer this question is William Sheridan Allen's *The Nazi Seizure of Power: The Experience of a Single German Town, 1930–1935* (Franklin Watts, 1984). Using a wide variety of sources including archival material, town records, and personal interviews, Allen traces the Nazi rise to power in one small town. Allen believes that Hitler was able to seize power in the spring of 1933 because the Nazis had been successful with the base population, those at the "lower" socioeconomic rungs. While an in-depth study of one particular town may not be representative of all of Germany, Allen's work does allow the reader to understand in a detailed fashion how one group of people responded to the Nazis.

To fully understand how the Nazi leadership managed to cement its hold over the population at large it is instructive to read some of the materials that were distributed to the German population. A good selection of these can be found in *Nazi Culture: Intellectual Cultural and Social Life in the Third Reich* (Schocken Books, 1981), which is edited by one of the leading scholars on the topic, George L. Mosse. Included are a prayer written for children, selections from a novel by Goebbels, and Hitler's argument that women were not worthy of equal status with men. Every aspect of German life—culture, economy, recreation, religion, and, of course, politics—was totally regulated. This collection helps illustrate that point.

Even as one probes the reactions of "ordinary" Germans, some readers will wish to examine the background of the man who was Nazism's central figure. Alan Bullock's *Hitler, A Study in Tyranny* (Harper & Row, 1990, abr. ed.) and Joachim Fest's *Hitler* (Vintage Books, 1975) are both solid and interesting studies. Neither work focuses in any measure on Hitler's anti-Semitism or how that portion of his ideology that resulted in the Final Solution was shaped. While this omission weakens the ultimate value of these books, it is instructive in and of itself, in that it demonstrates how much—if not most—of the world treats Nazism in general and Nazi anti-Semitism in particular. Most curricula dealing with World War II and the vast majority of studies of Nazi Germany treat the Holocaust as an addendum to the main story. It is seen as an important but *isolated* event. These works fail to recognize the degree to which anti-Semitism was ingrained into all aspects of Nazi ideology.

Another important insight into Nazism and its success in permeating every aspect of society is contained in Robert Jay Lifton's *Nazi Doctors: Medical Killings and the Psychology of Genocide* (Basic Books, 1988). Lifton, a medical doctor, asks a question that has disturbed him on both a personal and scholarly level: how were doctors—whose professional identity is, at least in theory, rooted in the responsibility to heal—able to allow themselves to participate in the Final Solution? A significant number of doctors, Mengele best known among them, played an intimate role in the running of the death and concentration camps. They were also the ones who carried out the pre-war euthanasia program against Germans who were mentally ill. Understanding how they were so easily able to participate in this endeavor sheds light on how German society in general responded to the Nazis. These questions lead to queries which are applicable to the German population at large and not just to the doctors.

One of the most remarkable endeavors in documenting the history of the Holocaust is Claude Lanzmann's film, *Shoah*. Because of its length and its intensity it was often difficult to fully grasp all the nuances contained therein. Consequently the book, *Shoah: An Oral History of the Holocaust* (Pantheon Books, 1987), which contains the text of the film, is useful. Of particular interest in relation to understanding the nature of Nazi Germany are the interviews with two high-ranking officials. One was assistant to the commissioner in charge of the Warsaw Ghetto and the other was part of the chain of command at Treblinka.

THE JEWISH DEATH-TOLL
1939-1945

This map shows the number of Jews murdered in Nazi-dominated Europe between 1939 and 1945. All the figures are approximate, but most of them are probably *underestimates*. In all, more than **5,950,000** deaths are shown even with these minimum figures.

NORWAY 868

ESTONIA 1,000

DENMARK 120

LATVIA

LITHUANIA

HOLLAND 106,000

BELGIUM 24,000

FURTHEST ADVANCE OF THE GERMAN ARMY 1942

GERMANY 125,000

4,565,000

POLAND

WESTERN USSR

LUXEMBOURG 700

CZECHOSLOVAKIA 277,000

FRANCE 83,000

HUNGARY 300,000

RUMANIA 264,000

AUSTRIA 70,000

YUGOSLAVIA 60,000

ITALY 7,500

GREECE 65,000

Approximate Jewish death-toll, country-by-country.

---·--- European frontiers of 1937.

© Martin Gilbert 1978

North Sea

Baltic Sea

Adriatic Sea

Black Sea

Mediterranean Sea

Jewish death-tolls throughout Europe during the Holocaust. (From *Jewish History Atlas* by Martin Gilbert [Weidenfeld & Nicolson, 1988]. Reprinted by permission of the author.)

Using a degree of subterfuge to get them to reveal themselves, Lanzmann demonstrates how lacking in remorse either of them are. These interviews are also useful because they constitute a wonderful response to those who are perverse enough to try to deny that the Holocaust occurred. Here are two people who played intimate roles in it. They were there and they do not deny it; how can anyone else do so?

We turn now to one of the more complex aspects of this topic: the response of the Jewish community. Every teacher who has broached this topic has been asked, How did Jews respond to this terrible persecution? It is one of the most difficult queries to answer, in part because of the great diversity of human nature and the myriad of different situations in which Jews found themselves.

One of the most efficacious ways of getting at this question is through the use of diaries. Though diaries have a limited focus and do not encompass the experiences of a broad array of individuals and communities, probing the response of one individual or community in depth is illuminating and has an immediacy missing from more general studies.

The diaries kept in the various ghettoes both by the Jewish leadership as well as by individuals reveal a tremendous amount about the way life was organized in these settings and how desperate were the attempts made to retain a semblance of normalcy. *The Warsaw Diary of Adam Czerniakow* (Stein and Day, 1982) allows the reader to follow the evolution of the ghetto. Czerniakow was the head of the Jewish Council of Warsaw. He oversaw the transfer of the Jews to the ghetto and the running of the ghetto from its establishment until the summer of 1942 when he was instructed by the Nazis to prepare lists of Jews for deportation. Instead of complying with their instructions, he committed suicide. Though parts of Czerniakow's diary are somewhat tedious and composed of many mundane details, as would be the case with any diary kept by a mayor of a city, the overall impact is quite powerful.

There are other important diaries which chronicle the Warsaw ghetto including *The Warsaw Diary of Chaim A. Kaplan* (Collier, 1973) and Emmanuel Ringelblum's *Notes from the Warsaw Ghetto* (Schocken Books, 1974). Ringelblum was trained as a social historian and his diary reflects his understanding of the importance of presenting as full and detailed a portrait of ghetto life as possible. The story of the resistance and the ghetto uprising is contained in Vladka Meed's *On Both Sides of the Wall: Memoirs of the Warsaw Ghetto* (Holocaust Library,

A scene from the Lodz ghetto. (YIVO Institute for Jewish Research)

1979). Meed joined the underground in 1942 and thanks to her Aryan appearance was able to smuggle Jews out and weapons into the ghetto.

There are a number of compelling novels about the Warsaw ghetto including John Hersey's *The Wall* (Vintage Books, 1988), which is based on Ringelblum's experiences, and Leon Uris's *Mila 18* (Bantam, 1983), which tells the story of the uprising itself. Though they take a measure of license with the facts, many readers, particularly younger ones, find such novels a valuable introduction to the topic.

The *Chronicle of the Lodz Ghetto, 1941–1944* (Yale University Press, 1987), which was edited by Lucjan Dobroszycki who survived the Lodz ghetto, tells the history of this unique ghetto. The ghetto was run by Mordecai Chaim Rumkowski who long after his death remains a controversial figure. Some despised him for his autocratic and self-aggrandizing behavior. He ran the ghetto with an iron fist and often included on deportation lists anyone who was critical of him. He had his own personal police force and lived in relative luxury. His dictatorial style has been captured in Leslie Epstein's novel *King of the Jews* (Summit Books, 1989). Others point out that because he made the ghetto economically profitable for the Nazis, it was not liquidated until the summer of 1944, long after most other ghettoes had been destroyed. More Jews survived in Lodz than in any other ghetto. That Rumkowski, a despicable character, was able to preserve the lives of so many Jews for so long illustrates some of the terrible moral dilemmas which faced individuals in leadership positions during this period. See also *Lodz Ghetto*, edited by Alan Adelson and Robert Lapides (Viking, 1989).

A diary of a different sort is Janusz Korczak's *Ghetto Diary* (Holocaust Library, 1978). It is a record of the struggle of a prominent doctor and child psychologist to protect and educate the children in his care. Korczak, well known for his work with children, tried to maintain a semblance of normalcy inside the ghetto orphanage. His gentleness and humanity provide a striking counterpoint to the Nazis' brutality. A fuller portrait of Korczak is contained in Betty Jean Lifton's biography *The King of Children* (Schocken Books, 1989). Ultimately he chose to go to his death at Treblinka with the children in his orphanage rather than take advantage of the opportunity to save himself. One of the most memorable portraits of this period is the description of Korczak leading the children to the *Umschlagplatz*, the place where people boarded the trains to be deported to the death camps. If resistance can be found in dignity, then Korczak was the ultimate resistance fighter. He may not have lifted a physical hand against the Nazis but his behavior was the ultimate contrast to theirs.

A portrait of an entirely different ghetto experience is contained in *The Terezin Requiem* (Avon Books, 1978) by Josef Bor. It is the story of the young orchestra conductor Raphael Schachter, who decides to conduct Verdi's Requiem with the camp orchestra and the five-hundred-voice choir. This is a fictionalized account of a performance which actually did take place and which was attended by high-ranking Nazi officials. Bor, himself a survivor of Terezin, has written a remarkable tribute to the human spirit in which he offers important insights into this strange camp which was used by the Nazis as a showcase to convince the Red Cross that the Jews were being well treated. It is one of the earliest works I read on the Holocaust and it has remained with me for many years. A companion volume, in a manner of speaking, contains the drawings and poems of the children of Terezin, *I Never Saw Another Butterfly* (Schocken Books, 1978). Pain, hope, bewilderment, and childlike faith permeate every page.

Jews in ghettoes and Jews in hiding had remarkably different physical and emotional experiences. A diary that describes the latter is *Young Moshe's Diary* (New York: Board of Jewish Education, 1965) by Moshe Flinker. Flinker, a native of Holland, hides with his family in Brussels until they are eventually caught and deported to Auschwitz where he and parents perished. The diary is among the most moving and compelling works to emerge from the Holocaust. Written by a teenager, it contains his struggles with profound theological problems: how does one who believes deeply in a just and merciful God make sense of the horror of the Holocaust? Well aware of what is happening to his fellow Jews, he expresses intense love for the Jewish people. His love is as strong as his conflict over the relative comfort in which he lives while his fellow Jews suffer: "Something devours my heart—a vast yearning to participate with my brothers in all that is happening to them." This diary is an extraordinary contrast with the other teenage diary which has captivated so much of the world's attention, *Anne Frank: The Diary of a Young Girl* (Pocket Books, 1985). Anne Frank had the vaguest sense of her Jewish identity; Flinker's heart and soul was bond up with his people. One can only marvel at what a Moshe Flinker would have contributed to his people had he been granted more than his fifteen years.

Two other personal memoirs, written not during the war but subsequent to it, also tell the story of children who were hidden during the Holocaust. Saul Friedlander's *When Memory Comes* (Avon Books, 1980) is the story of Friedlander's experience as a young boy in a highly assimilated Czech family which manages to escape to France. When his parents realize that they will soon be caught by the Nazis they leave him with a Catholic family. He is so taken with his Catholic education that in 1946 at the age of fourteen he decides to enter a Jesuit seminary in order to prepare for the priesthood. It is only when a priest says to him, "Didn't your parents die at Auschwitz?" that he comes to learn the full extent of the tragedy which had befallen him and his people. Friedlander intertwines this memoir with a diary he keeps many years later in Jerusalem.

The third memoir of a family in hiding written from the child's perspective is Nechama Tec's *Dry Tears: The Story of a Lost Childhood* (Oxford University Press, 1984). Tec and her family were hidden by Polish non-Jews who repeatedly risked their own lives to protect their guests. But this kindness coexisted with other, less positive sentiments. The elderly grandmother admitted to the young Tec that she opposed hiding Jews. "I would not harm a Jew," she said, "but I see no point in going out of my way to help one. Besides, it is outright stupid to risk Christian blood for Jewish blood. No amount of money could pay for that." But she tells the young Tec, "You and your family are not like Jews. If they wanted to send you away now, I would not let them."

When Tec's family leaves at the end of the war their saviours ask them not to reveal their true identity to the people of the town. (The Polish family obviously knew the mind-set of their neighbors. They lived in Kielce, the site of a pogrom in 1946. It was this final act of horror that prompted many Jews to conclude that there was no future for them in Poland and decide to leave.) The Polish rescuers expressed no sense of gratification at having participated in the rescue and survival of Tec's family. They were just anxious for them to leave.

An anthology of personal memoirs is contained in *Witnesses to the Holocaust: An Oral History* (Twayne Publishers, 1989). Edited by Rhoda Lewin, it contains the numerous personal recollections of survivors of concentration camps as well as survivors who were not in camps. It also contains the recollections of American liberators of the camps. They were the first witnesses from the West to come upon the victims of Nazi terror and their recollections form an important part of this story.

For those who do not have the personal memories of a Moshe Flinker, Saul Friedlander, or the countless others, these memoirs impart knowledge in a fashion that touches the heart even as it expands the mind.

The entire issue of Christians who rescued Jews is a relatively new area of research. It is axiomatic to observe that in virtually no area of the study of the Holocaust is there much "good news." There is little—if anything—that leaves one with a sense of hope or faith in the actions of humanity. This is particularly problematic because the Holocaust has become such a linchpin of contemporary Jewish identity.

The one area of the Holocaust which runs counter to this message of "everybody hates the Jews" is the story of those who risked their own lives and those of their family to aid Jews. It has been an arena of study which has been neglected for too long. When it was discussed it was usually in a purely anecdotal fashion and in terms of a few well-known cases, but even these stories were told in sketchy detail. In the *Encyclopaedia Judaica* more than a page is devoted to the story of the Frank family. But as Professor Nechama Tec observes in her highly readable *When Light Pierced the Darkness* (Oxford University Press, 1987), the only mention of those who risked their lives trying to save Anne and her family reads: "From July 9, 1942 until August 4, 1944 the Frank family remained in their hiding place, kept alive by friendly Gentiles. An act of betrayal resulted in their discovery by the German police." No names. No biographical details. No explanation of why they did what they did. Other works on Anne Frank compounded this omission. One of the ways of rectifying this lacuna is by reading Miep Gies's *Anne Frank Remembered* (Touchstone, 1988). It is essentially the other half or the "flip side" of the Frank family story, told from a perspective of looking into the attic from the outside.

Study of the action of the rescuers gives the lie to the oft-repeated claim "there was nothing anyone could do to help these hapless people." There was something some could do to help and many, far more than we thought, did.

There are a growing number of works which document the behavior of the rescuers. In addition to those already mentioned, there is Philip Hallie's study of Le Chambon, *Lest Innocent Blood Be Shed* (Harper & Row, 1980). Le Chambon was a Huguenot village in France which saved thousands of Jews. A cinematic parallel to Hallie's study is Pierre Sauvage's documentary film *Weapons of the Spirit.* Sauvage was a young child in Le Chambon; consequently his attempt to discover why the people of Le Chambon did what they did takes the form of a personal quest.

The Courage to Care (New York University Press, 1986), edited by Carol Rittner and Sondra Myers, contains the personal reflections of those who engaged in rescuing Jews. One is repeatedly struck by their matter-of-fact attitude and modesty about what they did. "We still don't think what we did in the war was a big deal. . . . We don't like to be called heroes," observed one man who hid thirty-six people in Holland. There were other acts of heroism which did not entail hiding Jews but which put those who performed them at equal risk. Walter Laqueur and Richard Breitman's *Breaking the Silence* (Simon & Schuster, 1986) tells the story of Eduard Schulte, one of Germany's top industrialists, who was responsible for transmitting the news in the summer of 1942 regarding the Nazi plans for genocide. His information resulted in the famous telegram sent by the World Jewish Congress representative in Geneva, Gerhart Riegner, informing Jewish leaders in Britain and America that "all Jews in countries occupied or controlled [by] German . . . after deportation and concentration in East [will] be exterminated at one blow."

A very readable novel which tells the remarkable story of Oskar Schindler, a German industrialist who saved thousands of Jews by giving them work in his factory, is Thomas Keneally's *Schindler's List* (Penguin, 1983). It is based on interviews the author conducted with the people Schindler saved. Siegfried Jagendorf's memoir, *Jagendorf's Foundry,* edited by Aron Hirt-Manheimer (Harper Collins, 1991) tells the extraordinary story of a Romanian Jew who started an ironworks labor force that saved 15,000 deportees.

What made these people do what they did? Is there anything that would enable us to predict such behavior? And given contemporary levels of moral behavior, is there any way that we can use what we know about them to inculcate such values in young people—or older ones as well—today? Can we use their example to teach goodness? These were normal people and not unique "do-gooders." Many are convinced that what they did was unextraordinary. They made a habit of virtue. We can do no less.

A place where there was no virtue was Auschwitz and the other death camps. The miracle of survival there remains one of the incomprehensible aspects of this topic. Primo Levi's *Survival in Auschwitz: The Nazi Assault on Humanity* (Collier/Macmillan, 1988) is a powerful and dispassionate account of how some inmates who were lucky enough not to be sent to the gas chambers or to die of disease were able to survive. It is a short but compelling account. Another powerful memoir of life in a camp is *The Holocaust Kingdom* (Holocaust Library, 1963) by Alexander Donat. Elie Wiesel's *Night* (mentioned earlier) remains one of the most riveting essays about the world of the death camps. Many people begin their excursion into this field with this book.

For those who are interested in how the concentration camps functioned and in the nature of the SS, which was responsible for them, Eugen Kogon's *The Theory and Practice of Hell: The German Concentration Camps and the System Behind Them* (Berkley Publishing Group, 1984) provides important insights. Much of this material is contained in Yahil and the other general histories. There are also many novels which try to capture the horrors of this existence. One of the most powerful is Tadeusz Borowski's *This Way for the Gas, Ladies and Gentlemen* (Penguin, 1976). Borowski, who survived the camps, reflects on the ability of human beings to endure the unendurable.

André Schwarz-Bart's novel, *The Last of the Just* (Atheneum, 1973), stands out as one of the masterful works on this topic. It chronicles the story of a young boy from the rise of the Nazis to his death at Auschwitz. The book is based on the Jewish legend of the thirty-six unknown righteous people who persist throughout Jewish history.

The horror of the transit camps and the ability of some of those held there to focus their energies not only on their own survival but on the survival of others as well is contained in *An Interrupted Life: The Diaries of Etty Hillesum* (Pocket Books, 1985). Hillesum, a well-to-do and highly assimilated Dutch Jew, was well aware of the fate that awaited her and the other inmates of the camp. Still, she maintained an indomitable spirit in the face of this frightful future. This is a poignant and powerful book.

The ability of people to survive the camps for even limited periods of time is something that continues to boggle the imagination. Terrence Des Près's *The Survivor: An Anatomy of Life in the Death Camps* (Oxford University Press, 1976) addresses "not the fact that so many died, but . . . the fact that some survived."

One of the too frequently ignored aspects of the Holocaust is Jewish physical resistance. While most Jews did not have the opportunity or ability to physically resist the Nazis, a significant number, given the terrible circumstances that faced them, did. The history of resistance is told in Yisrael Gutman's *Fighter Among the Ruins: The Story of Jewish Heroism During World War II* (B'nai B'rith, 1988) and in Yuri Suhl's edited volume *They Fought Back* (Schocken Books, 1975). Gutman explores both the varied forms of Jewish resistance as well as the question of why wasn't there more resistance.

One of the most dramatic attempts to revolt in a death camp occurred at Treblinka. Jean-François Steiner's novel *Treblinka* (Mentor, 1968) is a dramatic and compelling account of this important story. See also Samuel Willenberg's memoir, *Surviving Treblinka* (Basil Blackwell, 1989). Books such as these demonstrate that while the Warsaw ghetto uprising may be the best known instance of Jewish resistance, it does not stand alone.

Anthologies are helpful in providing a broad overview to various aspects of the Holocaust. One of the earliest anthologies to appear was *Out of the Whirlwind* (Schocken Books, 1976). Prepared for both the general reader and classroom use, it is a useful compilation of fiction and nonfiction material dealing with a range of questions and issues. Another important anthology which contains over sixty excerpts by victims and eyewitnesses is Jacob Glatstein's *Anthology of Holocaust Literature* (Atheneum, 1972).

One of the questions which seems to haunt the post-Holocaust generation, particularly those who live in "Allied" countries is what was known, when was it known, and what was and was not done? Specific interest is concentrated on the United States because it is difficult—particularly for Americans—to reconcile the mythic idea of a country which proclaimed itself the home of those seeking liberty and freedom from persecution with the fact that the same country barred its gates to those desperately in need of refuge during the 1930s and 1940s.

Allied officials were more concerned about the fact that they would have to aid Jews rather than that Jews were being killed. At times they actually worked to frustrate and prevent rescue. Disbelief, indifference, anti-Semitism, and political expediency all served to hamper rescue efforts.

One of the first works on this topic was Arthur Morse's *While Six Million Died: A Chronicle of American Apathy* (Overlook Press, 1985). It remains one of the most riveting. Morse argues that the State Department was home to numerous anti-Semites, a number of whom had a direct hand in thwarting American rescue efforts. David Wyman's first work on this topic, *Paper Walls: America and the Refugee Crisis, 1938–1941* (Pantheon Books, 1985), graphically demonstrates how American anti-Semitism in both official and popular circles helped to keep Jewish refugees out of this country. Wyman's second volume, *The Abandonment of the Jews: America and the Holocaust, 1941–1945* (Pantheon Books, 1986), earned the distinction of being one of the few—if not only—historical works on this topic to be on the *New York Times* best-seller list. Wyman is relentless in his condemnations of Roosevelt and the entire administration for their response to the persecution of the Jews. His meticulous research is very impressive.

One of the great areas of interest is what did the bystanders know about Final Solution? How much information was available to them? Walter Laqueur's *The Terrible Secret: Suppression of the Truth about Hitler's "Final Solution"* (Little, Brown, 1980), demonstrates that within a short time after the Nazis decided to annihilate the Jews, the Allies knew about it. In a forceful fashion he illustrates that not only the Allies but the Vatican and the International Red Cross all had the information regarding the annihilation of the Jews.

Bernard Wasserstein's *Britain and the Jews of Europe, 1939–1945* (Oxford University Press, 1988) reveals that at times British officials were more heartless than their American counterparts. They preferred to see a boat filled with Jews escaping persecution sink off the coast of Turkey rather than allow them to be rescued. Had the Jews been allowed to escape and enter Palestine, British officials worried, it would have the "deplorable effect" of "encouraging" other Jews to try to escape.

My work on the American press coverage of the entire period, *Beyond Belief: The American Press and the Coming of the Holocaust, 1933–1945* (Free Press, 1986), an analysis of the way in which four hundred American newspapers covered this topic, is at its heart an attempt to deal with the issue of information and knowledge, particularly in relation to public opinion. Unless we know what people knew and how they learned of it, we will never be able to fully determine the role of public opinion in formulating American policy. The press generally followed the government's lead and treated the news in a way that made it entirely "missable" or "dismissable." The shortcomings in press coverage, even after the news was verified and confirmed by the Allies, are legion. The gap between information and knowledge is striking. Even when the press had the information, it was often buried in inside pages where it could easily be missed. There is of course no guarantee that if the press had covered this in a more forthright fashion, American rescue policy would have been different. However, one can still ask, did the press fulfill its obligation to inform readers of events?

One of the most potent areas of interest is the behavior of the American Jewish community, which continued to maintain its faith in Franklin D. Roosevelt even while his record on rescue was dismal. Wyman is convinced that had American Jews been more forceful, there might have been a change in government policy. Other authors dissent. Richard Breitman and Alan Kraut's *American Refugee Policy and European Jewry 1933–1945* (Indiana University Press, 1988) argues that American Jews used all the means available to them—private pleas, mass public protest, and political pressure—to try to open America's gates to European Jews. They argue that American Jews were not, as some have contended, "docile" or paralyzed by fear of domestic anti-Semitism. Both those Jews who believed open protest was the most efficacious response and those who believed in quiet backdoor diplomacy "worked tirelessly to command the attention of the hydra-headed government bureaucracy in Washington." Jews were terribly frustrated by their inability to convince the Allies to act.

Haskel Lookstein's *Were We Our Brother's Keepers: The Public Response of American Jews to the Holocaust 1938–1944* (Vintage Books, 1988) condemns American Jewry. The Holocaust may have been "unstoppable" by American Jews, but, he argues, that it should also have been "unbearable." And it was not. Lookstein bases his work on the major newspapers and journals published in the Jewish community. He does not probe the activities of various Jewish organizations beyond what was published in these papers and magazines. Consequently there are many things we still do not know about American Jews' response.

Another Jewish community whose response has been scrutinized is Palestinian Jewry in Dina Porat's *The Blue and Yellow Stars of David: The Zionist Leadership in Palestine and the Holocaust, 1939–1945* (Harvard University Press, 1990). She demonstrates how leaders of the Jewish community in Palestine spent a great portion of their energies engaged in party squabbling rather than in rescue efforts. But the other part of the problem was that the Jewish community had little leverage with the British and yet had nowhere else to turn. They were caught in a bind between killers who were intent on murdering European Jews and British leaders who feared they might be saved. The British supported the dispatch of young Palestinian Jews to Hungary (including Hannah Senesh), to engage in what they knew would be futile attempts at rescue because, Porat argues, Britain would succeed in "removing from Palestine a number of active and resourceful Jews," especially since "the chances of many of them returning in the future to give trouble in Palestine are slight." If these were your only allies, how much hope was there for rescue?

There is an array of significant postwar questions. The Allied failure to prosecute Nazi war criminals is a fairly recent area of research. In the United States the FBI, CIA, and Departments of State and Defense all helped known war criminals escape from Europe. American officials "sanitized" the files of over four hundred German and Austrian scientists so that their war crimes would be hidden. Among them were Wernher von Braun and Arthur Rudolph, both of whom played a crucial role in America's space program and who during the war worked at Nordhausen where thousands of slave laborers died. This entire sordid saga has been documented in Tom Bower's *The Paperclip Conspiracy: The Hunt for Nazi Scientists* (Little, Brown, 1988).

Allan A. Ryan, Jr.'s *Quiet Neighbors: Prosecuting Nazi War Criminals in America* (Harcourt Brace Jovanovich, 1984) is written from personal experience. Ryan was director of the United States Office of Special Investigation at a time when revelations about the American role in the postwar harboring of approximately ten thousand Nazi war criminals were made and prosecution begun.

How the postwar world engages in remembrance is analyzed in a compelling fashion by journalist Judith Miller's *One By One By One: Facing the Holocaust* (Simon & Schuster, 1990). Miller examines how six different countries engage in remembering the Holocaust. She places special emphasis on how American Jews incorporate remembering into their communal agenda. It is a significant contribution to this topic.

For many people the Holocaust presents fundamental questions about faith in a just and merciful God. How can one believe in the face of such horror? Theologians have struggled and continue to struggle with this question. Two extremes are represented by the writings of Emil Fackenheim and Richard Rubenstein. In *After Auschwitz* (Bobbs-Merrill, 1966) Rubenstein offers one of the most radical theological reflections in reaction to the Holocaust. He questions whether it is

The *Einsatzgruppen*, the Nazi's mobile killing squads, murdering Jews at the site of mass graves in the Ukraine. (YIVO Institute for Jewish Research)

possible to maintain any faith in an all-powerful God in a post-Holocaust world. Fackenheim's *God's Presence in History* (Harper & Row, 1972) is a response to Rubenstein. Fackenheim argues that the Holocaust as an epoch-making event mandates a 614th commandment, "Thou shall not hand Hitler a posthumous victory," that is, by ceasing to be Jews. A selection of essays which explore a variety of responses is contained in John K. Roth and Michael Berenbaum's *Holocaust: Religious and Philosophical Implications* (Paragon House, 1989).

The question of guilt, responsibility, and forgiveness is creatively addressed in Simon Wiesenthal's *Sunflower* (Schocken Books, 1976). The first section of the book is a novella of a young German soldier who, from his hospital bed, asks forgiveness of a Jew for the atrocities he has committed. The Jew's response is silence. This story is followed by a symposium of responses by theologians, philosophers, and religious leaders. They were asked by Wiesenthal to respond to the following question: Should the Jew have responded? Should he have forgiven the soldier? Did he have the right to do so? Is there any way the soldier can absolve himself of the guilt for the atrocities he performed? This is an accessible volume which addresses some of the important post-Holocaust questions.

The experience of the survivors and of their children is a fitting place to end this excursion. They are the living reminders of an event about which millions of words have been written and yet which still remains largely beyond comprehension. Helen Epstein's *Children of the Holocaust* (Penguin Books, 1988), which started out as a *New York Times Magazine* cover story, opened a virtual floodgate of emotions for thousands of children of survivors who suddenly discovered that they shared certain legacies. Their childhood experiences had been different from others and continued to be so. Though other books have subsequently been published on this topic, Epstein's remains one of the more riveting. An anthology of survivors' voices is contained in Dorothy Rabinowitz's *New Lives: Survivors of the Holocaust in America* (Alfred A. Knopf, 1976). In addition to describing their experiences during the Holocaust, they discuss their experiences in rebuilding their lives in America. This book demonstrates that even after surviving the horrors of the Nazis, they faced many additional obstacles.

I conclude this essay knowing that I have only scratched the surface of a topic which has had and continues to have overwhelming historical implications. Readers may choose to "detour" from one particular path in order to conduct their own investigation into this whirlwind. I hope that this essay will provide some important guideposts for the reader. The books I have suggested will not answer all the readers' questions. While they answer some questions, they will serve more as catalysts for others, for even after the most often asked questions are answered, the Holocaust can never be fully explained. And this is how it should be.

ISRAEL AND ZIONISM

David Twersky

It is impossible to comprehend the modern Jewish predicament without reference to Israel and the changes its establishment have introduced into Jewish life. Those changes are quite literally revolutionary, in the deepest sense of the term. Stateless for two millennia, Jews are now both a global people living as minorities with varying degrees of acceptance in host countries and a majority in their own land. Hebrew has been reclaimed from the prayer book and religious texts and resurrected as a living, modern tongue. The image of Jews in the eyes of the world, as well as their self-image, has been irretrievably altered.

Understanding the people and events that contributed to the reality of modern Israel takes us on a complex journey with stops to examine the philosophical and intellectual climate of the nineteenth-century central and eastern Europe; and the historical forces that shaped the modern European state and the nationalisms that are still evident, for example, in the just freed or still struggling peoples emerging from half a century of Communist domination.

The story then moves on to Palestine, or Eretz Israel—the land of Israel—

where the founding fathers and mothers of Zionism laid the foundations for the modern Israeli reality. The story includes Turkish rule, the British mandate, the destruction of European Jewry (the reservoir Zionist leaders hoped to tap), and the struggle for statehood. The basic structures of the state-to-be came to life during this formative period. Political parties were formed, an army took shape, the return to the land, which had an almost mystical attraction for the early pioneers, took on the socialist kibbutz and moshav shapes.

Thus, the Zionist revolutions were intellectual and theological, touching the roots of how Jews thought about themselves, their world and their God; political, involving all of the currents of turn-of-the-century European social thought; geographical and economic, as one dominant focus of Jewish life in reality shifted back to the ancient homeland in Israel.

Finally, Zionism and the rise of Israel must be seen in the context of the changes that have affected Jews within the past century. The hold of Orthodoxy is weakened (though clearly not fatally), the once-marginal secular politics is mainstream and secular politicians lead Israel. Nazism in central Europe and Communism in eastern Europe effectively combined to put an end to the demographic and cultural dominance of European Jewry. These changes culminated in the decade from 1939 to 1949, during which time European Jewry was almost completely destroyed, the mantle of diaspora leadership passed over the sea to America, and an independent Jewish state was established in Israel. A Jewish Rip Van Winkle who fell asleep in 1939 would hardly believe his eyes on awakening ten years later.

Anyone interested in beginning to master these developments must confront what seems to be an endless and constantly expanding forest of books. To list all of the books about Israel and Zionism available in English would require a book itself. Instead what follows is a guide for those who want to set out upon the journey. If one takes the basic tour, a kind of intellectual safari back to one's roots, later the denser territory can be covered on one's own.

Zionism

There are those who argue that the study of Israel properly begins with an examination of the almost three-millennia-old relationship of the Jewish people to the land of Israel. Indeed, the tie is there, and must be acknowledged. A book which explores this dimension and explicates the spiritual underpinnings of Zionism is Abraham Joshua Heschel's *Israel: An Echo of Eternity* (Farrar, Straus and Giroux, 1987). A more scholarly presentation of the historical relationship of the Jewish people to Israel can be found in Lawrence Hoffman's *The Land of Israel: Jewish Perspectives* (University of Notre Dame Press, 1986). The tie to this particular land, Eretz Israel, was a powerful force in the debates of the early Zionists. Indeed, at one crucial point in the development of modern political Zionism, the movement rejected pleas that it adopt a "realistic" course by abandoning the hope for a return to Israel and instead persuade Great Britain to allow the establishment of a Jewish home in Uganda. (A splinter group, called "territorialists," broke away from the Zionist movement to pursue that path.) However arcane, these disputes are not merely historical. As they attempt to define Zionism, they are wrestling with the nature of Jewish identity and taking a stand on the often volatile combination of religious, cultural, and national strands combined in the modern Israeli experience. A historian sympathetic to a contemporary religious view is more likely to find a basis for that view in the inner dynamic of Zionism; a secularist will try and support his position by referring to the alleged anti-religious revolution inherent in Zionism. Thus Zionist historiography serves almost as a quasi-Constitutional debate.

In the absence of a constitution, Israeli liberals, especially, draw on what they see as secularizing and universal themes within Zionism to buttress their own positions in contemporary Israel. At the same time, religious Zionist thinkers have attempted to portray Zionism—and by extension the state of Israel—as the logical culmination of an unfolding process of religious eschatology. (Of course, the anti-Zionist Orthodox portrayed the movement as a false messianic one.) If many of the contradictions of modern Israeli society, especially the secular-religious divide and the nationalist-liberal one, are reflected in early Zionism, others, like the ethnic Ashkenazi-Sephardi tension, are not.

The traditionalist dimension of the Jewish return to Israel—paradoxical since the return was led by non-religious Jews—is fully explored in several books about the Zionist movement. Arthur Hertzberg's *The Zionist Idea* (Atheneum, 1969) remains the best place to start. The book is an anthology of the major Zionist thinkers and leaders and touches all of the ideological bases—socialist, liberal, Revisionist nationalist, and religious. This anthology remains the best source of primary Zionist thinking available. What makes the book even more valuable is Hertzberg's still unsurpassed introductory essay on Zionism, which places the phenomenon into the broad contexts of both late-nineteenth-century European and early modern Jewish histories. The author argues that "Zionism cannot be typed . . . as a 'normal' kind of national risorgimento." Seen from an inner Jewish perspective, he writes, Zionism draws on the sometimes subterranean tradition of messianism but with a critical difference. What Hertzberg calls the "Copernican revolution which modern Zionism announced" is that in drawing on messianism, the focus is shifted from the Jews and God to Jews and the nations of the world.

Shlomo Avineri's *The Making of Modern Zionism* (Basic Books, 1984) puts a greater emphasis than Hertzberg does on the influence of nineteenth-century European nationalist theory. In what amounts to an intellectual history, the author rejects the view that Zionism is chiefly a reaction to anti-Semitism, insisting instead that it be understood as the Jewish response to a universal, modern quest for self-determination. The nineteenth century, he writes, was the best for Jews since the destruction of the Temple, not the worst, thus Zionism was not a response to the pogroms that swept Russia in the 1880s but to the Emancipation—that body of ideas of freedom and nationalism generated from central Europe. Defining Zionism as "the quest for self-determination and liberation under the modern conditions of secularization and liberalism," he concludes that it should be viewed as legitimately a part of both "the Jewish history of dispersion and return" and "the universal history of liberation and the quest for self-identity."

David Vital's *Origins of Zionism* (Oxford University Press, 1980) is a scholarly treatment of many of these themes. The revolutionary secular-nationalist view in its most concise form can be found in Shmuel Almog's *Zionism and History: The Rise of a New Jewish Consciousness* (St. Martin's Press, 1987). The author argues that there was a "wide disparity in the conception of historical attachment" evident in the work of different Zionist thinkers and that "the dominant tendency had a negative attitude toward the recent past combined with hopes for a modern renaissance, that would draw its inspiration from both the ancient Jewish past and contemporary European culture." A modern reformulation of the Zionist "negation of the Diaspora" view can be found in Hillel Halkin's *Letters to an American Jewish Friend* (Jewish Publication Society, 1977).

An example of the tendency to tie historical inquiry to contemporary politics can be found in Amnon Rubenstein's *The Zionist Dream Revisited: From Herzl to Gush Emunim and Back* (Schocken Books, 1984). Rubenstein, who was dean of the Tel Aviv law faculty and a member of Knesset, is a liberal politician interested in drawing on the enlightened tradition in the work of Zionist movement founder Theodore Herzl to portray the annexation-minded Gush Emunim as an aberration of mainstream Zionism, rather than its very essence.

Walter Laqueur's *History of Zionism* (Schocken Books, 1989) is a readable and informed history of the politics of the movement from before its formal founding in 1896 by Theodore Herzl to the establishment of the state in 1948. Laqueur's book pays particular attention to the unfolding tensions between the Palestinians—that is, the growing Jewish settlement in Palestine led by Zionists called the *Yishuv*—and the Diaspora Zionist parties, a tension that presaged today's endless conferences and discussions about "Israel-Diaspora relations."

As the Yishuv grew in strength, and mass-based Zionist advocacy passed from Nazi- or Stalinist-dominated Europe to the United States, the tensions began to assume the shape with which we are still familiar. The specifics under discussion were, of course, far different, but the subtext was the gradual accumulation of power by the Yishuv at the expense of the Diaspora, a process that climaxed with the establishment of the state. Although he does not dwell on it, Laqueur is sympathetic to Avineri's view of Zionism as part of the liberal European tradition of the early nineteenth century.

A brilliant statement of Zionist aims can be found in Benjamin Halpern's *The Idea of the Jewish State* (Harvard University Press, 1969). In addition to Halpern's summative work which begins in Labor Zionism and progresses to the central objectives in the struggle for statehood, Yaacov Shavit's history of the Zionist right is a useful work. It is *Jabotinsky and the Revisionist Movement 1925–1948: The Right in Zionism and Israel 1925–1985* (London: Frank Cass, 1988). The best overall history can be found in Howard M. Sachar's monumental *A History of Israel: From the Rise of Zionism to Our Times* (Alfred A. Knopf, 1979). A very readable popular history of Israel is *The Siege* by Connor Cruise O'Brien (Simon & Schuster, 1986).

Leaders

There is an endless supply of books about the lives of Israeli leaders. David Ben-Gurion, the country's first prime minister, is the subject of numerous biographies, of which the best is *Ben-Gurion: The Burning Ground* by Shabtai Tevet (Houghton Mifflin, 1988). Tevet's book, which takes Ben-Gurion's story through the establishment of the state, adopts the view that the "Old Man's" politics were driven by the sense of impending doom in Europe and the need to establish a state as soon as possible. Ben-Gurion emerges as a rare mixture of statesman and machine politician. Michael Bar Zohar has written what amounts to an authorized biography of Ben-Gurion called *Ben-Gurion: A Biography* (Adama Books, 1986) but the English-language version of the book misses much of the notes and complexity covered in Tevet. Dan Kurzman's *Ben-Gurion: Prophet of Fire* (Simon & Schuster, 1984) takes the story up to his retirement, but departs from Tevet's central thesis. Kurzman writes that Ben-Gurion did not take the threat of the Holocaust seriously until it was too late—the same argument advanced by his critics from the right.

Of the autobiographical volumes, *My Life* by Golda Meir (Dell, 1976) captures much of the appeal and strength of the late prime minister, but shies away from the private and personal side of Meir's life. Unfortunately, the book also avoids much of the political turmoil in which Meir figured prominently, such as her long feud with David Ben-Gurion. *Trial and Error* by Chaim Weizmann (Westport, Conn.: Greenwood Press, 1972) is a good accounting of the life of the first president, a liberal who was frustrated in his political ambitions by the Palestinian labor leaders led by David Ben-Gurion. Jehuda Reinharz's *Chaim Weizmann, The Making of a Zionist leader* (Oxford University Press, 1985) is an excellent account of Weizmann's life and career as a scientist and as a Zionist leader. Abba Eban's *Autobiography* (Random House, 1977) and his *My People* (Random House, 1984) have all the eloquence and insight one would expect from the legendary foreign minister, but like other Israeli leaders, Eban at times places himself at the center of his story instead of the events in which he played a significant role. Thus, in Eban's work there is a greater emphasis on the role of diplomacy leading up to the United Nations vote in 1947 to partition Palestine and establish the State of Israel and less on the internal politics in the Yishuv or on the battlefield.

There are a number of biographies of former Prime Minister Menachem Begin, who led the right-of-center Likud to its first victory in 1977. Amos Perlmutter's *The Life and Times of Menachem Begin* (Doubleday, 1987) is the most comprehensive. Like all books about Begin, this one comes with a view: It is written from the vantage point of someone who grew up identifying with, and later achieved some distance from, Begin's political philosophy. It is far more incisive than Ned Temko's Begin biography, *To Win or To Die* (Morrow, 1987).

The best book about Shimon Peres, leader of the left-of-center Labor party, is Matti Golan's *Shimon Peres: A Biography* (St. Martin's Press, 1982). Anita Shapira's *Berl* (Cambridge University Press, 1985) is an in-depth look at the lesser known but influential Labor Zionist leader, Berl Katznelson, who died before in-

Theodor Herzl, the founder of Zionism, in Basel. (Library of The Jewish Theological Seminary of America)

dependence. The book is useful to anyone interested in the inner spiritual and political dynamics of the Labor movement. The book was a best-seller in its two-volume Hebrew edition when it appeared in 1980.

Ernst Pawel's *Herzl: The Labyrynth of Exile* (Farrar, Straus and Giroux, 1989) is an excellent biography of the founder of the Zionist movement, as is Amos Elon's penetrating analysis in *Herzl* (Schocken Books, 1985).

Closely linked to biographies of leaders are books by leaders which relate their side of an important story. For example, Menachem Begin's *The Revolt* (W. H. Allen, 1983) tells the story of the Irgun, the militant underground which Begin led during the struggle against the British mandate. Noteworthy as well is former Defense and Foreign Minister Moshe Dayan's account of his role at the Camp David peace talks, *Breakthrough: A Personal Account of the Egypt-Israel Peace*

Negotiation (Alfred A. Knopf, 1981) and former Defense Minister Ezer Weizman's *The Battle for Peace* (Bantam, 1981). Neither of these last two books is complimentary to Begin; both Dayan and Weizman broke with the Begin government within a few years of the signing of the peace accords, with Weizman ending up as a Labor party dove. Similarly self-serving although enlightening is former Prime and Defense Minister and chief of staff Yitzhak Rabin's *The Memoirs of Yitzhak Rabin* (Little, Brown, 1979).

In the Yishuv

The period between the Holocaust and the establishment of the state—1945–1948—is the background for *The Palestine Triangle* by Nicholas Bethel (Pomfret, Vt.: Andre Deutsch, 1979) and Christopher Sykes's *Crossroads to Israel* (Midland Books/Indiana University Press, 1973). Sykes was what would be called a central player in the jargon of today's Washington. The best of the books on this period is J. C. Hurewitz's *The Struggle for Palestine* (Westport, Conn.: Greenwood Press, 1968).

The historical moment between the end of the Second World War and the creation of the state is the context for I. F. Stone's *Underground to Palestine* (Pantheon Books, 1978). The book by the famous journalist provides a sympathetic account of the flight of survivors through the British blockade to preindependence Palestine. Leonard Slater's *The Pledge* (Simon & Schuster, 1970) covers the story of arms running during the same period, when the United States embargoed weapons shipments to Palestine.

Benjamin Morris's *The Birth of the Palestinian Refugee Problem 1947–1949* (Cambridge University Press, 1988) created a sensation when it first appeared because Mr. Morris departs from the first-generation Israeli historians' defensiveness about the refugee problem. In contrast both to those who have long argued that Palestinian refugees ran away due to the exhortations of their leaders in the belief they would soon return behind victorious Arab armies, and to Arab charges that they were all driven out as part of a plot to rid Israel of Palestinians, Morris asserts that the Israeli army and state bears some, but not all responsibility for what happened.

An opposing view is offered in *From Time Immemorial* by Joan Peters (Harper

& Row, 1985). Peters's lengthy book's most original claim is that most of the Palestinian Arabs emigrated into Palestine within the last century due to the improved economic conditions there resulting from Zionist activity and thus have less of a claim than they pretend to the territory of Palestine.

Wars and the Search for Peace

A good overview of Israel's wars can be found in Chaim Herzog's *The Arab-Israel Wars* (Vintage Books, 1983). Herzog, now president of Israel, was a distinguished general and military commentator before entering the diplomatic service and, later, political life. The book documents the development of Israeli military doctrine, the growth of the air force, and the experience derived from each of the country's wars, through the 1982 invasion of Lebanon. The best history of the Israeli defense force is *A History of the Israeli Army* by Ze'ev Schiff (Macmillan, 1986), although two books by central actors in the development are also interesting: Palmach-commander Yigal Allon's *The Making of Israel's Army* (London: Vallentine, Mitchell & Co., 1977) and Shimon Peres's *David's Sling* (London: Weidenfeld & Nicolson, 1970). Allon and Peres were on opposite sides of many of the debates that split Israel's national security policy elite during the fifties and sixties.

Genesis 1948 by Dan Kurzman (New American Library, 1972) is a detailed and readable account of the 1948 war of independence. *O, Jerusalem,* by Larry Collins and Dominique Lapierre (Simon & Schuster, 1988), is more popularly written and easier to digest, but lacks some of the depth of the Kurzman book. *Warriors at Suez* by Donald Neff (Brattleboro, Vt: Amana Books, 1987) takes a pro-Arab view of the 1956 war, arguing that Israel was acting in concert with England and France who were trying to regain their colonial influence in the Canal Zone. A more pro-Israel account can be found in Moshe Dayan's *Diary of the Sinai Campaign* (Westport, Conn.: Greenwood Press, 1979).

Ezer Weizman's *On Eagle's Wings* (Macmillan, 1979) tells the story of the development of the Israeli air force by someone who rose to lead it. *The Seventh Day,* edited by Avraham Shapira (Penguin Books, 1974) reflects the spiritual and intellectual impact of the 1967 war on a group of then-younger Israeli writers, including Amos Oz. Chaim Herzog's *The War of Atonement* (Little, Brown, 1975) remains the best book in English of the Yom Kippur War of 1973, during which President Herzog served as a commentator.

First Strike by Shlomo Nakdimon (Summit Books, 1987) tells the story of the 1981 bombing of the Iraqi Osiraq nuclear facility by the Israeli war planes with some sympathy for Begin's decision to order the attack. Nakdimon is a journalist with ties to the Likud and his book takes Begin's side—at the time the opposition Labor party accused the Likud leader of timing the bombing raid in early June 1981 in order to reap the political benefit in the national elections at the end of the month. The Osiraq raid takes on added significance in light of the 1991 Gulf war. Argentinian journalist Jacobo Timmerman's *The Longest War: Israel in Lebanon* (Vintage Books, 1983) is sharply critical of the 1982 war but his book is not as well researched or as analytical as *Israel's Lebanon War* by journalists Ze'ev Schiff and Ehud Ya'ari (Simon & Schuster, 1984). The latter is the best study of the country's foray into Lebanon in 1982. The authors believe the war was badly conceived and a failure from both a strategic and political point of view.

David Grossman's *Yellow Wind* (Delacorte, 1989) was written just before the start of the intifada—the Palestinian uprising which began in December 1987 and has yet to run its course. It relates a long journey of discovery and penetration by an Israeli journalist and novelist into the realities of Palestinian life in the territories. Schiff and Ya'ari have also written the best book on the intifada, *Intifada: The Palestinian Uprising—Israel's Third Front* (Simon & Schuster, 1990). The authors fault the Israeli political and military leaderships for failing to gauge the economic hardship and national despair of the Palestinian inhabitants in the territories. *Intifada* is especially informative about Palestinian internal politics, especially within the territories. A volume of essays by Amos Oz, *The Slopes of Lebanon* (Harcourt Brace Jovanovich, 1989) is worthwhile reading for those interested in the period between the Lebanon invasion and the intifada.

A sober assessment of Israel's options, written before the Gulf war, can be found in *The West Bank and Gaza—Israel's Options for Peace* (published by the Jaffee Center, 1989, and available from the American Jewish Congress). The study is the result of work done by retired army officers and strategic analysts brought together by Tel Aviv University's Jaffee Center for Strategic Studies. While it recommends an ultimate separation between Israel and the bulk of the territories, the Options Report also calls for an interim period of up to fifteen years during which both sides could test the other's peaceful intentions.

Deterrence without the Bomb by Avner Yaniv (Lexington, Mass.: Lexington Books, 1986) belongs to a sophisticated literature about Israeli strategy. Yaniv opposes the view, advanced by Shai Feldman and others, that Israel should rely more heavily on nuclear deterrence and less on territorial depth.

Yoram Peri's *Between Battles and Ballots* (Cambridge University Press, 1983) is the best book about the impact of Israel's army experience on its democracy. Michael Brecher's *Decisions in Israel's Foreign Policy* (Yale University Press, 1975) is the classic text study of how Israeli foreign policy is made. The book is a bit tough going on the casual reader but exhaustive.

The impact of Israeli arms sales on foreign policy is examined in Aaron Kleiman's *Israel's Global Reach: Arms Sales as Diplomacy* (Pergamon-Brassey's International Defense Publications, 1985). The author discusses how and why Israel's aggressive arms sales program became an economic necessity and an ethical and political dilemma. An account of the same subject wholly negative to Israel can be found in Benjamin Bet Halachmi's *The Israeli Connection* (Pantheon Books, 1987).

Harvard University scholar Nadav Safran's *Israel: The Embattled Ally* (Harvard University Press, 1981) provides a serious and detailed examination of Israel's wars and its developing strategic relationship with the United States. The book includes impressive chapters on the early years of Zionism, on political developments, and on the development of party politics in the country.

Yehoshafat Harkabi has written several books which plumb the depths of Israel's strategic and moral dilemmas about the Palestinians and the territories. Harkabi is a former head of military intelligence and the person responsible for the hardline explication of the PLO covenant, turned latter-day dove. In *The Bar Kokhba Syndrome* (Rossel Books, 1983) Harkabi attacks the conventional historical view that the first-century Bar Kokhba revolt against Rome was heroic. Given the lives lost and the impact of the revolt on Jewish history, Harkabi sees it as a major disaster. Harkabi makes clear that his intent is not only historical and that his sights are set on the contemporary versions of Bar Kokhba in the Israeli right as well. In *Israel's Fateful Hour* (Harper & Row, 1989) Harkabi makes a case for a compromise settlement that will allow for Palestinian self-determination in the territories and Israeli security without occupation.

A less passionate but more rigorously analytical case for a Palestinian state solution can be found in Mark Heller's *A Palestinian State: The Implications for Israel* (Harvard University Press, 1983). Heller argues that the occupation is strategically and morally more dangerous in the long run than a demilitarized Palestinian state. Former deputy mayor of Jerusalem Meron Benvenisti's *Conflicts and Contradictions* (Villard Books, 1986) is an eloquent essay on Palestinians and

Jews. Benvenisti's *The West Bank Data Project: A Survey of Israel's Policies,* published annually during most of the 1980s by the American Enterprise Institute, chronicled the creeping annexation—or liberation, if you prefer—of the West Bank by Jewish settlements. The reports served as context for Benvenisti's assertions that territorial compromise (or "land for peace") had been overtaken by the facts on the ground.

In recent years, interest in espionage has escalated as reports of Israeli success in this field have won an international audience. The Jewish connection to the craft of espionage goes back to the thirteen men dispatched by Moses to spy out the Promised Land, and the Israeli experience demonstrates that the skills did not wither despite thousands of years in which they were underused. Israeli intelligence services have attracted significant attention and a reputation for being among the best. *Every Spy a Prince: A Complete History of Israel's Intelligence Community* (Houghton Mifflin, 1991) by Yossi Melman, an Israeli journalist, and CBS reporter Dan Raviv is a recent and highly informative examination of the subject. The authors are not overwhelmed with either the omnipotence or malevolence of the Jewish state's intelligence agencies.

A more negative view is taken in the recent *By Way of Deception: The Making and Unmaking of a Mossad Officer,* by Victor Ostrovsky and Claire Hoy (St. Martin's Press, 1990). The Ostrovsky book attracted much attention when published, due less to its strengths than to attempts by the Israeli government to prevent its release. Ostrovsky describes the Mossad in highly uncomplimentary terms but his book fails to pass the threshold of credibility. *The Spymasters of Israel* by Stewart Steven (Ballantine, 1988) is a readable account detailing Israeli intelligence assignments globally.

Portraits

Portraits of the Israeli people and their culture betray the biases and personal idiosyncrasies of their authors. Among the best is *From Beirut to Jerusalem* by Thomas Friedman (Doubleday, 1990). Friedman was the celebrated *New York Times* correspondent in the Lebanese and Israeli capitals during much of the 1980s. Widely praised for its lucid style and penetrating insights, the book irritated some reviewers because of its implicit attempt to equate Arab and Israeli society. Notwithstanding that criticism, the Israel half of the book takes the

Street scene with Israeli soldiers. (Photograph by Bill Aron)

reader into many of the political and religious nooks and crannies of modern Israeli life. Friedman is a pessimist: he believes Arabs and Jews know each other well enough *not* to compromise in the near-term future.

Amos Oz's book of essays, *In the Land of Israel* (Vintage Books, 1984), created a sensation when it appeared in Hebrew, running weekly in the Labor paper *Davar*. The essays on blue-collar Sephardic reaction to liberals like Oz, and the author's discussions with West Bank Jewish settlers and ultra-Orthodox Jews in Jerusalem are without match.

Origins of the Israeli Polity by Moshe Lissak and Dan Horowitz (University of Chicago Press, 1979) is a good study of the development of the domestic politics in Palestine and Israel. *The Israelis: Fathers and Sons* by Amos Elon (Penguin Books, 1983) is a colorful and readable description of the dominant, European-ized, secular, and liberal Ashkenazi Israeli elite. It is the story of Israel the way one segment of the population would like it to be told. Originally published in 1971, the book's flaw is that in discussing the future it turned a blind eye to the rising impact of Sephardi, or North African, resentment, the emergence of the Likud, and the humbling of Labor Zionist hegemony. The book assumed contin-ued Labor/Ashkenasi rule; for example, Menachem Begin's name doesn't appear, even in a footnote.

Ze'ev Chafets's *Heroes and Hustlers, Hard Hats and Holy Men* (Morrow,

1987), written almost two decades later, takes a different view, more sympathetic to the political culture of the Israeli middle and working classes. Lawrence Meyers's *Israel Now* (Delacorte Press, 1982) is a good portrait by a sympathetic American journalist. More politically oriented, Peter Grose's *A Changing Israel* (Vintage Books, 1985) deals with domestic and economic issues, the burgeoning West Bank settlements, and Israel's changing relationship with the United States. Joyce Starr's *Kissing Through Glass: The Invisible Shield Between Americans and Israelis* (Contemporary Books, 1990) includes some useful descriptions of the ways in which Americans and Israelis interact and misperceive each other. The political nature of the relationship is explored in Nimrod Novick's *The United States and Israel* (Boulder, Colo.: Westview Press, 1986). Despite the end of the Cold War and the need to reformulate the meaning of Israel's strategic value to the United States, Novick's book retains much of its worth.

Israel: Building a New Society by Daniel Elazar (Indiana University Press, 1986) is an attempt to describe a political-cultural model for understanding Israeli society. Elazar, who has pioneered the study of American Jewish institutions, examines how the variegated Jewish past interacts with modern Israeli society created by pioneers to create a new political unit that escapes conventional categorization. S. N. Eisenstadt's *The Transformation of Israeli Society* (Boulder, Colo.: Westview Press, 1986) traces the impact of four factors on change and continuity in Israel. These are the country's nature as a pioneering society, its geographical position within an alien and hostile environment, its diminutive size and Jewish nature. Gad Yaacobi, a Labor party leader and former cabinet minister, has written a book on the way the government works, or doesn't work, *The Government of Israel* (Praeger, 1982). Yaacobi is a leading proponent of reforming Israel's electoral system to cut down on the large number of parties and stabilize the government. *Civil Religion in Israel: Traditional Judaism and Political Culture in the Jewish State* by sociologists Charles Liebman and Eliezer Don-Yehiya (University of California Press, 1983) is an excellent inquiry into the nexus of religion and state in the Jewish state. *Sands of Sorrow* is Milton Viorst's analysis of what has gone wrong in the Zionist dream (Harper & Row, 1987). Viorst believes Israel should settle with the PLO and agree to the establishment of a PLO-led state on the West Bank and Gaza Strip.

There are books, usually written by Israelis, which are more inner directed and less celebratory (or condemning). Reuven Gal, formerly the chief psychologist in the Israel Defense Forces, has drawn a complex portrait of the wounds not always visible inflicted on those serving in the defense of the Jewish state. The book is called *A Portrait of the Israeli Soldier* (Westport, Conn.: Greenwood Press, 1986). *Tin Soldiers on a Jerusalem Beach* by Israeli psychologist Amia Lieblich (Pantheon Books, 1978) describes the traumas that the endless wars have inflicted on men, women, and children.

Lieblich wrote *Kibbutz Makom* (Pantheon Books, 1981) after spending a year on a kibbutz interviewing its members. The book is an oral history of the multigenerational kibbutz and provides an in-depth insider's view of life on kibbutz, the collective villages which have left an indelible imprint on the history and life of the country.

A critical treatment of the life of Israel's Arab citizens—not the Palestinians in the territories—constituting over fifteen percent of the population, can be found in Ian Lustik's *Arabs in the Jewish State* (University of Texas Press, 1980). A more balanced version can be found in David Shipler's *Arab and Jew: Wounded Spirits in a Promised Land* (Penguin Books, 1987). Shipler was the *New York Times* correspondent in Israel during the early 1980s. His book concentrates on Jewish-Arab relations. He believes in a trickle-up theory of human relations, and supports efforts to foster greater understanding and empathy between the two peoples.

Keeping Up

Events in Israel can change at a frightening pace. Over the past four years, for example, the country has had to cope with the Palestinian intifada, a massive wave of Soviet Jewish immigration, and the Iraqi crisis. In order to keep apace, the interested reader might wish to subscribe to *The Jerusalem Post*, which publishes a weekly international edition; the new weekly newsmagazine, *The Jerusalem Report*, published in Jerusalem; or the *Forward*, published in New York. All three carry sophisticated and in-depth coverage of the ongoing political and security issues in the life of the Jewish state.

C H A P T E R   9

JEWISH MYSTICISM

Elliot K. Ginsburg

To enter the world of Jewish mysticism is to enter a world thick with meaning. Its practitioners place the cosmos beneath a numinous canopy: extending the realm of sacred signification from the supernal Source to the merest rose (emblem of divine immanence), from the elemental act of eating to abstruse patterns of speech. All the while, they forge surprising linkages and indulge in multivocal allusions (for a rose is not only a rose). Indeed, as Geoffrey Hartman has noted, Jewish mysticism exalts the analogical imagination. Still, understanding this mystical tradition (or, to be more precise, traditions, given the sheer variety of mystical creativity) does not always come easy. The neophyte often stands bedazzled, and not a little bewildered. I recall some questions from my students—fascinated, unsettled, newly opened up. Two examples:

It is early in an introductory course on Jewish mysticism. We are reading a passage from 3 Enoch, a mystical ascent text redacted in the fifth or sixth century of the common era in rabbinic circles. Enoch, primeval hero and apparent role model for the rabbinic mystic, has wended his way through the labyrinths of the multitiered cosmos. Arriving at the seventh heaven, he is transmuted into an

angelic being, now able to stand before the awesome divine throne. In the preserved version of the text, a mystical authority, Rabbi Ishmael, reports Enoch's
recollections:

> R. Ishmael said: The angel Metatron [as transmuted Enoch was re-
> named], Prince of the Divine Presence, the glory of the highest
> heaven, said to me: "When the Holy One, blessed be he, took me to
> serve the throne of glory, the wheels of the chariot and all the needs
> of the Shekhinah, at once my flesh turned to flame, my sinews to
> blazing fire, my bones to juniper coals, my eyelashes to lightning
> flashes, my eyeballs to fiery torches, the hairs of my head to hot
> flames, all my limbs to wings of burning fire, and the substance of my
> body to blazing fire . . ." (3 Enoch 15:1–2)

Here the words, like transmuted Enoch, are on fire. Despite the mediated nature
of the text (reported speech having undergone multiple recensions), something
of the intensity of mystical experience is preserved in it. And here the students'
questions begin: What does it mean that the heavenly traveler is smelted down
and recast in ecstatic fire? What do we learn about the nature of the religious
experience from this description? But, why would anyone want to come before
such a searing deity? What attracted so many Jewish mystics over the ages to such
encounters?

It is somewhat later in the course and we are ready to explore the rich imagery
of the divine developed in Zoharic kabbalah (so named after the Zohar, "Bible" of
medieval Jewish mysticism). Here the portrait of divinity is strikingly different.
These kabbalists conceived of divine unity not as the simple, unchanging perfection proposed by the rationalist philosophers but as a dynamic ecosystem, a complex whole. The one God was composed of diverse aspects—suggestively
symbolized as a texture of ever-shifting primal letters, as ever-dancing light, as
harmonizing antipodes. One of the key ciphers for expressing divine unity was
forthrightly sexual in nature, involving the coincidence, or coupling, of male and
female potencies. Divine unity was thus expressed through the figure of sacred
marriage: the joining of divine Groom and Bride—the Holy One and Shekhinah—and in a related image, the restitution of primordial androgyny. It is the
holy task of the Jew to bring about this divine unity through sacred action, i.e.,
the proper performance of the mizvot. For in this tradition, God and humanity
exist in symbiotic relationship, "a rousing below producing a similar rousing on
high." Although a full appreciation of this ritual schema would demand far more
explanation than we can offer here, let us plunge into the text.

> When Israel studies the Oral and Written Torah for their sake, the
> celestial counterparts [the feminine and masculine aspects of the di-
> vine] are aroused: "They are joined to one another" [Job 41:9]
> through a kiss and the Tabernacle [the divine structure exemplified by
> the male and female aspects of divinity] becomes one" [Ex. 26:6].
> Then blessing descends from them on high and peace fills the cosmos
> . . . Now when Israel learns Torah for its own sake, their Mother on
> high [Shekhinah, the divine female] sings unto Her lover [the Holy
> One], chanting: "Let him kiss me with the kisses of his mouth" [Cant.
> 1:2]. For it is the way of lovers to kiss each other mouth to mouth, so
> great is their love. This [supernal love] is symbolized by the two lovers
> in the Song of Songs who unite through a kiss. (Meir ibn Gabbai,
> *Tolaat Yaakov,* 1507)

This passage is suffused with sublime (and sublimated) erotic passion: divine unity
(symbolized both as the union of the lovers and the completion of the Tabernacle)
is effected by the mystic's activity. The rabbinic act par excellence, Torah study,
has here become a kind of divine "aphrodisiac."

One need not grasp all the allusions to begin asking interesting questions. To
the neophyte, the scenario described may seem quite shocking. Their "Mother on
high"? Divine coupling? This is Jewish?! After all, did not the biblical authors
engage in a polemic against the very notion of divine sexuality? Yet here, as Gershom Scholem has noted, "it is as though a kind of pagan mythology were resurrected in the heart of mystical Judaism." More astonishingly, texts like these did
not raise many eyebrows among the elite or arouse concerted opposition. Indeed,
in the post-medieval period kabbalah became the closest thing we have to a dominant Jewish theology. Instead, it was the highly abstract theology of Maimonides
(so dear to post-Enlightenment Jewish scholars) that triggered the more concentrated opposition.

This all-too-brief sampling of sources should alert us to the sheer variety of
trends found within Jewish mysticism, and to the continual surprises that befall
one in its study. One must be prepared to learn and unlearn, reconfiguring one's
understanding as one proceeds. Time and again, one comes to appreciate Gershom Scholem's dictum that one cannot predict *a priori,* on the basis of earlier
evidence, what will be considered authentically Jewish in a given era. That is, as
one studies Jewish mysticism, one is constantly reworking, expanding, and refin-
ing one's understanding of "Judaism," that compact term that brings together (but
also masks) the multifarious currents of Jewish culture and thought.

How does one enter into the study of Jewish mysticism? What are the questions to ask and what books should we take along on the journey? To these and related questions, this essay is addressed.

A person who returned to the scholarly study of kabbalistic literature after a twenty-year hiatus would barely recognize the field. Where once Gershom Scholem loomed magisterially over the terrain, the English reader now confronts a profusion of skilled authors, and a growing corpus of translated primary and secondary sources. Enriching (but some would say complicating) matters further, is the fluid nature of the field. For the past decade a debate has been taking shape over the nature of Jewish mysticism, the sources worthy of careful study, the respective merits of historical versus phenomenological[1] inquiry, and digging even deeper, the very nature of Judaism. Although my primary purpose is to enable the reader to confront key primary texts, this chapter will also allow readers to slowly enter into this second-order debate, to measure what is at stake.

According to Lurianic Kabbalah, every word of Torah has 600,000 "faces"—layers of meaning or entrances—one for each member of Israel who stood at the foot of Mount Sinai. Extending this image, we might say that each reader enters the study of Jewish mysticism through his or her own portal. For we come to the study of Jewish mysticism with different biographies and questions, not to mention different styles of learning. In the attempt to anticipate some of these differences, I have constructed a sequential narrative that gives readers a broad sweep of the tradition (the panoramic view from above), but which allows the reader with more specialized interests to plumb a given topic more deeply. Given the constraints of space, this bibliography cannot fully compass the range of worthy sources: It is intended to whet, rather than sate, one's appetite.

For one who wants to survey the broad sweep of Jewish mysticism, several works are crucial to have at hand. First and foremost are several of the more broadly gauged works of Gershom Scholem, the preeminent scholar of Jewish mysticism. These include his seminal *Major Trends in Jewish Mysticism* (Schocken Books, 1961) and his two volumes of thematic studies: *On the Kabbalah and Its Symbolism* (Schocken Books, 1969) and the newly published *On the Mystical Shape of the Godhead* (Schocken Books, 1991). Scholem's *Kabbalah* (Meridian, 1978), a collection of articles originally written for the *Encyclopaedia*

---

[1] The description and interpretation of the core structure of key mystical motifs and experiences.

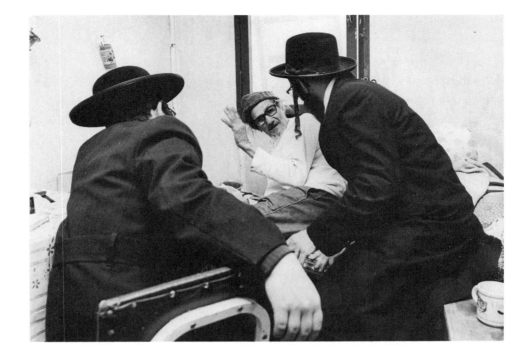

Two Hasidim consult a Yemenite Kabbalist for a mystical interpretation. (Photograph by Zion M. Ozeri)

Judaica, is also extremely useful as a reference tool; it is, however, too dry for sustained reading for the general reader.

The past decade has seen a blossoming of works directed to the serious lay reader. Of great value are the many germane articles found in the two-volume collection *Jewish Spirituality*, edited by Arthur Green (Crossroad, 1985, 1989). A valuable anthology of primary sources is Louis Jacobs's *Jewish Mystical Testimonies* (Schocken Books, 1978), which provides a welcome glimpse into the nature of mystical experience and appends Jacobs's succinct commentary. Ben Zion Bokser's anthology *Jewish Mystical Tradition* (Pilgrim Press, 1981) is also useful but lacks the commentary that graces the Jacobs volume.

Finally, essential to any serious study of Jewish mysticism is Moshe Idel's innovative *Kabbalah: New Perspectives* (Yale University Press, 1990), a work that has been likened to *Major Trends* in its synthetic ambitions, scholarly reach, and potential influence. In comparing them, we will glimpse some of the ferment currently enriching the field.

Major Trends and *New Perspectives* represent two different wagers regarding the nature of Jewish mysticism, and how it is to be approached. For example, Scholem organizes his book chronologically, charting the historical unfolding of key movements. Idel proceeds thematically, moving toward a description and interpretation of central mystical techniques and experiences. Scholem views mysticism as a romantic counterstroke to the classical phase of Jewish religiosity and speaks of various dialectical developments within the mystical tradition itself. Idel has amassed intriguing evidence that suggests far greater continuity between later mystical traditions, and esoteric aspects of ancient and Rabbinic Judaism. He is much more willing to seriously consider the mystics' claim that what they have is *kabbalah*, literally, a venerable "received tradition" conveyed from master to disciple. To put it all-too-baldly: Scholem masterfully points out the disruptions, reversals, and radical rereadings that suffuse the mystical tradition, while Idel attends to heretofore ignored points of continuity and focuses upon more subtle shifts of meaning.

I am very sympathetic to, and excited by, the revisionist work of Idel. Still, I would encourage most readers to begin with Scholem's *Major Trends* and to use it as a working guide for the study of Jewish mysticism. Idel, in most instances, is better appreciated at a later phase of one's study.

Having said this, there are attentive readers who find Scholem's lucid, nuanced prose too dense, and in the case of *Major Trends*, a bit dry. Happily, there are two recent books that provide responsible introductions to Jewish mysticism, in formats that are more easily accessible. These are Joseph Dan's *Gershom Scholem and the Mystical Dimension of Jewish History* (New York University, 1987) and David Ariel's *The Mystic Quest* (Schocken Books, 1992). Dan succinctly summarizes the research of Scholem, and provides considerable updating from *Major Trends*. Several chapters are enriched by Dan's own pioneering research. Ariel's book is a solid synthesis of the scholarship of Scholem and his students, most of which is still available only in Hebrew. Ariel writes well and his work is often inspired pedagogically. It should be noted, however, that neither Dan nor Ariel attempts to reflect on the most recent scholarly studies.

At this point, we may move to our sequential charting of Jewish mysticism—its key movements, underlying themes, and historical reverberations.

Mystical Experience and Its Expression

Although the focus of this essay is Jewish mysticism per se, it is useful to cast the net more widely at first, to reflect on mysticism as a worldwide phenomenon. The goal here is threefold: to characterize the term "mysticism," by distinguishing it from other intensive forms of religious experience and expression; to raise questions concerning the complex relationship between mystical experience and mystical expression; and to explore the relationship between the mysticism and religious authority, to locate the mystic vis-à-vis the tradition in which he or she is trained. By briefly considering these broad characterizations of mysticism we will be better equipped to place Jewish mysticism in a cross-cultural context, to appreciate its unique tonalities, and to come to it with fresh questions.

One of the best working definitions of mysticism is provided by Arthur Green in his article "Mysticism and Religion: The Case of Judaism," in J. Neusner, ed., *Take Judaism, for Example* (University of Chicago Press, 1983). Drawing on evidence found most commonly in the West, Green characterizes mysticism as a religious outlook that:

> (1) seeks out inner experiences of the divine, and to that end generally cultivates a life of inwardness; (2) longs to recover an original intimacy with God, the loss of which is essential to the ordinary human condition; and (3) involves itself with an esoteric lore that promises both to reveal the inner secrets of divinity and to provide access to restoration of divine/human intimacy.

From this we learn that mysticism is a path or discipline, something carefully cultivated and transmitted. A mystic is not merely someone who has these intense religious experiences (for a mystical experience alone does not a mystic make), but one who consciously seeks out such encounters time and again, and places them at the center of his or her life.

While Green focuses on the case of Judaism, other scholars consciously seek out cross-traditional paradigms. Useful overviews include the opening chapter of Ariel's *The Mystic Quest;* Louis Dupre's analysis, "Mysticism" in the new *Encyclopedia of Religion,* vol. 10, edited by Mircea Eliade (Macmillan, 1986); and Lawrence Fine's succinct discussion, in pages 305–7 of his "Kabbalistic Texts," in B. Holtz, ed., *Back to the Sources* (Summit Books, 1986). Finally, a classic characterization of mysticism, still worth reading, is William James, *Varieties of Religious Experience* (Vintage Books, 1990), Lectures 16 and 17.

Although mystical experiences vary widely in intensity, feeling-tone, and social ramifications, some scholars give added weight to a certain type of particularly concentrated mystical experience. The relationship between such events (generally held to be ineffable, or at least hard to describe) and their subsequent symbolization (mystical expression) has been the subject of much critical debate. Some scholars (e.g., Gershom Scholem) assert that the acme of mystical experience is a "zero" experience, an experience that is wholly unmediated and devoid of specific content. According to this view, both Jewish mystic and Buddhist mystic may indeed have virtually the same peak experience. They, however, subsequently interpret it differently, in accord with the theological resources and symbols which are at their disposal.

Other scholars (e.g., Louis Dupre and Steven Katz) claim that all experience is necessarily mediated, colored by one's (socially located) values and interpretive lenses. Prior preparation and expectation always shapes even the most intense mystical experience, however subtly. For them, the Jewish adept and Buddhist contemplative not only interpret their experiences differently, their experiences *are* different.

What are the arguments for and against these two viewpoints? For a detailed discussion, see Scholem's essay, "Mysticism and Religious Authority," in *On the Kabbalah and Its Symbolism* (mentioned earlier); S. Katz, "Language, Epistemology, and Mysticism," in his *Mysticism and Philosophical Analysis* (Oxford University Press, 1978); and Louis Dupre, "Unio Mystica: the State and the Experience," in M. Idel and B. McGinn, eds., *Mystical Union and Monotheistic Faith: An Ecumenical Dialogue* (Macmillan, 1989).

Related to this last question is the relationship between mystical experience and religious authority. Here the key questions are: Why do mystics tend to affirm their religious tradition and its sources of authority? Why do Christian mystics, e.g., tend to have a "Jesus experience" whereas kabbalists receive a revelation from Elijah or a vision of the Shekhinah? How do religions guard against conflicts between the mystic's experience and Tradition? And what factors determine whether a mystic becomes a conservative, reformist, or revolutionary actor? These questions are illumined by Scholem, both in his essay "Mysticism and Religious Authority" and in a related piece, "Mysticism and Society," *Diogenes* 58 (1967): 1–24. See also Steven Katz's stimulating essay "The 'Conservative' Character of Mysticism," in his *Mysticism and Religious Traditions* (Oxford University Press, 1983).

Some of the ways in which the revolutionary mystical impulse was restrained in Judaism was through charging the adept with social responsibility and by requiring intensive prior training in the exoteric tradition. Still, only rarely was mystical study actually postponed until an advanced age. The pronouncement "no kabbalah before forty"—known by legions of latter-day Hebrew school stu-

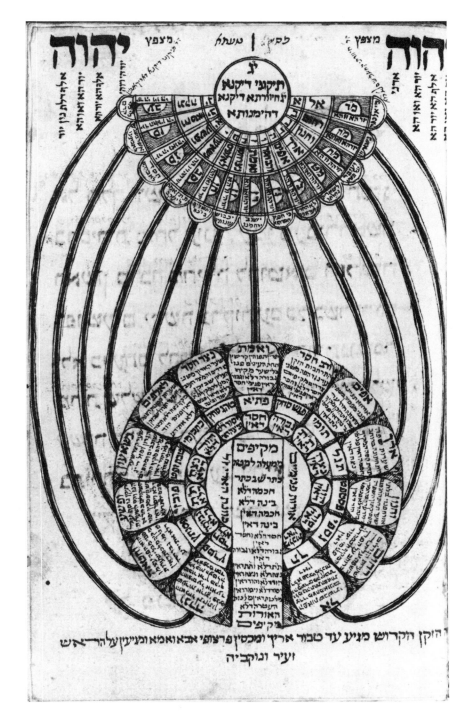

This chart depicts the thirteen attributes of God's mercy as interpreted in the Zohar and by Isaac Luria. (Library of The Jewish Theological Seminary of America)

dents—is a relatively late teaching, one which was generally acknowledged, if at all, in the breach.

The Tone of Jewish Mysticism

Primed with these overarching questions, we may now survey the more specific contours of Jewish mystical tradition. I would begin with Arthur Green's afore-mentioned "Mysticism and Religion: the Case of Judaism," published in J. Neus-ner, ed., *Take Judaism, for Example.* After a brief characterization of mysticism, Green provides a capsule history of the Jewish mystical tradition and elucidates exemplary texts. In my estimation this is the single best introduction to the liter-ature. Green's interpretations are models of clarity and profound pedagogy, as they disclose the mystical life pulsating beneath the text.

There are several other introductory essays that merit close reading. The opening lecture in Scholem's *Major Trends* is perhaps the classic synthetic portrait of Jewish mysticism. As a superb teacher, Scholem necessarily oversimplifies at times. Still his is a schema that will get the ball rolling: the careful student will refine the portrait as he or she proceeds, adding half-tints and nuances. Written in a different vein is A. J. Heschel's "The Mystical Dimension in Judaism," in L. Finkelstein, ed., *The Jews: Their Religion and Culture* (Schocken Books, 1971). Heschel offers more of an "insider's" view, writing in a way that intriguingly blurs the boundaries between academic scholar and mystically inflected theologian.

Finally, two other essays that are personal favorites: Moshe Idel's article "Qab-balah," published in the *Encyclopedia of Religion*, is helpful for those readers who wish to concentrate on kabbalah. By bringing in streams of mysticism neglected in the other essays (e.g., ecstatic and philosophical kabbalah), he rounds out the portraits of Scholem and Green. In another vein entirely is the passionately felt "Psychedelics and Kabbalah," in J. Sleeper and A. Mintz, eds., *The New Jews* (Vintage Books: 1971). Written by a youthful Arthur Green under the pen name Itzik Lodzer, the essay offers an experiential key for unlocking kabbalistic under-standings of the divine.

We are now ready to commence our more discrete studies. The topics will generally follow a chronological structure; at key junctures, however, thematic studies will be woven in.

The Dawn of Jewish Mysticism: Judaism in the Greco-Roman World

Most courses on Jewish mysticism follow Scholem's model and begin with rabbinic ascent mysticism, the so-called *Merkavah* (divine Chariot) and *Hekhalot* (celestial palaces) traditions, whose origins lie in late antiquity. Still, a less deterministic view of Jewish mysticism (and of Judaism) suggests the need to begin earlier, among the sundry Judaisms of the Hellenistic world. Indeed, I would argue, one cannot fully understand rabbinic ascent mysticism without some rudimentary knowledge of its pre-rabbinic parallels.

One of the hallmarks of Jewish life in the late Second Temple period–early Rabbinic period is its diversity. To survey the forms of Judaism in this period, and place its mystical expressions in historical context, the reader may turn to Michael Stone's wonderfully readable *Scriptures, Sects and Visions* (Philadelphia: Fortress Press, 1980). His discussions of apocalyptic and Wisdom literatures, the mystically colored piety found in the Qumran texts, and the relationship between Gnosticism and Judaism, are invaluable for those interested in mystical tendencies in Hellenistic Judaism. A more compressed discussion is Jacob Neusner's "Varieties of Judaism," in Green's *Jewish Spirituality*, vol. 1, mentioned earlier in this essay.

Perhaps the most common motif in these mystically inclined traditions is that of heavenly ascent, wherein the hero gains access to the celestial spheres: receiving revelations concerning the secrets of heaven and earth, and even, in some instances, beholding the divine Chariot and its Rider. Good introductions to this broad phenomenon of spiritual ascent include Alan Segal's *Paul the Convert* (Yale University Press, 1990), and in more expansive fashion, Christopher Rowland's *The Open Heaven* (Crossroad, 1982).

Perhaps the best-known sources of heavenly ascent are found in apocalypses: the formal name for those visions, written in the name of an ancient sage, which reveal the secrets of heaven and earth, often through an angelic mediator. One of the central works of Apocalypse, 1 Enoch, anticipates the motif of heavenly ascent stressed in the rabbinic hekhalot texts without, however, providing actual techniques of ascent. This text, and many other mystically tinged sources, including "The Apocalypse of Abraham" and "The Ascension of Isaiah," are ably translated and introduced in James Charlesworth, ed., *The Old Testament Pseudepigrapha*, 2 vol. (Doubleday, 1986). An excellent discussion of Enoch's ascent is found in Martha Himmelfarb's "From Prophecy to Apocalypse: The Book of the Watchers and Tours of Heaven," in Green's *Jewish Spirituality*, vol. 1. Himmelfarb carefully considers the question of whether the heavenly ascent reflected the author's own mystical experience or whether it remained (for him) an act of literary imagination.

Over the last fifty years, great interest has been generated in the Jewish sectarian community at Qumran, on the edge of the Dead Sea. Striking mystical elements have been found in the literature preserved by this community. On these elements, which often bear resemblance to hekhalot material, see David Halperin's eminently readable *The Faces of the Chariot: Early Jewish Responses to Ezekiel's Vision* (Tübingen: JCB Mohr, 1988; distributed by Coronet Publishers). The liturgical Songs themselves are readily available to the English reader in G. Vermes, ed., *The Dead Sea Scrolls* (3d ed., Penguin Books, 1988).

While the role of heavenly ascent in early Jewish-Christian circles has been discussed by Gershom Scholem in his *Jewish Gnosticism, Merkabah Mysticism, and Talmudic Tradition*, 2d ed. (Jewish Theological Seminary of America, 1960), by far the best general introduction is Alan Segal's *Paul the Convert*. Segal argues that Paul should be seen as a Jewish mystic with close affinities to both Apocalyptic and Merkavah traditions. His is a stirring, if controversial, analysis.

The writings of Philo, a first-century Jew who combined Platonic philosophy with biblical religion, evince a sort of intellectual mysticism, wherein the human psyche ascends unto the divine. Perhaps the best place to begin exploring the mystical aspects of Philo is in David Winston's cogent article "Philo and the Contemplative Life," in *Jewish Spirituality*, vol. 1.

Rabbinic Mysticism

Of all the forms of Jewish mystical literature, perhaps none retains the fire of ecstatic experience as fully as rabbinic ascent texts, generally called either Merkavah or Hekhalot mysticism. Here the mystical hero wends his way through the labyrinths of the multitiered cosmos, in his attempt to ascend unto (and hence, behold) the divine Glory. After considering this ramified ascent literature, we

Gershom Scholem, who pioneered
the study of Jewish mysticism, was
professor of Jewish Mysticism at the
Hebrew University. (Photograph by
Alfred Bernheim)

will briefly consider the second major genre of rabbinic mystical creativity: cosmogonic mysticism, i.e., speculations on the secrets of *creation.*

Of all the streams of Jewish mysticism, the Merkavah tradition appears to be
the longest-lasting, and perhaps, the slowest changing. Indeed, it has been
termed the dominant form of non-rational Jewish spirituality in the first ten centuries of the common era. Later absorbed into German Jewish Pietism and Spanish kabbalah, its reverberations were still felt in eighteenth-century Hasidism.
The one authentic letter of Israel Baal Shem Tov (c. 1700–1760) in our possession recounts one such visionary ascent. (It is printed in Jacobs's *Jewish Mystical
Testimonies.*) The best overviews of Merkavah mysticism are Scholem's somewhat
dated but still lucid lecture in *Major Trends* and Joseph Dan's recent article, "The
Religious Experience of the Merkavah," in *Jewish Spirituality*, vol. 1.

What is the nature of the religious experience underlying these soul ascents? What were the techniques used to induce ecstasy? And what understandings of the divine are implied in the hekhalot literature? These and related issues are addressed in Rachel Elior's splendid article, "The Concept of God in Hekhalot Literature," in J. Dan, ed., *Binah: Studies in Jewish Thought*, vol. 2 (Praeger, 1989). For discussion of the mystical perception of the so-called divine body in the hekhalot literature, see Scholem's excellent study of the *Shiur Komah*, in his newly available *On the Mystical Shape of the Godhead*, cited earlier.

Translated Texts

After this overview, the reader should be ready to encounter primary texts, still the central portal to the richness of this tradition. Brief extracts are found in Green's article, mentioned earlier, "Mysticism and Religion: the Case of Judaism," and in Jacobs's *Jewish Mystical Testimonies*. More extensive exposure is afforded by P. S. Alexander's translation and commentary to 3 Enoch, found in J. Charlesworth, ed., *Old Testament Pseudepigrapha*, vol. 1 (mentioned earlier). This text, which reworks the motif of Enoch's transformation from person to angelic being, his initiatory death and rebirth as "lesser YHWH," may contain important clues for given mystics' experiences and their lofty aspirations. A partial translation of *Hekhalot Rabbati*, perhaps the most influential ascent text, is found in David Blumenthal's introductory book *Understanding Jewish Mysticism*, vol. 1 (Ktav Publishing House, 1978). However, the translation (confusingly titled "Pirkei Heikhalot") is laced with errors and must be used with caution.

Perhaps the most accessible aspect of the Merkavah literature is the numinous hymns, which function both as the songs uttered by the celestial chorus and the libretto chanted by the adept which serves as a trigger for his own mystical ecstasy. A selection of these hymns is presented in T. Carmi, ed., *The Penguin Book of Hebrew Verse* (Penguin Books, 1981). Also found in the Carmi collection is a series of liturgical poems that draw heavily on the mystical ascent tradition. These include poems of the Eretz-Israeli liturgical poets Yannai and Eleazar Qalir, as well as the southern Italian poet Amittai ben Shephatiah. These hymns (and such well-known prayers as *El Adon* and the Sabbath "Crown" *Kedushah*) point to the potent influence that the mystical tradition exerted on the Jewish liturgical imagination. A striking example of a mystical hymnology that entered popular liturgy is *Perek Shira* (The Chapter of Song). In this work, all living creatures—like the angels on high—offer songs of praise to the Creator, each chanting an appropriate verse from Psalms. This hymn has been ably translated by Barry Holtz in Carl Rheins and Richard Siegel, eds., *The Jewish Almanac* (Bantam, 1980).

Rabbinic ascent mysticism has become something of a scholarly growth-field in recent years. The reader seeking deeper understanding of the tradition may consider three representative studies: Scholem's *Jewish Gnosticism, Merkabah Mysticism and Talmudic Tradition*, the book that reenergized the field; Ithamar Gruenwald's richly descriptive *Apocalyptic and Merkavah Mysticism* (Leiden: E. J. Brill, 1980); and *The Faces of the Chariot: Early Jewish Responses to Ezekiel's Vision* by David Halperin. Halperin's is a work of brilliance and imaginative daring (witness his use of psychoanalytic categories to probe Merkavah experience). Despite its grand scope, the book is quite accessible, for Halperin explains terms clearly and nowhere presupposes specialized knowledge. One need not agree with all of his key contentions to be enlivened by this study. The book also contains a highly useful and comprehensive annotated bibliography.

The Secrets of Creation

Our second category of mystical literature concerns the Secrets of Creation, works which attempt to explain "what is left unsaid" in the biblical accounts. For a rich, erudite discussion of rabbinic speculation on divine emanation, see Alexander Altmann's "A Note on the Rabbinic Doctrine of Creation," in his *Studies in Religious Philosophy and Mysticism* (Salem, N.H.: Ayer, 1975). *Seder Rabba di-Vreshit*, a fascinating work of cosmogonic speculation, is discussed in the present author's *The Sabbath in the Classical Kabbalah* (SUNY Press, 1989). This source adumbrates the later kabbalistic understanding of the Sabbath as mystical wedding ceremony.

Surely the most important of the mystical treatises on Creation is *Sefer Yezirah* (The Book of Creation), a work which correlates divine creativity with the permutation of the twenty-two Hebrew letters and ten elemental numbers (or *sefirot*). This work is translated and briefly explicated by David Blumenthal in his *Understanding Jewish Mysticism*, vol. 1. Aryeh Kaplan's translation, *Sefer Yetzirah* (Samuel Weiser, 1991), with extensive commentary, is newly available as well.

The correlation between *Yezirah*'s theory of divine creativity and the human creativity implied in the tradition of the golem (the artificial being created via letter combinations) is explored in Moshe Idel's new book, *The Golem* (SUNY

Press, 1990). See also Scholem's "The Idea of the Golem" in *On the Kabbalah and Its Symbolism*.

The mystical speculations and *midrashim* from the late tenth to mid-twelfth centuries are only beginning to be studied in adequate fashion. The results promise to revolutionize our understanding of medieval Jewish mysticism. Unfortunately, the most important explorations of these transitional texts are as yet either in Hebrew or of a highly technical nature. For the time being, the interested reader may refer to Scholem's summary remarks in *Kabbalah*, pp. 30–35, and chapter 3 of Dan's *Gershom Scholem and the Mystical Dimension in Judaism*.

Multiple Streams: Jewish Mysticism in the Twelfth and Thirteenth Centuries

Martin Buber has spoken of historical periods marked by a sudden outbreak of the spirit, times of religious ferment and creativity. In Jewish history, the twelfth and thirteenth centuries were surely such a time. In this period, four expressions of elite Judaism came to the fore or matured. One can point to the highly developed religious philosophy, of which Maimonides was the high-water mark; the halakhic creativity of the Tosafists, those Rhineland legalists and Talmudic commentators; the emergence of kabbalah in its sundry forms; and the growth of distinct mystical pietist movements (called *hasidut*) in the Franco-German Rhineland and in Egypt. Although the impact of mysticism was registered in religious philosophy and among some of the Tosafists, mystical experience and expression stood at the heart of the last two streams, kabbalah and hasidut. In good rabbinic fashion, let us consider the second first.

Mystical Pietism

Jewish Sufism in Egypt

From the time of Bahya Ibn Pakuda (d. 1080), some Jewish seekers had drawn on Sufi teachings to fashion a theology that stressed inwardness. Perhaps the most striking exemplars of such religiosity were the Egyptian hasidim, who were both observant Jews and students of Sufi piety. The prime movers of this Jewish Sufism were the scions of the Maimonides family, who seem to have extended and rendered more explicitly mystical Maimonides's teachings on prophecy. To attain communion with God, the Pietists drew on such Sufi-derived practices as ablution, solitary meditation, and the sustained recitation of holy names. The best introduction to this movement is Paul Fenton's lucid essay "Judaism and Sufism," in his edition of Obadiah Maimondes's *Treatise of the Pool* (Cambridge, Mass.: Institute for the Study of Human Knowledge, 1981).

There is some evidence that these Pietists, whose tradition seems to have endured into the fourteenth century, influenced the ecstatic kabbalah that developed in the Land of Israel in the late thirteenth century. These points of possible contact are briefly explored in Fenton's essay and in Moshe Idel's *Studies in Ecstatic Kabbalah* (SUNY Press, 1988).

The Mystical Pietism of Hasidei Ashkenaz (Franco-German Pietists)

Considerably more has been written about the ethico-social and mystical activities of these Pietists, who flourished from around 1170 to the mid-thirteenth century. The recipient of venerable mystical traditions which apparently spread from the Middle East through Byzantium and Italy, they preserved the *Hekhalot* traditions, engaged in mystico-magical speculations on the golem, and developed complex exegetical means of decoding hidden dimensions of Scripture, the liturgy, and *Sefer Yezirah.* Their goal was to engender visionary experience of the divine Glory (the visible manifestation of the Godhead).

The best brief introductions to Hasidei Ashkenaz remain Scholem's masterly lecture in *Major Trends* and Joseph Dan's more up-to-date discussion in *Gershom Scholem.*

Most scholars of Hasidei Ashkenaz focus on either their social-penitential program or on their esoteric theology. The historian Yitzhak Baer exemplifies the first trend. His celebrated Hebrew essay "The Socio-Religious Orientation of Sefer Hasidim" has recently been translated in J. Dan, ed., *Binah*, vol. 2. Cut from wholly different cloth is the revisionist work of Ivan Marcus, *Piety and Society* (Leiden: E. J. Brill, 1981). Whereas most scholars have noted only graded differences between the generations of Pietists, Marcus distinguishes between two stages of historical development: a radical phase which stressed social-religious reform while espousing sectarian consciousness; and a second "conservative" phase, wherein traditional rabbinic authority was reaffirmed, and Pietism reinterpreted as a largely privatistic program whose penitential rituals were now open to all. While Marcus's reading of the Pietist socio-religious program is controversial, his pathfinding book makes for exciting, intellectually sophisticated reading.

The central text expressing the religious and moral teachings of the central group of Pietists is the aforementioned *Sefer Hasidim*. Ivan Marcus is currently preparing a translation and introduction to this work for Yale University Press. For the time being excerpts may be found in Ben Zion Bokser's *Jewish Mystical Tradition*. An important meditation on love and fear of God, written by the Pietist mystic Eleazar of Worms, is printed in Jacobs's *Jewish Mystical Testimonies*.

Hasidei Ashkenaz was a multivocal movement, speaking to the common Jew and the elite at once. The spectrum of prayer techniques, from those aimed at the unlettered man or woman to those appropriate for the mystic, is ably discussed in Ivan Marcus's "Devotional Ideals of Ashkenazic Pietism," in *Jewish Spirituality*, vol. 1. The famous hymn *Shir ha-Kavod* (The Song of the Glory) is a striking example of a Pietist-penned prayer which can be read on both exoteric and esoteric-mystical levels of meaning. A particularly good translation of *Shir ha-Kavod* can be found in the Birnbaum Prayer Book (Hebrew Publishing Co., 1977). A less precise rendering may be found in Bokser's anthology.

The deepest layer of mystical doctrine focuses on the celestial realm, and more specifically on the multileveled structure of the Godhead. These speculations are discussed by Scholem in *Major Trends* and in clearer, nuanced fashion by Joseph Dan in chapter 3 of his book, *Jewish Mysticism and Jewish Ethics* (University of Washington Press, 1986). The connection between mystical and magical practice in Hasidei Ashkenaz is explored by Scholem in his article "The Golem" and by Idel in chapters 5 and 6 of his *Golem*.

Finally, special mention must be made of recent studies by Moshe Idel, Asi Farber, and Elliot Wolfson which strongly suggest that the esoteric theology of Hasidei Ashkenaz was actually quite close to the concerns typical of kabbalah. At present most of these studies are inaccessible to the general reader, but Idel's views are compactly expressed in his *Kabbalah: New Perspectives*, especially in chapters 6 and 8. The interested reader should also be on the lookout for Elliot Wolfson's work-in-progress on visionary experience in medieval Jewish mysticism (including Pietism). His specialized studies to date suggest that this will be a landmark book.

The Origins of Classical Kabbalah

At this juncture, we are ready to begin our trek from the Rhineland to southern France and northern Spain, to explore the emergence and growth of kabbalah. *Kabbalah*—meaning "received tradition"—is the most common term used for the variegated stream of Jewish mysticism and esoteric speculation, especially as it developed from the late twelfth century onward. Following the leads of Scholem and Idel, we may distinguish between two broad modes of classical kabbalah: a relatively small "ecstatic" current which cultivated a spiritual path leading to mystical *union* with God and a larger, more ramified tradition whose primary goal was theosophy (experiential knowledge of the hidden life of divinity) and theurgy (the attempt to act on—to augment or restore—the deity). The theosophical kabbalists generally stopped short of claiming the radical absorption in God expressed in ecstatic kabbalah. Rather, they attested to a mystical communion wherein some distinction between devotee and divinity was maintained, however tenuously. Some readers may wish to survey the formative stage of kabbalah—its history and symbolic universe—before proceeding to more discrete studies. Recommended are Idel's essay "Qabbalah," mentioned earlier in this chapter, and the introductory chapter of my book, *The Sabbath in the Classical Kabbalah*, cited earlier.

The best in-depth study of the early stages of kabbalah, from around 1180 to 1280, remains Scholem's *Origins of the Kabbalah* (Princeton University Press, 1990). It is a work of luminous and comprehensive scholarship. The best collection of primary sources in this period is Joseph Dan, ed., *Early Kabbalah* (Paulist Press, 1986). The texts are expertly translated by Ronald Kiener; because the notes are brief, however, it is best to study these often enigmatic sources with a more knowledgeable guide.

Provençal Kabbalah

The origins of Kabbalah constitute a complex puzzle that has not been fully solved by scholars. Although intriguing evidence has been uncovered suggesting an older theosophic tradition, the dominant tendency has been to associate the beginnings of kabbalah proper with the emergence of *Sefer ha-Bahir* (The Book of Clarity), in the intellectually charged rabbinic culture of Provence in the latter decades of the twelfth century. The themes in the deeply mythic *Bahir* run a wide gamut, ranging from mystical rationales for the commandments to esoteric symbolism of the Hebrew alphabet to theosophical speculations on the mysteries of Creation and God's inner life. Brief introductions to the *Bahir* are found in Scholem's *On the Kabbalah and Its Symbolism* and in chapter 5 of Dan's *Gershom Scholem*. By far the most comprehensive and penetrating treatment is found in chapters 1 and 2 of Scholem's *Origins*. Parts of this work, however, may prove rough going for the non-specialist. Excerpts from the *Bahir* text are found in *Early Kabbalah*, while the complete text is competently rendered in Aryeh Kaplan's bilingual edition, *The Bahir* (York Beach: Samuel Weiser, 1989). Finally, Joseph Dan provides a succinct account of the *Bahir*'s interpretive strategies in "Midrash and the Dawn of Kabbalah," found in Geoffrey Hartman and Sanford Budick's superb collection, *Midrash and Literature* (Yale University Press, 1986). The more contemplative strand of Provençal mysticism is treated in masterly fashion in Scholem's *Origins* and in admirably compact fashion in Dan's *Gershom Scholem*, chapter 6.

Gerona Kabbalah

By the early thirteenth century, kabbalah had taken root in Spain, most notably in the Catalonian towns of Barcelona and Gerona. Gerona, in particular, harbored an astonishing array of mystical personalities: poets, polemicists, moralists, contemplatives. If Azriel of Gerona was its most profound contemplative, it was the halakhist and exegete, Nahmanides, who lent the kabbalah a new sense of authority and prestige. For a brief overview, see Dan, *Gershom Scholem*, chapter 7; for the best in-depth discussion (including a splendid analysis of Azriel), see Scholem, *Origins of the Kabbalah*. Key Gerona texts are found in *Early Kabbalah*, while some of Nahmanides's mystical teachings are found in Charles Chavel's edition of Nahmanides's multitiered *Commentary on the Torah*, 5 vols. (Shilo Publishing Co., 1971). Many of his mystical teachings there are telegraphed by the phrase "according to the way of truth."

At this point, the reader may wish to pursue a thematic course: focusing on contemplative prayer and meditation, central preoccupations of the Provençal-Spanish adepts. Scholem laconically introduces the theme in *Kabbalah*. A detailed study of mystical contemplation in one early mystic is Scholem's, "The

Concept of Kavvanah in the Early Kabbalah," in A. Jospe, ed., *Studies in Jewish Thought* (Wayne State University Press, 1981). Finally, a wonderfully readable essay is Daniel Matt's "Ayin: the Problem of Nothingness in Jewish Mysticism," in Robert K. C. Forman, *The Problem of Pure Consciousness: Mysticism and Philosophy* (Oxford University Press, 1990). A significant portion of this essay is devoted to Geronese mystics' accounts of the contemplative return to the divine source (the divine Nothing), accomplished in the course of prayer.

Ecstatic Kabbalah

The central figure in this influential tradition was Abraham Abulafia (1240–92), a highly creative mystic and itinerant seeker, who taught in settings as diverse as Spain, Italy, Greece, and the Land of Israel. Abulafia's mystical theory is a striking mixture of rationalism and emotionalism. The kabbalist seeks to untie the knots that chain the soul to material forms, so that it may merge with the cosmic stream of life, "he and He becoming one entity." Abulafia's kabbalah has been called a Judaized yoga, replete as it is with breathing exercises, postures, and highly developed forms of recitation and meditation.

The best place to begin studying ecstatic kabbalah is Scholem's lecture in *Major Trends.* This provides an excellent overview for the more detailed studies of Moshe Idel, the preeminent scholar of Abulafian mysticism. Of special merit is his *The Mystical Experience in Abraham Abulafia* (SUNY Press, 1987), an erudite, frequently exciting analysis of Abulafia's mystical techniques; his use of music, both as an analogy for mystical experience and as a means for attaining ecstasy; and the experience of mystical union with the divine. A final chapter focuses on the erotic imagery used by ecstatic kabbalists to portray the connection between Lover and beloved.

Although Abulafia's teachings attained only limited influence in his native Spain (due to a rabbinic ban), he exerted an important influence on the development of kabbalah in Italy and the eastern Mediterranean lands. His teachings entered into Safed kabbalah and, in its wake, east European Hasidism. The reverberations of Abulafian teachings are explored in Idel's excellent "Hitbodedut as Concentration," in *Jewish Spirituality,* vol. 1, and in more technical fashion in *Studies in Ecstatic Kabbalah* (SUNY Press, 1988). David Blumenthal has translated and glossed the teachings of a sixteenth-century Abulafian in his *Understanding Jewish Mysticism,* vol. 2 (Ktav Publishing House, 1982). Perhaps the most extensive collection of ecstatic texts is found in Aryeh Kaplan's *Meditation and Kabbalah* (Samuel Weiser, 1982).

The Religious Vision of the Zohar

Late-thirteenth-century Castile was the gathering point for a wide variety of mystical trends: contemplative Gerona kabbalah; ecstatic kabbalah; mythic meditations on the problem of evil; even anti-mythic kabbalistic philosophy. Several adepts attempted to combine several of these trends. The richest synthesis, and the fateful one from the historical point of view, was that accomplished by Moshe de Leon and his circle, author(s) of the "Bible of Spanish Kabbalah," the Zohar.

The Zohar represents a new departure in kabbalistic literature. For the first time there is a voluminous work, a broad canvas of symbolic interpretation and mystical speculation covering the whole world of Judaism as it appeared to its author. Over the centuries the Zohar took on quasi-canonical importance, standing alongside the Bible and the Talmud. It was studied, contemplated, chanted, and popularized, penetrating into virtually every Jewish community. Surely it was the best loved of all mystical works. The eighteenth-century hasidic master Pinhas Koretzer went so far as to say, "The Zohar has kept me Jewish."

For years the best English introduction to the Zohar was the two lectures in *Major Trends*. It still makes compelling reading; nonetheless, I would urge most readers to begin elsewhere, with Daniel Matt's introduction to his *Zohar: Book of Enlightenment* (Paulist Press, 1983). In a lively style, Matt places the work in historical relief, discusses the drama of authorship, and offers a lucid introduction to the symbolism of the ten *sefirot*, as the dynamic inner aspects of the Godhead were called. Next I would turn to Arthur Green's splendid "The Zohar: Jewish Mysticism in Medieval Spain," in P. Szarmach, *An Introduction to the Medieval Mystics of Europe* (SUNY Press, 1985). This article not only provides an excellent entree into the world of Zoharic spirituality and symbolic creativity, but helps the reader learn how to read the Zohar in a way that is both careful and religiously alive. Other introductory guides to Zoharic symbolism and hermeneutics include Lawrence Fine's excellent discussion in *Back to the Sources* (Schocken Books, 1990) and the present author's *The Sabbath in the Classical Kabbalah* ("How to Read a Zoharic Text").

The Zohar is a work to enter slowly, to puzzle over, to savor. What the Zohar says of the Torah may be said of *The Book of Enlightenment* itself, namely, that "it discloses its secrets to those who love her," to those who pursue a love affair with the text. The best place to begin is with Daniel Matt's anthology *Zohar: Book of Enlightenment*. Matt employs a rather daring strategy of translation, rendering the sonorous Aramaic text as a poem. Even more impressive, albeit less controversial, is Matt's lucid commentary, which opens up the often recondite text to the general reader. He is sensitive to the experiential aspects of Zoharic mysticism and avoids flattening the multitiered richness of the symbolism. The major drawback to the Matt work is its small scope, treating but two percent of the Zohar corpus.

More expansive in nature is the three-volume classic, *The Wisdom of the Zohar*, edited by Fischel Lachower and Isaiah Tishby (Oxford University Press, 1989). Its recent appearance in English translation is cause for celebration. While the sonorities of the Zohar's original language are lost in David Goldstein's otherwise superb translation, its mysterious power remains largely intact. The book is organized thematically, each chapter consisting of an introductory essay, written by Tishby, followed by a rich sampling of primary sources.

Much less helpful than Lachower/Tishby and Matt is the venerable five-volume *Soncino Zohar*, translated by H. Sperling and M. Simon, 2d ed. (Soncino Press, 1984). The translation (which is limited to the central stratum of the book, the so-called *guf ha-zohar*) is serviceable, if not always a model of precision. However, the Soncino edition lacks a commentary. Bereft of reference to the Zohar's symbolic language and sefirotic structure, it is of rather limited value for most beginners.

Kabbalistic Symbolism

With a basic understanding of the symbolic system of classical kabbalah under our belt, we may now turn to explicitly thematic studies. Indeed, these are often the most exciting ways to enter into kabbalah. I have here focused on three topics, by way of example: Symbols of the Male and Female; Ritual Life; and Torah, Language, and Hermeneutics (i.e., the theory and practice of interpretation).

Sexual and Gender-Related Symbolism

One of the most arresting features of theosophic kabbalah lies in its use of sexual and gender-encoded symbolism when imaging the deity. As Scholem noted, the adepts located the mystery of sex within the Godhead itself. Thus the Zohar: divine perfection can occur only when "Male and Female are together," when divine androgyny is realized. This model of divine sexuality has ramifications for the understanding of human sexuality and for such institutions as (heterosexual) marriage. We shall begin by focusing on the engenderment of divinity and then proceed to human sexuality.

For the theoretically minded, a fine introduction to the import of gender-related symbolism in religious life is Caroline Walker Bynum's "The Complexity of Symbols," in C. Bynum, S. Harrell, and P. Richman, eds., *Gender and Religion* (Beacon Press, 1988). From there I would turn to studies that discuss Shekhinah, that rich cipher of divine immanence, usually (although not exclusively) conceived in female-related terms. The best introductory discussions include Arthur Green, "Bride, Spouse, Daughter: Images of the Feminine in Classical Jewish Sources," in Susannah Heschel, *On Being a Jewish Feminist* (Schocken Books, 1983); and Green's "The Song of Songs in Early Jewish Mysticism," reprinted in Harold Bloom, ed., *The Song of Songs* (Modern Critical Interpretations Series, Chelsea House, 1988). Newly available to the English reader are Tishby's excellent essays in volume 1 of *The Wisdom of the Zohar*, and Scholem's classic "The Shekhinah," in *On the Mystical Shape of the Godhead*, mentioned earlier. A more popular treatment is provided by D. Ariel in *The Mystic Quest*, chapter 6, "Shekhinah: The Feminine Aspect of God." The best-known treatment of the divine female is surely Raphael Patai's *The Hebrew Goddess*, 3d ed. (Wayne State University Press, 1990). This is a provocative, highly speculative book which attempts to discern points of continuity between the various feminine God-images found in the ancient Near East with those found in later (generally mystical) Jewish sources. Applying comparative and quasi-Jungian methods, Patai finds suggestive parallels amidst the materials but does not corroborate his points in sufficiently thorough fashion. Patai's book is well worth reading, but needs to be supplemented by more conventional (i.e., cautious) scholarship.

More specialized studies that illumine divine engenderment include Elliot Wolfson's "Female Imaging of the Torah: From Literary Metaphor to Religious Symbol," in *From Ancient Israel to Modern Judaism: Essays in Honor of Marvin Fox*, vol. 2, edited by J. Neusner et al. (Scholars Press, 1989); and Moshe Idel's

"The Land of Israel in Medieval Kabbalah," in L. Hoffman, ed., *The Land of Israel: Jewish Perspectives* (University of Notre Dame Press, 1986). Finally, the present author's *The Sabbath in the Classical Kabbalah* explores the image of Shekhinah as the mystical Sabbath Bride.

Given the nature of divine sexuality, what is the nature of human sexuality? These issues are raised in David Biale's brief meditation "Eros: Sex and Body," in A. Cohen and P. Mendes-Flohr, *Contemporary Jewish Religious Thought* (Free Press, 1988); in Moshe Idel's "Sexual Metaphors and Praxis in the Kabbalah," in David Kraemer, ed. *The Jewish Family* (Oxford University Press, 1989); in Jeremy Cohen's illuminating discussion of sexual life and procreation in *"Be Fertile and Increase, Fill the Earth and Master It": The Ancient and Medieval Career of a Text* (Cornell University Press, 1989); and in *The Sabbath in the Classical Kabbalah*, appendix 2, which treats the sacramental significance of marital intercourse.

Tishby devotes a chapter to "Conjugal Life" in volume 3 of *The Wisdom of the Zohar*, while Scholem reflects on the ambivalence of Lurianic kabbalists to human sexuality in *On the Kabbalah and Its Symbolism*. Of special note is Charles Mopsik's engaging "The Body of Engenderment in the Hebrew Bible, the Rabbinic Tradition and the Kabbalah," in M. Feher, ed., *Fragments for a History of the Human Body*, part 1 (New York: Zone, 1989). Mopsik argues that in kabbalah the body is the prime locus for acquiring knowledge of the divine world.

Ritual Life

The academic study of kabbalah has often reduced Jewish mysticism to a mode of thinking, rather than viewing it in an active sense, first and foremost, with a deeply experiential core. To understand kabbalah, one must explore its ability to shape the inner life of the adept, via the mime of ritual.

An excellent place to begin the study of ritual is with Scholem's splendid "Tradition and New Creation in the Ritual of the Kabbalists," in *On the Kabbalah and Its Symbolism*, or Daniel Matt's fine overview, "The Mystic and the Mizvot," in *Jewish Spirituality*, vol. 1. Moshe Idel sheds valuable light on techniques used for triggering mystical experience in chapter 5 of his *Kabbalah: New Perspectives*, while part 5 (found in vol. 3) of Tishby's *Wisdom of the Zohar* is devoted to the inner meaning of the Life of Torah—prayer and mystical communion, study, celebration of fasts and festivals. Finally, David Ariel provides a highly enjoyable account of kabbalistic ritual in chapter 9 of *The Mystic Quest*.

To deepen one's understanding of kabbalistic ritual, the reader may wish to focus on a given ritual or ritual-complex. One such option is that of the Sabbath, which in kabbalah became a day of cosmic transformation. Interestingly, the kabbalistic understanding of the Sabbath was highly influential, coloring Sabbath celebration in virtually every Jewish community in the post-medieval period.

Perhaps the best way to begin is with A. J. Heschel's classic *The Sabbath* (Farrar, Straus and Giroux, 1975), which is replete with mystical references. A complementary work is Arthur Green's beautifully written "Sabbath as Temple: Some Thoughts on Space and Time in Judaism," in S. Fishman and R. Jospe, *Go and Study* (Washington, D.C.: B'nai B'rith, 1982). Green argues that, in the wake of the Temple destruction, primary Jewish allegiance slowly shifted from the spatial realm to that of time, the dimension left untouched by the conquerors. Drawing on rabbinic and mystical sources, he shows how the Sabbath was reconstituted as a symbolic Temple in time.

On the mystical Sabbath, see my article "The Sabbath in the Kabbalah," in *Judaism* 31 (Winter 1982): 26–36. Adin Steinsaltz offers a moving "Additional Note on the Kiddush Ritual" in his introduction to kabbalah, *The Thirteen-Petalled Rose* (Basic Books, 1985). More detailed studies include my synthetic analysis of mythic motifs and rituals, *The Sabbath in the Classical Kabbalah* (SUNY Press, 1989); and *Israel in Time and Space* (Feldheim, 1987), written by the eminent theologian-scholar Alexandre Safran. Finally, the reader interested in text study may consider *Sod ha-Shabbat* [*The Mystery of the Sabbath*] (SUNY Press, 1989), my translation of and critical commentary to Meir ibn Gabbai's systematic roadmap for the mystical celebration of the Sabbath.

I also suggest that reading be supplemented with several recordings of mystical Sabbath table-songs and hymns. Excellent Yemenite, Sefardic, and hasidic recordings are readily available. I will mention only one by name here: Pierre (Pinchus) Pinchuk's 1929 rendition of *Raza de-Shabbat* (The Mystery of the Sabbath), the sonorous Zoharic hymn of mystical union that is chanted just before the evening service on Friday night. This lyrical expression of mystical transport is, to my mind, without equal. (It is available from Menorah records under the title "*Maoz Tzur* and Other Hits"!)

Torah, Language, and Hermeneutics

In normative Judaism, language has long been regarded as the medium of creation. It is through speech that God asserts order over chaos. In speculative kabbalah, language is not only the medium by which God creates, it is, in its primal form, the very *substance* of divinity. God, according to this symbolic schema, is an elaborate texture of Hebrew letters, the primordial essence of Torah. To study Torah, therefore, is to decode the inner life of divinity.

On the mystical understanding of Torah, there is an embarrassment of riches. One might start with Scholem's seminal "Revelation and Tradition as Religious Categories," found in his *The Messianic Idea in Judaism* (Schocken Books, 1971). This article affords keen insight into the interpretive process in Rabbinic Judaism and kabbalah. Another excellent essay is Frank Talmage's "Apples of Gold: The Inner Meaning of Sacred Texts in Medieval Judaism," in Green's *Jewish Spirituality*, vol. 1. Talmage offers nuanced appreciation of mystical allegory and symbolism.

Other important articles include Scholem's panoramic "The Meaning of Torah in Jewish Mysticism," in *On the Kabbalah and its Symbolism,* and two tightly focused pieces in Hartman and Budick's *Midrash and Literature* (Yale University Press, 1986): Moshe Idel's "Infinities of Torah" and Betty Roitman's "Sacred Language and Open Text." A superb comparison of hermeneutical strategies in theosophic and ecstatic kabbalah is Moshe Idel's "Kabbalistic Hermeneutics," in *Kabbalah: New Perspectives*, while Elliot Wolfson's groundbreaking essay "Circumcision, Vision of God, and Textual Interpretation," in *History of Religions* 27-2 (1987): 189–215, illumines all three themes limned here: gender, ritual, and mystical interpretation. Finally, Michael Fishbane's essay "Hermeneutics," in A. Cohen and P. Mendes-Flohr, *Contemporary Jewish Religious Thought,* is the perfect capstone to this section.

A cultural detail. The reverberations of kabbalistic hermeneutics have been deeply registered in contemporary critical theory, resulting in some writing of an unusually high order. It has informed the essays of Walter Benjamin, *Illuminations* (Schocken Books, 1969) and *Reflections* (Schocken Books, 1986), as well as Harold Bloom's *Kabbalah and Criticism* (Continuum Books, 1983) and George Steiner's *After Babel* (Oxford University Press, 1975). The kabbalistic embrace of multitiered truths, typified by the four-fold method of exegesis (PaRDeS), has inspired Michael Fishbane to attempt "to reframe modern text study through the schemata of sacred learning—wherein each level of interpretation requires a different orientation to the text and discloses different dimensions of truth." These variegated strategies for reading are explored in the essay "The Teacher and the Hermeneutical Task: A Reinterpretation of Medieval Exegesis," which can be found in his book *The Garments of Torah* (Indiana University Press, 1989).

From the Zohar to Safed: Kabbalah in the Fourteenth to Sixteenth Centuries

At this point, we resume our chronological narrative. The fourteenth to sixteenth centuries were a time of kabbalistic expansion, into North Africa, Italy, Poland, and, most notably, into the Byzantine region (home to a vital, if underexplored, mystical tradition).

Perhaps the best overviews of the period are J. Dan's chapter "From the Zohar to Safed" in his *Gershom Scholem,* and Scholem's discussion in *Kabbalah.* More specialized studies are found in Bernard Dov Cooperman, ed., *Jewish Thought in the Sixteenth Century* (Harvard University Press, 1982).

The reader may also wish to explore the philosophically sophisticated kabbalah that flourished during the Italian Renaissance. Its de-emphasis of mythic themes stands in stark contrast to the preoccupations of Zoharic kabbalah. A particularly intriguing introduction to Italian kabbalah is David Ruderman's graceful study of the late Renaissance physician, naturalist, and kabbalist Abraham Yagel, *Kabbalah, Magic, and Science* (Harvard University Press, 1988). Ruderman shows that the Jewish tradition of naturalistic learning authorized and encouraged Yagel to integrate his kabbalistic concerns with his scientific ones.

The Safed Revival and Lurianic Kabbalah

The expulsion of the Jews from the Iberian peninsula set off a series of shock waves. Numerous refugees and their children—along with other Jews of Near Eastern origin—eventually found their way to the small Galilean town of Safed, which became the setting for a mystical renaissance. In Safed one could find mystics of every stripe: mystic-legalists; poets; contemplatives; moralists; exegetes; synthesizers-systematizers, like the great Moshe Cordovero; and gifted myth-makers, like Isaac Luria. These mystics formed intentional communities or *havurot,* and (imbued with a heightened messianic awareness) developed and disseminated new rituals that articulated their mystical worldview.

There are several good introductions to Safed spirituality: Scholem's chapter in *Major Trends*; R. J. Z. Werblowsky's "Safed Revival," in *Jewish Spirituality*, vol. 2; and Lawrence Fine's introduction to his anthology *Safed Spirituality* (Paulist Press, 1984). Insight into the Safed community at large is provided in Solomon Schechter's somewhat dated but still beautiful essay "Safed in the Sixteenth Century," in his *Studies in Judaism*, second series (Jewish Publication Society, 1958).

Mystical Piety and Practice

In a series of essays, Lawrence Fine has opened various Safed mystical techniques to the general reader. One leading example is his "The Contemplative Practice of Yihudim in Lurianic Kabbalah," found in *Jewish Spirituality*, vol. 2. Safed mystical techniques are also discussed by Moshe Idel in his *Kabbalah: New Perspectives* and his "*Hitbodedut* as Concentration," in *Jewish Spirituality*, vol. 1. Other aspects of Safed spirituality are discussed in Scholem's *On the Kabbalah and Its Symbolism*, chapter 4; and Louis Jacobs's essay, "The Uplifting of Sparks," in *Jewish Spirituality*, vol. 2. Of special merit is R. J. Z. Werblowsky's *Joseph Karo—Lawyer and Mystic* (Jewish Publication Society, 1977). This book not only provides a study of the great legalist's mystical experiences but offers a clear-eyed analysis of Safed spirituality more generally (not avoiding its more extreme, often bizarre, manifestations).

The most comprehensive collection of texts is Lawrence Fine's aforementioned *Safed Spirituality*, which includes directives for ethical life and religious fellowship, mystical poems, as well as an important spiritual manual. Also noteworthy is Louis Jacobs's translation of Moses Cordovero's work of mystical ethics, *The Palm Tree of Deborah* (Sepher-Hermon Press, 1981). Finally, Aryeh Wineman's *Beyond Appearances* (Jewish Publication Society, 1988) is an especially delightful, warm-hearted collection of mystico-ethical tales, culled from Safed and post-Safed kabbalah. Such narratives constituted an enormously popular genre in the post-medieval period and were one of the main channels for the dissemination and popularization of kabbalah. Get hold of this book and enjoy!

Lurianic Theology and Its Influence

Perhaps the best-known aspect of Safed mysticism is the mythic theology developed by Isaac Luria (the Ari) and his disciples: the famous three-fold dialectic of divine contraction (*zimzum*), shattering of the vessels (*shevirah*), and ultimate restoration (*tikkun*). In this schema, both divinity and cosmos have undergone a deep trauma, one that can only be overcome by the slow accretion of sacred deeds and mystical piety. Scholem has argued that this activist mythos—whose outlines can only be sketched here—"may be described as a mystical interpretation of Exile and Redemption, or even as a great myth of Exile. Its substance reflects the deepest religious feelings of the Jews of that age," still reeling from the Spanish Expulsion. In giving mystical voice to the yearnings of a broken, exiled people, Luria and his school created the last theological system to gain near-universal acceptance among the rabbinic elite.

While a relatively succinct account of the highly complex, almost baroque Lurianic mythos is provided in *Major Trends,* the most profound analysis is found in the opening chapter of Scholem's *Sabbatai Sevi: The Mystical Messiah* (Princeton University Press, 1973). A particularly compelling explication of Lurianic kabbalah is provided by Harold Bloom in his *Kabbalah and Criticism,* mentioned earlier.

Mystical Radicalism and Heresy: The Case of Sabbateanism

While Jewish history knows no shortage of messianic longing, no movement had so widespread an appeal or lasted as long as that unleashed in 1665 by Shabbetai Zevi, the mystical "messiah" from Smyrna and his prophet, the twenty-year-old Nathan of Gaza, "the first great theologian of heretical kabbalah." I suggest that the reader begin with a brief historical overview of Shabbetai Zevi and the messianic movement, that he (along with Nathan) helped spawn. Particularly recommended are Scholem's account in *Kabbalah;* J. Dan's *Gershom Scholem,* chapter 11; and Cynthia Ozick's engaging essay "The Fourth Sparrow: The Magisterial Reach of Gershom Scholem," in Harold Bloom's collection, *Gershom Scholem* (Modern Critical Views Series, Chelsea House, 1987).

Scholem's chapter in *Major Trends* provides the best succinct overview of Sabbatean theology, while the essays in his *Messianic Idea in Judaism* allow the reader to explore both the historical antecedents and the reverberations of Sabbateanism (up to the Doenmeh, latter-day adherents of Sabbateanism). Particularly recommended is Scholem's classic essay "Redemption through Sin." By far the richest study, however, is Scholem's monumental *Sabbatai Sevi*, a book that leaves one now overwhelmed, now exhilarated. Scholem captures the pathos and tragedy of this multivocal movement and digs deep into the complex personalities of the "mystical messiah" and his prophet. Despite the welter of details and the tour de force scholarship, the narrative rarely flags. Scholem's book is a deeply moving meditation on exile and the human longing for redemption.

While Scholemian scholarship has (deservedly) defined the field, several other English-language writers have made worthy contributions. One is the sociologist Stephen Sharot, in his lively book, *Messianism, Mysticism, and Magic* (University of North Carolina Press, 1987). Sharot argues that Scholem overstates the influence of Sabbateanism in the non-Sefardic orb, and roots his own explanation of Sabbateanism's successes in more concrete social-historical factors. A second work is Elisheva Carlebach's *The Pursuit of Heresy* (Columbia University Press, 1990), an excellent study of the inner turmoil that visited Sabbateans and anti-Sabbateans alike in the generations after the apostasy.

Popularization of Kabbalah

The sixteenth through eighteenth centuries represented the high-water mark of kabbalah's influence, as mystical teachings and rites penetrated into ever-wider sectors of Jewish society (primarily in the Middle East, central and eastern Europe, and Italy).

An excellent example of a kabbalistic ritual that has shaped popular celebration is the Tu Bi-Shvat (Jewish Arbor Day) seder. Little do most contemporary Jews know of its mystical origins! For a succinct discussion of this oddly compelling ritual, see Arthur Waskow, *Seasons of Our Joy* (Beacon Press, 1990).

Chava Weissler has studied the spread of Lurianic customs in Yiddish literature, and has investigated the extent to and manner in which kabbalistic material appears in texts for and by women. Her "Women in Paradise," *Tikkun* 2:2 (1987), traces a Zoharic women's motif in several genres of Yiddish literature. Weissler's study of the religious lives of central and eastern European Jewish women (*Voices of the Matriarchs*, to be published by Beacon Press) contains an analysis of "The

Tkhine of the Matriarchs," a meditation authored by a woman who wrote kabbalistically in Hebrew and non-kabbalistically in Yiddish.

Finally, the presence of "practical kabbalah" (amulets, incantations, dibbuks, and exorcisms) in popular piety is well known. Joshua Trachtenberg's venerable *Jewish Magic and Superstition* (Atheneum, 1970) and T. Schrire's *Hebrew Magic Amulets* (Behrman House, 1982) are recommended reading.

Eastern European Mysticism: The Case of Hasidism

From the sixteenth century on, east-central Europe was home to a growing number of gifted Jewish mystics. Still, most of these figures have not yet been adequately studied in English. One exception is Judah Loew, the MaHaRaL of Prague, whom legend links with the creation of the Golem. The MaHaRaL, who had a powerful influence on the Polish school of Hasidism, is the subject of a fine, accessible study by Byron Sherwin, *Mystical Theology and Social Dissent* (Oxford University Press, 1982).

Hasidism, a popular pietistic revival movement with a strong mystical inflection, surely represents one of the great success stories in Jewish religious history. (One measure of its success is that it was its traditionalist critics who have become known as the *mitnaggedim*, "*the* opponents.") At the height of its popularity, in the early nineteenth century, Hasidism claimed the allegiance of over half of eastern European Jewry. One of the salient features of Hasidism is the astonishingly diverse galaxy of religious leaders (*zaddikim* or *rebbeim*) that emerged during its formative period, from around 1760 to 1815.

For a brief overview of Hasidism, I would suggest three sources. The first is Scholem's final lecture in *Major Trends*. His portrait is lucid, succinct, and sensitive to the varieties of hasidic piety. Different hasidic models of mystical leadership are explored in the second source, Arthur Green's "Typologies of Leadership and the Hasidic Zaddiq," in *Jewish Spirituality*, vol. 2. Finally, one of the striking features of Hasidism lay in its cultivation of the life of prayer as a means to mystical communion. Arthur Green and Barry Holtz's anthology *Your Word Is Fire: The Hasidic Masters on Contemplative Prayer* (Schocken Books, 1987) is a rare gem: a thematically arranged collection of hasidic teachings of great spiritual depth.

Two other books are recommended for students seeking to deepen their understanding of hasidic mystical piety: Gershon Hundert's anthology, *Essential Papers on Hasidism* (New York University Press, 1991); and Joseph Weiss's *Studies in Eastern European Jewish Mysticism* (Oxford University Press, 1985). This second book focuses on the origins of the hasidic movement and the teachings of some of its most gifted subsequent exponents.

The following works are suggested for readers wishing to delve more deeply into specific aspects of hasidic piety.

The Figure of the Baal Shem Tov

The charismatic Israel ben Eliezer, or the Baal Shem Tov (the BeSHT), is the figure around which the nascent hasidic fellowships coalesced. For those in search of the historical BeSHT, see now Murray Rosman's pioneering study, published in the Hundert volume. Drawing on Polish archival evidence, Rosman contradicts the widely held notion that the BeSHT was a lay mystic, widely scorned by the rabbinic establishment. Rather, the evidence suggests that he was a highly respected figure, honored as a healer and kabbalist. The Baal Shem Tov of legend is glimpsed in Dan Ben-Amos and Jerome Mintz's excellent translation of the classic *In Praise of the Baal Shem Tov* [*Shivhei ha-Besht*] (Schocken Books, 1984). This enormously popular work—written to inspire and enlighten the hasidic faithful—makes for delightful reading.

The Institution of the Zaddik

The term *hasid* is a relational term, always raising the question: a hasid of whom, of which zaddik? Still, the institution of the zaddik—the so-called mystic in the marketplace—evolved considerably over the first decades of hasidic history, as Hasidism grew from an elite mystical fellowship to a mass movement. A fine introduction to the role of the zaddik in hasidic life is Green's "Typologies of Leadership and the Hasidic Zaddiq," previously mentioned. Samuel Dresner provides a detailed discussion of the role of the zaddik in the early stages of Hasidism in *The Zaddik* (Schocken Books, 1960).

Thematic Studies in Hasidic Mystical Theology
Contemplative Mysticism in Hasidism

The best place to begin mining this rich vein of Jewish spirituality is with two pieces by Arthur Green, perhaps our most profound student of hasidic piety. Early hasidic piety was energized by two contradictory longings: for a spirituality born of pure devotion (unmediated by the mizvot and the strictures of Halakhah) over against a spirituality shaped and enriched by the commandments. This tension, and its not-uncomplicated resolution, is explored first in Green's daring "Hasidism: Discovery and Retreat," in Peter Berger, *The Other Side of God* (Doubleday Anchor, 1981); and now in greater detail, in his *Devotion and Commandment: The Faith of Abraham in the Hasidic Imagination* (Cincinnati: Hebrew Union College Press, 1989). The book is a succinct, graceful study that makes for fine reading.

Other aspects of hasidic contemplative piety are explored in the Weiss volume, while the experiences of mystical communion and the more radical *unio mystica* (mystical oneness with God) are explored by Scholem in "*Devekut:* or Communion with God," in *The Messianic Idea in Judaism* (mentioned earlier); and by Moshe Idel in both *Kabbalah: New Perspectives,* and his "Universalization and Integration: Two Conceptions of Mystical Union in Jewish Mysticism," in M. Idel and Bernard McGinn, *Mystical Union and Monotheistic Faith* (Macmillan, 1989). Of special note is Daniel Matt's essay "Ayin" (discussed on p. 184).

Prayer

Perhaps the primary vehicle for mystical communion was prayer. The best synthetic discussion of hasidic prayer is Louis Jacobs's *Hasidic Prayer* (Schocken Books, 1973); an excerpt appears in the Hundert volume. Also, see the Weiss collection and *Your Word Is Fire,* discussed earlier.

Daily Life as Worship

One of the most intriguing, and controversial, aspects of hasidic spirituality is *avodah be-gashmiut,* "service through corporeality." Here the body becomes the locus for mystical experience, and daily life the setting for worship. Important essays on this topic include the deeply insightful (if controversial) work by Martin Buber in *The Origin and Meaning of Hasidism* (Humanities Press International, 1988); and Louis Jacobs's "Eating as an Act of Worship in Hasidic Thought," in S. Stein and R. Loewe, *Studies in Jewish Religious and Intellectual History* (University of Alabama, 1979). A particularly vivid, albeit pious, account of lived religiosity is Aaron Wertheim's "Traditions and Customs in Hasidism," in the Hundert volume.

We have been concentrating, thus far, on literary studies of hasidic piety. Still, there are other means of entering into this thickly textured world. Music, for example, is one of the primary vehicles for mystical communion and exaltation in this tradition. Among the many excellent recordings of hasidic *niggunim* (melodies) are those put out by Chabad (Lubavitch), Bratslav, Bobov, and Modzitz. Get hold of some and enjoy!

Film can also open up the world of hasidic piety. Two works of the experimental filmmaker Zalmen Jofen, himself a Lubavitcher Hasid, are especially recommended. The first is *Prayer,* a seven-minute silent film imbued with a liquid, near-sensual quality. I know of no other visual work that gives such powerful expression to inward states of prayer. The longer *Rituals and Demonstrations* affords a glimpse into the world of sacred study, a wedding, a *farbrengen* (communal gathering) with the *rebbe,* an *upsheren* (the ritual hair-cutting of a three-year-old boy), etc. Both films are available from Taryag Media, Inc., 719 Crown Street, Brooklyn, New York 11213, and from various Jewish video clubs.

Chabad and Bratslav

Two schools have exerted special attraction on students of Jewish mysticism: Chabad (spelled "HaBaD" in scholarly articles) at once the most deeply mystical of sects and the most popular; and Bratslav, a much smaller group, whose spiritual master is Nahman of Bratslav, 1772–1810. The best introduction to Chabad mysticism is Rachel Elior's brilliant essay, "HaBaD: The Contemplative Ascent to God," in Green's *Jewish Spirituality,* vol. 2. Naftali Lowenthal's fine new volume *Communicating the Infinite* (University of Chicago Press, 1990) traces the emergence of the Chabad school as a mass movement. Louis Jacobs discusses the mystical teachings of an early figure, Aaron of Starosselye, in his succinct *Seeker of Unity* (Basic Books, 1966), and translates and annotates an important theoretical tract by Dov Baer of Lubavitch, *On Ecstasy* (Rossel Books, 1982). A full range of

Chabad texts—including Shneur Zalman of Liadi's masterwork, *Tanya*—is available in English through Kohus publications.

Perhaps no other hasidic master has kindled more interest in the reading public than Nahman of Bratslav. An enormously inventive and complex man, his was a life torn between the presence and absence of God. Arthur Green's groundbreaking biography, *Tormented Master* (Schocken Books, 1981), combines textual mastery and psychological insight. Nahman's multitiered tales, classics in their own right, have been ably translated by Arnold Band in *The Tales of Nahman of Bratslav* (Paulist Press, 1978). These narratives are a source for endless interpretation. Helpful readings are provided by Green, Band, and also by Adin Steinsaltz in his *Beggars and Prayers* (Basic Books, 1985). Nahman's dreams provide additional fascination. Arthur Green has translated them in Jay Mirsky and David Stern, *Rabbinic Fantasies: Imaginative Narratives from Classical Hebrew Literature* (Jewish Publication Society, 1990).

Hasidic Homilies

Virtually all the genres of hasidic literature had their origins in the spoken word. Perhaps the central literary genre of hasidic teaching is the homily. The best introduction to these hasidic sermons—and how to read them—is Arthur Green's "Teachings of the Hasidic Masters," in Holtz's *Back to the Sources* (Schocken Books, 1990). Of the hundreds of published homiletical works, only a small handful have made their way into English. My two favorites are Green's translation, *Menahem Nahum of Chernobyl: Upright Practices, Light of the Eyes* (Paulist Press, 1982), and Joseph Dan's anthology *The Teachings of the Hasidim* (Behrman House, 1983). The strengths of the two volumes are complementary: The Dan volume—which presents textual excerpts—affords a panoramic view of hasidic teachings on key themes. Brief annotations are offered. The Green volume, by contrast, offers a concentrated encounter with complete texts, written by one particularly intriguing, and relatively accessible, master. A generous commentary facilitates study.

Tale Literature

Hasidism, Martin Buber once said, was "mysticism become ethos." One of the best windows into the popular aspects of the tradition is the tale literature, i.e., narratives told by Hasidim in praise of their masters. Perhaps the best-known genre of hasidic literature, it was actually the last to appear in print. The classic collection of tales is *In Praise of the Baal Shem Tov*, edited by Ben-Amos and Mintz, discussed above. A recommended anthology is Buber's *Tales of the Hasidim* (two vols. in one, Schocken Books, 1991), which also draws on tales embedded in the homiletical literature. Spirited retellings include Elie Wiesel's *Souls on Fire* (Summit Books, 1982), and this writer's personal favorite, Jiri Langer's *Nine Gates to the Hasidic Mysteries* (Attic Press, 1988).

Latter-day Reverberations: Jewish Mysticism in the Twentieth Century

Most studies of hasidic spirituality focus on the formative period prior to 1815. A few notable exceptions may be found: Heschel's fervent, theologically inflected *A Passion for Truth* (Farrar, Straus and Giroux, 1986) contrasts Menahem Mendel of Kotzk with Kierkegaard. Mordechai Joseph Leiner of Izbica is studied in Joseph Weiss's "A Late Utopia of Religious Freedom," in *Studies in Eastern European Jewish Mysticism*, and now in M. Faierstein's *All Is in the Hands of Heaven* (Ktav Publishing House, 1989). Finally, Nehemiah Polen explores one modern hasidic master's attempt to grapple with radical evil in "Divine Weeping: Rabbi Kalonymous Shapiro's Theology of Catastrophe in the Warsaw Ghetto," in *Modern Judaism* 7:3 (1987): 253–69.

Perhaps the outstanding creative figure in recent Jewish mysticism is Abraham Isaac Kook, both an Orthodox Zionist and a mystic of deep, transcultural vision. While Kook has been avidly studied in Israel, relatively little has appeared in English. The best English-language introduction to his kabbalah is the anthology *Abraham Isaac Kook*, translated and introduced by Ben Zion Bokser (Paulist Press, 1978). A brief discussion of Kook's mysticism is also found in Ariel's *The Mystic Quest* (mentioned earlier).

In recent years Jewish mystical creativity has enriched other realms of Jewish culture and thought: literature, critical theory, visual art, philosophy, and theology (including feminist thought), psychology, even political discourse. This fascinating phenomenon lies beyond the mandate of the present essay. I will here mention only Martin Buber, the best-known Jewish thinker to grapple with—

and reformulate—the mystical tradition. Although influenced by Jewish mysticism throughout his life, young Martin Buber was himself a profound mystic. His essay "The Life of the Hasidim," reprinted in his *Hasidism and Modern Man* (Humanities Press International, 1988) is at once a romantically tinged reading of hasidic mysticism and a spiritual manual for latter-day seekers.

In conclusion, we might note several works that responsibly re-present kabbalah in a contemporary, non-scholarly vein. These include Adin Steinsaltz's aforementioned *Thirteen-Petalled Rose*, Edward Hoffman's psychologically oriented *The Way of Splendor* (Shambhala, 1981), and Herbert Weiner's fine tour guide, *Nine and One Half Mystics: The Kabbalah Today* (Macmillan, 1986); and two works that constitute spiritual manuals of sorts: Aryeh Kaplan's *Jewish Meditation: A Practical Guide* (Schocken Books, 1985); and a book by the "*zeyde* of the Jewish Renewal Movement—Zalman Schachter-Shalomi—a vibrant, deceptively simple book, *The First Step: A Guide for the New Jewish Spirit*, written with Donald Gropman (Bantam, 1983).

When all is said and done, we must still ask: why study the Jewish mystical tradition? What might we learn from studying these complex, often arcane, texts; from listening to their inner music? How might they touch, unsettle, and enrich our lives? Let me suggest a partial answer to these questions.

Studying Jewish mysticism deepens and enlarges our understanding of Judaism. It is eloquent testimony to Scholem's dictum that one cannot predict, on the basis of earlier evidence, what will ultimately be considered authentically Jewish.

The mystical tradition contains some of the most precious resources for Jewish spiritual and theological renewal. It, perhaps more than any other Jewish path, provides models for a life of inwardness. It contains a deep reservoir of symbols, and gives us a language to express moments of ecstasy and wonder, hope and fear, moments of transcending and realizing the self. It helps us understand the metaphorical nature of our God-language, and cautions us against freezing our images of the divine into a powerful few.

We dwell in the shadow of the Holocaust, in a world that is newly fraught with ecological and nuclear dangers. Kabbalah's stress on our cosmic responsibility (broadened and universalized, to be sure) takes on added resonance in such a world, where the planet's well-being is at stake. Kabbalah's vision of a divine-human partnership, where it is the human task to heal the fissures and uplift the divine sparks scattered throughout the world, becomes (to many) newly compelling.

Until now, I have been speaking on a grand scale, suggesting some of the large gifts that the study of Jewish mysticism may afford. Most of the gifts we attain, however, are small ones: minute insights made into a text, the sudden pleasure we feel when the electricity leaps across the synapses and a new connection is made, a better question framed—when we see a world in a grain of sand. But in order to discover such delights we must close this book—and open those others described above.

JEWISH PHILOSOPHY : MEDIEVAL AND MODERN

Michael Paley and Jacob J. Staub

The Value of Jewish Philosophy

What can and should a Jew in the contemporary world believe? There is a common notion, widespread in many Jewish circles today, that the simple and straightforward answer to this question is: "Almost anything. The guidance one can expect from the Jewish tradition is primarily in the areas of action—ritual and ethics."

It was Moses Mendelssohn, initiating the Jewish enlightenment in late-eighteenth-century western Europe, who first made the systematic claim in his book *Jerusalem* (University Press of New England, 1983) that Judaism cares about how you act rather than what you believe. Arguing for the social and political integration of Jews into Western societies, Mendelssohn sought to assure non-Jews that Jews were just like everyone else, except for their adherence to Jewish practice.

For a variety of reasons, Jews of all stripes have since found it convenient to let Mendelssohn's claim go unchallenged. Those interested primarily in halakhic (legal) practice have often been content to avoid the philosophical challenges of the modern era by assuming that they are not relevant to the observance of the commandments. Liberal Jews, on the other hand, have interpreted the alleged Jewish preference for deed over creed as a license for the broadest kind of theological pluralism and for their own claim that the essential core of Judaism is neither Halakhah nor belief, but rather individual and social ethics.

There is a kernel of truth to Mendelssohn's idea. It is in fact the case that Jewish communities in the pre-modern world were led by halakhic authorities whose governance focused primarily on behavior. And it is also true that the specific contents of Aggadah—narrative theology—have never been enforced normatively in a way comparable to that of Halakhah.

The diversity of belief that has existed throughout Jewish history, however, should not be taken as an indication that Jewish authorities didn't care what a person believed as long as one observed the commandments. In fact, Jewish communities frequently have been split over issues of belief. For an insightful description of a notable case that extended over several centuries, see Daniel Jeremy Silver, *Maimonidean Criticism and the Maimonidean Controversy* (Leiden: E. J. Brill, 1965). In addition, Menachem M. Kellner's work *Dogma in Medieval Jewish Thought* (Oxford University Press, 1987) illustrates persuasively that Jewish thinkers throughout the medieval period cared very much about the specifics of Jewish belief.

Moving beyond Mendelssohn's argument is important for any Jew who is interested in the ultimate philosophical questions of our age and who seeks wisdom and guidance from his or her intellectual heritage. It is reassuring to know that the best Jewish minds of the past and present have indeed cared passionately about ideas, and that they have regarded clear and persuasive thinking as critically important to the life of the Jew.

Jews today may be freed by social and cultural circumstances to pursue the truth from sources of their own choosing. As they do so, however, they need not feel orphaned from their past. Jews who are willing to devote the time and effort to the study of Jewish philosophy are likely to find that their own questions are not new, and that a wide range of thoughtful, challenging, and satisfying answers to those questions are available for their consideration.

Where to Begin

Many people who would otherwise be interested in studying Jewish philosophy find themselves intimidated, put off by the apparent difficulty of technical philosophical writing. Those seeking an easy entry back into Jewish culture are certainly more quickly rewarded by beginning with rabbinic midrash, hasidic tales, or discussions of the reasons for Jewish practice. But philosophical study has its own rewards, and those who are interested in the more elaborate perspectives of serious Jewish thinkers through the ages can now find a wealth of resources in English translation. We will first look at overviews and general works on both medieval and modern Jewish philosophy. In the next section we will turn to the individual philosophers.

The reader who begins uninitiated either in Jewish history or Jewish philosophy will be well served by Robert M. Seltzer's *Jewish People, Jewish Thought* (Macmillan, 1980). Seltzer does a masterful job of providing a clear, nontechnical, and intelligent introduction to the various periods of Jewish history and then relating the Jewish thought of the periods to the historical circumstances out of which they emerge. His bibliographies are well selected and are designed to be helpful to those interested in pursuing a topic further. Parts 3 and 4 deal respectively with the medieval and modern periods.

The reader who prefers to begin by investigating particular issues in Jewish philosophy should turn to *Contemporary Jewish Religious Thought* (Free Press, 1988), a comprehensive guide to the full range of topics in Jewish philosophy, edited by Arthur A. Cohen and Paul Mendes-Flohr. The volume is particularly suited to those who prefer to bypass introductory surveys. Each article is written by an expert on the topic with a definite perspective of his or her own. The results are designed to stimulate and provoke, thus engaging the reader immediately in the universe of discourse of Jewish thought.

The best source book for excerpts of texts organized topically is Nahum N. Glatzer's *The Judaic Tradition* (Northvale, N.J.: Jason Aronson, 1987). The selections span the full range of Jewish history and are not confined to philosophical topics or writers. The beginner will thus be well served by being introduced to a wider Jewish perspective before focusing specifically on philosophical approaches.

Those who first prefer to define terms and have clear information about the names and basic perspectives of philosophers should consult Steven T. Katz's *Jewish Philosophers* (Bloch Publishing Co., 1975). While the articles that Katz assembles are taken from the *Encyclopaedia Judaica* and are thus written in a dry style, they provide the most authoritative and comprehensive catalog of the field that is available. Read from cover to cover, this may not be the best book to generate excitement; it is, nevertheless, useful to consult as factual questions arise. Katz's two essays, written especially for the volume, also open up the field in exciting ways.

Those with more traditional backgrounds may enjoy Louis Jacob's *Principles of the Jewish Faith* (Northvale, N.J.: Jason Aronson, 1988), which is structured around Maimonides's thirteen principles of faith and offers a fascinating tour through the history of Jewish discussions about each of the principles. If you are willing to wade through some dense writing, you are likely to find Jacobs's erudition and insightfulness a real treat.

Reading medieval Jewish philosophy presents its own unique challenges. Medieval philosophers wrote in the idiom of the leading philosophical systems of their day—Muslim Kalam, Neoplatonism, and Aristotelianism—frameworks with which most readers today are not likely to be familiar. To understand them, however, it is not necessary to embark on a crash course in classical philosophy. There are a sufficient number of introductions and surveys to guide you, and a slow, careful reading of primary texts quickly yields an acquaintance with the terms and concepts required for a satisfying understanding of their questions, arguments, and conclusions.

The single best survey of medieval and modern Jewish philosophy remains *Philosophies of Judaism* by Julius Guttmann (Schocken Books, 1973). Guttmann presents careful and generally reliable summaries of the thought of Jewish philosophers from Philo through Rosenzweig. One appreciates his succinctness and clarity particularly when his effort is contrasted to more recent attempts at surveys of the field like Collette Sirat's *A History of Jewish Philosophy in the Middle Ages* (Cambridge University Press, 1985), which is far less helpful as an introductory survey.

Isaac Husik's *A History of Mediaeval Jewish Philosophy* (Atheneum, 1974) is a monumental achievement that is best suited for those who prefer digests. His introduction offers a difficult but worthwhile capsule summary of the basic approaches of the various medieval philosophical schools. He then provides a chapter on each of the medieval Jewish philosophers in which he methodically summarizes the contents of each of their works. The result is very dense prose with occasional oversimplifications of complex positions. The information made available, however, serves as a useful encyclopedia. Don't read it to get inspired by the field; once your interest has been aroused elsewhere, however, Husik becomes an indispensable guide.

The clearest and most reliable capsule portrait of the "typical" medieval Jewish philosopher can be found in H. A. Wolfson's *From Philo to Spinoza* (Behrman House, 1977). This short volume brings together two of Wolfson's earlier essays that succeed in presenting the field in a clear and exciting way.

Readers who are impressed with this initial excursion into Wolfson's corpus, and who want to become immersed in the field in all of its technical and challenging aspects, should be aware that it was Wolfson who, almost single-handedly, created the modern academic discipline of medieval Jewish philosophy. Recognizing a unity of purpose in all Jewish philosophers from the first-century Philo until the seventeenth-century Spinoza, Wolfson devoted his life's work to tracing their sources. His many volumes—including *Crescas's Critique of Aristotle* (Harvard University Press, 1929), *The Philosophy of Spinoza* (Harvard University Press, 1983), *The Philosophy of Kalam* (Harvard University Press, 1976), *Repercussions of the Kalam in Jewish Philosophy* (Harvard University Press, 1979), and two volumes of his collected essays, edited by George H. Williams and Isadore Twersky, *Studies in the History of Philosophy and Religion* (Harvard University Press, 1973 and 1977)—comprehensively survey the sources and development of Jewish philosophy for the entire period. Wolfson's work may frustrate those who want to move immediately to the implications of medieval philosophy. He is far more interested in documenting the historical sources and influences of philosophers than in addressing the contemporary significance of their work.

Readers who prefer primary sources to both surveys and secondary studies may want to go directly to J. David Bleich's *With Perfect Faith* (Ktav Publishing House, 1983). Bleich's anthology of medieval philosophical texts is organized around Maimonides's thirteen principles. Each section and passage is preceded by short, helpful introductions. The primary value of the volume, however, lies in the selection of excerpts, each of which enables the reader to get directly at the core of the central issues, and to observe the medieval thinkers in their discussions with one another.

Entry into the world of modern Jewish philosophy may be less intimidating. The beginner should consult the works of Robert Seltzer and Julius Guttmann, mentioned above. Other very readable surveys written for adult study are S. Hugo Bergmann's *Faith and Reason* (Schocken Books, 1963), and Simon Noveck's two books, *Contemporary Jewish Thought: A Reader* and *Great Jewish Thinkers of the*

Twentieth Century (Washington, D.C.: B'nai B'rith, 1985). These works assume no philosophical background and provide a basic familiarity with the names in the field.

Still at an introductory level but more ambitious in exposing the reader to the complexities of the thinkers' ideas are: Eugene B. Borowitz's *Choices in Modern Jewish Thought: A Partisan Guide* (Behrman House, 1983), Eliezer Berkovits's *Major Themes in Modern Philosophies of Judaism* (Ktav Publishing House, 1974), and William E. Kaufman's *Contemporary Jewish Philosophies* (University Press of America, 1986). Each of these works is a partisan guide, as Borowitz freely admits in his subtitle. Borowitz, whose clarity of presentation transcends everything else, is a preeminent spokesman for liberal Judaism; Berkovits actively and sometimes belligerently engages his subjects from the perspective of modern Orthodoxy; and Kaufman writes as a disciple of Mordecai Kaplan and the school of pragmatism.

A more technical guide, but one that truly immerses the reader in the nuts and bolts of the field, is Norbert M. Samuelson's *An Introduction to Modern Jewish Philosophy* (SUNY Press, 1989). Samuelson places each of the modern Jewish philosophers clearly in the context of the general philosophical milieu to which they were responding. Kenneth Seeskin's *Jewish Philosophy in a Secular Age* (SUNY Press, 1990) is also very much worth reading as an excellent example of the emerging discipline of constructive Jewish theology—the attempt not only to study what thinkers in the past said but also to develop out of that study a persuasive philosophy of Judaism for our time.

Samuelson is a key figure behind the Academy for Jewish Philosophy, an organization of Jewish philosophers that meets annually to discuss critical philosophical issues. The published proceedings of its papers reflect some of the best emerging work in contemporary Jewish philosophy. These papers are collected in *Studies in Jewish Philosophy* (University Press of America, 1987), edited by Norbert M. Samuelson, and *Creation and the End of Days* (University Press of America, 1986), edited by Samuelson and David Novak.

Medieval Philosophers

The enterprise of medieval Jewish philosophy can be defined quite simply. It was the attempt of Jewish thinkers in the medieval period to come to terms with the fact that the fundamental beliefs that they inherited from biblical and rabbinic traditions were apparently in conflict with the dominant scientific and philosophical theories of the cultures in which they lived.

Had they chosen to retreat inward, ignoring the surrounding cultures, the Jewish heritage would have been much less rich and vibrant. They were unable to do so, however, because of their conviction that the human species had been created in God's image and thus was obligated to employ all of its God-given faculties, including reason, in pursuit of the truth. For an excellent description of this view, see Herbert Davidson's article "The Study of Philosophy as a Religious Obligation," in *Religion in a Religious Age*, edited by S. D. Goitein (Association for Jewish Studies/Ktav Publishing House, 1974).

Had they simply indulged in apologetics, defending traditional beliefs against competing world views, the development of Jewish thought would have stagnated. To their credit, medieval Jewish philosophers chose instead to view rational philosophy and traditional Jewish teachings as two, mutually correcting avenues that led to the truth. Apparent contradictions between them were not taken as sources of embarrassment, but rather as spurs to further investigation. Perhaps Scripture was being interpreted incorrectly. Perhaps philosophers had proceeded based on incorrect premises. Only when records of divinely revealed teachings and the conclusions of the divine gift of human reason were measured against each other could one be assured that the quest for the truth had been pursued to its limits.

The issues and conflicts that engaged them were serious indeed. Jewish tradition, from the Bible and onward, had presented God as the Creator of the universe, passionately concerned with human affairs and with the Jewish people in particular; God was the Revealer of the Torah who rewarded obedience to its commandments and punished their violation; and God was seen as the Governor of nature and of a history that would one day culminate in messianic redemption.

All of these founding principles of Jewish life came into conflict with the outlook of Greek philosophy. The God of Plato and Aristotle, and of their later Hellenistic and Islamic proponents, was an Unmoved Mover, blissfully self-contemplating and uninvolved in the affairs of the universe—definitely not one who revealed Scripture and commandments and who was capable of miracles. Indeed, the Greek concepts of unity and perfection demanded an unchanging and uninvolved God. Jewish thinkers were clearly committed to the unity and perfection of God. Accepting these Greek conceptions, they could not bring themselves to believe that the literal and traditionally interpreted meaning of Scripture could possibly be its true teaching. Out of their struggle, medieval Jewish philosophy emerged.

Intellectual history doesn't always fit as neatly into our categories as we would prefer. By the above definition, the first "medieval" Jewish philosopher was Philo Judaeus, who lived hundreds of years before the Middle Ages, in first-century Alexandria, the first cultural setting in which Jews were fully immersed in Hellenistic culture. Living in a milieu that was witness to the rise of Neoplatonic philosophy, Philo responded prolifically, recasting the nature of God and the account of Creation and Revelation, and reinterpreting allegorically the stories and commandments of Scripture.

Philo's writings provide a fascinating portrait of a Jew struggling nobly to integrate the disparate sources of his intellectual heritage. *The Essential Philo*, edited by Nahum N. Glatzer (Schocken Books, 1971), is a well-edited, topical primary source. Selections of Philo's works, edited by Hans Levy, can also be

Medieval Jewish philosophers were concerned with scientific, as well as theological, inquiry. These fourteenth-century astronomical tables were intended for use as a perpetual calendar. (Library of The Jewish Theological Seminary of America)

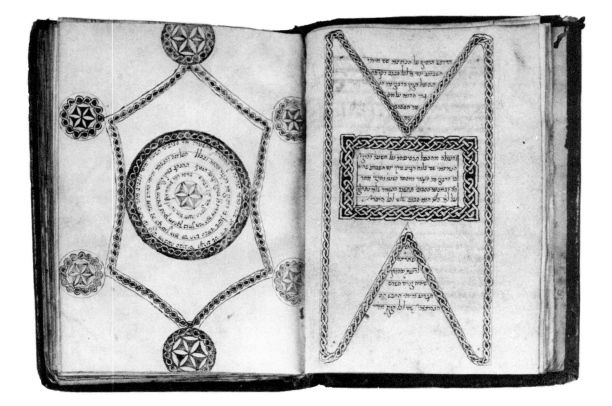

found in *Three Jewish Philosophers* (Atheneum, 1973). For further exploration, the reader can refer to H. A. Wolfson's *Philo: Foundations of Religious Philosophy in Judaism, Christianity and Islam* (Harvard University Press, 1962), and David Winston's *Philo of Alexandria* in the Classics of Western Spirituality series (Paulist Press, 1981). For the full Philo corpus see *Philo of Alexandria,* translated by F. H. Colson and G. H. Whitaker (Harvard University Press, 1929–62).

While Philo's work was related to the development of subsequent Neoplatonic philosophy in late antiquity, it did not have a direct impact upon the later development of Jewish philosophy in the Middle Ages. Medieval Jewish philosophy proper begins much later, in the Muslim world of the ninth century, after the heritage of Greek philosophy and science had been translated by Islamic scholars and had permeated Muslim culture. There are several fine books available to readers interested in the cultural background of the period: Norman Stillman's *The Jews of Arab Lands* (Jewish Publication Society, 1979), Bernard Lewis's *The Jews of Islam* (Princeton University Press, 1984), and S. D. Goitein's *Jews and Arabs* (Schocken Books, 1974).

The ninth century also saw the rise, in the Jewish community, of the Karaite movement. Best known for their challenge to the halakhic authority of Rabbinic Judaism, the Karaites also accused the rabbinic version of Judaism of being theologically primitive in its acceptance of traditional anthropomorphic midrashim. Selections from the writings of Karaite thinkers can be found in Leon Nemoy's *The Karaite Anthology* (Yale University Press, 1952); the best presentation of the movement in all of its facets is Zvi Ankori's *Karaites in Byzantium* (AMS Press Inc., 1959).

The rabbinic leader who was most effective in responding to the Karaite challenge, Saadia Gaon, was, not coincidentally, also the first great medieval Jewish philosopher. Henry Malter's *Saadia Gaon: His Life and Work* (Sepher-Hermon Press, 1969) is a very readable introduction to Saadia's career, though it is now dated by subsequent developments in the field.

Saadia's philosophical work, *The Book of Beliefs and Opinions,* is available unabridged in a fine translation by Samuel Rosenblatt (Yale University Press, 1989) and in a useful abridged translation by Alexander Altmann in the volume *Three Jewish Philosophers,* mentioned previously. As the initiator of the medieval philosophical enterprise, Saadia's writing is more connected to the rabbinic tradition and his work may thus be more accessible to beginners than that of subsequent philosophers. Of particular note are his introductory chapter on the necessity to pursue philosophy, his third chapter on the rationality of the commandments, and his chapters on reward and punishment. The book's opening discussions of Creation and the existence and nature of God provide a clear picture of the intellectual challenges that he and his compatriots faced.

The preeminent Jewish Neoplatonist was Solomon Ibn Gabirol, whose book *The Fountain of Life* (Philosophical Library, 1962), portrays the universe as having emanated from God, first into an ethereal upper world, and only then into the coarse matter of our universe. Gabirol's philosophical influence on subsequent generations was limited, but there are important connections to be made between his outlook and that of later kabbalists. He is best known for his outstanding poetry, much of which reflects his philosophy and which is available in a dual-language edition, *Solomon Ibn Gabirol: Selected Religious Poems*, edited by Israel Davidson (Jewish Publication Society, 1974).

Bahya Ibn Pakuda, who probably lived in eleventh-century Muslim Spain but about whom little else is known, was interested in the internal meaning of the commandments. His book is available in Menachem Mansoor's translation, entitled *The Book of Direction to the Duties of the Heart* (Oxford University Press, 1984). In it, Bahya assimilates the contemplative psychology of both Neoplatonism and the mystical Muslim Sufis as he distinguishes between the external, mechanical observance of the commandments and the internal states of the soul (the duties of the heart) that must accompany that observance. Bezalel Safran's article on Bahya in Isadore Twersky's *Studies in Medieval Jewish History and Literature* (Harvard University Press, 1979), although a bit imaginative, is ultimately a very helpful attempt to place Bahya's work in historical context—as a reaction against the rapid acceptance of Greek values by the Jewish elite of his time. The best overall description of that world can be found in Eliyahu Ashtor's three-volume work, *The Jews of Muslim Spain* (Jewish Publication Society, 1978–85).

Bahya was not alone in his misgivings about the philosophical enterprise. The most powerful and influential voice of protest was that of Judah Halevi, who lived in eleventh-century Spain, a time in which the full force of the challenge of Aristotle's philosophy was being felt. In his book *The Kuzari*, which is available in an unabridged translation by Hartwig Hirschfeld (Schocken Books, 1987) and in an abridged translation by Isaak Heineman that appears in *Three Jewish Philosophers*, Halevi argues that philosophy and reason are inferior to prophecy and direct religious experience. Despite his opposition to philosophy as a religious enterprise, Halevi's own arguments are well schooled in the philosophy of the period, and his discussions of prophecy and prayer are particularly helpful. The book is written as a dialogue, in which a rabbi seeks to answer the questions of the Khazar king, a very readable format.

The twelfth-century philosopher and physician, Moses Maimonides. (Library of The Jewish Theological Seminary of America)

While all of the preceding works are interesting and valuable, the culminating and dominating figure of the period is Moses Maimonides. Commonly called by his acronym, the Rambam (*Rabbi Moses Ben Maimon*) was born in Muslim Spain in 1135, but did most of his writing in North Africa, and particularly in Egypt. His life involved a delicate balance between serving as a halakhic authority and leader of the Egyptian Jewish community, while exploring philosophical questions to which the answers would have been deeply subversive of his followers' faith. No completely satisfying biography has yet been written, but the reader may want to look at A. J. Heschel's *Maimonides* (Farrar, Straus and Giroux, 1982) or another work with the same title by David Yellin and Israel Abrahams (Sepher-Hermon, 1989). Even more insightful about the challenges Maimonides faced as a communal leader is *Crisis and Leadership* by Abraham Halkin and David Hartman (Jewish Publication Society, 1985).

The Rambam's great work of philosophy is *The Guide of the Perplexed*, the greatest achievement of the period. In this work, he recasts the entire range of Jewish beliefs as he addresses those Jews of his period whose faith had been shaken by Aristotelian philosophy. His best-known contribution is his discussion, in part I, of God. This position—referred to as negative theology—maintains that there is absolutely no relation between God's attributes and anything in the created world. Maimonides then proceeds systematically to reinterpret all biblical references to God in ways that accord with his notion of divine perfection. For an illuminating discussion of his negative theology, look at David B. Burrell's *Knowing the Unknowable God* (University of Notre Dame Press, 1986).

In part II of *The Guide*, the Rambam refutes the Aristotelian claim that the world was not created, while acknowledging that creation cannot be demonstrated; he then presents prophecy as the reception by a philosophically trained prophet of the unchanging overflow from God. In part III, he argues that divine providence protects individuals only to the extent that they come to know God, reinterprets the meaning of the commandments as pedagogical devices designed to move people toward the true conception of God, and then concludes the book with an evocative description of the mystical bliss attained by one who achieves true knowledge of God.

Isadore Twersky's *A Maimonides Reader* (Behrman House, 1972) excerpts important sections of *The Guide* while at the same time including substantial sections of the Rambam's code of Jewish law, *The Mishneh Torah*, as well as other important writings such as his Introduction to Perek Helek and his ethical work, "Eight Chapters." Twersky's introduction is helpful, and one should also note his *Introduction to the Code of Maimonides* (Yale University Press, 1980). While the latter is not primarily about the Rambam's philosophy, it is a major contribution to an understanding of the relationship between his rather startling philosophical ideas and his career as a halakhic authority.

There are many translations of *The Guide*, but the best one is that of Shlomo Pines, *The Guide of the Perplexed* (University of Chicago Press, 1974), available in a two-volume paperback edition. In addition to the precision of Pines's authoritative translation, the volume includes two illuminating introductory essays, one by Pines and the other by Leo Strauss. The precision of the Pines translation, however, often leads beginning students to complain about its difficulty. This is because, as the Rambam himself confesses, he did not want to write in a way that would make the work's controversial ideas too accessible to the uninitiated, whose faith might be shaken by them. He believed that a reader who was forced to work to comprehend the text would then be less liable to be shocked or offended by the work's conclusions. The book is therefore filled with apparent contradictions. M. Friedlander's earlier translation, *A Guide for the Perplexed* (Dover, 1956), is less careful about remaining true to the difficulties of the original and may thus be more inviting for an initial reading. The reader can thus choose between accuracy and ease.

Maimonides is so pivotal an authority in Jewish history that contemporary interpreters—even as they pursue their studies with the seriousness and attempted objectivity demanded by scholarship—continue inevitably to view him through the lenses of their own perspectives. The wonder is that the Rambam's own complexity, together with the intentional ambiguity of *The Guide*, bears these interpretations well, so that the book is illuminated in part by each of them. The reader interested in this phenomenon should look at Leo Strauss's *Persecution and the Art of Writing* (University of Chicago Press, 1988), for the Rambam as a closet nonbeliever obfuscating his message for political reasons; David Hartman's *Maimonides: Torah and the Philosophic Quest* (Jewish Publication Society, 1977), for a Maimonides heroically balancing commitment to the halakhah and the Jewish community with devotion to reason; Menachem M. Kellner's *Maimonides on Judaism and the Jewish People* (SUNY Press, 1991), for the Rambam as a model of moderation and tolerance for halakhic Jews; and Yeshayahu Leibowitz's *The Faith of Maimonides* (Adama Books, 1987), for a Maimonides with unwavering opposition to all kinds of idolatry, including that of nationalism.

Other important collections of essays about Maimonides and his philosophy include: *Studies in Maimonides*, edited by Isadore Twersky (Harvard University Press, 1990); *Essays on Maimonides*, by Salo W. Baron (AMS Press Inc.); *Maimonides: A Collection of Critical Essays*, edited by Joseph A. Buijs (University of Notre Dame Press, 1990); and Marvin Fox's *Interpreting Maimonides* (University of Chicago Press, 1990).

Maimonides's older contemporary and fellow Aristotelian, Abraham Ibn Daud, is worth reading, both on his own merits and for the light that his work sheds on that of the Rambam. Norbert Samuelson has translated and edited his work of philosophy, *The Exalted Faith* (Fairleigh Dickinson University Press, 1986). Samuelson's explanations are very clear and the reader who works through them will emerge with a thorough grounding in the field. Gerson D. Cohen has edited and translated Ibn Daud's work of historiography, *The Book of Tradition*

(Oxford University Press, 1967). Cohen's accompanying essays are particularly helpful in setting the cultural scene of early-twelfth-century Muslim Spain, the milieu out of which both Maimonides and Ibn Daud emerged.

The Guide sparked controversies almost immediately. Because of the Rambam's universally acknowledged stature as a halakhic authority, his ideas could not be ignored. Jewish communities everywhere, but especially in Christian Europe, were split into proponents and opponents of the philosophical enterprise. Daniel Jeremy Silver's work, mentioned at the start of the chapter, documents the controversies in very readable fashion, and Bernard Septimus's *Hispano-Jewish Culture in Transition* (Harvard University Press, 1982) is the clearest and most insightful analysis of the subject.

The most interesting of the post-Maimonidean philosophers is Rabbi Levi ben Gerson, or Gersonides, who lived in fourteenth-century Provence. Gersonides was much less guarded than the Rambam about exploring the implications of Aristotelian philosophy in an open way. His major philosophical work, *The Wars of the Lord,* is a brilliant attempt to resolve six issues that Maimonides had left unclear in *The Guide.* Seymour Feldman is engaged in translating *The Wars* in three volumes, two of which have appeared thus far (Jewish Publication Society, 1984 and 1987). Other helpful translations and studies of sections of *The Wars* are Norbert Samuelson's *Gersonides: On God's Knowledge* (Toronto: Pontifical Institute, 1977), a translation of and commentary to part 3, in which Gersonides argues that God's knowledge does not extend to the changing particulars of our world; J. David Bleich's *Providence in the Philosophy of Gersonides* (Yeshiva University Press, 1973), an introduction to and translation of part 4, in which Gersonides makes divine providence over an individual contingent on his or her level of knowledge; and Jacob J. Staub's *The Creation of the World According to Gersonides* (Scholars Press, 1982), a translation of and commentary to sections of part 6, in which Gersonides argues that God created the world out of preexistent matter, and then proceeds to read the text of Genesis in a way that reinforces his point. Gersonides's commentary on the Torah may be the best demonstration of the way medieval philosophers understood Scripture. A translation of it has yet to be published, but readers should look for Robert Eisen's excellent forthcoming study of Gersonides's commentary on Exodus.

The era of medieval Jewish philosophy closes with Hasdai Crescas's *The Light of the Lord,* an attempt to refute the premises of his philosophical predecessors and thus to question the value of the whole enterprise. Crescas led the Jewish community of Christian Spain at the beginning of the fifteenth century, when philosophy had lost its power over the besieged community, and the Aristotelian outlook was beginning to give way to modern science. *The Light* has yet to be translated in its entirety and is most easily accessible through Wolfson's *Crescas's Critique of Aristotle,* cited above.

Jewish philosophy waned after the Spanish Expulsion of the Jews in 1492. For a sample, look at Menachem M. Kellner's translation of Isaac Abravanel's *Principles of Faith* (Oxford University Press, 1985), and for a broad overview consult Bernard D. Cooperman's *Jewish Thought in the Sixteenth Century* (Harvard University Press, 1982) and *Jewish Thought in the Seventeenth Century,* edited by Isadore Twersky and Bernard Septimus (Harvard University Press, 1986). While Jewish writers continued to address philosophical issues, the era had passed in which philosophy had the power to provoke new formulations of Jewish thought. When Jewish philosophy was next attempted in earnest, the modern era had begun to present a whole new set of challenges.

Modern Philosophers

Ironically, the modern period of Jewish philosophy begins with Benedict (Baruch) Spinoza, probably the least Jewish of any Jewish philosopher. The aim of a Jewish philosopher was to translate and validate Judaism in philosophical terms; Spinoza stood against this mission. He inherited the full legacy of both Jewish and classical philosophies, but instead of attempting to harmonize them, he unfurled a stunning critique. His principal view is that all being is this-worldly, and that there is nothing beyond it. What we see or can see is all we get; there is nothing else. In his fine pair of books, *Spinoza and Other Heretics: The Marrano of Reason* and *The Adventures of Immanence* (Princeton University Press, 1989), Yirmiyahu Yovel argues that Spinoza's move from transcendence to immanence marks the key departure of modern Jewish thought from what preceded it. Perhaps best known for having been excommunicated by the Jewish community of Amsterdam in 1656, Spinoza constructed his philosophical system by turning away from Torah and tradition and toward science and mathematics.

It is easy to see the roots of our own worldview in Spinoza's works. His most accessible text is *A Theologico-Political Treatise,* which can be found in *The Chief Works of Benedict de Spinoza,* translated by R. H. M. Elwes (Dover, 1951). In this treatise, Spinoza offers his thoroughgoing critique of prophecy and prophets, miracles and magic, revelation and redemption. The reader will quickly understand the intensity of the Jewish community's reaction to Spinoza's perspective. He grants no special status to the authority of scriptural stories and claims that he examines them from the perspective of empirical facts and laws. For him, biblical accounts of miracles, for example, reflect more on the scientific naïveté of the observers than on the supernatural activity of God in history. Spinoza's masterpiece of systematic philosophy is *The Ethics*, also found in *The Chief Works*.

Ze'ev Levy's *Baruch or Benedict: Some Jewish Aspects of Spinoza's Philosophy* (New York: Peter Long, 1990) examines the Jewish context of Spinoza's thought. A useful guide to Spinoza's Jewish heritage is the two-volume *The Philosophy of Spinoza* by H. A. Wolfson, mentioned earlier in this chapter. Wolfson is at his best when he traces the terms and concepts from classical and medieval philosophy with which Spinoza was working. Understanding the ways that he turned the medieval system on its head only contributes to an appreciation of the revolutionary nature of his thought. Because of his excommunication, the inclusion of Spinoza in the history of Jewish philosophy has remained controversial, at least until recently. His work had a direct and immediate impact on Western philosophy. Its influence on the thinking of Jews, by contrast, was delayed until the Jewish community began to emerge from its cultural isolation at the end of the eighteenth century. At that point, as Jews began to emerge from the ghetto, they were forced to confront the ideas of their surrounding culture—to address the challenge of whether Judaism continued to remain viable in light of contemporary philosophical currents.

The outstanding figure of the period referred to as the Haskalah or Enlightenment, was Moses Mendelssohn. Mendelssohn was the first to pick up the threads of the medieval enterprise in order to articulate an approach to Judaism in the language of the general philosophy of the time. In many ways, Mendelssohn is more significant as a historical figure than he is as a philosopher. Thus, Alexander Altmann's magnificent biography, *Moses Mendelssohn: A Biographical Study* (University of Alabama Press, 1973), is a good place to start. Mendelssohn tried to clarify where Judaism could embrace the new religion of reason and where it could not. His most philosophical book is *Jerusalem* (University Press of New England, 1983).

Subsequent modern Jewish philosophy, like modern philosophy in general, is tied to the destiny of the two dominant modern thinkers: Kant and Hegel. Taken together, their thought constitutes a rejection of religious authority, and the embrace of human autonomy as the ultimate value. As Spinoza had discarded the supernatural, Kant and Hegel conducted an onslaught against the nature of revealed religion. Divine commandments were finite and were thus to be rejected as enslaving. This notion of freedom, a human-oriented freedom, flew in the face of the traditional Jewish belief that obedience to divine law set one free. Kant became the father of the religion of reason, a practical, ethical religion that demanded of individuals that they make autonomous, ethical choices without reference to laws, divine or human. Hegel emerged as the father of the religion of spirit, a religion that articulated a vision of all reality as unified and spiritual. Hegel also held that history was progressive—that we know more now than we did in the past, and that it is knowledge which sets us free. The future, unfettered of the bonds of revealed religion, would lead to absolute spirit. A passionate and accessible contemporary work that deals with the challenges of Kant and Hegel is *Encounters Between Judaism and Modern Philosophy*, by the eminent philosopher Emil Fackenheim (Schocken Books, 1983).

Jewish philosophers of the nineteenth century were compelled to cope with these new perspectives. These philosophers understood philosophy itself as an activity that purified and liberated the mind. The greatest of these nineteenth-century philosophers was Nachman Krochmal. Krochmal understood that Jews of his time would have to confront the challenge of Hegel, and his book, *Guide for the Perplexed of the Time*, translates traditional Jewish concepts into the language of German idealism. Currently, this work is available only in Hebrew. Look, however, for the forthcoming English translation.

In the *Guide*, Krochmal attempted to demonstrate that the idea of historical progress and even of absolute spirit had been present in Judaism long before it was to be found in other religions. A useful description of Krochmal can be found in Guttmann's *Philosophies of Judaism* and in N. Rotenstreich's *Jewish Philosophy in Modern Times* (Holt, Rinehart & Winston, 1968). Simon Rawidowicz's article on Krochmal in his *Studies in Jewish Thought* (Jewish Publication Society, 1974) is also worth reading.

Krochmal is also important because of his pioneering work in what became the School of the Science of Judaism. This school began to conduct historical and philological studies of Jewish texts and sources—research that would have a profound effect on shaping the modern Jewish outlook. A useful context for the importance of Krochmal is provided by a series of very fine essays in the second part of *Jewish Spirituality: From the Sixteenth-Century Revival to the Present*, edited by Arthur Green (Crossroad, 1989).

As Krochmal was the first Jewish Hegelian, Hermann Cohen was the Jewish answer to Kant. In Cohen's early years, his work essentially recast Judaism into Kantian terms. While Cohen believed that it was important to preserve Jewish identity for historical reasons, there was no place in his system for "heteronomously" commanded religion. He believed that ethics would one day develop to a point where religion—and its odd belief in divine authority—would disappear. In the latter part of his life, however, Cohen recognized the need for religion—a religion of reason and ethical monotheism. From this new perspective, Judaism would not resume its legal character of old, but would rather provide the vehicle for the individual Jew to approach the infinite Divine. Ethic and spirit would constitute the "correlation" between God and the individual. These later views are articulated in *The Religion of Reason Out of the Sources of Judaism,* which has been translated by S. Kaplan (Frederick Ungar, 1972). Selections from Cohen's writings may be found in *Reason and Hope,* translated and selected by Eva Jospe (W. W. Norton, 1971). Cohen is a fine writer, and *The Religion of Reason* is an excellent introduction to the flavor of late-nineteenth-century Jewish thought in western Europe. A useful introduction and biography can be found in Bergmann's *Faith and Reason* cited above. Fackenheim's *Encounters* is also very helpful in approaching Cohen's work. Finally, for a look at Cohen's ongoing influence upon the best of contemporary Jewish philosophy, Menachem Kellner's collection, *The Pursuit of the Ideal: Jewish Writings of Steven Schwarzschild* (SUNY Press, 1990), is well worth reading.

The two great figures of twentieth-century Jewish philosophy are Franz Rosenzweig and Martin Buber. In their work, we witness the Jewish response to a new philosophical movement, existentialism. In the early part of the century, over one hundred years after the political emancipation of the Jewish people in western Europe, the world that they confronted was one in which religious authority was diminished and the Jewish community seemed to be completely integrated with secular society. Jewish versions of Hegel's idealism were no longer sufficient to convince Jews of the value of their heritage. What was needed instead was an evocation of the spiritual depth of Jewish experience. Rosenzweig stands at the center of the new movement. The best way to meet Rosenzweig is in Nahum N. Glatzer's *Franz Rosenzweig: His Life and Thought* (Schocken Books, 1961). Reading this biography and collection of excerpts from his writings, one follows the young, assimilated Jew's inspiring journey from his near-conversion to Christianity back to his passionate embrace of the totality of Jewish life. Countless readers have found in Rosenzweig's path the model they seek in order to transcend their alienation from Judaism. Reflecting his personal experience, Rosenzweig's writings testify to the fact that one need not have been immersed in the traditional Jewish world from an early age in order to have access to the power of that world. Rosenzweig's contribution is best understood as a fresh and self-conscious look at Judaism, and for its recognition that Judaism can enhance and bring meaning to Western culture.

The critical chapter in Glatzer's volume is entitled "The New Thinking." For Rosenzweig, modernity and Judaism are not at odds, but are in fact in desperate need of each other. In his magnum opus, *The Star of Redemption,* translated in a complex fashion by William Hallo (University of Notre Dame Press, 1985), Rosenzweig continues his project of the new thinking. In this text, Rosenzweig moves the encounter with the Divine from the level of a people set in history to the realm of a passionate faith relationship between the individual and God. The traditional concepts of creation, revelation, and redemption all take on new meaning, focused in the present and based on relationship to divine love, rather than on divine authority. The best collection of essays about Rosenzweig's thought has been edited by Paul Mendes-Flohr in *The Philosophy of Franz Rosenzweig* (University Press of New England, 1987). In a short collection of his writings edited by Nahum N. Glatzer, *On Jewish Learning* (Schocken Books, 1965), Rosenzweig transforms the law, the commandments, and the observance of the liturgical cycle, providing a new rationale for traditional Jewish observance. Of particular note is his exchange of letters with Martin Buber, at the end of the volume, in which the two great thinkers debate what a modern Jew can believe about the content of the revelation at Sinai.

Buber indeed represents another approach to the meaning of Judaism in the modern world. For Buber, modern Judaism is based on the encounter between each person and God. In the volume *On Judaism,* edited by Nahum N. Glatzer (Schocken Books, 1972), Buber notes that traditional religion, with its laws and rituals, obstructs the divine encounter—a position at odds with that of Rosenzweig.

Buber's central philosophical work is *I and Thou,* his statement of the dialogical principle. It is a work of great power and vision. The traditional translation of the work is by Ronald G. Smith (Scribners, 1984). The preferred translation, however, containing an interesting and controversial prologue, is by Walter Kaufmann (Scribners, 1978). Buber's is an attractive response to the modern secular world, a world devoid of religious intensity. *I and Thou* is a difficult book, best read slowly and only after reading Buber's *The Knowledge of Man,* edited by Mau-

Martin Buber (Library of
The Jewish Theological
Seminary of America)

rice Friedman (Humanities Press International, 1988) which includes an appendix with a wonderful dialogue between Buber and the psychologist Carl Rogers.

There are numerous essays on Buber's *I and Thou*. The best collection is probably the Library of Living Philosophers volume, *The Philosophy of Martin Buber*, edited by Paul Schilpp and Maurice Friedman (La Salle, Ill.: Open Court, 1967). This entire volume is full of interesting articles, including one by the noted French philosopher Emmanuel Levinas.

Buber the philosopher is balanced by Buber the Jewish personality and teacher. While *I and Thou* is certainly Buber's best-known work, it may not be as helpful for the beginner as his more Jewish material, such as *On Judaism* or *Israel and the World* (Schocken Books, 1963). In these volumes, Buber is able to draw a picture of a spiritual revival in Judaism that digs deep into the tradition but is not bound by it. Also of great interest are his biblical insights in *The Kingship of God*

(Humanities Press International, 1988) and *The Prophetic Faith* (Macmillan, 1949). In addition, Buber's penetrating analysis of the relationship between Judaism and Christianity in *Two Types of Faith* (Macmillan, 1986) and his powerful response to the theological challenges posed by the existence of evil in *The Eclipse of God* (Humanities Press International, 1988) are both excellent starting places to understand Buber's response to the predicaments of the modern age.

A healthy portion of the energy of Jewish thinkers in the twentieth century has been devoted to articulating the significance of the revival of Jewish nationalism and the establishment of the Jewish state. Those interested in studying Zionist thought for the first time may want to begin with a history of the Zionist movement, for which either Walter Laqueur's *A History of Zionism* (Schocken Books, 1989) or Shlomo Avineri's *The Making of Modern Zionism* (Basic Books, 1984) is an excellent start.

The single best collection of Zionist writings remains Arthur Hertzberg's *The Zionist Idea* (Atheneum, 1969). Hertzberg has assembled a stunning array of excerpts from the full range of Zionist thinkers. Moreover, his introductory essay provides a penetrating and illuminating analysis of the various, often conflicting, currents in Zionist thought that help the reader to understand the ongoing controversies surrounding the purpose and meaning of the Zionist enterprise.

From the point of view of their influence on subsequent Jewish thought, two Zionist thinkers stand out as especially worthy of further, more intensive study. Ahad Ha'am, the pen name (meaning "one of the people") of Asher Ginzberg, was the founder of cultural and spiritual Zionism, a perspective in the pre-State period that understood the significance of the Jewish return to the Land as being greater than the establishment of political independence. For Ahad Ha'am, the purpose of the new Jewish community in the Land of Israel was to become the center of the much-needed cultural and spiritual revival of Judaism in the modern era, a beacon of light to be followed by Jewish communities in the Diaspora.

Ahad Ha'am became an important figure for a large segment of Diaspora Jews who were concerned by the emphasis of other Zionists on "normalization"—the belief that the Jewish state would render the Jewish people no different from any other nation. Selections of his writings are available in *Ten Essays on Zionism and Judaism* (London: G. Routledge and Sons, 1922) and *Selected Essays of Ahad Ha-Am* (Atheneum, 1970), collected and translated by Leon Simon, whose biography, *Ahad Ha-am* (Jewish Publication Society, 1960) is also of interest.

Most of the early Zionist thinkers were secularists who believed that the nationalist revival would render secondary the religious component of Judaism. It is thus ironic that one of the most influential of the pre-State Zionist writers was Abraham Isaac Kook, the first Chief Rabbi of Palestine. The dominant figure of religious Zionism, Kook can be seen as the bridge between a Jewish past and future.

It is within the context of traditional religious categories that Kook developed his response to modernity, a startling reaffirmation of messianism. While others in the Orthodox camp were rejecting the pioneering work of secular Zionist settlers, Kook viewed them as unwitting tools of a divine plan. His work thus represents an attempt to re-infuse the secular project of Zionism with a sense of redemptive holiness that is at once radically particularistic and broadly universal. His teachings continue to influence Israel's religious community.

The best short biography of Kook can be found in Bergmann's *Faith and Reason* (mentioned earlier). Jacob Agus's *The Banner of Jerusalem* (Bloch Publishing Co., 1946) also provides a useful presentation. The most accessible sampler of his Zionist writings is in Hertzberg's *The Zionist Idea*. The bulk of his work is found only in Hebrew, but a great deal of his most stunning spiritual statements has been translated in the Classics of Western Spirituality series by Ben Zion Bokser in *Abraham Isaac Kook* (Paulist Press, 1978). Bokser also edited *The Essential Writings of Abraham Isaac Kook* (Amity House).

Jewish thinkers in America have faced their own set of unique challenges. The millions of Jewish immigrants from eastern Europe at the turn of the century arrived prepared to embrace American culture unequivocally. Leaving behind traditional communal structures that had been responsible for the preservation of Jewish culture and practice, they found a society that was unprecedented in its willingness to integrate them. By the 1920s, Jewish leaders were already concerned about the corrosive effects of American Jews' freedom upon their Jewish identities.

The foremost thinker to address these issues was Mordecai M. Kaplan. In his first and most important work, *Judaism As a Civilization* (Jewish Publication Society, 1981), he addressed the challenges facing American Jewry in a comprehensive and visionary way. The first to acknowledge that Judaism had always functioned as much more than a religion, he stressed the need to establish organic communities in which Jewish life could be nurtured. Recognizing that Jewish civilization had, contrary to rabbinic claims, always evolved to meet the changing needs of the time, he called for the ongoing reconstruction of Jewish beliefs and practices in light of the best insights and values of contemporary Western culture.

Kaplan subsequently wrote many other works, the best of which are *The Future of the American Jew* (Reconstructionist Press, 1981), in which he explores the implications of his approach for such issues as the Chosen People idea and the status of women in Judaism; *The Meaning of God in Modern Jewish Religion* (Reconstructionist Press, 1975), a wonderful attempt to reinterpret the significance of Jewish holidays in light of contemporary values; *A New Zionism* (Reconstructionist Press, 1959), a clear statement of a devoted follower of Ahad Ha'am; and *The Religion of Ethical Nationhood* (Macmillan, 1970), a call for Judaism to lead the international community toward peace and justice. Mel Scult, Emanuel S. Goldsmith, and Robert M. Seltzer have also edited a valuable collection of essays on Kaplan's thought in *The American Judaism of Mordecai M. Kaplan* (New York University Press, 1990). Finally, for a brief introduction to Kaplan and an indication of his ongoing effect on the Reconstructionist movement, look at *Exploring Judaism: A Reconstructionist Approach*, by Rebecca T. Alpert and Jacob J. Staub (Reconstructionist Press, 1985).

Attempting to reconstruct Judaism in accordance with the rational, scientific outlook of the first half of the century, Kaplan sought to articulate a Judaism without supernaturalism. Abraham Joshua Heschel, the other preeminent thinker who addressed American Jews, had other objectives in mind. For him, the great challenge was not to bring reason into Judaism but rather to demonstrate that the power of the traditional Jewish outlook is still persuasive in an era of secularism, humanism, and technology. It was the American technological context, impersonal and anti-community, that presented Heschel with the foil for his critique.

In addressing the problem, Heschel focuses not only on the Jewish world but on the individual Jew. His greatest systematic statement is in *God in Search of Man* (Farrar, Straus and Giroux, 1976) and its companion volume, *Man Is Not Alone* (Farrar, Straus and Giroux, 1976). Heschel was devoted to restoring the notion of asking religious questions, and his statement in *The Insecurity of Freedom* (Schocken Books, 1972) is an inspiring exploration. Heschel's poetic ability is gripping, and brings the traditional outlook of Jewish faith alive with a power unmatched elsewhere.

In his last book, *A Passion for Truth* (Farrar, Straus and Giroux, 1986), Heschel grapples with the most vexing issue of our times, the Holocaust, through a presentation of two great religious personalities, the Hasidic master Menahem Mendel of Kotzsk, and the philosopher Kierkegaard. Readers should also note Heschel's beautiful recollection of the lost world of eastern European Jewry in *The Earth Is the Lord's* (Farrar, Straus and Giroux, 1978) and his most accessible work, *The Sabbath* (Farrar, Straus and Giroux, 1975).

The classic statement of Modern Orthodoxy is indisputably that of Joseph B.

Abraham Joshua Heschel
(Photograph by Rabbi
Joel Orent)

Soloveitchik, in his classic article, "The Lonely Man of Faith" (*Tradition* magazine, Summer 1965). In it, this preeminent halakhic authority explores the nature of faith for the halakhic Jew. The mentor of generations of Orthodox rabbis and scholars, Soloveitchik represents an approach to halakhic Judaism that is informed by philosophical erudition and does not shrink from the challenges of modern thought. The volumes of his translated writings are well worth reading: *Halakhic Man*, translated by Lawrence Kaplan (Jewish Publication Society, 1984); *The Halakhic Mind: Jewish Tradition and Modern Thought* (Free Press, 1986); and *On Repentance*, translated by Pinchas Peli (Paulist Press, 1984).

Perhaps the most well known of Soloveitchik's disciples is David Hartman, whose work may be the best current attempt to have halakhic Judaism address the challenges of our day. Hartman does not shrink from addressing such thorny issues for Orthodoxy as pluralism among Jews and inter-religious dialogue. Hartman is also at the forefront of discussions in Israel about the Jewish meaning of the State. Readers are advised to begin with Hartman's *A Living Covenant* (Free Press, 1985) or his later work, *Conflicting Visions* (Schocken Books, 1990), which includes an extended conversation with the modern sage and philosopher, Yeshayahu Leibowitz.

The epigraph introducing *Conflicting Visions* is taken from the Talmud: "The tablets and the broken fragments of the tablets were deposited in the Ark" (Berakhot 8b). The line aptly characterizes the current state of the enterprise of Jewish philosophy—an endeavor that seeks to retain the old, even as it creates something new. Three fine attempts to do just that have recently appeared: Judith Plaskow's *Standing Again at Sinai* (Harper & Row, 1990), a first-rate presentation of the feminist approach to issues of Jewish belief; Neil Gillman's *Sacred Fragments* (Jewish Publication Society, 1990), an engaging attempt at creating a new theological approach within the context of the Conservative movement; and Arthur Green's *See My Face, Speak My Name: A Contemporary Jewish Theology* (Northvale, N.J.: Jason Aronson, 1992), a moving and powerful expression of the contemporary meaning of traditional Jewish belief that combines Jewish mystical teachings with the most current insights available in the social sciences. The appearance of these works bodes well for what is yet to come as Jewish thinkers continue the age-old quest to formulate systems of thought that address new generations.

CHAPTER 11

JEWISH WOMEN'S STUDIES

Sue Levi Elwell

Women have always been an integral part of Judaism and Jewish tradition. Women were the matriarchs, the mothers of Israel, the wives and the sisters and the companions to the patriarchs and kings and prophets. They were the wives and sisters and mothers of sages, and, occasionally, they were sages themselves. Jewish women have always made history, and some have left records of their lives and deeds. But until relatively recently, Jewish women's stories remained untold. The history and Torah that most Jews have studied has been incomplete, for the stories of men have not been complemented by stories of women of faith, women of courage, women of insight, and women of wisdom.

It is only in the last twenty years that scholars and teachers have begun to write about the ways that women, both as individuals and as members of groups, have challenged, influenced, and, at times, changed the course of Jewish history and Jewish communal life. The nineteenth-century women's movement influenced several early studies of Jewish women, most notably Nahida Remy's *The Jewish Woman* (Bloch Publishing Co., 1915). The contemporary women's studies movement provided a context for Jewish scholars and educators to pose new questions about women's contributions to Judaism and to examine the centrality of gender in Jewish life and Jewish learning. Jewish women's studies is now well established as an interdisciplinary area of inquiry, including studies in history, religious thought, sociology, literature, and political science.

So where does one begin to learn about Jewish women? What are the primary texts? Where does one learn about Jewish women's past, and the changing role of Jewish women in the present? What are the major social, religious, psychological, and historical issues for contemporary Jewish women? As we search for sources, we find that many of the most innovative and thoughtful responses to such questions have appeared in articles published in a range of popular and scholarly journals. Some of these important pieces have been anthologized, and several of the introductory works in the field are collections. Other essential contributions have appeared as book chapters. Because this essay is primarily concerned with book-length studies, the work of some of the most provocative scholars and thinkers in this field may be underrepresented, and the serious student of Jewish women's studies must turn to publications such as *Lilith, Bridges, Tikkun,* and *Response,* as well as the academic *Journal of Feminist Studies in Religion* for the latest work by scholars such as Rachel Adler, Rebecca Alpert, Marcia Falk, Paula Hyman, T. Drorah Setel, Ellen Umansky, and Chava Weissler.

Six basic resources open the world of Jewish women's studies to the newcomer. First of all, Susan Weidman Schneider's comprehensive *Jewish and Female: Choices and Changes in Our Lives Today* (Simon & Schuster, 1985) is an excellent introduction to the issues and realities of Jewish women's lives in late-twentieth-century America. Compiled by the editor of *Lilith* magazine, *Jewish and Female* speaks with sensitivity to women seeking a way to bring together their "femaleness" and their Judaism; both the traditionalist and one who has felt alienated from Judaism may find assistance in this full volume. The networking directory included in the book was one of the first compilations of its kind, providing readers access to resources including programs on alcoholism, battered women, female cantors, displaced homemakers, divorce, intermarriage, lesbian and gay services, rape crisis centers, ritual objects, scholars and scholarship, single women, Holocaust survivors and their children, and Yiddish and Ladino. While somewhat dated, it is still an excellent guide to services for Jewish women across this continent.

Schneider's accessible and comprehensive work is complemented by four anthologies, whose order of publication mirrors the growth and development of Jew-

ish women's studies. *The Jewish Woman: New Perspectives*, edited by Elizabeth
Koltun (Schocken Books, 1976), grew out of a special issue of *Response* magazine
that Koltun edited in 1973. The twenty-five essays collected in the volume represent first attempts at a critical examination of women and *halakhah* (Jewish
law), Jewish women's historical legacy, and new rituals to celebrate the passages
of women's lives. Several of the contributions are now considered classics, and the
volume continues to be required reading for all newcomers to the field.

The seventies opened with the question: "Can a woman be a Jew?" Koltun's
collection represents a strong affirmative response. The issues raised in Susannah
Heschel's 1973 collection, *On Being A Jewish Feminist* (Schocken Books, 1983),
reflect both greater readiness to challenge the Jewish religious and communal
establishment and a sober awareness of the seriousness and depth of that challenge. In the ten years following the original *Response* collection, an increasing
number of Jewish women were ready to identify themselves as feminists, and to
address the issues that preoccupied them *as feminists* from a Jewish perspective.
Heschel's anthology includes essays on several "family secrets": dysfunctional Jewish families, addictive-compulsive behaviors in the Jewish community, the continued absence of women from Jewish communal leadership, lesbians who are
proud to claim their Jewish identity. The development of a distinctly feminist
theology is offered as a first step toward healing the community and bringing in
those who are no longer content to be invisible.

Although it was initially published in 1972, Evelyn Torton Beck's collection,
Nice Jewish Girls: A Lesbian Anthology (Beacon Press, 1989), did not receive the
recognition it deserved until it was bought by a major publishing house and reissued in an revised and updated edition. Only in the late 1980s did the Jewish
community begin to acknowledge both the presence and the contributions of the
gay and lesbian Jewish community. Beck's anthology, the first to challenge the
Ashkenazi bias of most contemporary Jewish writing, also explored the pain of
being a feminist and lesbian in Israel. It was followed by *The Tribe of Dina: A
Jewish Woman's Anthology*, edited by Melanie Kaye/Kantrowitz and Irena Klepfisz
(Beacon Press, 1989), a rich collection of essays, reminiscences, poetry, midrash,
political writings, interviews, and photographs. Dedicated to Jacob's daughter
Dina, "who went out to see the daughters of the land," these writings begin to
reconstruct the lost legacy of Jewish women.

The sixth work on the "read these first" list differs in tone and texture from
the other books discussed here, for it is written by a woman who defines herself
both as an Orthodox Jew and a feminist. Blu Greenberg's *On Women and Juda-*

ism: A View from Tradition (Jewish Publication Society, 1983) is a thoughtful collection of essays that reflects the author's love for and commitment to a tradition she acknowledges as deeply patriarchal, yet offering a range of opportunities to women for spiritual growth and communal support. The essay that opens the book, "Feminism: Is It Good for the Jews?" examines Greenberg's understanding of the feminist challenge to Judaism, and suggests that in the rush toward equality women must not forget how the roles of wife, mother, and nurturer have sustained Jewish women and Jewish families throughout the ages. As Greenberg continues to question both feminism and Judaism, she recognizes that she is committed to having the best of both of these worlds she inhabits. Greenberg is optimistic about a future where both men and women can explore all aspects of their Judaism.

Once you have begun to get a sense of the breadth of issues raised in this field, you will want to pursue your own areas of interest. The balance of this chapter introduces works that discuss religious life and law, theology, women's spiritual quest, biblical studies, new texts and new traditions, history, Israel, Jewish lesbian experience, women's fiction and poetry, feminist literary criticism, and essential reference guides.

Several recent works examine the role of women in traditional Jewish religious life and law. Rachel Biale's *Women and Jewish Law: An Exploration of Women's Issues in Halakhic Sources* (Schocken Books, 1984) is a detailed, yet accessible, study of traditional sources. With great sensitivity to the distance between some modern readers and the texts in question, Biale presents a wealth of rabbinic and contemporary halakhic (legal) information and argumentation. *Chattel or Person? The Status of Women in the Mishnah* by Judith Romney Wegner (Oxford University Press, 1988) is a sophisticated analysis and close reading of essential Talmudic texts. Wegner's reading is informed by her training as a jurist and a Jewish scholar, and a keen understanding of feminist theory. Julie Ringold Spitzer's *Spousal Abuse in Rabbinic and Contemporary Judaism* (National Federation of Temple Sisterhoods, 1985) analyzes rabbinic texts on this timely topic.

How do thoughtful modern women respond to the tradition? The only book-length, systematic study of Jewish feminist theology available to date is Judith Plaskow's *Standing Again at Sinai: Judaism from a Feminist Perspective* (Harper & Row, 1990). Plaskow's provocative study examines the traditional areas of God, Torah, and Israel under the lens of contemporary feminist scholarship. She suggests new images of God and ways to speak to God, poses important questions about rethinking the canon of texts that we hold sacred, and proposes new ways of thinking about the Jewish community. Her important final chapter, which describes a new "theology of sexuality," suggests new images of God as lover and companion that have implications for the erotic connections that fuel our lives.

Women's spiritual quests are emerging as a new genre of Jewish writing. In *Words on Fire: One Woman's Journey into the Sacred* (Harcourt Brace Jovanovich, 1990), Vanessa Ochs explores the world of traditional Jewish Torah study from the perspective of a contemporary woman. Tamar Frankiel's *The Voice of Sarah: Feminine Spirituality and Traditional Judaism* (San Francisco: HarperCollins, 1990) presents traditional Judaism through the loving eyes of a thoughtful, observant Jew.

The spiritual quest often leads to a search for a usable past. The last twenty years have been a very fertile period for feminist bible studies, and a number of notable scholars have addressed the biblical text. *Discovering Eve: Ancient Israelite Women in Context*, by Carol Meyers (Oxford University Press, 1988), is an essential resource. Phyllis Trible's pioneering *God and the Rhetoric of Sexuality* (Philadelphia: Fortress Press, 1978) is an accessible scholarly work. Athalya Brenner's *The Israelite Woman: Social Role and Literary Type in Biblical Narrative* (Sheffield, England: JSOT Press, 1985) is a compact, provocative study by an Israeli Bible scholar. Savina Teubal's *Sarah the Priestess: The First Matriarch of Genesis* (Athens, Ohio: Swallow Press, 1984), and her more recent *Hagar the Egyptian: The Lost Tradition of the Matriarchs* (Harper & Row, 1990) show how traditional readings of the biblical text have ignored a vibrant women's culture of connection and mutual support.

In addition to the monographs above, several excellent collections of feminist scholarship on the Hebrew Bible include the works of Jewish scholars writing from a Jewish perspective. Esther Fuch's article, "The Literary Characterization of Mothers and Sexual Politics in the Hebrew Bible," appears in *Feminist Perspectives on Biblical Scholarship*, edited by Adela Yarbro Collins (Scholars Press, 1985). Drorah Setel's "Prophets and Pornography: Female Sexual Imagery in Hosea," in *Feminist Interpretation of the Bible*, edited by Letty Russell (Philadelphia: The Westminster Press, 1985), exposes the essentially pornographic imagery utilized in the Book of Hosea, and raises serious questions about reading this prophetic portion as part of public worship.

Challenge of the texts that stand at the center of public Jewish prayer often leads to a reconsideration of the form and content of traditional prayer itself. Since the late 1960s, Jews across the country have been wrestling with the androcentric language of the traditional liturgy. The first fruits of this struggle were the early feminist Passover *haggadot,* many of which were duplicated and passed from hand to hand. The San Diego Women's Institute for Continuing Jewish Education published their first haggadah in 1979, and others have appeared since, including such diverse interpretations as *Spring Festival for Women: A Feminist Haggadah* (Lebanon, N.H.: New Victoria Publishers, 1974), created by a small feminist collective that developed its haggadah after nine years of celebrating the seder together, to *The Telling: A Loving Hagadah for Passover* (Oakland, Calif.: Rakhamim Publications, 1983), edited by Dov ben Khayyim, which includes both traditional Hebrew blessings and blessings that have been reformulated in the feminine voice. *The Shalom Seders,* three haggadot compiled by New Jewish Agenda (Adama Books, 1984), are all non-sexist and egalitarian, while leaving the traditional Hebrew unchanged. *On Wings of Freedom: The Hillel Haggadah for the Nights of Passover,* edited and translated by Richard N. Levy (B'nai B'rith Hillel Foundation and Ktav Publishing House, 1989), is a poetic, egalitarian translation of the traditional text with a wonderful commentary. The traditional Hebrew is left unchanged.

The first Sabbath prayer book to recognize the need to include women's voices in the liturgy was *V'Taher Libenu,* the prayer book of Congregation Beth El of the Sudbury River Valley (1980). While the editors were scrupulous about alternating between masculine and feminine God-language in the English sections, the only Hebrew prayer that was altered was the *amida;* the matriarchs's names were added to those of the patriarchs. In 1984, The Women's Institute for Continuing Jewish Education in San Diego issued *On Our Spiritual Journey: A Creative Shabbat Service.* This abbreviated service was designed by a *havurah* (religious fellowship) composed solely of women, but could certainly be used by a congregation of men and women. The compilers attempted to integrate both male and female images of God and to offer alternatives to the traditional Hebrew blessing formulations. While the results are, at times, uneven, they reflect the pathbreaking nature of this work.

By the end of the 1980s, both the mainstream and the alternative Jewish community had produced *siddurim* (prayer books) that provided alternatives to the traditional representation of God as male in both Hebrew and English, added the matriarchs to the patriarchs in the *amida* prayer, *and* included women's writings as sources for prayer and reflection. *Or Chadash,* the Sabbath prayer book of the P'nai Or Religious Fellowship (Philadelphia, 1989), was published as a working document in a loose-leaf notebook. The explanatory notes are as important as the prayers themselves, for the editors provide a rationale for a guide that challenges traditional notions of the interaction between human beings and the Creator that we call prayer. *Or Chadash* includes a rich offering of poems, songs, and prayers that celebrate the experience of *all* Jews.

Kol Haneshamah, the experimental Sabbath evening prayer book of the Reconstructionist movement (Reconstructionist Press, 1989), provides egalitarian translations of all of the Hebrew portions of the text (and transliterations of many prayers), as well as including a thoughtful commentary. Most notably, the volume includes an extensive alternative *amida* including new, inclusive prayers in English and Hebrew.

The editors of *The Gates of Repentance* (New York: Central Conference of American Rabbis, 1978) attempted to use egalitarian language in the English translation in the *mahzor* (High Holiday prayer book) for the Reform movement, but were unable to find satisfactory alternatives to "Our Father, our King." *Wings of Awe*, a High Holiday mahzor compiled by Richard Levy (B'nai B'rith Hillel Foundation, 1985), offers a rich bounty of translations and interpretations, and parenthetically includes the matriarchs whenever the Hebrew text invokes the patriarchs. While other traditional Hebrew prayers are not complemented by alternative formulations, Levy is scrupulous about maintaining egalitarian translations throughout the text.

Work with traditional liturgy and rituals has been complemented by the development of new ritual and liturgical texts. Penina Adelman's *Miriam's Well: Rituals for Jewish Women Around the Year* (Fresh Meadows, N.Y.: Biblio Press, 1990) is a rich source of guidance and wisdom for those seeking to create and participate in the celebration of Rosh Hodesh (the new month). Adelman teaches through example and story, and introduces the reader to a wide range of sources that can deepen the communal experience of this reclaimed ritual.

The cycles of women's lives are being celebrated in a wide range of settings and by women from many Jewish backgrounds, and many of these rituals have been described and analyzed in the periodical literature. In addition, several book-length publications include new rituals for the passages of Jewish women's lives. *A Ceremonies Sampler: New Rites, Celebrations and Observances of Jewish Women*, edited by Elizabeth Resnick Levine (San Diego: Women's Institute for Continuing Jewish Education, 1991), includes twenty-two ceremonies and rituals that mark biological, developmental, and spiritual changes including pregnancy, infertility, divorce, rabbinic ordination and mourning. Several rituals for naming baby girls and welcoming them into the covenant are presented in Anita Diamant's *The New Jewish Baby Book*. Egalitarian *ketubot* (marriage documents) are described in Diamant's *The New Jewish Wedding* (Summit Books, 1986), as are suggestions for transforming the traditional Jewish wedding into an experience that focuses on the equality of the two partners entering into the covenant of marriage. *Midlife, A Rite of Passage & The Wise Woman: A Celebration* by Irene Fine (San Diego: Women's Institute for Continuing Jewish Education, 1988) provides both ceremonies and analysis of rituals for celebrating the process of menopause, and for women over sixty, claiming the status of elder in the Jewish community. Fine discusses the impact of public, communal celebrations of what have been, traditionally, private passages, and confronts the gynephobia and ageism that is so pervasive in both traditional and modern cultures. The range of ceremonies presented attests to the hunger of many Jews for increased opportunities for celebration.

Ritual provides a bridge from the past to the present, and from the present to the past. What are the sources of Jewish women's past? In 1976, two Jews who were frustrated by the lack of available material on Jewish women compiled a book of sources on Jewish women from ancient times until the present. The resulting study, *Written Out of History: Our Jewish Foremothers,* by Sondra Henry and Emily Taitz (Fresh Meadows, N.Y.: Biblio Press, 1990), remains the single one-volume study of Jewish women's history, and is an accessible "first book" for many newcomers to the field, despite the absence of critical analysis and complete documentation.

The recently published *Jewish Women in Historical Perspective,* edited by Judith R. Baskin (Wayne State University Press, 1991), is an essential resource. Baskin's work includes twelve essays by leading scholars on Jewish women's lives from biblical times to the present, providing a comprehensive overview of the field of Jewish women's history.

In addition, there are several excellent one-volume scholarly studies of women in particular historical periods. Bernadette J. Brooten's *Women Leaders of the Ancient Synagogue: Inscriptional Evidence and Background Issues* (Scholars Press, 1982) is an indispensable source of information on an otherwise lost chapter of history. Deborah Hertz's *Jewish High Society in Old Regime Berlin* (Yale University Press, 1988) includes valuable material about the Jewish women who led the literary salons of Berlin. Marion Kaplan's *The Jewish Feminist Movement in Germany: The Campaigns of the Judischer Frauenbund, 1904–1938* (Westport, Conn.: Greenwood Press, 1979) is another example of a well-researched rescue operation of a crucial development of modern Jewish history ignored by mainstream Jewish historians. *Women of Theresienstadt: Voices from a Concentration Camp,* by Ruth Schwerteger (St. Martin's Press, 1989), is a brief study of female inmates of Hitler's "model ghetto."

Studies of Jewish American women include *The Jewish Woman in America,* by Charlotte Baum, Paula Hyman, and Sonya Michel (New American Library, 1977). Written for the general reader, the book focuses on the economic, social, and family lives of Ashkenazi women in the first half of the twentieth century, and includes a provocative chapter on the portrayal of Jewish women in American Jewish fiction. Another readable overview is provided by Jacob Rader Marcus in his *The American Jewish Woman, 1654–1980* (New York and Cincinnati: Ktav Publishing House and The American Jewish Archives, 1981). In a companion volume, *The American Jewish Woman: A Documentary History* (1981), Marcus, the founder of the American Jewish Archives, brings together an invaluable collection of material by both well-known and otherwise forgotten American Jewish women.

Sidney Stahl Weinberg's *The World of Our Mothers: The Lives of Jewish Immigrant Women* (Schocken Books, 1990) is a well-organized study of immigration and adaptation that is useful both to the general reader and the scholar. Weinberg skillfully weaves together her extensive reading of both fiction and nonfiction by immigrant women with interviews with informants from similar backgrounds. Her book provides an excellent and necessary complement to Irving Howe's widely read *World of Our Fathers* (Schocken Books, 1989). Susan A. Glenn's *Daughters of the Shtetl: Life and Labor in the Immigrant Generation* (Cornell University Press, 1990) is an engaging scholarly analysis of Jewish women's activities in the Labor movement.

Linda Gordon Kuzmack's comparative study, *Woman's Cause: The Jewish Woman's Movement in England and the United States, 1881–1933* (Ohio State University Press, 1990), examines the simultaneous development of Jewish feminist movements on both sides of the Atlantic.

Few scholarly studies speak as eloquently as Jewish women through history have spoken for themselves. One of the most important documents in pre-modern Jewish literature is *The Memoirs of Glückel of Hameln,* (Schocken Books, 1977), a delightfully written narrative that offers rare insight into Jewish life in seventeenth-century Germany. Glückel's handwritten manuscript was not transcribed and published in the original Yiddish until one hundred seventy years after her death, and shortly thereafter it was translated into modern German by Bertha Pappenheim, one of Glückel's descendants.

At the end of the nineteenth and in the first quarter of the twentieth century, a number of Jewish women took pen in hand to record the stories of their lives. Most interesting are the immigrant narratives, particularly Mary Antin's *From Plotzk to Boston* (Markus Wiener, 1986) and Anzia Yezierska's autobiographical

Red Ribbon on a White Horse (Persea Books, 1988). Elizabeth Stern's *I Am a Woman and a Jew*, written under the pseudonym Leah Morton (Markus Wiener, 1986) depicts the confusion caused by acculturation and assimilation in America more directly than do the autobiographical works of her better-known peers Edna Ferber and Fanny Hurst.

Historians Ruth Rosen and Sue Davidson rescued the letters of Maimie Pinzer from oblivion, and through *The Maimie Papers* (The Feminist Press, 1977) we learn of one woman's successful journey from prostitution to social reformer. Sophie Trupin's unique story of Jewish life on the Great Plains is told in *Dakota Diaspora* (Berkeley: Alternative Press, 1984). Kate Simon's three-part autobiography presents one woman's view of growing up Jewish in New York: *Bronx Primitive: Portraits in a Childhood* (Harper & Row, 1983), *A Wider World: Portraits in an Adolescence* (Harper & Row, 1987), and *Etchings in an Hourglass* (Harper & Row, 1990). Faye Moskowitz's stories in *A Leak in the Heart: Tales from a Woman's Life* (Boston: David R. Godine, 1987) are powerful, beautifully crafted evocations of a midwestern girlhood. Kim Chernin's *In My Mother's House: A Daughter's Story* (Harper & Row, 1984) not only reconstructs Chernin's mother's story, but also tells her own.

Anne Frank's *Diary of a Young Girl* (Pocket Books, 1990) remains the classic Holocaust memoir, now complemented by the haunting poetry of *An Interrupted Life: The Diaries of Etty Hillesum* (Pantheon Books, 1983) and *Etty Hillesum: Letters from Westerbork* (Pantheon Books, 1986). In addition to the many Holocaust memoirs written in the last thirty years, *Women of Exile: German Jewish Autobiographies Since 1933*, edited by Andreas Lixl-Purcell (Westport, Conn.: Greenwood Press, 1988) is a powerful collection of previously silent voices.

Several excellent biographies tell the stories of outstanding and memorable Jewish women. *Rachel Varnhagen: The Life of a Jewish Woman*, by Hannah Arendt (Harcourt Brace Jovanovich, 1974), is a study of the intellectual and social world of one eighteenth-century saloniere and her struggle with her Jewish identity. Ellen Umansky's *Lily Montagu and the Advancement of Liberal Judaism: From Vision to Vocation* and the companion volume, *Lily Montagu: Sermons, Addresses, Letters and Prayers* (New York: Edwin Mellen Press, 1984 and 1985) explore Montagu's pivotal role in the development of liberal Judaism. Eve Merriam's biography, *Emma Lazarus: Woman with a Torch* (Citadel Press, 1956), remains one of the most accessible studies of the poet who is remembered for writing the poem for the base of the Statue of Liberty. *Solidarity Forever: Rose Schneiderman and the Women's Trade Union League*, by Gary Edward Endelman (Arno Press,

Emma Lazarus, author of
the poem at the base of the
Statue of Liberty.
(Library of The Jewish
Theological Seminary
of America)

1982), is the only biographical study of this important labor leader. Elisabeth
Israels Perry's *Belle Moskowitz: Feminine Politics and the Exercise of Power in the
Age of Alfred E. Smith* (Oxford University Press, 1987) is a fascinating study of
one of Governor Smith's most influential political advisers. Joan Dash's well-
researched *Summoned to Jerusalem: The Life of Henrietta Szold* (Harper & Row,
1979) tells of the complex, brilliant woman whose accomplishments included
founding the Hadassah movement and medical center in Jerusalem. *Jewish
Grandmothers*, edited by Sydelle Kramer and Jenny Masur (Beacon Press, 1976),
is an engaging collective biography that inspired oral history projects in many
Jewish communities. Emma Goldman's autobiography, *Living My Life* (2 vols.,
Dover) is complemented by a number of biographical studies, including Alix
Kates Shulman's *To the Barricades: The Anarchist Life of Emma Goldman* (Crow-

Henrietta Szold, the founder of Hadassah. (Library of The Jewish Theological Seminary of America)

ell, 1971) and Alice Wexler's *Emma Goldman: An Intimate Life* (Pantheon Books, 1984) and *Emma Goldman in Exile: From the Russian Revolution to the Spanish Civil War* (Beacon Press, 1989).

Two important areas of Jewish women's studies are that of Israeli women and lesbian women. While the comprehensive study of women's lives and experiences as shapers of Israeli politics, society, and culture remains to be written, several works explore aspects of Israeli women's experience. Ada Maimon's *Women Build a Land* (Herzl Press, 1962), and *The Plough Woman: Memoirs of the Pioneer Women of Palestine*, edited by Rachel Katznelson Shazar (Herzl Press, 1975), are complementary commentaries on women's lives during the first two decades of the state. Israeli women's memoirs include *Woman of Violence: Memoirs of a Young Terrorist 1943–1948*, by Geula Cohen (Holt, Rinehart & Winston, 1966), *Han-*

nah Senesh: Her Life and Diaries (Schocken Books, 1973), and Golda Meir's *My Life* (Dell, 1976).

Lesley Hazelton's *Israeli Women: The Reality Behind the Myths* (Simon & Schuster, 1977) was the first contemporary feminist critique of Israeli women written in English, followed by *Daughters of Rachel: Women in Israel*, by Natalie Rein (Penguin Books, 1980). Melford Spiro's pioneering work on kibbutz women is presented in *Gender and Culture: Kibbutz Women Revisited* (Schocken Books, 1980). Scholarly studies include *Ginger and Salt: Yemini Jewish Women in an Israeli Town*, an anthropological analysis by Lisa Gilad (Boulder: Westview Press, 1989). Marcia Freedman's memoir, *Exile in the Promised Land* (Ithaca, N.Y.: Firebrand Books, 1990), is a painful commentary on how the Zionist vision has betrayed not only women but all who are considered "outsiders." Myra [Miriyam] Glazer's collection *Burning Air and a Clear Mind: Contemporary Israeli Women Poets* (Athens, Ohio: Ohio University Press, 1981) provides a forum for Israeli women's voices that are too rarely heard. Letty Cottin Pogrebin's *Deborah, Golda, and Me: Being Female and Jewish in America* (Crown Publishers, 1991) describes her personal decision to return to Judaism and attempt to reconcile her Jewish identity with her commitment to feminism.

The field of Jewish lesbian writing is producing a rich harvest. Since the initial publication of *Nice Jewish Girls* in 1972, many Jewish lesbians have explored their Jewishness in print. Alice Bloch's *The Law of Return* (Boston: Alyson Publications, 1983) is a moving account of a young woman's sojourn in Israel where she explores her Judaism, her feminism, and her lesbianism. Leslea Newman's *A Letter to Harvey Milk* (Ithaca, N.Y.: Firebrand Books, 1988) is an anthology of short stories, many autobiographical. In *My Jewish Face and Other Stories* (San Francisco: Spinsters/Aunt Lute Book Company, 1990), Melanie Kaye/Kantrowitz chronicles her own political growth with sharp humor and keen insight. Much of the poetry of Adrienne Rich and Irena Klepfisz explores the dark corners of Jewish historical consciousness from a uniquely Jewish lesbian perspective.

Twice Blessed: On Being Lesbian, Gay and Jewish (Beacon Press, 1989) is an anthology on Jewish lesbian and gay issues and experiences edited by Christie Balka and Andy Rose which includes essays by lesbian and gay Jews, their parents, and rabbis who have worked in the gay community.

The expanding body of historical, biographical, and autobiographical studies of Jewish women's lives is complemented by an equally bountiful body of Jewish women's fiction. Until recently, twentieth-century Jewish fiction seemed to be an entirely male enterprise. However, readers have begun to hear the strong, insistent, richly colored voices of Jewish women writing in English. Those voices are changing the ways that we see the worlds that we inhabit.

The first contemporary anthology of Jewish women's fiction was *The Woman Who Lost Her Names: Selected Writings by American Jewish Women*, edited by Julia Wolf Mazow (Harper & Row, 1981). This collection includes both previously published and unpublished pieces by both well-known and not-yet-known writers whose lives span a hundred-year period. Two subsequent short story anthologies, *America and I*, edited by Joyce Antler (Beacon Press, 1990), and *Shaking Eve's Tree*, edited by Sharon Niederman (Jewish Publication Society, 1990), further widen the world of Jewish women's writing, carrying on Mazow's broad vision.

Beyond the anthologies, readers will want to explore the works of writers such as Anzia Yezierska, beginning with *The Bread Givers* (Persea Press, 1975), and Esther Broner's *A Weave of Women* (Indiana University Press, 1985), a visionary portrayal of a community of women in the old city of Jerusalem. Esther Kreitman's

Some recent liturgical innovations by women have revived *Rosh Hodesh* rituals, celebrating the new month. (Photograph by Lori Grinker/Contact Press Images)

Deborah (St. Martin's Press, 1984) is a recently discovered autobiographical novel by the sister of I. J. and I. B. Singer. Nessa Rapoport's *Preparing for Sabbath* (Biblio Press, 1988) is a contemporary Jewish woman's coming-of-age novel. Deena Metzger's haunting *What Dinah Thought* (Viking Penguin, 1989) also explores Israel through the eyes of a modern woman, a woman in search of a mythic past that will inform her present. Anne Roiphe's *Lovingkindness* (Warner Books, 1989) is an intense exploration of the parallel spiritual struggles of a woman and her adult daughter. Other recent fiction includes Meredith Tax's popular novel on the rise of the labor movement, *Rivington Street* (Avon Books, 1990), Lynne Sharon Schwartz's *Disturbances in the Field* (Bantam, 1985), and Rhoda Lerman's *God's Ear* (Henry Holt, 1988). Two new voices are heard in *Secret Correspondence*, by Marcia Golub (Ticknor & Fields, 1990), and *Missing*, by Michelle Herman (Columbus, Ohio: Ohio State University Press, 1990).

As Marcia Cohn Spiegel has noted in her introduction to *Women Speak to God: The Prayers and Poems of Jewish Women*, which she edited with Deborah Lipton Kremsdorf (San Diego: Women's Institute for Continuing Jewish Education, 1987), Jewish women have been writing poems and songs since biblical times, but until recently, many of these songs have been lost or buried. While women's poems have begun to appear in general anthologies of Jewish poetry, there are only a small number of collections devoted entirely to the work of Jewish women poets. Those include: *Sarah's Daughters Sing: A Sampler of Poems by Jewish Women*, edited by Henny Wenkart (Ktav Publishing House, 1990), and *Bubbe Meisehs by Shayneh Maidelehs: An Anthology of Poetry by Jewish Granddaughters about Our Grandmothers*, edited by Leslea Newman (Santa Cruz, Herbooks, 1989).

Jewish women poets whose work reflects a particularly Jewish consciousness include (in alphabetical order): Amy Blank, Ruth Brin, Chana Bloch, Marcia Falk, Leah Goldberg, Pamela White Hadas, Shirley Kaufman; Irena Klepfisz, Gertrud Kolmar, Else Lasker-Schuler, Diane Levenberg, Alicia Ostriker, Linda Pastan, Marge Piercy, Dahlia Ravikovitch, Adrienne Rich, Muriel Rukeyser, Ruth Whitman, Zelda, and Linda Zisquit, to name just a few.

For the reader interested in literary criticism, three recent books examine Jewish writing from a feminist perspective: Nehama Aschkenasy's *Eve's Journey: Feminine Images in Hebraic Literary Tradition* (University of Pennsylvania Press, 1987), Esther Fuchs's *Israeli Mythogonies: Women in Contemporary Hebrew Fiction* (SUNY Press, 1987), and Marlene E. Heinemann's *Gender and Destiny: Women Writers and the Holocaust* (Westport, Conn.: Greenwood Press, 1986).

No listing of books on Jewish women would be complete without Aviva Can-

Women registering to vote, New York City, 1936. (ILGWU Records, Labor-Management Documentation Center, Cornell University)

tor's essential bibliography, *The Jewish Woman: 1900–1985* (Fresh Meadows, N.Y.: Biblio Press, 1987). First published in 1979, and augmented by two supplements, and finally the preparation of a second edition, with additional citations by Ora Hamelsdorf, the bibliography reflects the outpouring of new work on and by women. Cantor's incisive introductory essay establishes the boundaries of Jewish women's studies, and her bibliographic annotations are thoughtful, if subjective. My own *Jewish Women's Studies Guide* (University Press of America and Biblio Press, 1987) is a compilation of syllabi that integrates the study of women into university and adult education courses.

As the twentieth century draws to a close, there are an increasing number of resources for exploring the lives, the contributions, and the challenges of Jewish women. As the field of Jewish women's studies continues to expand, we can look forward to a growing scholarly and popular literature which celebrates the full diversity of the Jewish community.

CHAPTER 12

HEBREW LITERATURE

Alan Mintz

It is hardly an exaggeration to observe that the revival of Hebrew as a modern spoken language has something of the miraculous about it. There surely can be few other instances in which an ancient tongue has been brought back to life to become the everyday speech used at all levels, high and low, of a new nation. Whether in law, science, the military, or in affairs of the heart or the slang of children in the schoolyard—Hebrew has established itself in ways hardly imagined by the most extravagant Zionist visionaries. Yet at the same time, the student of Jewish history recognizes a logic behind the miracle. Hebrew was never abandoned in the millennia following the Bible. In addition to being the language of prayer and learning, Hebrew served as the poetic idiom for writing of love, wine, and fame, and as the mode of communication among scholars. Far from being dead, Hebrew never ceased to develop.

These dual qualities of miraculous revival and historical persistence mark the paradox of Hebrew reborn. On the one hand, with its new terms and expressions, Modern Hebrew represents the dynamic reality of Israeli society, the revolutionary creation of the Jewish people. On the other hand, Modern Hebrew carries within it the successive layers of earlier Jewish experience, the evolution of Jewish civilization from the Bible to the Talmud and on through the Middle Ages. In language, as in perhaps no other area of human culture, are the revolutionary and the traditional forced to coexist.

An extraordinary literary flowering has been based upon the revival of Hebrew. Interestingly, the usual relationship between literature and the spoken language, in which the former grows out of the latter, has been uniquely reversed in the case of Hebrew. By the time of World War I, there were still only scattered pockets of Hebrew speakers in Eretz Yisrael (the Land of Israel), while modern Hebrew literature, beginning in the late eighteenth century, had already run through a whole cycle of stylistic revolutions, from classical to romantic to modern, and produced scores of masterworks. These literary developments had taken place, moreover, in eastern Europe, and it was not until the 1920s that the institutions of Hebrew literature (the writers, journals, and publishing houses) came to Eretz Yisrael and the growing numbers of speakers of the language "caught up" with its literature. (A book written sixty years ago which remains a good account of this phenomenon is Shalom Spiegel's *Hebrew Reborn* [Schocken Books, 1962].)

Modern Hebrew literature makes two essential claims—beyond its inherent artistic pleasures—on the attention of American readers. Most importantly, this literature provides a window onto the soul of Israeli society for anyone who is concerned with this most extraordinary Jewish experiment. Amos Oz, A. B. Yehoshua, Aharon Appelfeld, Yaakov Shabtai, and Yehuda Amichai are the writers who furnish the best vantage onto this passionate actuality, and consequently much of the following survey will focus on them and others of their generation, who began writing in the 1960s. The second claim made by modern Hebrew literature is that it is the best source for understanding the human side of the great transformation that engulfed Jewish society during the past century. History and philosophy may tell us many things, but it is only the great works of literature which show us how individuals experienced the dislocations which accompanied the loss of religious faith and the emergence of radically new forms of Jewish identity. These insights are embodied in the poetry and novels that preceded the creation of the State of Israel, and it is to this background we shall first turn.

A word about translations and editions before going on. The good news is that a decent, representative selection of modern Hebrew literature does exist in English translation. This being said, however, it needs to be pointed out that because of the vagaries of publishing much of it is not in print at any one time. Thus, unfortunately, there will be many references below to books not currently in print, but I have tried to limit these to well-known editions that have been in recent circulation and are likely to be on the shelves of municipal, synagogue, and community center libraries. It should also be kept in mind that for many complex reasons it is not always the best that gets translated. Some novelists could arguably be said to be overrepresented in translation, while other writers (for example, S. Yizhar, Amalia Kahana-Carmon, and in particular, Uri Zvi Greenberg, who many consider the greatest Hebrew poet of the twentieth century) have virtually no presence in English. These disproportions will be pointed out as we go along.

The European Background

Haskalah means enlightenment, and it is the name given to the first hundred years of modern Hebrew literary activity, a period ending around 1881. In its various guises, the Haskalah sought to open the Jewish mind to Western learning, promulgate fundamental reforms of community life, and purge the "superstitious" elements in Jewish religion. For the modern reader, the greatest (and most accessible) writer of this time is Sh. J. Abramovitsh (1836–1917), who took the pen name of Mendele Mokher Seforim (Mendele the Bookpeddler) after the narrator of many of his stories. Abramovitsh's fiction, written in both Hebrew and Yiddish, moves between the poles of wicked and hilarious satire of traditional Jewish life and of broadly sentimental pathos for the worsening plight of Russian Jewry. Two wonderful late stories embody these extremes: "Shem and Japheth on the Train," in Robert Alter, ed., *Modern Hebrew Literature* (Behrman House, 1975), and "Burnt Out," in David G. Roskies, ed., *The Literature of Destruction: Jewish Responses to Catastrophe* (Jewish Publication Society, 1989).

In both stories, the narrator, Mendele, is accosted by a group of exiled east European countrymen who appear at first to be the epitome of small-minded self-pity, but as Mendele comes to understand their story from the inside, his attitude changes from ridicule to pathos. This scheme is played out in larger terms in a short comic novel, *The Travels and Adventures of Benjamin the Third*, translated from the Yiddish by Moshe Spiegel (Schocken Books, 1968), in which a latter-day Don Quixote and Sancho Panza set out from their *shtetl* to find the lost Ten Tribes. They do not get very far from home, but their antic misadventures reflect on the contradictions of the Jewish situation in Russia at the end of the century. Two other Abramovitsh novels exist in English and are worth looking for: *Fishke the Lame*, translated by Gerald Stillman (Thomas Yoseloff, 1960), and *The Mare*, in Joachim Neugreschel's *Great Tales of Jewish Occult and Fantasy* (Wings Books/ Outlet Book Co., 1991).

Implicit in the Haskalah critique of Jewish society was the self-confident belief that reform would purchase acceptance by the surrounding culture. The widespread pogroms in southern Russia in 1881 and again in 1903–5 were signals that this conviction could not be sustained. The destruction taking place within Russian Jewry was felt at the spiritual as well as political and social levels. The structures of plausibility that had sustained Jewish faith inscribed within the world of Torah and the commandments were collapsing, and this internal catastrophe, which reflects the crisis of Judaism, is one of the dominant themes of Hebrew literature during what is called the Revival period (1881–1918).

A good place to sample this literature is in works of Mordecai Ze'ev Feierberg (*Whither? and Other Stories*, translated by Hillel Halkin [Jewish Publication Society, 1973]). Like his creator, Nahman, the hero of *Whither?*, grows up within the lap of hasidic piety in the Ukraine only to lose his faith during adolescence. Feierberg's achievement lies in his depicting the stages of knowledge and experience that inexorably lead up to the crisis and in making intelligible to us the true pathos of this calamity.

Life of course went on in the aftermath of losing one's faith, yet the void that ensued offered particular temptations to bad faith, among them emigration, assimilation, and "conversion" to a new political ideology like communism and socialism. The fiction of Yosef Haim Brenner (1881–1921), the preeminent prose writer of the generation, describes the struggles of young men and women to live authentically in this moment of cultural upheaval while remaining faithful to the Jewish nation. Unfortunately, Brenner's best work, especially his stunning autobiographical first novel *In Winter*, has not yet been translated. We do have, however, Brenner's ambitious last novel, *Breakdown and Bereavement*, in an excellent translation by Hillel Halkin (Cornell University Press, 1971). The novel, which is set in Eretz Yisrael where Brenner lived from 1909 until his death in the Arab riots of 1921, follows the career of a young intellectual who has failed at being a pioneer and winds up in the old religious community of Jerusalem. Like the works of Dostoevsky, which Brenner admired and translated into Hebrew, *Breakdown and Bereavement* succeeds in making philosophical speculations about good and evil within the framework of the novel. In addition to this novel, an important short story "The Way Out" is to be found in translation in Robert Alter's *Modern Hebrew Literature* (mentioned earlier).

The magisterial poetic voice of the era belongs to Hayim Nahman Bialik (1873–1934). Bialik's career, which reached its zenith at the turn of the century, proceeded along two tracks. For the Hebrew readers of his time, Bialik wore the mantle of *the* national poet who explored in verse the dilemmas of a generation: the emergence from the *beit midrash* (study house) to the modern world, the meaning of tradition, and the response to anti-Semitism. At the same time, Bialik wrote confessional lyric poetry of great subtlety which chronicles his path toward romantic despair, and it is this personal verse which has been rediscovered by a new generation of Israeli readers. Reading Bialik in translation is sometimes difficult because of the pervasiveness of allusions to Jewish sources. A good place to begin is the six poems of Bialik's explicated in *The Modern Hebrew Poem Itself*, edited by Stanley Burnshaw, T. Carmi, and Ezra Spicehandler (Harvard University Press, 1989). An impressive earlier translation is A. M. Klein's version of *In the City of Slaughter*, Bialik's epic poem on the Kishinev pogrom and his empassioned indictment of Jewish political passivity; it is included in Roskies's *The Literature of Destruction* (previously mentioned). Bialik was also an important essayist and short story writer; see in the Alter anthology "The Short Friday" and "Revealment and Concealment in Language."

By many counts the greatest writer in Hebrew literature is S. Y. Agnon (1888–1970), who was awarded the Nobel Prize in Literature in 1966. Although he was influenced by earlier Hebrew literature, Agnon in many ways stands as a phenomenon unto himself. His work marks an extraordinary intersection between the rabbinic tradition, in which he was steeped in his native Galicia, and the modernist aesthetic he learned from Flaubert, Mann, Kafka, and Hamsun during his long sojourn in Germany. In addition to mastering realist and surrealist narrative techniques, Agnon was adept at using the naive materials of the tradition, especially the hasidic tale, for sounding profound existential themes. More than any other Jewish writer in any language, Agnon internalized the crisis of Judaism, or at the very least the crisis of the bourgeois religious artist in the modern world.

Even though only a small percentage of Agnon's oeuvre is available in English, in absolute terms this turns out to be not so little: four major novels, several novellas, and scores of short stories. For the reader approaching Agnon for the

S. Y. Agnon reading his acceptance speech upon receiving the Nobel Prize for Literature in 1966. (Library of The Jewish Theological Seminary of America)

first time, the best way may be his 1935 novel *A Simple Story*, freshly translated by Hillel Halkin (Schocken Books, 1985). Set in a small, traditional Jewish town in Poland, the novel tells the story of a family of shopkeepers whose son Hirshl is attracted to a poor relative who has become a maidservant for the family. Hirshl is dissuaded from following his amorous feelings and steered toward a more suitable match. But the consequences of this repression are severe; he goes insane and is brought back to himself only through an unconventional form of psychoanalysis. The story is told in a naturalistic mode, although additional readings of the novel reveal an elaborate network of symbolic images and motifs.

A second step in gaining an acquaintance with Agnon might be the *Twenty-one Stories*, edited by Nahum Glatzer (Schocken Books, 1971), which offers a good selection of the various genres in which Agnon worked. Especially recommended in that collection are "Agunot" and "The Tale of the Scribe" as examples of the pseudo-naive story; "The Doctor's Divorce" and "Metamorphosis" as examples of realistic narrative; "The Lady and the Peddler" as allegorical grotesque; and "A Whole Loaf," "At the Outset of the Day," and "Night" as surrealistic, dreamlike stories.

Agnon left an immense number of writings unpublished at the time of his death in 1970, and these have been appearing in a constant stream since that time. One of the most interesting items of this posthumous work is the novel *Shira*, translated by Zeva Shapiro (Schocken Books, 1989), which is set among the German Jewish refugees in the university circles of Jerusalem in the late 1930s. The protagonist, Manfred Herbst, is a professor of Byzantine studies at the Hebrew University; in his scholarship, politics, and family life he embodies the liberal cultural synthesis of German Jewry. This balance is disturbed when Herbst becomes attracted to a nurse from Poland named Shira, who arouses feelings in him which can be evaded but not suppressed. The story of Herbst's decline is left unfinished, but the novel remains a fascinating study in the interrelationship among intellect, art, and eros.

Other translations to look for are *Two Tales: Betrothed and Edo and Enam*, translated by Walter Lever (Schocken Books, 1966) and *In the Heart of the Seas*, translated by I. M. Lask (Schocken Books, 1967). Two of Agnon's greatest novels exist in not entirely satisfactory English versions, but they are nevertheless worth seeking out for the abundant gifts that shine through: *The Bridal Canopy*, translated by I. M. Lask (Schocken Books, 1967) and *A Guest for the Night*, translated by Misha Louvish (Schocken Books, 1968).

The State of Israel Period

Although such older figures as S. Y. Agnon and Haim Hazaz continued to write prolifically after the establishment of the State of Israel in 1948, the literary spotlight turned to a much younger generation of writers who grew up in Eretz Yisrael rather than in Europe. They did not know the Yiddish culture of their grandparents; they were raised in Zionist-socialist youth movements; and most important of all, they grew up with Hebrew as their native tongue. This group—which includes S. Yizhar, Moshe Shamir, Hanoch Bartov, Aharon Megged, and Nathan Shaham—were catapulted into a premature adulthood by their participation in the War of Liberation. Thematically, their fiction represents the formative experience of having one's personal liberty enlisted in a common exalted cause. The debt that the individual owes to friends, kibbutz, movement, country, cause—the exploration of this responsibility in its many guises is a major preoccupation of these writers. Artistically, their fiction harks back to the canons of Tolstoy and Russian realism and eschews the formalist experiments of modernism. Protagonists tend to be positive heroes whose struggles embody the ideological conflicts of the group.

Several works of most of these writers are available in English. The exception, unfortunately, is the writer who is generally regarded as the best of the lot, S. Yizhar (b. 1916); some of his shorter fiction can be sampled in *Midnight Convoy and Other Stories*, translated by Misha Louvish et al. (Jerusalem: Israeli Universities Press, 1969), and his powerful story "The Prisoner" appears in the anthology edited by Robert Alter, mentioned previously. Here is one suggested work for each of the other writers, although the reader can profit from other titles he or she comes across: Moshe Shamir (b. 1921), *The Hittite Must Die*, translated by Margaret Benaya (East and West Library, 1978); Aharon Megged (b. 1920), *Asahel*, translated by Robert Whitehill and Susan G. Lilly (Taplinger, 1982); Hanoch Bartov (b. 1926), *The Brigade*, translated by David S. Segal (Jewish Publication Society, 1968); and Nathan Shaham (b. 1925), *The Other Side of the Wall*, translated by Leonard Gold (Jewish Publication Society, 1983).

Before moving on, it's worth mentioning three talented writers, contemporary to or somewhat younger than those just mentioned, whose work has developed along separate individual tracks. Benjamin Tammuz wrote picaresque novels about young heroes who do not fit into their surroundings; see *Requiem for Na'aman*, translated by Mildred Budny and Yehuda Safran (New American Library, 1982). David Shahar (b. 1926) has created a many-volume cycle of novels about Jerusalem during the Mandate period which mix present events with the recollection of past experience in a way reminiscent of Proust; the first volume in the cycle is *The Palace of Shattered Vessels*, translated by Dalya Bilu (Houghton Mifflin, 1976). See also his collection of short stories, *News from Jerusalem*, translated by Dalya Bilu et al. (Houghton Mifflin, 1974). Yoram Kaniuk (b. 1930) is a novelist with a decided flare for the comic grotesque; his interesting experiment *Adam Resurrected*, translated by Seymour Simkes (Harper & Row, 1978), applies this technique to the obsessions with the Holocaust at the root of Israeli consciousness.

Beginning around 1960, a group of younger writers called by some critics the

Amos Oz (Photograph by
Eric Feinblatt. Courtesy of
Harcourt, Brace, Jovanovich)

New Wave—among them Amos Oz, A. B. Yehoshua, Aharon Appelfeld, and
Yaakov Shabtai—introduced into Israeli fiction a new perspective and a new narrative style. The mood was revisionist in an existential mode. Some of the great
myths upon which the state was founded, especially the heroic idealism of the
founding fathers of social Zionism, were taken apart and evaluated in light of their
truthfulness to individual experience. What added to the vitality of this new reck-
oning was the innovative means by which it was carried out. Oz's experiments
with figurative images, Yehoshua's use of allegory and monologue, Appelfeld's
insistence on understatement and narrative gaps, Shabtai's attempts to represent
the density of narrative events and human interrelationships—all this ferment
opened an exciting chapter in the development of Israeli literature.

The revisionist thrust can be seen most pointedly in the early kibbutz stories of Amos Oz (b. 1939) contained in *Where Jackals Howl and Other Stories*, translated by Nicholas de Lange and Philip Simpson (Bantam, 1982), and in his first novel, *Elsewhere, Perhaps*, translated by Nicholas de Lange (Harcourt Brace Jovanovich, 1985). Although only a small percentage of Israelis live on kibbutzim, the institution has always been taken to embody the best ideals of the society as a whole as a kind of working example of utopian ideology. Oz's stories examine the kibbutz from another angle; they see the kibbutz as a failed yet fascinating attempt to impose rationality upon the chaos of human need and emotion. A just society in which individuals work for the sake of the community was the vision of a generation of larger-than-life founders. It is their children, however, who pay the price for the imposition of these heroic ideals. In such masterful stories as "A Hollow Stone," "The Way of the Wind," and "Before his Time" (reprinted also in the Alter anthology), Oz probes the ironic gap between romantic idealism and its human consequences. Oz's narrative style is extremely readable but tightly wound; the dense description of objects sets up patterns of images that interconnect and deepen the import of the stories.

Oz's later fiction displays an ambitious attempt to comprehend the changes in Israeli society and to meditate on some of the enduring themes of Jewish history. In *The Hill of Evil Counsel*, translated by Nicholas de Lange (Bantam, 1982), Oz returns to his childhood in pre-independence Jerusalem and writes of a period in which relations between Arabs and Jews were still fluid and fraught with possibility. *Unto Death*, translated by Nicholas de Lange (Harcourt Brace Jovanovich/ Harvest, 1978), contains the novellas *Crusade* and *Late Love*. The former is unique among Oz's works because it is an allegory set in medieval Europe; it is an attempt to see the Jews through Christian eyes, and its relevance to the present is always apparent. *My Michael*, translated by Nicholas de Lange (Harcourt Brace Jovanovich/Harvest, 1984), examines the rapidly changing Israeli society of the 1950s from the perspective of a young married woman who is losing her grip on her sanity. *A Perfect Peace*, translated by Hillel Halkin (Harcourt Brace Jovanovich, 1985) returns to the subject of the kibbutz, while *Black Box*, translated by Nicholas de Lange (Harcourt Brace Jovanovich, 1988), a comic novel in letters, chronicles the rise of religion in recent years and the newly assertive presence of oriental Jews as forces in Israeli society. The latest novel by Oz to appear in English, *To Know a Woman*, translated by Nicholas de Lange (Harcourt Brace Jovanovich, 1991), deals with the moral dilemmas of a Mossad agent who has left the service for private life. Oz is also the author of two volumes of reportage and political essays: *In the Land of Israel*, translated by Maurie Goldberg-Bartura (Vintage Books, 1984) and *The Slopes of Lebanon,* translated by Maurie Goldberg-Bartura (Harcourt Brace Jovanovich, 1989).

The most respected and widely read novelist writing in Israel today is A. B. Yehoshua (b. 1936). Yehoshua is the scion of a Sephardic family which has been in Israel for many generations. Raised in Jerusalem, Yehoshua has lived for years in Haifa, which serves as the setting of many of his works. His early stories, which can be found in *Three Days and a Child,* translated by Miriam Arad (Doubleday, 1970), *Early in the Summer of 1970,* translated by Miriam Arad (Berkley Publishing Group, 1981), and *The Continuing Silence of the Poet: Collected Stories* (Penguin Books, 1991) are starkly existential. They feature nameless protagonists who live in isolation from meaningful contact with others and who are driven to extremity by the deprivation that underlies the tedium of their lives. One of the best known of Yehoshua's stories, "Facing the Forests," which is also available in the Alter anthology, integrates the existential theme with a broadly national allegory. The story concerns an aging university student who takes a job as a fire watcher for a forest which has been built by Zionist agencies with monies from the diaspora. The forest has been built over the ruins of an Arab village, and the discovery of this fact, plus the inability of the watcher to abide his solitude, lead to a violent consummation.

In two later novels, *The Lover,* translated by Philip Simpson (Dutton/Obelisk, 1985), and *A Late Divorce,* translated by Hillel Halkin (Dutton/Obelisk, 1985), the focus on the isolated individual broadens to include a larger cast of figures. Following Faulkner, Yehoshua gives each character his or her own dramatic voice and makes the novels a succession of these monologues without third-person narrative commentary. The effect is to give us immediate and direct access to the inner thoughts of a gallery of interesting characters. *The Lover* is set during the Yom Kippur War in 1973 and concerns the tangled relations within a single family. The novel is notable for containing one of the most ambitious attempts to portray the inner life of an Arab character, a teenager named Naim, who falls in love with the daughter of the owner of the auto repair garage in which he works. The description of another character's desertion from the army and his concealment within the ultra-Orthodox quarters of Jerusalem is also a stunning piece of writing. *A Late Divorce* concerns a man who returns to Israel from America to obtain a divorce from his mentally-ill wife. Yehoshua uses the situation to give dramatic embodiment to radical thoughts he has about the relationship of Israel to the diaspora, which he expresses in a series of essays contained in another volume: *Between Right and Right,* translated by Arnold Schwartz (Doubleday,

1981). A later novel, *Five Seasons*, translated by Hillel Halkin (Dutton, 1990) turns away from the monologue format to explore the mind of a man who has cared for his wife during a long bout with cancer and who attempts to reconstruct his life in the year after her death. In this finely crafted novel, Yehoshua brings to fruition his portrayal of daily experience as it is shaped by the forces of the unconscious.

Less well known but of great importance is the fiction of Yaakov Shabtai (1934–1981), whose early death robbed Israeli literature of one of its most inventive writers. If Haifa is the characteristic setting for Yehoshua's novels, and Jerusalem and the kibbutz for those of Oz, in the case of Shabtai it is Tel Aviv, the first Hebrew city, which is the presiding presence in his writings. In *Past Continuous*, translated by Dalya Bilu (Schocken Books, 1989), Shabtai traces the fortunes of a network of families over two generations. The major pattern is a decline from the grandiosity and ideological single-mindedness of the fathers and mothers to the hedonism and confused self-doubt of the sons and daughters. The melancholy nature of thematic material is transformed by the brilliant tour-de-force of the novel's style. Writing in long, rhythmic sentences (in the Hebrew there are no paragraph breaks whatsoever!), Shabtai creates a trancelike momentum which carries the reader throughout this fascinating novel. See also Shabtai's other novel, *Past Perfect*, translated by Dalya Bilu (Viking Penguin, 1987).

In the works of the writers discussed so far, the Holocaust moves in the wings but rarely commands center stage. The one major writer of fiction for whom this is assuredly not the case is Aharon Appelfeld (b. 1932). The formative years of Appelfeld's childhood were spent in the forests of central Europe hiding from the murderers of the rest of his family. From the DP camps on the Italian coast, Appelfeld came to Eretz Yisrael, where he was educated in Youth Aliyah villages and urged to forget his wartime experiences. Instead, he made the Holocaust the center of a prolific stream of novels and short stories which have immeasurably expanded the boundaries of Israeli fiction.

The central feature of Appelfeld's writing is the principled decision to refrain from writing about the Nazis, the concentration camps, and the fascination with the whole apparatus of evil which is the staple of most popular writing on this subject. To this end, Appelfeld usually sets his plots in the period just before the Holocaust or in the aftermath, as reflected in the lives of survivors. The dominant theme is the power and pervasiveness of denial in the Jewish psyche. *Badenheim 1939*, translated by Dalya Bilu (David R. Godine, 1980), tells the story of a summer resort frequented by assimilated Viennese Jews which is gradually being prepared for deportation by the town's "Sanitation Department." The refusal or disinclination to see the threat raises the persistent question in Appelfeld's work as to how the Jews, one of the cleverest and most accomplished groups in Europe, could manage to ignore the evident signs of the disaster to come. *The Age of Wonders,* translated by Dalya Bilu (David R. Godine, 1989), describes, through the eyes of his young son, the disintegrating world of an Austrian Jewish writer whose work is rejected as "anti-Austrian" as the Nazi era progresses. Other Appelfeld titles worth looking for include *Tzili: The Story of a Life,* translated by Dalya Bilu (Dutton, 1983); *The Retreat,* translated by Dalya Bilu (Dutton, 1985); *To the Land of the Cattails,* translated by Jeffrey M. Green (Perennial Library, 1987); *The Immortal Bartfuss,* translated by Jeffrey M. Green (Harper & Row, 1989); and *The Healer,* translated by Jeffrey M. Green (Grove Weidenfeld, 1990).

Two other writers whose fiction is eminently worth reading are Shulamith Hareven and the young writer David Grossman. Hareven's *City of Many Days,* translated by Hillel Halkin (Popular Library, 1978), is a densely and colorfully imagined novel set in Jerusalem of the Mandate period as seen through the experience of a spirited woman. See also her allegorical *The Miracle Hater,* translated by Hillel Halkin (North Point Press, 1988). Grossman's *See Under: Love,* translated by Betsy Rosenberg (Simon & Schuster, 1990), is considered the most important piece of fiction about the Holocaust since Appelfeld began publishing in the early 1960s. Its challenging form, which adopts many of the devices of postmodernism, makes it a breathtaking reading experience.

Compared to Hebrew fiction, the achievements of Hebrew poetry in the twentieth century are even more profound and extensive, yet, alas, the barrier of translation does not grant the English reader much access to this golden territory. (Herein lies a powerful motivation for learning Hebrew!) Yehuda Amichai, the great poet of the postwar period, is really the only one whose poetry has a substantial and extensive presence in English translation. There are, however, some good anthologies which offer a sampling of Hebrew verse. One of the most interesting of these is *The Modern Hebrew Poem Itself,* edited by Stanley Burnshaw, T. Carmi, and Ezra Spicehandler (mentioned earlier). The period covered stretches from Bialik to Amichai; each poem is reproduced with the Hebrew original, a prose translation, a transliteration of the Hebrew, and a commentary. A useful volume is Ruth Finer Mintz, editor and translator, *Modern Hebrew Poetry; A Bilingual Anthology* (University of California Press, 1982). *Israeli Poetry, A Contemporary Anthology,* selected and translated by Warren Bargad and Stanley F. Chyet (Indiana University Press, 1986), includes substantial selections (the translations only, with biographical introductions) from more recent poets, including David Avidan, Amir Gilboa, Dahlia Ravikovitch, Meir Wieseltier, and Yona Wallach. Three titles in the Jewish Publication Society's bilingual poetry series deserve special mention. *The Syrian–African Rift and Other Poems*, by Avot Yeshurun, translated by Harold Schimmel (Jewish Publication Society, 1980), presents poetry by an older poet whose idiosyncratic modernism has been rediscovered and admired by a younger generation of writers. The poetry of Gabriel Preil in *Sunset Possibilities and Other Poems*, translated by Robert Friend (Jewish Publication Society, 1985), is remarkable for its simple imagistic beauty but also for the fact that it was written wholly in America and thus represents the work of dozens of other poets who wrote Hebrew on these shores. Dan Pagis's *Points of Departure*, translated by Stephen Mitchell (Jewish Publication Society, 1982) offers selections from the work of an important poet whose Holocaust experience hovers in the background of poems with science fiction themes. The work of another Israeli poet, Nathan Zach, is considered by most critics to be as important as that of Amichai's; it can be sampled in *The Static Element*, translated by Peter Everwine and Shulamit Yasny-Starkman (Atheneum, 1982).

One of the reasons Yehuda Amichai's poetry works so well in English is that he was influenced more by English literary models than by the Russian and German literature which had helped to shape such earlier poets as Abraham Shlonsky and Uri Zvi Greenberg. Although he was brought to Israel from Germany by his parents at the age of twelve in 1936, his coming of age during the last years of the British Mandate and his service in the British army in World War II oriented him toward the more conversational rhythms of such English poets as Auden. The result is that rather than sounding grandly poetic, Amichai's verse better resembles human speech; it is further marked by great wit and playfulness. Many of the poems are built around stunning metaphors which yoke together ideas or things drawn from vastly disparate realms. Yet beneath this clever play of language, Amichai's poetry meditates on very profound themes. Recollections of Amichai's Orthodox upbringing generate much reflection on the disappearance of God from the world. His service as a soldier in many wars is the basis of poems about the relationship between public duty and private experience. Contemplation on erotic love is another dominant theme, and many of these poems have been brought together in a bilingual edition, *Love Poems* (Harper & Row, 1981). Amichai can also be thought of as a Jerusalem poet, and his poems about his city have similarly been brought together in a bilingual edition, *Poems of Jerusalem* (Harper & Row, 1988). Other important collections of poetry in translation include: *Songs of Jerusalem and Myself,* translated by Harold Schimmel (Milkweed Editions, 1987); *Amen,* translated by Amichai and Ted Hughes (Harper & Row, 1977); *Time,* translated by Amichai (Harper & Row, 1979); *Great Tranquillity; Questions and Answers,* translated by Glenda Abramson and Tudor Parfit (Harper & Row, 1983); *The Selected Poetry of Yehuda Amichai,* translated by Stephen Mitchell and Chana Bloch (Harper & Row, 1986).

Books in English *about* modern Hebrew literature have begun to appear in significant numbers only during the past decade, largely as a result of increased teaching of the subject in the universities. An earlier study by a poet and scholar who lived much of his life in America before emigrating to Israel is Simon Halkin's *Modern Hebrew Literature; Trends and Values* (Schocken Books, 1950). Robert Alter's *After the Tradition* (Dutton, 1969) includes essays about a number of Hebrew writers. The literary response to the Holocaust and its relations to earlier Hebrew literature has been treated in David Roskies, *Against the Apocalypse: Responses to Catastrophe in Modern Jewish Culture* (Harvard University Press, 1986), and Alan Mintz, *Hurban: Responses to Catastrophe in Hebrew Literature* (Columbia University Press, 1984). Increasing attention has been recently given to the representation to the "other" in Hebrew literature: women, oriental Jews, and Arabs. See Gila Ramras-Rauch, *The Arab in Israeli Literature* (Indiana University Press, 1989). Israel has an active and controversial theater which often makes interesting use of material from the Bible and Jewish history; a good overview (with illustrations of stage sets) is Glenda Abramson, *Modern Hebrew Drama* (St. Martin's Press, 1980). The pleasure of reading Agnon can be enhanced by several critical studies: Arnold J. Band, *Nostalgia and Nightmare: A Study in the Fiction of S. Y. Agnon* (University of California Press, 1968); Baruch Hochman, *The Fiction of S. Y. Agnon* (Cornell University Press, 1970); Ann Golomb Hoffman, *Between Exile and Return: S. Y. Agnon and the Drama of Writing* (SUNY Press, 1991); and Gershon Shaked, *Shmuel Yosef Agnon: A Revolutionary Traditionalist* (New York University Press, 1989).

A thematic study of the inner lives of young Hebrew writers at the turn of the century can be found in Alan Mintz, *Banished from Their Father's Table: Loss of Faith and Hebrew Autobiography* (Indiana University Press, 1989). Readers interested less in literary criticism than in the ideas and personalities of Israeli writers can consult two collections of interviews: Chaim Chertok, *We Are All Close: Converstions with Israeli Writers* (Fordham University Press, 1989), and Joseph Cohen, *Voices of Israel; Essays on and Interviews with Yehuda Amichai, A. B. Yehoshua, T. Carmi, Aharon Appelfeld, and Amos Oz* (SUNY Press, 1990).

YIDDISH LITERATURE

David G. Roskies

Last summer, as I drove my son to nursery school by bicycle, we came upon the familiar movie vans parked on both sides of Riverside Drive. At 116th Street, with its quaint carriage entrance at the corner—a favorite of all fashion photographers—we noticed two old Fords and a Pontiac, a green-and-yellow city bus and yellow checkered cab, all lined up in mint condition. Workers had just finished repainting the street lamps brown and had installed a hackstand and walk-in phone booth of the kind that Clark Kent used when he had nowhere else to change. On our way home that afternoon we learned that the crew was setting up to film I. B. Singer's *Enemies, A Love Story* (New American Library, 1989), which explained the flashback effect to forty years ago. When the movie was released I was astonished to discover other dissemblances: that the exterior shots of Central Park West in a driving blizzard were the very ones shot on Riverside Drive in the heat of the summer; that the Catskill vacation scenes were shot in the Laurentian Mountains outside of Montreal, my hometown, where, in turn, most of the "Lower East Side" was reconstituted.

All of this has made me think about why there is more of I. B. Singer's work available in translation than that of any other Yiddish writer, living or dead; about Singer's fortunate decision, made very late in life, to describe the American urban landscape; and about Singer as a possible guide to reading modern Yiddish literature as a whole. Singer himself is the master dissimulator, whose best work affects a storytelling style, exploits the rhythms and linguistic layers of Yiddish, and draws heavily from the work that came before him. So to the extent that Singer's work is neatly divided between fantasy and reality, and that his own life is not-so-neatly divided between the Old Country and the New, Singer can indeed serve as a guide to what in Yiddish literature is worthy of being read and reread.

For readers hungry to know about the real lives of Yiddish authors there is embarrassingly little to go by. Singer himself has written two memoirs: *In My Father's Court* (Fawcett, 1980) recalls the domestic dramas that Jews from all walks of life enacted before his father, an Orthodox rabbi, and *Love and Exile*, which brings together three autobiographical novellas (Farrar, Straus and Giroux, 1986). Whereas the father is busy enforcing God's Torah, the son is off pursuing his carnal desires while dabbling in philosophy and kabbalah on the side. If this sounds familiar, it is because similar plots and love triangles reappear in Singer's fiction as well. And so it goes with the few available memoirs of Singer's illustrious precursors. Yiddish writers do not bare their souls.

The founding fathers of Yiddish literature were Mendele Mokher Seforim (Mendele the Bookpeddler), pen name of Sholem Yankev Abramovitsh (1836–1917); Sholem Aleichem (literally "Peace be with you," the standard Yiddish "Hello"), pen name of Solomon Rabinovitsh (1859–1916), and Isaac Leib Peretz (1852–1915). Mendele's memoir *Of Bygone Days* focuses exclusively on the folkways of his native *shtetl* in White Russia where he lived until his father's death in 1850. In the book's delightful preface, "Mendele the Bookpeddler" pays a visit to "Sholem Yankev Abramovitsh," now living in Odessa, to convince the real author . . . to write his memoirs! Though "Abramovitsh" protests that Jewish life is like an anthill in which the individual has no role to play, "Mendele" and the other guests finally prevail. Dan Miron's pathbreaking *A Traveler Disguised: A Study in the Rise of Modern Yiddish Fiction in the Nineteenth Century* (Schocken Books, 1973) goes a long way toward explaining why this first generation of Yiddish moderns could not address their audience other than through masks—the folksier, the better.

Sholem Aleichem's *From the Fair*, translated by Curt Leviant (Penguin Books, 1986), likewise makes no pretense at truthfulness. Billed as a biographical novel, it charts the rise and fall of a storyteller from his roots in a semilegendary *shtetl* to his "banishment from Eden" and the beginnings of his adult life as a government-appointed rabbi. Only Peretz (who dropped his many pseudonyms once he became an established writer) wrote a truly modern, introspective, and self-consciously *literary* memoir. It reveals his lifelong struggle between heart and mind, a split which philosophy, science, and even art could not resolve. (The memoir is included in Ruth R. Wisse's *A Peretz Reader,* discussed later in this essay.)

Perhaps the most revealing Yiddish literary autobiography is the most fanciful, Itzik Manger's *The Book of Paradise,* translated by Leonard Wolf (Hill & Wang, 1986), which recounts "The Wonderful Adventures of Shmuel-Aba Abervo"—before he was actually born! Paradise, it turns out, is a turn-of-the-century Galician *shtetl* where biblical heroes, hasidic rabbis, and lower-class Yiddish-speaking angels fall in love, write Purim plays, get drunk, and have to contend with Christians who steal their Messiah Ox. The hero, who alone retains total recall of life in Paradise, can regale the *shtetl* elders down on earth in much the same way as the baby Jesus had once inspired the Magi in Bethlehem.

Yiddish writers, in fact, became so much the property of the folk that their lives took on paradigmatic meaning. Mendele was hailed *der zeyde,* the Grandfather of Yiddish literature. Sholem Aleichem, Mr. How-Do-You-Do?, was a household name on both sides of the Atlantic. Peretz was the standard-bearer of Yiddish culture, the "Prince of the Ghetto," as Maurice Samuel once crowned him. (Howe and Greenberg provide minibiographies of the major figures in their *Treasury of Yiddish Stories* of which more, below.) These writers were thus free to reinvent their own lives just as they reinvented the collective life of all east European Jews as embodied by their mythic birthplace, the *shtetl.*

The *shtetl,* or Jewish market town of eastern Europe, is arguably the greatest single invention of Yiddish literature. What the Western is to American popular culture, the *shtetl* novella is to the Yiddish imagination. Its symbolic landscape is etched into the Yiddish psyche. Main Street is dominated by the marketplace and is occupied solely by Jews. Instead of the saloon, there is the *besmedresh* (the house of study); instead of the church, the *shul.* The *kohol-shtibl,* where the Jewish notables meet, replaces the sheriff's office. And of course there is the train depot, either nearby or somewhat removed, through which unwelcome news and travelers arrive in town.

With this symbolic map firmly in place, the variations on the theme of the small town in a dangerous world were almost inexhaustible. Ruth R. Wisse has

Yiddish writer I. L. Peretz. (YIVO Institute for Jewish Research)

Sholem Aleichem (YIVO Institute for Jewish Research)

anthologized some of the most celebrated examples in *A Shtetl and Other Yiddish Novellas* (Wayne State University Press, 1986). But except for Mendele's ethnographic memoir *Of Bygone Days*, mentioned earlier, the literary image of these *shtetlekh* was anything but rosy, as becomes clear in this anthology. The title piece, I. M. Weissenberg's *A Shtetl* (1906), opened in the house of study with a scene of class warfare. Weissenberg's animus was partly fueled by Sholem Asch's *The Shtetl*, in *Tales of My People*, facsimile of 1948 ed., translated by Meyer Levin (Salem, N.H.: Ayer Company Publishers, 1970), that appeared two years before. Whereas Asch had written the first of many ecumenical fantasies in which the prayers of Jewish and Christian believers ascended to the same God, Weissenberg charted the rising tide of anti-Semitism and political reaction that culminated with the czarist forces carting the *shtetl* revolutionaries off to prison at novella's end. By 1909, the *shtetl* had become the scene of *ennui* and existential despair in David Bergelson's *At the Depot* (in the Wisse anthology)—a script worthy of Ingmar Bergman.

As World War I and the Bolshevik revolution added the physical destruction of the *shtetl* to its earlier economic and social decline, Yiddish (and Hebrew) writers ever more exploited the *shtetl* as a symbol for Jewish collective survival. Joachim Neugroschel's *The Shtetl: A Creative Anthology of Jewish Life in Eastern Europe* (Overlook Press, 1990) and my own *The Literature of Destruction* (Jewish Publication Society, 1989) provide a horrific contemporary panorama of the *shtetl* under siege. Against this background we can view I. B. Singer's masterpiece, *Satan in Goray*, translated by Jacob Sloan (Avon Books, 1978), which refracted the apocalyptic events in eastern Europe through the lens of Jewish heretical movements in seventeenth- and eighteenth-century Poland.

Much of Yiddish literature is dedicated to burying the *shtetl*, not to praising it. This fact is sometimes obscured in translation when the word *shtetl* itself is rendered as "village," to suggest a bucolic Paradise Lost, just as the rough-and-tumble *besmedresh* is invariably translated as "synagogue," to underline the image of a Holy Community engaged in constant study and prayer. Zborowski and Herzog's *Life Is With People* (Schocken Books, 1962), which eliminated the goyim, history, and geography from its idealized portrait of a timeless, archetypical *shtetl*, did much to further this sentimental myth of origins. The Howe and Greenberg *Treasury of Yiddish Stories*, 2d rev. ed. (Viking Penguin, 1990), remains the standard introduction to modern Yiddish writing probably because of its focus on the *shtetl* and on issues of social concern. Yet even Howe and Greenberg were hard pressed to find many examples of a united community that withstood the sources of seduction from within and the forces of destruction from without.

The collapse of a religious civilization as embodied by *shtetl* culture is not a happy sight, however favorably predisposed the viewer might be toward a secular tomorrow. The happy endings assembled by Howe and Greenberg—in Peretz's "Devotion Without End" (1904), Singer's "The Little Shoemakers" (1945), and Itzik Manger's "The Adventures of Hershel Summerwind" (1947)—are few and far between and are all written against the backdrop of prior destruction. The counterexamples, notably those written by Lamed Shapiro, are among the most memorable in the anthology. Few Yiddish writers could chart the trajectory of modern violence as precisely as Shapiro in "White Chalah" (1919), just as few could so subtly describe the aesthetic and erotic desires that could drive a young yeshiva student away from the *shtetl* altogether ("Eating Days," 1926–27).

The Janus-faced *shtetl*, half haven, half hell, is key to the two major trends in modern Yiddish literature. Yiddish literature was born out of rebellion: the rebellion of sons against their fathers; secular pursuits against religious discipline; the individual against the collective. It was born when young writers escaped the medieval *shtetl* for the big city and beyond; when they abandoned the traditional forms of Jewish self-expression—synagogue sermon and poetry, rabbinic commentary, the sacred tales and lives—for European forms and forums—the satiric newspaper sketch, the lyric and epic poem, the novel and short story, drama and melodrama, the literary essay. This rebellion produced many works that were Jewish in language or subject matter but otherwise indistinguishable from comparable works in Russian, Polish, German.

At the same time that modernism gripped the imagination of these writers, a second, almost contradictory, countermovement emerged: an attempt to reclaim "lost" Jewish forms in the name of cultural renewal. Suddenly, and almost concurrently, Peretz discovered the beauty of Yiddish love songs, medieval romances, and hasidic tales; Sholem Aleichem turned to writing folk monologues; S. Ansky began recording Yiddish folklore and custom. Thanks to these pioneering efforts, the Pantheon Fairy Tale and Folklore Library can today include a superb volume of *Yiddish Folktales*, edited by Beatrice Silverman Weinreich (Pantheon Books, 1990), and Ruth Rubin could write a popular history of the Yiddish folk song, *Voices of a People* (Jewish Publication Society, 1979).

The folklore revival bore immediate fruits in Jewish eastern Europe: Chagall reinvented Jewish folk art, Itzik Manger rehabilitated the *Purim-shpil* (the folk plays performed on the holiday of Purim), I. B. Singer wrote monologues for Jewish demons—not to speak of Ansky's *The Dybbuk*, the all-time favorite of the Jewish theater repertoire. What is most extraordinary, and perhaps unique to Yiddish literature, is that no writer abandoned one mode for the other. The modern and the pseudo-folk voices coexisted. Peretz continued to experiment with new literary forms even as he perfected his *Stories in the Folk Vein*, selections from which are included in the *I. L. Peretz Reader*, described below. Sholem Aleichem continued writing novels about middle class morals and mores even as he put the finishing touches on *Tevye the Dairyman* (see below). And I. B. Singer began his career as a realistic novelist even as he immortalized "Gimpel the Fool."

Thus to become a Yiddish writer meant catching up on several centuries' worth of secular cultural development. That is how Abramovitsh came to write

The Travels of Benjamin the Third (1878), a marvelous spoof on *Don Quixote* (in Neugroschel's *The Shtetl: A Creative Anthology*). When the young Solomon Rabinovitsh launched his literary career in the late 1880s under the pen name of Sholem Aleichem, he wanted nothing less than to write the great "Jewish Novel" à la Turgenev. The result was seen in two novels that dramatized the struggle of the artist in traditional society: *Stempenyu* (in Neugroschel's *The Shtetl*) and *The Nightingale Or, The Saga of Yosele Solovey the Cantor*, translated by Aliza Sherrin (G. P. Putnam, 1985). These fictional "folk artists" were Sholem Aleichem's shorthand for the struggle between Judaism and Hellenism, between class and national loyalty on the one hand and the call to artistic self-expression on the other.

But Sholem Aleichem's real genius was released only when he put the novel aside in favor of old-fashioned literary forms. *The Adventures of Menahem-Mendl*, translated by Tamara Kahana (Perigee, 1979), is a zany, fast-clipped, and tragicomical exchange of letters between that peripatetic *schlemiel* (a ne'er-do-well) and his emasculating wife, Sheyne-Sheyndl. "The Haunted Tailor," the famous tale about a she-goat that kept turning into a he-goat, imitates the style of an old storybook, Hebrew captions and all (translated by Leonard Wolf in Howe and Wisse, eds., *The Best of Sholom Aleichem* (Northvale, N.J.: Jason Aronson, 1989). And the Tevye stories in *Tevye the Dairyman and The Railroad Stories*, translated by Hillel Halkin (Schocken Books, 1988) is a series of monologues narrated "live" to "Sholem Aleichem."

The discovery that one could be modern and traditional at the same time revolutionized the way that Yiddish was written thereafter. Tevye—engaged in a three-way dialogue with God, his horse, and himself—has profitably been compared to Job. Then, in *The Railroad Stories* (published in the same volume as *Tevye*), Sholem Aleichem took traditional storytelling on the road to confront the whole welter of modern Jewish problems, from apostasy and suicide to anti-Semitism and the white slave trade. The resulting tension between *what* is being told and the folksy manner *in which* it is being told; between narrators using a language of faith to chronicle the collapse of a religious civilization, made possible the later writing of Isaac Bashevis Singer.

Singer's demons are witty and learned, very much in the Yiddish tradition. Where Singer differs from the founding fathers of Yiddish literature is that in stories such as "The Mirror," in *Gimpel the Fool and Other Stories* (Farrar, Straus and Giroux, 1957), and "The Last Demon," in *The Collected Stories* (Farrar, Straus and Giroux, 1982), he enlivens the ubiquitous forces of evil, while Mendele and Peretz cut the devil down to allegorical size. Mendele's *The Mare,* in Joachim Neugroschel's *Great Tales of Jewish Occult and Fantasy* (Wings Books/ Outlet Book Co., 1991), costars Ashmedai, king of the demons, who is merely a stand-in for the czar. Which is not to say that Mendele's allegory has lost its punch. The book, written 120 years ago, is as trenchant a critique of Jewish liberalism as anything that appears in the pages of *Commentary.* And Izzy the Madman, whom the mare inducts in the ways of the world, could profitably be played by Woody Allen.

Peretz's demons are wittier still, as part of his sustained attempt to modernize Yiddish folklore. Peretz began writing pseudo-folktales at the turn of the century in order to dramatize for secular readers the ways of achieving transcendence— through nature, music, love, and self-sacrifice. Peretz's Hasidim are of a piece with Martin Buber's.

Yet while Peretz the neoromantic sometimes borders on the sentimental, there is a dark side to his writing that emerges ever so clearly in Ruth R. Wisse's recent *I. L. Peretz Reader* (Schocken Books, 1990). Here is Peretz's harrowing panorama of *shtetl* decay, its innocent title—"Impressions of a Journey through the Tomaszow Province" (1891)—beguiling the reader into unrelieved squalor and suffering. Here is Peretz the parodist exposing the hallowed traditions of Jewish passivity to harsh cross-examination in "Bontshe Shvayg" (Bontshe the Silent). Here is Peretz exploring the pathology of the *shtetl* intellectual in "The Mad Talmudist"; the sexual warfare of the *shtetl* home in "Bryna's Mendl"; and the split of heart and mind in his own anguished memoirs.

And so a Yiddish writer like I. B. Singer who came of age after the Great War was heir to two traditions—one that tried to stay on the cutting edge of what was then considered modern and the other that channeled the modern back into the forms of the past. Indeed, this tension became still more pronounced in the new urban centers of Yiddish culture—in St. Petersburg, Kiev, Warsaw, Lodz, Berlin, New York.

S. Ansky's "The Dybbuk" makes the point in its original title: "Between Two Worlds" (and so do I in my forthcoming anthology, *The Dybbuk and Other Writings* by S. Ansky, translated by Golda Werman [Schocken Books, 1992].) One of Ansky's worlds centered in St. Petersburg and Paris, where Russian was the lingua franca and revolutionary politics made the world go round. The other centered in the endangered *shtetlekh* of the Ukraine and Galicia where no effort was spared to rescue the ethos, the heroes, and artifacts of the folk. Younger writers, meanwhile, intent on liberating Yiddish from the folk and from anything resembling a

"The Dance of Death": a still from the 1937 Yiddish film of S. Ansky's play, *The Dybbuk.* (From the Rutenberg & Everett Yiddish Film Library, a collection of the National Center for Jewish Film, Brandeis University)

traditional worldview, made Kiev their center of operations. Here David Bergelson's hypnotic prose style and existentialist outlook on life made him the major Yiddish novelist of the twentieth century. (The newly revised *Treasury of Yiddish Stories* contains two shorter works of Bergelson, as does the aforementioned Wisse anthology of *shtetl* novellas.)

In Kiev as well, Der Nister ("The Hidden One," pen name of Pinkhes Kahanovitsh, 1884–1950) transformed the hasidic tale into an arena for monks, mystics, and medieval dreamers to seek redemption through art and other untraditional channels. Young Bovo, the hero of "A Tale of Kings" (1920), actually succeeded. Joachim Neugroschel has brought together the largest sampling of Der Nister's symbolist tales in *Great Tales of Jewish Occult and Fantasy* (Wings Books/Outlet Book Co., 1991). When Der Nister was later forced, under pressure from the Communist Party, to abandon storytelling in favor of critical realism, he produced the only novel in Yiddish to rival Dostoyevsky: *The Family Mashber*, translated by Leonard Wolf (Summit Books, 1987). Set in nineteenth-century Berdichev, then the commercial hub of the Ukraine, it exploited Der Nister's inside knowledge of Bratslav Hasidism—and portrayed it as an aspect of family pathology.

During Peretz's lifetime, his home in Warsaw was the obligatory pilgrimage site for all Yiddish hopeful writers. Bergelson and Der Nister both payed homage to the master. Others, like Abraham Reisen and Sholem Asch, were so taken by Peretz that they decided to stay for a while. Almost overnight, Asch became the most protean figure in Yiddish literature, producing in short order *The Shtetl, God of Vengeance,* a naturalist drama about lesbianism, in Joseph C. Landis's *The Great Jewish Plays* (Horizon Press, 1972), two novels about the hardships of the mass immigration to America (*America, Uncle Moses*), and a historical novel about the Cossack revolt of 1648–49, *Kiddush Ha-Shem,* translated by Rufus Learsi (Salem, N. H.: Ayer, 1975). Moving back and forth across Europe himself, he wrote a sweeping trilogy of historical upheaval in *Three Cities,* of Petersburg, Warsaw, Moscow (Carroll & Graf, 1983)—a big-screen adventure that still awaits its Cecil B. De Mille.

Warsaw, now boasting the largest Yiddish-speaking population in Europe, was also home to I. J. Singer, I. B.'s older brother. Not to be outdone by Asch, and recently disabused of his faith in Bolshevism, I. J. Singer became the chronicler of Jewish "homelessness" (see Anita Norich's *The Homeless Imagination in the Fiction of Israel Joshua Singer* [Indiana University Press, 1991]). Whether it was the hero of *Steel and Iron,* translated by Joseph Singer (Funk & Wagnalls, 1969), living under German occupation during World War I, or the legendary *Yoshe Kalb,* translated by Maurice Samuel (Schocken Books, 1988) or *The Brothers Ashkenazi,* translated by Joseph Singer (Carroll & Graf, 1985), Jewish manufacturers who took industrial Lodz by storm, Singer's verdict was everywhere the same: Jewish life and dreams were built on sand. With the knowledge of hindsight, and with greater literary skill than his brother, I. B. Singer delivered a sweeping indictment of Polish Jewry through the prism of its leading city, Warsaw, and of its leading fictional family in *The Family Moskat,* translated by A. H. Gross (Farrar, Straus and Giroux, 1988).

But what of New York City, where both brothers Singer sought refuge in the 1930s? Here the Jewish Labor movement first came into being. Here the professional Yiddish theater first got off the ground, and here modern Yiddish poetry was first created. According to Hutchins Hapgood, whose *The Spirit of the Ghetto*

(Harvard University Press, 1983), richly illustrated by Jacob Epstein, remains the most vivid guide to the Lower East Side, it was all over even while the mass immigration was in full swing. Hapgood was a Boston Brahmin turned muckraker. His "deep throat" was the famous Abraham Cahan, soon to become czar of the *Jewish Daily Forward*. The two men saw little hope for a viable Yiddish counter-culture surviving under American democratic conditions. But they were wrong, as any reader of Irving Howe's *World of Our Fathers* (Schocken Books, 1989) must surely know. Not only did Yiddish culture continue to flourish on the Lower East Side, later in Harlem, and other places north, south, and west, but it soon exported its goods back across the Atlantic.

The "world history" of the Yiddish theater has been pieced together by Nahma Sandrow in *Vagabond Stars* (Limelight Editions, 1986), with American Yiddish vaudeville (called *shund-teater*) occupying center stage. For a more specialized study, see Mark Slobin's *Tenement Songs: The Popular Music of the Jewish Immigrants* (University of Illinois, 1982) that comes complete with an audio cassette. The future that Hapgood denied could happen is the story of Ruth R. Wisse's *A Little Love in Big Manhattan* (Harvard University Press, 1988). Choosing as her heroes the two "lions" (*leyb* in Yiddish) of American Yiddish poetry, Moyshe-Leyb Halpern and Mani Leyb (Brahinski), Wisse also surveys the Yiddish literary scene from the beginning of this century until the death of Mani Leyb, in 1953.

Surprising but true: modern Yiddish poetry began in the New World and spread from there to the Old. Thanks to the bilingual *Penguin Book of Modern Yiddish Verse*, edited by Irving Howe, Ruth R. Wisse, and Chone Shmeruk (Viking Penguin, 1988), it is now possible to redraw the map of Yiddish beginning with Peretz, but then moving to America and back again. Howe's "Introduction" to Yiddish poetry in this volume is first-rate. Take, for example, the school of the Yiddish grotesque that began with Moyshe-Leyb Halpern in America and reached its apogee in Poland between the two world wars. Halpern's preoccupation with death (Peretz's, among others), his unerring eye for bourgeois hypocrisies, his "antipoetic" images and brutal rhymes—these were the underpinnings of Uri Zvi Greenberg's "Mephisto" (1921), of Yisroel Shtern's "Men Who Hunger" (c. 1928), of Leyzer Volf's "The Coarse Old Maid" (1928), of Israel Rabon's "A Funeral" (1933), and of Itzik Manger's ballads. Indeed, Yiddish modernism was a school for scandal, its members roguishly subverting just about everything that one normally associates with Yiddish—the voice of Labor, a mother's tears, a matinee idol's mixture of satire and schmaltz.

Yet because they starved and struggled alongside the rest of the Yiddish-

speaking masses, modern Yiddish poets the world over had to fight on all available
fronts. Thus the six poets whom Howe, Wisse, and Shmeruk selected as "the
strongest, the most characteristic, and the most accessible in translation" for the
Penguin Book of Modern Yiddish Verse—Moyshe-Leyb Halpern, Itzik Manger,
Moyshe Kulbak, Peretz Markish, Jacob Glatstein, and Abraham Sutzkever—
these poets all doubled as prose writers, playwrights, literary critics, editors, and
journalists. Those, in addition, whose career spanned the first half of the twentieth century were forced to temper their youthful exuberance, experimentation,
and iconoclasm when faced with the historical fate of the Jewish people.

Glatstein co-founded the ultra-modernist movement called Introspectivism,
earning him Cynthia Ozick's scorn as an aging "idolator" in her story "Envy, or
Yiddish in America," in *The Pagan Rabbi* (Dutton, 1983)—co-starring a thinly
disguised Isaac Bashevis Singer. With equal skill Ozick redeemed the full range of
Glatstein's verse in her translations in the *Penguin Book of Modern Yiddish Verse*.
She began with the apocalyptic mindscape of "1919," moved on to the sexual
combat of a man and two women seated at "Evening Bread." Then, in response
to Hitler and the imminent destruction of Polish Jewry, Glatstein emerged as the
greatest "national poet" in the Yiddish language; indeed, as the towering presence
among Jewish-American poets as a whole. When not delivering a dramatic monologue in the persona of Rabbi Nahman of Bratslav, Glatstein the nonbeliever
found a way of addressing a diminished God ("I pray from a tongue-tied page,
/ my woebegone God"). When not assessing the fate of his beloved language, he
was casting a satiric glance at anemic suburban Judaism. Other translators who
have tried their hand at Glatstein include Benjamin and Barbara Harshav, in
American Yiddish Poetry: A Bilingual Anthology (University of California, 1986),
very richly illustrated, and Richard J. Fein, in *The Selected Poems of Yankev
Glatshteyn* (Jewish Publication Society, 1988).

Abraham Sutzkever's modernism expressed itself in diametrically opposite
ways. Not New York, but the forests outside Vilna provided the very young Sutzkever with his "world of a thousand colors" ("In the Sack of the Wind"). Not free
verse and urbane speech rhythms but a profusion of rhymes and metrical schemes
displayed the poet's virtuosity. Then came the Nazis, in 1941. With ghetto walls
blocking all access to nature, survival itself became a nightmare ("How?"). And
so the poet cast about for new analogies, new meaning, new rhyme, and he fashioned an epic of "The Lead Plates at the Rom Press" being melted down into
bullets for the uprising to come. Fated to survive the Holocaust, Sutzkever chronicled "The silence of those who are no longer there" through the fleeting image of
"Deer at the Red Sea." The irreconcilables of natural beauty and human barbarity,

of national destruction and rebirth finally translated into a tightly wrought sequence of metaphysical *Poems from a Diary,* the last of which (and the last in the Penguin anthology) contemplated the contradictory meanings of a blade of grass from Ponar, the slaughter site of Vilna Jewry. In *The Fiddle Rose* (Wayne State University Press, 1990), translator Ruth Whitman has selected some of Sutzkever's poetry from 1970 to 1972, revealing a lyrical muse that defies all the ruptures of this tragic century.

The example of Sutzkever points to another aspect of postwar Yiddish writing: that literature became a memorial on paper to places and people that no longer existed. Thus Sutzkever's *landsman,* Chaim Grade, announced in the Yiddish preface to *The Agunah,* translated by Curt Leviant (Menorah Publications, 1978) that henceforth he planned to rescue from oblivion the one place on the *shtetl* map where no Yiddish writer before him had dared to tread: the synagogue world of prayer and Talmud study. Grade's many novels and novellas set in and around Vilna and culminating with *The Yeshiva,* translated by Curt Leviant (Menorah Publications, 1979) and *Rabbis and Wives,* translated by Harold Rabinowitz and Inna Grade (Schocken Books, 1987), and *My Mother's Sabbath Days* (Schocken Books, 1987), stand as a memorial to the dead. As do the agnostic prayers of Jacob Glatstein. As do the metaphysical poems of Abraham Sutzkever.

Which brings us, inevitably, to the matter of catastrophe itself. Yiddish has been fated to become the memory bank of Jewish national disaster. This process began long before the Holocaust, as shown in my own book, *Against the Apocalypse: Responses to Catastrophe in Modern Jewish Culture* (Harvard University Press, 1986) and illustrated with a wealth of examples in the companion volume, *The Literature of Destruction* (Jewish Publication Society, 1989). As these two books demonstrate, Yiddish writing in the Nazi ghettos and concentration camps not only brought together the sum of all previous responses to catastrophe but also anticipated the themes, styles, and searching questions that were to characterize the literature of the Holocaust.

Many are the ways that Yiddish writers turned historical experience into fictional form. Leyb Rochman employed subtle novelistic techniques when recasting the day-by-day terror of the Nazi occupation in *The Pit and the Trap: A Chronicle of Survival,* translated by Moshe Kahn (Holocaust Library, 1983)—just as Elie Wiesel did in *Night* (Bantam, 1982), first published in Yiddish in 1956. By the same token, much of the poetry written in the Nazi ghettos and camps must be understood against the backdrop of earlier songs. This layering process is amply illustrated in *We Are Here: Songs of the Holocaust,* edited by Eleanor Mlotek and Malke Gottlieb (Education Department of the Workmen's Circle, 1983) and in

I. B. Singer was awarded the Nobel Prize for Literature in 1978.
(Photograph by Barbara Pfeffer)

Pearls of Yiddish Song, compiled by Eleanor and Joseph Mlotek (Workmen's Circle, 1988). The Mloteks, for example, made the astonishing discovery that *Eyli Eyli,* sung as a religious hymn during the Holocaust, was originally performed on the New York Yiddish stage—in 1896! In addition to singing—the most public vehicle of group memory—Yiddish-speaking Jews produced hundreds of *yizker-bikher,* memorial volumes to their destroyed communities in eastern Europe. These have been excerpted and ably described by Jack Kugelmass and Jonathan Boyarin in *From a Ruined Garden: The Memorial Books of Polish Jewry* (Schocken Books, 1985).

In a sense, *everything* written in Yiddish, even the most highbrowed experimental poetry, can be read as a response to the terrible upheavals in modern Jewish life. Benjamin Harshav sees *The Meaning of Yiddish* (University of California Press, 1990) in the achievements of Yiddish modernism against the backdrop of these exhilarating and terrifying changes, many of them, as he stresses, undertaken voluntarily by a people that wanted out—out of the "ghetto" at any price. As Harshav tells it, Sholem Aleichem too must be understood as a modernist rebel!

If Yiddish functions primarily as metaphor for Jews and Americans of the present generation, reading Yiddish literature in translation greatly enriches that metaphoric field. Those Yiddish works that appear on the surface to be most folksy, most true to the norms of "*shtetl* society" emerge upon closer inspection to be careful acts of camouflage, studied attempts on the part of very modern writers to reimagine themselves as members of the folk. Peretz, Sholem Aleichem, and Manger taught I. B. Singer everything he needed to know about the art of folk simulation. The *shtetl* itself, it turns out, was a useful myth of origins invented by writers who could never go home again.

When Yiddish writers turned to unabashedly modern pursuits—the writing of novels, memoirs, expressionist or introspective verse—there were always countervailing forces pulling them back to the fold. The murderous attempts of Hitler and Stalin to solve the Jewish Problem once and for all convinced Yiddish writers that they could not remain above the fray. Many perished, among them the stellar group of Soviet-Yiddish writers whom Stalin purged between 1936 and 1952. Howe and Greenberg captured their collective fate in the title of their book *Ashes Out of Hope: Fiction by Soviet-Yiddish Writers* (Schocken Books, 1978). This reengagement with the folk and its fate, as we have seen, was often accompanied by a negotiated return to the forms of folk creativity as well: to folk songs, folktales, and the whole legendary landscape of Jewish eastern Europe. And when they lost their Yiddish-reading audience to mass murder or assimilation, Yiddish writers turned increasingly to other media. I. J. Singer adapted his novels for Maurice Schwartz's Yiddish Art Theater and won a ticket to America in the bargain. I. B. Singer preferred to let Barbra Streisand and Paul Mazursky write the screen adaptations for him. Anyway, on the screen, the best one could hope for was a Yiddishized English—and that Riverside Drive in the heat of the summer would look like Central Park West in the snow.

CHAPTER 14

THE JEWISH NOVELIST IN AMERICA

Mark Shechner

Prologue

From the start, writing by Jewish novelists in America has been a vast enterprise. Seen from afar, the house of Jewish letters may resemble a bustling sweatshop, where writers arranged by rank and by file turn out books the way garment makers used to turn out apparel for the American clothing market. If that image belies the isolation and enclosed sensibility of the writer's enterprise, it does suggest the scale of the Jewish entry into American letters along with the hothouse atmosphere in which that literary endeavor has flourished. Writing remains, as tailoring once was, a principal Jewish occupation. Plainly, a reader's guide must proceed by exclusions, by ignoring certain books that were once read by thousands and by omitting entire careers that once appeared to define the Jewish presence itself. If the reader should find scant mention of writers once as prolific and acclaimed as Edna Ferber, Sholem Asch, Ben Hecht, Jerome Weidman, Maurice Samuel, Waldo Frank, Clifford Odets, Arthur Miller, Budd Schulberg, Leon Uris, and

Herman Wouk, or find Edward Lewis Wallant, Norman Mailer, and Chaim Potok given less than their due, it is not for any failure to appreciate their contributions to American writing.

We must also be prepared to turn a blind eye to such literary forms as poetry, theater, and film and restrict our survey of memoirs and autobiographies to writers who had significant careers in fiction. We must say virtually nothing of the Yiddish language and must skip over the culture and literature the immigrants brought with them and continued to produce in Yiddish decades after their arrival. (For this topic see chapter 13, "Yiddish Literature" in this book.) Moreover, we are bound to favor a writing that declares its Jewish self-consciousness, however that may be conceived, as historical consciousness or as covenant or as folk culture, though, ironically, we need say little about Talmud, Torah, and Halakhah, which have small bearing on a literature whose well-springs were secular and even anti-religious. What follows, then, is a personal canon, a declaration of what I would cite as the enduring legacy of Jewish fiction in America.

In the Beginning

In the beginning there was Abraham Cahan, whose *The Rise of David Levinsky* (1917; Harper & Row, 1966), though not the first Jewish novel written in America, is the earliest to have stood the test of time. It comprehended better than any other the disruptions of immigration and the ironies of acculturation. As a socialist and reformer, of both American and Jewish life, as the editor of *The Jewish Daily Forward,* as the proprietor of the "Bintel Brief" letters column to that paper, and as a peripatetic walker in the city, Cahan was uniquely positioned to write the moral history of the immigrant generation: to document its experiences, underscore its conflicts, and summarize its achievements. *The Rise of David Levinsky* is the testament of a man whose life's work was observing the culture of his people, giving it voice, and forming the institutions through which it could realize itself and gain entry into America.

As a novel about a man who starts out as a *yeshiva bokher* in Russia and ends up as a tycoon in America, *The Rise of David Levinsky* is a quintessential statement of the collision between spirit and money, Jewish values and American promises. It portrays the Jewish soul in the throes of its transformation by capitalism, opportunity, and the need to look out for number one. During and after the

Abraham Cahan, editor
of the *Jewish Daily Forward,*
which guided a generation
of immigrant Jews toward
Americanization. (YIVO
Institute for Jewish Research)

great immigration, this transformation became one of the chief themes of Jewish life in America. The "Bintel Brief" column of Cahan's *Jewish Daily Forward* was a compendium of life in convulsive change, as immigrants and their children set about learning how to cope with the unique American conjunction of opportunity and peril.

The Rise of David Levinsky was a typical American novel of the Progressive era. Jewish in its histories and locales, it was American in its plot, exploring themes of fortune and failure, ambition and mobility, hardship at the bottom and hardship at the top. Like a garment, it was cut from a standard pattern, borrowed in this case from William Dean Howells's 1885 novel, *The Rise of Silas Lapham.*

But *David Levinsky* had another dimension that distinguished it from the documentary and the didactic: it was an experiment in creating a modern self, whose interiority went deeper than anything Jewish writers had attempted before.

The character of David Levinsky signaled the entry of the individual into Jewish-American literature. Though typical he is not generic, and he is the first in a line of Jewish heroes who become individuals by virtue of being neurotics. David Levinsky's conflicts and his instinct for defeat in love—the moral counterweight to his success in business—are forerunners of the more probing, psychological literature that emerged some twenty years later with the stories of Delmore Schwartz and flowered after the war in the novels of Saul Bellow and Isaac Rosenfeld, Bernard Malamud, Philip Roth, Harold Brodkey, Joseph Heller, and E. L. Doctorow.

In 1917, this struggle to compose a unique self for purposes of survival was a distinctly American concept, and *The Rise of David Levinsky* was a Jewish novelty, though a novelty against the backdrop of a people discovering, *en masse*, self-reliance. As the Jews cast off their traditional habits and ways, their rituals and beliefs, it was to America that they looked for moral guidance and models of character. The great paradigm shift saw the Jews become a desanctified people and a people for whom the ceremonies of self-reliance were to be substituted for those of common purpose and common destiny. It is not surprising then that so many early books should be stories of separation and conflict: between parents and children, between tradition and exploration, between *shtetl* austerities and American horizons. Such books became blueprints of how, in a single generation, a culture founded upon "Thou Shalt Not" would find its new moral sanction in "The Pursuit of Happiness."

For more by and about Cahan, see his *Yekl: A Tale of the New York Ghetto* (1896), in *The Imported Bridegroom and Other Stories of Yiddish New York*, (Dover, 1978); Ronald Sanders, *The Downtown Jews: Portraits of an Immigrant Generation* (1969; Dover, 1987); Isaac Metzker, ed., *A Bintel Brief: Sixty Years of Letters from the Lower East Side to the Jewish Daily Forward* (1971; Schocken Books, 1990); Abraham Cahan, *The Education of Abraham Cahan* (Jewish Publication Society, 1969), translated by Leon Stein et al. from the 1926 Yiddish autobiography *Bleter fun mein leben*.

Perhaps no novel from these years better epitomizes these struggles than Anzia Yezierska's *Bread Givers*, subtitled *A Struggle between a Father of the Old World and a Daughter of the New* (1925; Persea Books, 1975). Etched out on a smaller social canvas than Cahan's *The Rise of David Levinsky*, but in swifter, more jagged strokes, it was a doxology of liberation on the part of a young woman, Sara Smolinsky, for whom the shackles of life as a scholar's daughter were not to be suffered in a world where striking out and forging ahead were canonized in the national liturgy as inalienable rights. *Bread Givers* reads like a "Bintel Brief" letter in novel form. The father, a talmudic scholar cursed with four daughters, is desperate to match them with husbands who will sustain him in his old age and safeguard his privileged leisure. Sara's sisters tragically give in to their father's demands while Sara ferociously holds out for her own destiny. "Woe to a man who has females for his offspring" is the father's battle cry. "My will is as strong as yours" is Sara's retort. "I'm going to live my own life. Nobody can stop me. I'm not from the old country. I'm American!" It is not amiss to say that *Bread Givers* is the first Jewish feminist novel.

An immigrant herself, who did not arrive in America until she was sixteen, Yezierska set about with a passion to Americanize herself: to teach herself English and to express her wild yearnings in prose. It was as a factory worker, in her thirties, that she began writing the stories of immigrant life that would launch her career, which included an arid detour through Hollywood as a screenwriter and a brief, intimate relationship with the philosopher John Dewey. Like Cahan, however, Yezierska knew Americanization to be a tainted blessing. One might be liberated, but for what? To be independent, desanctified, and alone. With Sara Smolinsky, as with David Levinsky, the heart does not open toward the new life but grows rigid and prohibitive and, ironically, talmudic, as her form of self-assertion is a dedication to scholarship and study.

In life, Yezierska found the successes that her writing had thrust upon her unpalatable, as her talent dried up in Hollywood. After a brief stay there, which she describes ruefully in her autobiography *Red Ribbon on a White Horse* (1950; Persea Books, 1988), she returned to the claustral cityscape that had formed her gifts. Rebel against Jewish life though she might, only Hester Street and its sorrows ignited her imagination, and it was after the Hollywood fiasco that she would come back to New York and write her masterwork, *Bread Givers.* There were other books, before *Bread Givers* and after: *Hungry Hearts* (1926; Persea Books, 1985), the collection of stories for which Samuel Goldwyn offered $10,000; *Children of Loneliness* (1923), *Salome of the Tenements* (1923), *Arrogant Beggar* (1927), and *All I Could Never Be* (1932). All are marked by the same rawness and desire, out of which one of Yezierska's heroines declaims: "I am a Russian Jewess, a flame, a longing. A soul consumed with hunger for heights beyond reach. I am an ache of unvoiced dreams, the clamor of suppressed desires." Of Yezierska's novels, only *Bread Givers* is in print, though there are two anthologies of her work: *The Open Cage: An Anzia Yezierska Collection,* edited by Alice Kessler-Harris, with an afterword by Yezierska's daughter, Louise Levitas Henriksen (Persea Books, 1979), and *How I Found America: Collected Stories of Anzia*

Yezierska, introduced by Vivian Gornick (Persea Books, 1991). There one can experience in full measure that "ache of unvoiced dreams" and "clamor of suppressed desires," which remain as stirring and unsettling as they were some sixty-five years ago.

Jews and the Left

Any account of the evolution of Jewish writing in America must come to terms with one overwhelming fact about that history: that in the early years much of it was associated with radical ideas and left-wing movements. Throughout the first half-century of Jewish writing in America, radicalism seemed indigenous to the Jewish profile. In the 1930s especially, the Depression and fears of fascism drove many Jewish intellectuals and writers into revolutionary postures and sponsored an outpouring of "proletarian" and "popular front" novels. Since political and social agendas usually outweighed literary ones in such books, most of them have little more than historical interest today, though some, like Mike Gold's *Jews Without Money* (1930; Carroll & Graf, 1984), transcend their *parti pris* through raw documentary force.

There has been no lack of efforts to explain Jewish leftism, though explanations hardly seem necessary. The greater part of the Ashkenazi Jews came to America a dispossessed people: landless, excluded, and persecuted, and discovered in America routines of labor so exploitative, when work could be found, that it is a wonder that they were not all converted to revolutionism at once. The Triangle Shirtwaist fire of 1911, in which 146 workers died, remains a symbol of the working conditions that immigrants encountered in America. There are, however, reasons why the Jews among the immigrants produced much of this literature, and not others who suffered from the same Malthusian economics: 1. Their exclusion from opportunities predisposed some toward programs that promised a world reformed to abolish Jewish isolation. 2. Yiddish-speaking Jews already constituted a de facto workers' internationale of their own and looked upon internationalist movements as instruments for initiating others into their brand of brotherhood. 3. The immigrants imported the revolutionary idealism of Russia. Marxism provided a rallying point for these insurrectionary sentiments. 4. Marxism itself was a rigorous ideology whose basic tenets existed in canonical texts, allowing the Talmudic strain in Jewish culture to express itself in political terms. The road from the Yeshiva to the barricade was paved with volumes of *Kapital*. 5. The Jewish prophetic tradition, detached from the Law, attached itself to other eschatologies that combined moral righteousness with Millenarian visions.

Mike Gold's *Jews Without Money* might well stand for the whole corpus of revolutionary testaments produced by the Jewish-radical fusion. Though it is a self-consciously "proletarian" novel, a fable of working-class life with a revolutionary moral, its staying power derives not from any formulas that Gold brought from the Communist party, for which he worked as editor of *The New Masses*, but from a searing recollection of his childhood among those whom Jacob Riis called "the other half."

Born Iztchok Granich in 1893 on New York's Lower East Side, the son of Rumanian immigrant parents, Gold changed his name to Irwin as a youth and during the Palmer raids of 1919–20 took the name of Mike Gold, an abolitionist hero who had fought in the Civil War. Everywhere around him he saw poverty and demoralization; his own father, a manufacturer of suspenders, failed in business and Gold had to leave school and go to work at the age of twelve. The experience of poverty in an environment of predatory capitalism became the source of his revolutionary ardor and grist for his literary mill.

Behind *Jews Without Money* were assumptions about literature as revolutionary action. Melodramatic though those assumptions could be—all labor was misery, all ownership exploitation—they showed Gold the way to convert the impressions of his childhood into a theater of radical initiation, bringing, in effect, Dickens together with Engels. In Gold, the theater of the grotesque merged with the documentary of conditions to form one of the most graphic literatures of disaffection America ever produced.

Jews Without Money is a contra-*Levinsky*, a look at Jewish life through the other end of the telescope. If Abraham Cahan and Anzia Yezierska depicted the immigrant experience as an ascent, however jagged, Michael Gold was intent on the fall, which was as American as the rise. *Jews Without Money* is a reminder of how immigrant society in America fell into classes and that the vast majority of the Jews did not, like David Levinsky, go into business, or like Sara Smolinsky, light out for the university. They were working people who were either self-employed at marginal levels, as pushcart vendors, or worked in whatever trades were open to them in the urban ghettos of America. For more about Gold, see *Mike Gold: A Literary Anthology*, edited by Mike Folsom (International Press, 1972).

The Landscape of Dreams

The great Jewish book of the 1930s was Henry Roth's *Call It Sleep* (1934; Avon Books, 1976), though few reviewers of the time were prepared to appreciate its power. Its emotionalism was too raw and its psychologism too radical for an age that professed to have other, more social, uses for literature. It was not until 1964, when the paperback reprint was given a front-page review in *The New York Times Book Review* by Irving Howe, that the book enjoyed anything like widespread acclaim. The ordeal of the child, David Schearl, who comes to America with his mother to encounter a father who is suspicious, estranged, and given to capricious rages, is perhaps better appreciated now than in the thirties, when its brand of literary impressionism was looked on with a certain condescension.

Call It Sleep is the story of a young boy's initiation into the mysteries of his own being: the mysteries of sex and those of religion, the mysteries of origin, and those of the world around him which appears to be ruled by ominous and alien symbols. At the center of it is a grotesque family romance, dominated by a father whose smoldering rage ionizes the atmosphere. The novel's prologue, in which he and his mother are greeted at Ellis Island by a fearful and accusatory father, is a preview of all that is to befall David. Virtually a babe in arms, he is guilty of unnamed crimes.

Unlike anything else Jewish writers were doing in the 1930s, *Call It Sleep* was a book about symbols (basements, closets, fiery coals, rosaries), terrors, secret powers, and hidden meanings. It exposed the dark side of the psyche and read more like German Expressionist drama than anything else in Jewish-American writing. The forty pages at the end of *Call It Sleep* are the most powerful sustained writing ever done by a Jewish writer in America.

While other novelists were writing social dramas with occasional Marxist flavoring, Roth was writing a Freudian dissection of the soul in crisis. If Abraham Cahan in *The Rise of David Levinsky* invented the self for the Jewish novelist in America, it is astonishing that just seventeen years later Henry Roth, making the leap into modernism, would dismantle the self, not to restore a lost communality but to declare the vulnerability of the naked ego, alone and isolated in a strange world. The spectacular cadenza in which David hurtles through the night streets and sticks the handle of a milk ladle onto the third rail of the trolley tracks, not only brings the motifs of the book to a stunning climax but sums up a relationship to the New World that distinguishes it sharply from the Old: America is a place where loneliness can drive you insane.

Footnote to the Thirties

The pre-war literary culture was rich in writing by and about Jews, and though most of it is time-bound, a portion retains both freshness and a documentary value. Foremost among these novels are those by Daniel Fuchs, *Summer in Williamsburg* (1934; Carroll & Graf, 1983), *Homage to Blenholt* (1936; Omnigraphics, 1990), *Low Company* (1937). The three novels were assembled into *The Williamsburg Trilogy* by Basic Books in 1961. Of the three, the first, a social portrait of a Williamsburg (Brooklyn) adolescence, an urban romance, and a bemused disquisition on adolescent movie-going, is the best known, though I am partial to the *Homage to Blenholt*, in which the funeral of a corrupt Commissioner of Sewers occasions a degree of civic mourning that is usually reserved for heads of state or oriental despots. In it Fuchs demonstrated a capacity for broad social satire that would later stand him in good stead as a Hollywood screenwriter. Indeed, *Low Company*, a hard-boiled novel about a gangland takeover of prostitution in Neptune, New Jersey, would be made into a film, *The Gangster*, in 1947. In all these Fuchs would demonstrate an ear for common speech, an eye for social detail, and a gift for irony. In Hollywood, where he would work continuously after 1940, Fuchs wrote or collaborated on a series of popular screenplays, including *Panic in the Streets* (1950), *Love Me or Leave Me* (1955), and *Jeanne Eagels* (1957).

Meyer Levin, regarded by some as the great neglected figure among the Jewish novelists, wrote his best book, *The Old Bunch*, in 1937 (Carol Publishing Group, 1985). A novel about the fracturing of the Jewish community and the capriciousness of destiny in the New World, it traces a group of poor Jewish boys out of the ghettos of the Chicago West Side into the mainstream of American life. A quintessential Chicago novel in the manner of Theodore Dreiser, James T. Farrell, and Nelson Algren, *The Old Bunch* is dense in the gritty urban detail of downtown realism and ghetto naturalism: it is a fiction inspired by stockyards and rail yards and a life in which the impossibility of romance takes on a romantic coloration of its own. In later years Levin would divide his time among fiction, journalism, and drama, and nowadays is probably best remembered for his book about the Leopold and Loeb case, *Compulsion* (Simon & Schuster, 1956), *The Settlers* (1972; Bantam, 1987), and for the stage adaptation he did of Anne Frank's diary, which her father denied him permission to produce. This episode would eventually lead to a strange and vivid book, the autobiographical *The Obsession* (Simon & Schuster, 1973), Levin's bitter account of his struggles with Otto Frank and a diatribe on the politics of Jewish letters in the postwar years. See also Levin's edition of *Classic Hasidic Tales: Marvelous Tales of Rabbi Israel Baal Shem and of his Great-Grandson, Rabbi Nachman, Retold from Hebrew, Yiddish, and German Sources*, published 1932 as *The Golden Mountain* (Penguin Books, 1975).

Fuchs and Levin both were social writers, like most of the Jewish novelists who published in the 1930s. From Mike Gold's *Jews without Money* in 1930 to Meyer Levin's *Citizens* ten years later, the social muse is in the ascendant and the song of protest is the most plangent. The plays of Clifford Odets, of which *Waiting for Lefty* (1935) and *Awake and Sing* (1935) remain the most memorable, are the dramatic counterparts of this fiction. If much of this literature seems to retain more documentary than imaginative appeal, it is nevertheless needful in reminding us how Jewish life and the Jewish spirit came of age in America, through bitter days and arid scenes.

The Advent of Modernism

It is common knowledge that Jewish writing through the 1930s was inspired largely by the social muse, which could construct vivid tableaux of exploitation and grief even while being imaginatively constricted and compositionally banal. In due course, however, as both social integration and success came to American Jews, Jewish writers would cast off purely social agendas and adopt psychological and spiritual ones. Parable and myth, psychological complexity and moral ambiguity, Jamesian strategy and Joycean virtuosity begin to assert their presence in the fiction written by American Jews.

Precursors could be found in the novels of Nathanael West (Nathan Weinstein), most notably *Miss Lonelyhearts* (1933) and *The Day of the Locust* (1939) (reprinted in one volume by New Directions, 1969), but West's sense of Jewish identity was marginal and it was as an American rather than as a Jew that he wrote and was read. And Roth's *Call It Sleep,* a virtual handbook of modernist clichés, was *sui generis,* a brilliant interlude that made no impact on its time and left no legacy except a certain backwash of wonder and speculation.

The Jewish writers' modernization in America—their connection to the European avant-garde—can be traced back to a slim volume of stories that appeared in 1938 under the title of its lead story, *In Dreams Begin Responsibilities and Other Stories,* by Delmore Schwartz (New Directions, 1978). Schwartz's writing was more auspicious than Roth's because it had an intellectual context: *Partisan Review* magazine which, from the late 1930s on, was a rallying point for disaffected and militant writers and intellectuals. The stories in *In Dreams Begin Responsibilities* could not be characterized as "Bintel Brief" letters writ large, because Schwartz was primarily a psychological writer, the tormented stations of the soul being the keynotes of his writing. Irving Howe once called him a "comedian of alienation," which captures something of the ironic and tangential relation he bore to his time. Indeed, what would make him auspicious was that at first glance *he had no relation to his time,* preferring to establish an ongoing relation to eternity. If America was going to produce a Franz Kafka, it looked for a while as though Schwartz was the prime candidate. Certainly, the pathos of his first story, in which a young Delmore sits in a movie theater and watches in horror the scene of his as yet unmarried parents' courtship in a Coney Island restaurant, was like nothing the social muse could inspire.

Schwartz did not fulfill himself in fiction. His main impact would be in poetry, though that would prove fleeting, as insomnia, alcohol, drugs, and finally madness ground him down. He is, as most readers know, the Von Humboldt Fleisher of Saul Bellow's novel *Humboldt's Gift.* It was as a releasing agent and a guide to an alternative tradition that Schwartz affected literature. A disciple of Rimbaud and Wallace Stevens, Pound and Eliot, he claimed new horizons for others, like Saul Bellow and Isaac Rosenfeld, who would seize upon his epigrams and work them up into strategies. It was Schwartz who showed the way out of the ghettos of realism (and the realisms of the ghetto) into the more capacious worlds of symbol and allusion, parable and myth, neurosis and alienation. For more by and about Schwartz, see his selected poems, *Summer Knowledge* (New Directions, 1959), and the biography by James Atlas, *Delmore Schwartz: The Life of an American Poet* (1977; Harcourt Brace Jovanovich, 1985).

Saul Bellow

What Schwartz inaugurated in American Jewish letters was the Europeanization of the self, and it is not too much to see Saul Bellow as the fulfillment of Schwartz's failed promise. It was in the Schwartz mode, as an underground man *à la* Dostoevski, that Bellow made his entry into American literature with *Dangling Man* (1944; Penguin Books, 1988) and *The Victim* (1947; Penguin Books, 1988), "post-socialist novels," whose basic strategies are neither the dissection of society nor the amelioration of its cruelties. Each is a subtle evocation of individual psychopathology, though in the context of real history. In *Dangling Man* the historical context is wartime; in *The Victim* it is the postwar malaise that would descend upon Jewish intellectuals for whom the bull market of fortune could not cauterize the wounds of war. While others celebrated, they despaired.

Probing the spirit in crisis would become the axial line of Bellow's thought, though he would take an occasional detour, as he did in his third novel, *The Adventures of Augie March* (1953; Penguin Books, 1984), an idiosyncratic return to the sprawling Chicago novel of Dreiser, Farrell, and Levin. But that book is now the least memorable of Bellow's performances, substituting panorama for penetration and the vast cityscape for the vivid cameo. Far more acute was *Seize the Day* (1956; Penguin Books, 1984), in which Tommy Wilhelm, a neurotic son, finds himself in a squeeze play between two fathers, a remote and narcissistic real father and a seemingly nurturing but utterly predatory therapist-father, who places a high price tag on the love he offers—Tommy's last penny for falling lard futures.

In *Seize the Day,* all the elements of Bellow's worldview are held in perfect equipoise. It is a comedy of capitalism, in which profit and loss are blended into health and neurosis, so that Tommy Wilhelm's final wipeout in the commodities market makes him one of Sigmund Freud's "Characters Wrecked by Success." In the figure of Tamkin, guru and commodities maven, rabbi, broker, therapist, and thief, Bellow conjured up one of his greatest inventions.

Seize the Day would inaugurate the main phase of Bellow's career, which would include *Henderson the Rain King* (1959; Penguin Books, 1984), the play *The Last Analysis* (Viking Penguin, 1965), *Herzog* (1964; Penguin Books, 1984), and *Mr. Sammler's Planet* (1970; Penguin Books, 1984). It is possible to talk about these books, Bellow's collective chef d'oeuvre, together, since they are thematically united. They are Bellow's therapeutic novels, foregrounding issues of illness and recuperation and suggesting that to fall ill is to suffer from culture or history. Virtually all of Bellow's heroes are patients or convalescents: Tommy Wilhelm in *Seize the Day*, Eugene Henderson of *Henderson the Rain King*, Bummidge of *The Last Analysis*, Moses Herzog of *Herzog*, and Artur Sammler of *Mr. Sammler's Planet*. All except Sammler are neurotics who seek relief from their symptoms and throw themselves into one curative scheme or another in their febrile searches for remedy. Tommy Wilhelm submits to a therapist-shaman who betrays him; Henderson sets off for Africa and meets up with a healer-dealer who cures him; Bummidge conducts autotherapy in front of closed-circuit TV; Herzog hands himself over to women and, when that fails, tries to kill his ex-wife's lover. Only Sammler deflects the neurotic question, since, as a Holocaust survivor, he suffers from history directly, not symptomatically.

From *Humboldt's Gift* (1975; Penguin Books, 1984) to the present, Bellow's work has turned into something of a long finale, a gathering together of impressions and memories as if, time running short, there is ever so much to say. The sprawling *Humboldt's Gift* is the most vigorous of these books, especially in those pages devoted to the failed poet and prophet, Von Humboldt Fleisher, who is Schwartz in every detail. Bellow can be a very funny writer and in *Humboldt's Gift*, the figure of Humboldt/Schwartz, whose antics grow more outrageous as his schizophrenia grows more dire, permits Bellow to release his comic impulses in a virtually uninhibited way. Humboldt's fate is black, but never too black for wisecracks.

Since *Humboldt's Gift*, Bellow has remained productive, though his recent writing has lost something of its bite. However, a blunted Bellow is worth a dozen other writers at their sharpest. His later writing includes two novels, *The Dean's December* (1982; Washington Square Press, 1985) and *More Die of Heartbreak* (1987; Dell, 1988); two novellas, *The Bellarosa Connection* (Penguin Books, 1989) and *A Theft: A Novella* (Penguin Books, 1989); a collection of stories, *Him With His Foot in His Mouth and Other Stories* (1984; Pocket Books, 1985); and a memoir of Israel in the wake of the Six-Day War, *To Jerusalem and Back* (1976; Penguin Books, 1985). It is all marked by the same sardonic wisdom, the same epigrammatic briskness, the same suave urbanity, the same keen perception. Bellow is the most visual of our writers. But the newcomer to Bellow who wants to catch him at his best should start with *Seize the Day* and follow it up with the difficult but dazzling *Herzog*. There may not be two better novels in all of postwar American literature.

In treating of Bellow we are compelled to mention his boyhood chum and early comrade-in-books, Isaac Rosenfeld, whose death of a heart attack in 1956, at the age of thirty-eight, was a blow to literature. Rosenfeld's promise, though troubled and erratic, was genuine. He was the only Jewish writer of his generation to write fiction in Yiddish as well as in English, and while the accumulated harvest of writing was small, the freshness and penetration of his mind is still palpable in much of it. He left behind one novel, *Passage from Home* (1948; Markus Wiener, 1988), and several collections edited posthumously by friends and admirers: *Alpha and Omega*, short stories (Viking Penguin, 1966), *An Age of Enormity*, essays (World Publishers, 1962). See especially Mark Shechner, ed., *Preserving the Hunger: An Isaac Rosenfeld Reader* (Wayne State University Press, 1988), a representative sampler of Rosenfeld's essays and his fiction. Rosenfeld's writing is still capable of surprising, and delighting, those who come upon it for the first time.

Bernard Malamud

Bernard Malamud's Jewish patrimony was altogether different from Saul Bellow's. Whereas Bellow came on the scene as an apostle of modernism, a disciple of Dostoevski (*The Victim* was based on the plot of Dostoevski's *The Eternal Husband*), an intellectual, who would become a professor at the University of Chicago's Committee on Social Thought, and an anthropologist of the urban middle class, Malamud was something much homier and more available to the common reader: a child of Yiddish folk culture whose first principle was an abiding love for the little man, *dos klayne mentschele*, as the grandfather of Yiddish literature, Mendele Mokher Seforim, had called him.

This may not have been apparent in Malamud's first novel, *The Natural* (1952; Avon Books, 1980), in which a bizarre event in the history of American baseball, the shooting of Philadelphia Phillies player Eddie Waitkus by a woman he had engaged for the night, was yoked together, in metaphysical fashion, with Golden Bough fertility myths, to create the mythical figure of Roy Hobbs, pitcher, slugger, and tragic Osiris of the American cornbelt. It was a strained performance, and anyone who saw the 1983 film, with Robert Redford in the leading role,

288

Bernard Malamud (Photograph by Barbara Pfeffer)

would be justified in wondering where the Jewish content was. But, given Mala-mud's subsequent career as a celebrant of Jewish folk myth and spiritual lore, in stories like "Angel Levine" and "Idiots First," *The Natural* may not be so alien from that world as might first be supposed, though Roy Hobbs finally is a player and not a zaddik.

Soon afterward, Malamud returned to native grounds with his two subsequent books, *The Assistant* (1957; Avon Books, 1980) and his first collection of stories, *The Magic Barrel* (1958; Farrar, Straus and Giroux, 1958). In the first, *dos klayne mentschele*, as an elderly Brooklyn grocery store owner, Morris Bober, is given homage as a hero of durability and fortitude, who tolerates a meager existence in a failing business because it is his lot to do so. For many readers, *The Assistant* remains the representative Malamud novel, for its celebration of endurance and conscience. The old grocery store, redolent of dust and neglect, the insistent weight of moral implication that leaves no act, no dialogue, no transaction free of ethical valence, the sense of moral combat between Jew, Morris Bober, and Gentile, Frank Alpine, the sustained note of lamentation—the still, sad music of daily existence—are all Malamud trademarks, and have been taken by many readers as his definitive Jewish credentials.

Yet precisely the throb of ethical pressure in *The Assistant* raises a problem that runs through Malamud's work: the Jewish content is wholly atmospheric and resistant to definition. When Morris Bober tries to define, for Frank Alpine, his Jewish identity in terms of the Law, he is hard put to specify what the Law is and ends up stuttering out a formula: "I suffer for you." When challenged on that, he adds, "I mean you suffer for me." To be sure, this elusiveness is typical of most Jewish writing in America, and Malamud can hardly be chastened for not knowing what no other writer is in firm possession of. It is precisely this conjunction of liturgical ignorance and tonal clarity about Jewish life that defines the entire Jewish-American literary corpus.

Malamud's minimalist sensibility, his feel for Depression-era marginality, has generally found its best vehicle in his short stories, and it was with the publication of *The Magic Barrel* in 1958 that Malamud's reputation as a master was made. Some of those stories are among the most consistently anthologized of any in the postwar canon: "Angel Levine" and "The Magic Barrel" are classic modern short stories, and from a second collection, *Idiots First* (Farrar, Straus and Giroux, 1963), "The Jewbird" and "Idiots First" have enjoyed similar ongoing appreciation. The reader who is in search of the essential Malamud should begin with the story collections: *The Magic Barrel, Idiots First, Pictures of Fidelman* (1969), and *Rembrandt's Hat* (1974; Farrar, Straus and Giroux, 1986), though the quintessence of Malamud is available in his personal selection of stories, *The Stories of Bernard Malamud* (1983; Plume, 1984).

The novels are more erratic performances, and though all have their moments of grace, it is generally conceded that Malamud never mastered the broader architecture of the novel. A novel that is interesting for its autobiographical reflections of Malamud's own days as a composition instructor at Oregon State University (where he was not permitted to teach literature), is *A New Life* (1961; Farrar, Straus and Giroux, 1988), which examines the ironies of a new world within the new world, a land so alien from Jewish experience or sensibility that one might wonder if the grocery store of *The Assistant* and the English Department of *A New Life* can possibly be on the same planet. In *The Fixer* (1966; Washington Square Press, 1989) Malamud stepped out of the personal mode to write a historical novel around the actual case of Mendel Beiliss, a Jew who was tried and acquitted on charges of ritual murder in czarist Russia at the turn of the century. Malamud's Yakov Bok, like the real Beiliss, is acquitted, but not before he is subjected to humiliating persecution and converted to revolutionism.

Malamud has never been given proper credit for his courage and his willingness to take risks. Consider the range of themes in his novels: life at the margins of existence in *The Assistant*, the ironies of liberation in the Far West in *A New*

Life, the pariah's lot in czarist Russia in *The Fixer.* In 1971 he would publish *The Tenants* (Farrar, Straus and Giroux, 1988), in which two inhabitants of an abandoned building in the South Bronx, Harry Lesser (Jewish) and Willie Spearmint (black), grow increasingly hostile to each other until, in a fit of rage, they beat each other to death. Then, in 1979, Malamud would publish what might arguably be his best novel, *Dubin's Lives* (Farrar, Straus and Giroux, 1979), about a Jewish writer who leaves his wife for a younger woman and discovers, like S. Levin in *A New Life* had, that liberty comes with a price tag. Finally, in *God's Grace* (1982; Avon Books, 1983), Malamud attempted a curious and awkward theological parable in which a paleologist named Calvin Cohn finds himself shipwrecked with a chimpanzee named Buz in a post-nuclear-holocaust world.

I don't believe we have fully come to terms with Malamud yet, surely not so long as critics continue to see him as either a placid moralist or an expert in timeless wisdom and contemporary ethics. The variety of his experiments will finally be recognized for what they are: signs of an imagination more restless, more daring, and more experimental than it is commonly thought to be. Malamud, whose voice was given to him by an ancient culture, will one day be understood to be the most modern of American writers.

Philip Roth

The first thing to observe about Philip Roth's career is a certain relentlessness that bears resemblance to a military campaign. Its basic marching orders are to press forward. From *Goodbye Columbus and Other Stories* in 1959, Roth's literary output has seldom lost a step, and if he has experienced any of the blocks that are common to the writer's trade, they are not visible in his accumulated work, which includes eighteen novels.

To me, the early books have aged badly. Time has dealt harshly with the stories in *Goodbye, Columbus and Other Stories* (1959; Houghton Mifflin, 1989) and the novels *Letting Go* (1962; Fawcett, 1984) and *When She Was Good* (1967; Penguin Books, 1985), because Roth has gone so far beyond them that they now seem like voices from some far base camp of our literature. Certainly there is some clever social satire in "Goodbye, Columbus" and a few of the accompanying stories. It was Roth's verbal agility, his sense of the absurd, his quickness to skewer easy social targets, that occasioned the adulation he received as well as the blows he took from members of the Jewish community who found his irreverence toward his Jewish characters instigation enough to call him to his senses.

Because of this criticism and because of Roth's own fear of remaining merely clever, his next two novels were rather obstinately sober and fussily high-minded. *Letting Go,* in point of bulk (680 pages in the Farrar, Straus and Giroux 1982 edition), compared favorably to Bellow's *Augie March* and Levin's *The Old Bunch.* A book about the failures of love among graduate students, it is long and portentous. *When She Was Good,* a curious novel about the tragic life of a small-town girl, is today the least read and least appreciated of all of Roth's novels.

These books must be regarded as Roth's juvenilia, his investigations into his talent and his discovery that he was not fated to be the Salinger or Dreiser or Henry James of Jewish experience. Roth's own voice did not come easily, and when it came it proved to be irreverent, desperate, satirical, and unsociable. The book in which it made its debut was *Portnoy's Complaint* (Fawcett, 1984), an exhibition so spectacular in both content and voice that it remains, twenty-two years since publication, Roth's signature book. *Portnoy's Complaint* paraded itself as a "breakthrough" novel in which psychoanalysis made its appearance as both setting and viewpoint. It was the opposite of everything the prior two books had aspired to be: raucous where they were controlled, raunchy where they were sober, irresponsible where they were dutiful. Its blend of cultural rebellion, comic mayhem, and textbook Freudianism brought Roth a mass audience and a movie contract, though not the universal approbation of literary critics or Jewish parents. The book was an exorcism, and as exorcisms will, it dealt in excess.

The Breast (1972; Penguin Books, 1985) is a footnote. A Kafkaesque parable of an English professor who is transformed overnight into a man-sized female breast, it reads like a dream that a patient such as Alex Portnoy might have produced for his analysis. Potentially hilarious though the situation was, Roth kept the humor in check and told the story as a case history, albeit a case history narrated by the patient. Roth did not, however, jettison his comic gift in subsequent novels, he just depersonalized it and projected it outward: satirically toward President Richard Nixon, in *Our Gang* (1971), a bitter diatribe on one President Trick E. Dixon, and affectionately toward baseball in a *slapstick noir* about a team without a home field, *The Great American Novel* (1973; Penguin Books, 1985). The former book is scattershot, while the latter book is mayhem in which the baseball evolves into a metaphor for Jewry and the wandering team becomes the diaspora. That the team comes to grief is the historical message of the parable, though along the way there is much of the madcap comedy that was, in the seventies, Roth's trademark.

But *The Breast, Our Gang,* and *The Great American Novel* were diversions from the main line of Roth's writing, the pseudo-autobiographical: autobiographical because Roth's own life has provided its basic situations, pseudo because they were so densely elaborated into "art" that no single image or event is dependably "true." In recent years, Roth would attempt to cast off his art altogether and tell his story directly, in *The Facts* (1988; Penguin Books, 1989) and *Patrimony* (Simon & Schuster, 1991), though neither is an artless performance. Indeed, what often makes Roth's books so fascinating is the tension between confession and craft that keeps us wary of Roth's cat-and-mouse game with the truth, and with us.

In my estimation, *My Life as a Man* (1973; Penguin Books, 1988) remains Roth's best novel, in part because it is abundant in social manners and in part because the counterpoint of life and art is cleverly built into the book's structure. A novel about the marital misadventures of a novelist, it contains "useful fictions," the writer's own efforts to turn his marriage into fiction, plus a long coda entitled "My True Story." The book approaches the question of truth through theme and variations, making it plain one's "true story" need be no truer than one's fictions.

If we concede the next novel, *The Professor of Desire* (1977; Penguin Books, 1985) to be an interregnum, then Roth's next major opus is the trilogy of novels that appeared in rapid succession over a period of four years: *The Ghost Writer* (1979; Fawcett, 1982), *Zuckerman Unbound* (1981; Fawcett, 1982), *The Anatomy Lesson* (1983; Fawcett, 1984). We can speak of them together because Roth conceived of them as "Zuckerman variations," as one character calls them. Though there is no continuous narrative that requires us to read them in sequence, they are discrete windows on the life of the novelist Nathan Zuckerman, whose adventures at times parallel Roth's own. All are fables of martyrdom: *The Ghost Writer* a fable of the artist as a martyr to language, *Zuckerman Unbound* a fable of the artist as a martyr to his fame, *The Anatomy Lesson* a fable of the artist as a martyr to his critics.

The martyred artist in *The Ghost Writer* is Nathan Zuckerman, who has outraged his family and community with a short story which hangs family laundry out for public inspection. In his flight from censure, Zuckerman finds brief respite in the home of one E. I. Lonoff, a writer who refuses to be martyred except by sentences. In Lonoff's home, Zuckerman meets a young woman whom he fancies to be Anne Frank, and whose story of escape and flight he freely dreams up. This tinkering with Anne Frank was a gambit that most critics deemed successful, prompting some to proclaim *The Ghost Writer* Roth's most achieved piece of work. Certainly it is a daring conception in which Roth demonstrated that he could hit and sustain new notes, notes of wonder, mystery, and delicate irony.

One admires these books not for their plots or characters, though in *Zuckerman Unbound* Roth invents one Alvin Pepler, who is his most splendid grotesque, but for the delight of watching Roth do his exercises and practice his scales. If ever a writer piped at his ease, surely it is Roth in the Zuckerman trilogy. Published together as *Zuckerman Bound* in 1985 (Farrar, Straus and Giroux, 1985), the novels were given an epilogue, *The Prague Orgy*, in which Zuckerman's trials of personal martyrdom are drowned in the greater martyrdom of a nation, Czechoslovakia. It is a report from Eastern Europe, which Roth has long been scouting, not only as a writer but as the editor of a series for Penguin Books, *Writers from the Other Europe.*

The final Zuckerman novel to date is *The Counterlife* (1986; Penguin Books, 1989), which brings the Zuckerman variations to a furious conclusion with a Zuckerman fugue. In five episodes it counterpoints the lives of two brothers, Nathan and Henry Zuckerman, as they struggle with their heart problems (amorous and medical), their Jewish identities and faiths, and their brotherhood. As in a repertory theater, they trade lives and predicaments as snappily as actors change costumes. An elegant novel, it describes an elaborate counterpoint between the inertia of history and the agility of the imagination, demonstrating that a novel can contradict itself repeatedly and become all the more convincing. Is it any wonder that Roth's last novel to date is entitled *Deception: A Novel* (Simon & Schuster, 1990)? It plays not only with the question of truth and illusion in marriage and love, but also the question of what the writer is doing every time he puts words to paper.

Keeping the counterpoint alive on a larger scale are the recent autobiographical books, *The Facts* and *Patrimony*, the latter a tender story of Roth's father's last year. Indeed in *The Facts*, putatively a straightforward if miniature life story, Roth introduces the voice of a fictional Nathan Zuckerman who, as Roth's kibitzing alter ego, announces at the end that the author has got it all wrong.

After thirty-two years, Roth's career is still evolving, and still astonishing for its variety as well as for its virtuosity. Under its present marching orders, it promises books to come. About all we can predict is that each will be a surprise, since the capacity for surprise has been Roth's patrimony as an artist from day one.

Postwar Potpourri

The years following the war brought Jewish writers into American letters in unprecedented numbers, and novels by, about, and for Jews inundated the markets in a flow that has never stopped. Jews had come of age in American culture, and the children and grandchildren of butchers, grocers, fish peddlers, junk dealers, cutters, pressers, tailors, furriers, and rabbis made their way into the cultural arena by the force of their ambition and the keenness of their intellects. Given the Jewish proclivity for literacy and learning, Jews in any society will aspire to literature when granted the opportunity. The literature they have produced has not been unified in theme or form; they have followed their own paths and obeyed their own muses. From among the hundreds of novels and stories for which these writers are responsible, the best one can do is identify a handful that stand out in one's recollection.

Given the politicized nature of Jewish life everywhere, it is not surprising that some of this literature should be saturated in politics, and of the political novels that bear remembering, I would place E. L. Doctorow's *The Book of Daniel* (1971; Fawcett, 1987) at the head of the list. A fable of the 1950s and the wave of anti-Communism that swept America, it is a fictionalized rendering of the arrest, trial, and execution of Julius and Ethel Rosenberg, told from the vantage point of one of the children. (There is also an actual book by the Rosenberg children, Robert and Michael Meeropol, *We Are Your Sons: The Legacy of Julius and Ethel Rosenberg* [1975; University of Illinois Press, 1986]). It is a novel that links the radical generations of the 1930s and the 1960s through the figure of Daniel Isaacson, whose parents are executed as spies in the 1950s, and who becomes a radical in the 1960s. What saves the book from being just a novel of protest is Doctorow's fascination with Daniel Isaacson's inner life and the psychic disturbances that afflict him as a result of his orphanage. Doctorow's novel is, I would say, the best of the novels to come out of the Jewish-Left fusion, precisely because Doctorow subordinated his political sentiments to his novelist's instincts and allowed the book to resonate beyond the case at hand.

Another political novel that is of continuing historical interest is Lionel Trilling's *The Middle of the Journey* (1947; Harcourt Brace Jovanovich, 1980), in which one of the characters, Gifford Maxim, a blood-and-iron ideologue who has changed ideologies, was fashioned after Whittaker Chambers, whose charge of espionage in the late 1940s against State Department undersecretary Alger Hiss set off one of the most controversial political trials in recent American history. As writing, Trilling's book, a parable of the revolutionary Left in decline, is somewhat wooden, and yet it communicates something of that ideological moment in the postwar era when, to quote Yeats, the best lacked all conviction and the worst were full of passionate intensity.

I do not regard Joseph Heller's celebrated *Catch-22* (1955; Dell, 1985) as the equal of either of these two novels in either style, political savvy, or intellectual sophistication. Its antic tap dance on the tragedy of war gained a certain cachet in the 1960s, when black humor reflected the mood of an anti-war generation. However, when read apart from that context, *Catch-22* seems to be a whimsical and turgid performance. However, Heller's subsequent novel, *Something Happened* (1974; Dell, 1989), a domestic novel about the pressures and insecurities of American middle-class life, is a far better book. Its grinding rhythms and density of specification about daily life among the new suburbanites make it far more politically telling than the gallows humor of *Catch-22,* and it can be read as a fictionalized version of C. Wright Mills's popular sociology text of the 1950s, *White Collar* (Oxford University Press, 1951).

Some noteworthy pieces of shorter fiction can be added to this list. The stories in Tillie Olsen's collection, *Tell Me a Riddle* (1961; Dell, 1989) are not themselves overtly political, though they are the decay products of a Left sensibility in retreat. A novella by a little-known writer, Meyer Liben, entitled "Justice Hunger" strikes me as a subtle portrait of the depressive mental aftermath of thirties revolutionism. It can be found in *Justice Hunger and Nine Stories* (1967; Schocken Books, 1986). Also, Isaac Rosenfeld wrote a brilliant short story entitled "The Party" about the last days of the Trotskyist Socialist Workers Party. It has been reprinted twice, in Isaac Rosenfeld, *Alpha and Omega* (Viking Penguin, 1966), and Mark Shechner, ed., *Preserving the Hunger: An Isaac Rosenfeld Reader* (Wayne State University Press, 1988).

It may be, however, that comic writing, pound for pound, substantially outweighs political writing by Jewish novelists since the war. Philip Roth has always had a comic edge, as have Joseph Heller, Saul Bellow, Wallace Markfield, Stanley Elkin, Bruce Jay Friedman, Mordecai Richler, Alan Lelchuk, and Max Apple. For many of them, the Yiddish theater and the Borscht-belt stage were formative cultural influences. A few representative books in which the reader may catch the flavor of this comedy would include Roth's *Portnoy's Complaint* or *The Great American Novel,* Markfield's *Titelbaum's Window* (Alfred A. Knopf, 1970), Elkin's stories in *Criers and Kibitzers, Kibitzers and Criers* (1966; Thunder's Mouth Press, 1990) or *The Rabbi of Lud* (Scribners, 1989), Richler's *Joshua Then and Now* (1980; Bantam, 1985), and Max Apple's *The Oranging of America and Other Stories* (1977; Penguin Books, 1987). In all of them there is an anarchistic *schadenfreude* that seeks to overthrow every piety, every solemnity, every symbol that in our daily lives we may hold dear. So mutinous and chaotic does this comedy get that Jewish comic novelists might be regarded as revolutionaries who have chosen language as their insurrectionary medium. If they are Marxists, they belong to the Groucho school. Certainly in stable times, their brand of revolutionism has given a lot more pleasure.

Finally, there is the whole middle range of Jewish writing that has not necessarily made a great stir but which has produced over the years some fine books, and for every book I can name here there may be a half dozen others no less deserving that I have yet to read. Some belong to the tradition of the Jewish *Bildungsroman,* the book of growing up and coming of age in America. Herbert Gold's *Fathers: A Novel in the Form of a Memoir* (Random House, 1966); Mordecai Richler's *St. Urbain's Horseman* (Alfred A. Knopf, 1971), E. L. Doctorow's *World's Fair* (Fawcett, 1986), and Alan Lelchuk's *Brooklyn Boy* (McGraw-Hill, 1990) are representative novels on that theme. Otherwise, picking and choosing at random, I'd say, read anything by Harold Brodkey, especially the thick collection of a lifetime of story writing, *Stories in an Almost Classical Mode* (Random House, 1989). Brodkey may be the slowest and most meticulous writer in America, having produced just three collections of stories in some forty years of writing. But he has a delicacy of sensibility and an exactitude of expression that few American writers can match. He is a writer to be read slowly and savored.

I would send you to Leslie Epstein's *King of the Jews* (1979; Summit Books, 1989), a historical novel about the demented patriarch of the Lodz ghetto during the Shoah, "King" Rumkowsky, who played Haman toward his people and fool toward the Nazis, in an apparent effort to buy time for his ghetto and its people. He failed utterly but left behind a legend of rage and confusion, which Epstein captures with great fidelity. Read anything by Mark Helprin, but especially *A Dove of the East and Other Stories* (1975; Harcourt Brace Jovanovich, 1990) and *Ellis Island and Other Stories* (1981; Dell, 1984). And don't miss Art Spiegelman's illustrated book about his father's experiences of the Shoah and life at Auschwitz, *Maus: A Survivor's Tale* (Pantheon Books, 1986), in which the Jews are represented as mice, the Nazis as cats, and the Polish people as pigs. It caused much stir when it first appeared but is considered a landmark publication, now followed by *Maus II* (Pantheon, 1991).

This is not a coherent picture of Jewish literary culture in America, which defies all attempts to see it in a unified way. Like our culture itself, our literature has all the internal schism and complexity that we look for in a rich, diverse, and open civilization, which is what Judea in our time has surely become.

Literature of Aliyah

One might well conclude from all the foregoing that Jewish writing in America has been largely divorced from normative Judaism and from the myths, the lore, and the consciousness of collective destiny that marked Jewish life in the Old Country, until its unity was shattered in the nineteenth century by the Haskalah or Enlightenment. That is a portion of the truth: the Enlightenment has been the main patrimony of Jewish writers in America, and our literature has been one that largely shuns tradition and seeks new horizons of value and experience. "I am an American, Chicago born," boasts Augie March in the auspicious first line of Saul Bellow's novel.

The full story is more complicated. There have been two lines of sentiment in coexistence as, if you like, thesis and antithesis in a great dialectic of Jewish consciousness: the centrifugal and the centripetal, the outward bound and the inward looking, the line of Haskalah (Enlightenment) and the line of Halakhah (Law), the line of universalism and that of particularism. If the outward bound, inaugurated by Cahan, Yezierska, Gold, Fuchs, and Henry Roth, has been the dominant mode of this century, it was because the circumstances of American life have favored it and the laws of literary success have sponsored it. But the other has always been there in the shadow of its twin, biding its time and awaiting circumstances favorable to its reception. Cynthia Ozick's name has been widely associated with this literature, though she is by no means alone.

Before Ozick, Meyer Levin, who kept a foot in both camps, devoted much of his life after the war and the Holocaust agitating for an American literature of Jewish identity. As a journalist, he was with the troops who liberated concentration camps in Poland. After the war he documented, and filmed, the illegal immigration that moved Jewish refugees from Europe into Palestine and eventually broke the will of the British Mandate. See his autobiography *In Search* (1950). His novel about the days of the Yishuv in Palestine, *The Settlers* (1972; Bantam, 1987), might be thought of as his effort to do for Israel what in *The Old Bunch* he had done for Chicago: write a novel of origins. Other writers devoted to Jewish consciousness during the 1920s and 1930s were Ludwig Lewisohn, whose autobiographies, *Upstream* (1927) and *Mid-Channel: An American Chronicle* (1929; Ayer, 1975), are of more interest than his novels, *The Case of Mr. Crump* (1926) and *The Island Within* (1928; Ayer, 1975), and Maurice Samuel, a popular journalist and champion of Jewish causes, whose books about the Zionist movement, the establishment of Israel, and the Yiddish language and literature retain their freshness long after his fiction has gone out of print. See in particular *The Gentleman and the Jew* (1952; Behrman House, 1977), *Harvest in the Desert* (1944; Westport, Conn.: Greenwood Press, 1982), and *The World of Sholom Aleichem* (1943; Macmillan, 1986).

The problem with all three as writers, however, was that they were journalists and advocates first and moved all too easily from advocacy to fiction, employing the latter as an extension of the former. If, in the twentieth century, it is the literature of Jewish universalism that earns so much more cachet among American readers, it is not simply because it arouses less tension and is more easily assimilated by most Americans. It is also, in the main, just better written.

Things are changing, and there are writers devoted to the religious life and national destiny of the Jewish people who are devoted to their craft. Cynthia Ozick is surely the only disciple of Henry James to ever declare for the Jewish Covenant with God, but there are a host of others for whom Jewish identity has been central: the late Edward Lewis Wallant, the late Arthur A. Cohen, Chaim Potok, E. M. Broner, Hugh Nissenson, Anne Roiphe, Rhoda Lehrman, Jay Neugeboren, Susan Fromberg Schaeffer, Tova Reich, Steve Stern, and Rebecca Goldstein, to name but a few. For all, the devotion to Jewish identity has been crucial, and while one would be hard pressed to find a single article of belief uniting them all, their writing constitutes a testament of collective identity, prompting me to call it a literature of Aliyah, to distinguish it from the literature of the Haskalah, to which it is sharply opposed. As the term *Aliyah* suggests, this is a literature of return, since the vast bulk of it is motivated by a desire to be reconnected to Jewish existence by writers who started out as Enlightenment Jews and had to forge a connection on their own. Some of it is conversion literature, which is in itself problematic, since there is no ready-made way to return to customs and beliefs one has never had, and it is often the drama of repossessing a lost history that is enacted in these books.

A recent instance is Anne Roiphe's *Lovingkindness* (1987; Warner Books, 1989), in which a middle-aged Jewish mother, with a secular Left-liberal upbringing, is confronted with a daughter who discovers Orthodox Judaism in Israel, changes her name from Andrea to Sarai, and accepts an arranged marriage to a young man from Detroit who has had a similar conversion. When the young man's parents stage a kidnapping of their son to restore him to "normality," the woman is faced with a choice between her own brand of secular, open-ended Judaism and her daughter's covenanted life. Her decision to make peace with her daughter's life is not so much an endorsement of halakhic Judaism as it is a statement of her own liberal principle: live and let live.

Roiphe's novel calls to mind the Judea chapter in Philip Roth's *The Counterlife*, in which Nathan Zuckerman visits his brother Henry in a fundamentalist kibbutz in Israel. Henry, having taken the name of Hanoch, has apprenticed himself to one Mordecai Lippman, a gun-toting radical settler with messianic plans for the Judea: to drive out the Arabs. Henry has made a fundamentalist conversion; Nathan remains staunch in his diaspora cosmopolitanism. The standoff between the brothers highlights the tension in Jewish consciousness that has been sharpened of late by the reawakening of Orthodox Judaism and prophetic fundamentalism to an eminence undreamed of by the Labor-Zionist founders of Israel.

By no means, however, is the literature of Aliyah necessarily conversion literature. Much of it is an effort to draw upon Jewish myth and lore for an alternative vision of reality, and writers like Arthur A. Cohen, Steve Stern, and Ozick have found ways to reframe biblical and hasidic stories as commentaries on modern problems and events. Cohen, in *In the Days of Simon Stern* (1973; University of Chicago Press, 1987), blends a Messiah legend into an American fable of social mobility, as his would-be savior of the Jews, Simon Stern, is a self-made millionaire who devotes his riches to a compound on New York's Lower East Side, a sort of Third Temple, to house the remnant of European Jews who have survived the Holocaust. The scheme goes badly, the temple is destroyed, and Simon Stern, reflecting on the cyclical nature of history, vows to rebuild it. Stern himself is not just a Jewish philanthropist, he is a *lamed vov zaddik*, one of the thirty-six hidden saints for whose sake the world continues to exist, and his fortunes are being chronicled by a blind scribe, one Nathan of Gaza, who shares a name with the prophet of the false Messiah of the seventeenth century, Sabbatai Zvi. *In the Days of Simon Stern* is an ambitious effort to bring traditional lore to bear on the Holocaust and the theological problem it raises for believing Jews: the silence of God and the tarrying of the Messiah. It is, unfortunately, a dense and difficult book, a philosophical tract strung out along a narrative frame in which there is scarcely a moment of irony or humor or a fresh line of dialogue. However, it did suggest a methodology for Jewish fiction: the mythic or midrashic technique, though its refinement would await more skilled practitioners. For more by Cohen, see especially his novel *A Hero in His Time* (1976; University of Chicago Press, 1987).

More resourceful as fiction, if less ambitious as philosophy, are the stories of Steve Stern in *Lazar Malkin Enters Heaven* (1986; Penguin Books, 1989). Stern, whose injection of visionary moments into common lives recalls the stories of Bruno Schulz, is a miniaturist whose parables of Jewish life in "The Pinch," a Jewish community in Memphis, Tennessee, bring the *shtetl* to the Mississippi and the landscape of Hasidism to the American neighborhood. In the title story, "Lazar Malkin Enters Heaven," the Angel of Death drags Lazar Malkin off into a heaven that looks exactly like a backyard only "sensitive." In "Schimmele Fly-by-Night," a young boy in conflict with his father awakens from his first spree of drinking to find himself borne aloft by birds, as if grubby pigeons might be angels. It is all quite brisk and vivacious if also rather formulaic—yoking ancient and modern to gain perspective by incongruity. But it is a formula deftly applied; here are worlds brought together with charm and brio.

The mythic technique has been exploited most fully by Cynthia Ozick, whose stories and novels since her early confrontation with modernism, *Trust: A Novel* (Dutton, 1983), have been excursions into "the midrashic method," narrative commentary on social situations or holy texts. Since issues of conduct and value invariably occupy Ozick, her fiction has the insistent quality of moral fable and admonition. In a famous manifesto, "Toward a New Yiddish," she argued that the only Jewish literature ever in diaspora that had any staying power was literature that was "centrally Jewish," by which she meant "whatever touches on the liturgical," ("Toward a New Yiddish," *Art & Ardor: Essays* [Dutton, 1985]), and it is plain that she has herself endeavored to be "centrally Jewish" and to create a fiction of liturgical significance.

Much of her best writing is in the short stories and novellas found in three collections: *The Pagan Rabbi and Other Stories* (1971; Dutton, 1983); *Bloodshed and Three Novellas* (Alfred A. Knopf, 1976); and *Levitation* (Dutton, 1983). There one sees the midrashic method in incisive miniature. Sometimes the subject is Jewish life and culture itself, as in Ozick's most famous story, "Envy; or, Yiddish in America" (in *The Pagan Rabbi*) in which the rage and envy felt by a neglected and obscure Yiddish writer toward one who is world-famous in translation is a poignant reminder of one consequence of the Holocaust: the death of Yiddish and the isolation of its writers. That the envied writer, Yankel Ostrover, was plainly modeled on Isaac Bashevis Singer and that the other writer, Edelstein, was a composite of several living Yiddish writers is no small part of the notoriety the story has long enjoyed.

Another story in which the midrashic devices are more apparent is Ozick's modern golem story, "Puttermesser and Xanthippe," in *Levitation.* Drawing upon the legend of the golem created by Rabbi Loew to save the Jews of seventeenth-century Prague, Ozick invents Puttermesser (Yiddish for butter knife), a woman and "an unmarried lawyer and civil servant of forty-six" who, out of frustrated desires and messianic longings, fashions a female golem, Xanthippe, from the dirt around her houseplants. First merely a domestic slave and then a political aide, Xanthippe goads Puttermesser into running for mayor of New York and into thinking of herself as the city's redeemer. Xanthippe, alas, quickly becomes a monster of excess, political and sexual, and must finally be destroyed. The story is a many-layered parable into which we may read a host of morals: power corrupts; "too much paradise is greed" (one of Ozick's own tag lines); keep your appetites on a short leash; pure reason is not enough in human affairs; don't hurry the Messiah. Moreover, there is a morality built into the method itself and its implicit argument that the dilemmas of humankind are unchanging and that Jewish lore and law may still cast light on basic issues of value.

Ozick's problem as a fiction writer is that she places no value upon aesthetic delight; literature for her is a moral form and "with certain rapturous exceptions, literature *is* the moral life" (*Art & Ardor*). She composes homiletic texts with specifically Jewish morals, and on occasion has condemned the "iconic" as opposed to the moral weight of modern writing, even going so far as to call Wordsworth's "Tintern Abbey" Moloch. Gratefully, at times, her instinctual writer's wisdom knows when the prohibition against the aesthetic won't do, and she can write with a combination of ethical assertion and verbal attack that is virtually without parallel in American literature. However, unlike any other major writer in America, she does not define herself as an entertainer, and readers are challenged to take her on her own implacable terms. In particular, the longer fictions make demands on the reader, who is never invited to relax with them. It is said of her books, especially the intricate and overbearing *Trust*, that they reward study more than they reward reading, and while that may be harsh, it does suggest something of Ozick's exacting requirements of her readers.

Two recent novels are cases in point: *The Messiah of Stockholm* (Vintage Books, 1988) and *The Shawl* (Alfred A. Knopf, 1989). The former, a parable on literature and idolatry, features a man's search for the lost manuscript of Bruno Schulz's last book entitled *The Messiah*, which disappeared during the war after Schulz was murdered by a Nazi officer, and his manuscript, left with friends for safekeeping, was lost. It is being sought by one Lars Andemening, a deluded book reviewer living in Stockholm who dreams himself to be the son of Schulz. He is presented with something that purports to be the manuscript by book dealers who may or may not be swindling him, and in a rage he sets the manuscript afire and burns it. The novel is difficult to follow; its plot line as tangled as a bird's nest and as murky as a Swedish fog. What stays with the reader is the lesson: the cost to civilization of all the lost books, the hundreds, perhaps the thousands, that disappeared with the murder of writers. A second, subtler point, has to do with the idolatry of texts. The manuscript is an idol which does not draw Andemening toward God, toward other humans, or toward moral awareness, but only deeper into his delusion of being Schulz's son. It is an icon, a grail, which Ozick has repeatedly warned us against. The very same moral is drawn more painfully in *The Shawl*, in which a Holocaust survivor, Rosa Lublin, has invested all of her life's energy into the shawl of her daughter, who was murdered before her eyes in a concentration camp. Retired in Florida, she is a bitter recluse obsessed with the shawl, which has been left behind in New York. What she must learn is that the shawl, like Andemening's *Messiah*, is an idol that stands between her and life and that in the very act of cherishing the memory of the dead, she has denied the living: herself and those who have attempted to draw close to her.

In spite of, or possibly even because of, her moral demands upon her readers and her insistence that those demands are based in Jewish tradition, Ozick has come to symbolize those pressures in Jewish life that point the way back from the margins toward the center, even if her version of the center may be no less eccentric than anyone else's these days. For that reason, one needs to approach her through her essays, for though she frequently denies that her polemics are in any way guides to her fiction, no reader of her fiction can afford to be in the dark about the morality of reading that she has sought to sponsor in our literary culture at large. For that, see Ozick *Art & Ardor*, cited earlier, and *Metaphor and Memory* (Alfred A. Knopf, 1989). See also the novel not discussed in this essay, *The Cannibal Galaxy* (Dutton, 1984).

This dialectic is far from played out, and there is reason to think that the tension out of which it springs is permanent, a given of the Jewish condition. The Jewish past is too fragmented, too various to ever be put back together into a single tradition. The schismatic is now the normal, and all the old doctrines are in disarray, the doctrines of emancipation as well as those of commitment. For the moment all we can see is that Jewish writers feel more powerfully than ever about their identities as Jews; that for them the search for the way is the way itself and that the tension between their restlessness and their commitment may not only be the root of their literary dynamism but arguably the very essence of the Jewishness they seek.

C H A P T E R   1 5

THE BAR/BAT MITZVAH BOOK

Rita Berman Frischer

As a library professional often asked to recommend books for the emerging adolescent, I am strongly concerned with the growing need for quality Jewish books for this age group. Twelve- or thirteen-year-olds are ready to engage some of the most basic issues of Jewish life and thought. They are developing their critical thinking skills, filtering the outer world through their own growing internal awareness. Because they frequently withdraw while mulling over what is presented, they may evaluate religion by confused criteria or solely by its sometimes disappointing practitioners. Some become disaffected about Judaism without ever sharing their perceptions or clarifying their misconceptions.

The ceremonial act of becoming *bar* or *bat mitzvah* is intended to work *with* these changes, beginning a new, expanded phase of Jewish understanding and responsibility. But in today's world, being called to the Torah at twelve or thirteen often marks the *end* of Jewish active learning for those not in secondary day schools. Grades, extracurricular activities, body changes, emotional confusions, and a myriad of other distractions easily divert many adolescents from further exploration of Judaism just when such insights could deeply affect their evolving sense of self.

The Jewish educational system recognizes this and tries to provide tempting options so teens will stay in structured classes: social programs, speakers, courses in ethics, sexuality, comparative religion, or Hebrew as a language made applicable for high school language credit. But for these youngsters, with or without formal Jewish schooling, there is a further step to take: reading books that can open the door to more mature levels of Jewish concern, understanding, and identification.

Most of the books mentioned here will not be exhaustive studies of belief and observance but *introductions* to Jewish living and literature—first, or maybe second, steps down a path that can take travelers as far as they are willing to go. Because reading levels are variable and levels of maturity unpredictable, I will often indicate throughout the following recommendations which titles I consider books for *now*, meaning those that can be used and enjoyed right away, and others that might best be considered as *bar/bat mitzvah* gifts which are, like children's clothes, big enough to grow into. Such books, while accessible to *advanced* readers in their early and mid-teens, are primarily investments to serve someday as foundations for good home Jewish libraries.

The "Bar/Bat Mitzvah Book" Itself

A bar/bat mitzvah book is usually an anthology of fact and fiction, chosen to provide present satisfaction and future challenge to the reader. Few such collections, however, are in print. Abraham I. Katsh's collection *Bar Mitzvah Illustrated* (Shengold, 1976), however, has been around thirty-five years. It is more informational than literary, presenting the history and customs of becoming *bar mitzvah* along with an overview of the holidays and basic precepts of Judaism.

The Bar Mitzvah Book, edited by Moira Paterson (Praeger, 1975), was definitely intended as a resource for the future and should be reprinted. An unusual, almost experiential book, profusely illustrated with many color plates, its chapters by different authors, writing about history, mysticism, law, philosophy, heroes, and martyrs, vary in age appeal. Until someone reissues this, look for it in bookshops or libraries.

A brief and readable book, designed for anyone from ten up, Bert Metter's *Bar Mitzvah, Bat Mitzvah: How Jewish Boys and Girls Come of Age* (Clarion Books, 1984) addresses itself directly to the young reader, giving history and facts

surrounding the ceremony, including some understated comments on past rabbinic reaction to excessive celebrations. The remembrances of a number of well-
known Americans include not a single theme party but emphasize instead the
sense of accomplishment and solemn meaning.

Bar and *bat mitzvah* are sometimes used in young people's fiction as pivotal
events, building character while advancing plot. Many of these novels are also
readable by youngsters one or two years younger than the requisite age of passage.
Of the fiction in print about *bar mitzvah*, Barbara Cohen's *King of the Seventh
Grade* (Lothrop, 1982) is still a favorite though its theme is slightly dated among
Reform Jews since the patriarchal lineage ruling came into effect. Vic, the terror
of the Hebrew School, is shocked the day his divorced parents disclose to him and
the rabbi that his mother never converted. Suddenly, becoming *bar mitzvah*, even
being Jewish, is a matter of choice and Vic, who couldn't wait to escape *cheder*,
finds himself feeling bereft of his identity.

In *Good If It Goes*, by Gary Provost and Gail Levine-Freidus (Macmillan,
1990), David Newman finds that if you are Max Levine's grandson, *bar mitzvah* is
no matter of choice. It's a responsibility that even supersedes Shrimp League bas-
ketball.

Pink Slippers, Bat Mitzvah Blues, by Ferida Wolff (Jewish Publication Society,
1989), has Rabbi Pearlman trying to involve Alyssa in his post–*bat mitzvah* confir-
mation class even though he sympathizes with the time conflicts caused by her
love of dancing and the complete dedication demanded by her ballet teacher. An
example of the Jewish Publication Society's increasingly modern and attractive
list for young readers, this novel would be an especially good *bat mitzvah* gift for
someone who dances better than she reads.

A similarly entertaining book is *Turning Thirteen*, by Susan Beth Pfeiffer
(Scholastic, 1988), in which Becky, having convinced her best friend into a joint
bat mitzvah, one day looks up into Heaven and realizes she doesn't believe in God.
How can she become *bat mitzvah* without believing in God? Rabbi Greenberg, a
woman, comes to the rescue. Though light, the book has something to say to the
recreational reader about Judaism as a religion not only of faith but of action. The
kids sound real and the families are fondly portrayed.

Like Everybody Else (Scribners, 1980) is another *bat mitzvah* novel set in a
recognizable suburban milieu. Barbara Girion's twelve-year-old heroine, Saman-
tha Gold, enjoys being the daughter of a well-known children's author. Then her
mother writes her first book for adults and the New Jersey town they live in turns
upside down. Mom, busy being interviewed by *People* magazine, doesn't have time
to pick the color scheme for Sam's *bat mitzvah* party; the Sisterhood cancels

Mom's speech to protest her "shocking" book. Sam does some serious thinking about what a woman owes her family and herself and decides, in plenty of time for her *bat mitzvah* speech, exactly what a "woman of valor" is today. A funny book that young people love; look for it in gift shop or library.

A personal favorite is a story called "Forgetting Me, Remember Me," in *Two Truths In My Pocket*, a collection of stories by high school librarian Lois Ruby (Viking, 1982). Tracy Lynn is MBD, Minimally Brain Damaged, so her wealthy Texas family assumes she isn't interested in or capable of becoming *bat mitzvah*. However, while they concentrate on the big doings surrounding her brother Alan's upcoming *bar mitzvah* extravaganza, color-coordinating their outfits right down to her father's custom-made Texas boots, only Tracy is interested enough in the religious aspects of the event to insist that she herself take on the mother's

Learning to bind *tefillin*, phylacteries worn during morning prayers, in accordance with Deut. 6:8: "And thou shalt bind them for a sign upon thine hand, and they shall be as frontlets between thine eyes." (Photograph by Maxine Margulies)

"burden" of learning the blessing for the candles. At the *bar mitzvah*, innocently described in ostentatious detail by Tracy Lynn, she triumphantly blesses the lights and vows that if it takes until she's eighteen, with Rabbi Feibush's help, she will become *bat mitzvah* herself.

Bible and Commentary

Since becoming *bar* or *bat mitzvah* is rendered significant by being called to the Torah, basic biblical studies, while they may not be immediately appreciated, are most appropriate gifts. Standard works, of all denominations, are dealt with extensively in other chapters of this book; emphasis is placed here on books which younger readers, unable or unwilling to cope with more sophisticated approaches to text, can handle.

The Torah: A Modern Commentary, by W. Gunther Plaut and Bernard J. Bamberger (Union of American Hebrew Congregations, 1981), is adapted by the Reform movement from the 1962 translation of the Jewish Publication Society, with added cantillation (guides to chanting melody), commentaries, and gleanings from Talmud, Midrash, classical and modern sources. Both it and the new JPS Torah Commentary series, overseen by Nahum Sarna with each volume prepared by a different biblical scholar (Jewish Publication Society, 1989–), are more accessible to young readers than such traditionally comprehensive works as *The Pentateuch and Haftorah*, edited by J. H. Hertz (Soncino Press, 1961).

At present, however, the Reform movement is bringing out a still more modern aid for the *bar* or *bat mitzvah* struggling with interpretation of his or her *parasha* and *haftarah*. The first large-size paperback volume of *A Torah Commentary for Our Times, Genesis*, by Harvey J. Fields (Union of American Hebrew Congregations, 1990), to be followed by the rest of the series, demonstrates a six-step approach: overview, current translation into accessible idiom, themes contained in the text, commentary, amplifications culled from talmudic, midrashic, or other sources, and suggested questions for thought and discussion. *The Rabbi's Bible*, by Solomon Simon and Morrison David Bial (Behrman House, 1966), issued in three volumes (*The Torah, The Early Prophets*, and *The Later Prophets*), is still in print and contains well-organized abridged texts with commentary appropriate for adolescent study.

Hannah Goodman's *The Story of Prophecy* (Behrman House, 1965) may well appeal to youngsters who have spent six months learning to chant the words of one of these prophets. Goodman's excitement over the lives and messages of her subjects is enhanced by drawings, maps, and liberal use of textual excerpts.

The Book of Adam to Moses, by children's author and novelist Lore Segal (Schocken Books, 1989), is in modernized language, illustrated with Leonard Baskin's striking black woodcuts. Segal has drawn from the translations of Martin Buber, Franz Rosenzweig, King James, and Martin Luther and simplified the Bible story for young readers without sacrificing its grandeur. See also her *Story of King Saul and King David* (Schocken Books, 1991).

Showing a feminist approach, *Moses Ark: Stories from the Bible,* by Alice Bach and J. Cheryl Exum (Delacorte Press, 1989), includes thirteen tales, symbolic of Jacob's twelve sons *plus* his often overlooked daughter, Dinah, with several centered on heroic women. The tales are expanded with carefully researched details of the period to interest young readers eleven to fourteen; brief afterwords point up puns and wordplay in the original Hebrew, set context, or explain unresolved details.

Alfred J. Kolatch uses a question-and-answer format to good advantage in *This Is the Torah* (Jonathan David, 1988), considering every aspect of Torah from history and sanctification, through writing and reading, organization, translation, division into weekly and festival reading and *aliyot.* This accessible book "for now" has, in addition to a bibliography and notes, a good index which also qualifies it for the "later" reference shelf.

Jewish Thought – An Introduction

No one is more skeptical than the thoughtful teen just beginning to wrestle with religious doubts. *The Nine Questions People Ask About Judaism,* by Dennis Prager and Joseph Telushkin (Touchstone/Simon & Schuster, 1986), was labeled by author Herman Wouk as "the intelligent skeptic's guide to Judaism" and addresses major questions that young people ask such as "Can one doubt God's existence and still be a good Jew?" The authors discuss the need for organized religion, differences between Judaism and other religions and creeds, the sometimes disappointing schism between religious and ethical practices, and the relationship, actual and potential, between young Jews and their religion. They take a rational, measured, and persuasive approach that can be understood by thoughtful youngsters even in early teens.

Rabbi Milton Steinberg's beautifully written *Basic Judaism* (Northvale, N.J.: Jason Aronson, 1987), lyrical in language and concise in presentation, is often considered the best single-volume work on basic Jewish belief. This brief nondenominational work provides an invaluable overview not just of fact but of intense feeling.

Herman Wouk's *This is My God* (Simon & Schuster, 1986) transmits his religious commitment with a novelist's skill. Without supplying specific guidelines, he offers an inspiring sense of the joy of living a Jewish life. Both of these works call for a certain maturity of understanding in the reader.

The Reform movement's Commission on Jewish Education publishing arm has a very readable text for teens, *Understanding Judaism,* by Eugene B. Borowitz (Union of American Hebrew Congregations, 1979). This book addresses the issues of revelation versus tradition from a values-based approach, balancing its Reform view with Orthodox and Conservative responses by rabbis from those movements.

An even simpler introductory work is *Why Be Different? A Look Into Judaism,* a text by Janice Prager and Arlene Lepoff (Behrman House, 1986), an illustrated paperback that addresses all the basic issues briefly and effectively.

The Big Issues . . . Life, Death, and God

For most modern parents, talking values and ethics may be much easier than talking theology. Teenagers, busily testing family values and rebelling against religious verities, may use strident disbelief to create havoc. Some go to *shul*, grumbling all the way that they're only going to see their friends. Some refuse to go altogether, asserting that since they don't believe in God anyhow, there's no point.

But in what God don't they believe? That's the question raised by *Finding God: Ten Jewish Responses,* by Rifat Sonsino and Daniel B. Syme (Union of American Hebrew Congregations, 1986). Teens will be surprised to find how many Jewish attitudes exist on such basic theological concepts as the nature of God, our knowledge of God, God's relationship with the world and the Jewish people, what God expects from each of us, and why evil exists in the world if God is all-powerful. They may be equally surprised to find that disbelief in a strict biblical or rabbinic God concept does not mean a Jewish model of faith does not exist for them. Philo, Maimonides, or Fromm may provide a theological perspective from which teens and young adults can reflect on Judaism in a whole new light. These brief, well-organized summaries, averaging ten pages each, may motivate youngsters to explore one or more of these philosophies in more detail.

UAHC tackles other difficult issues for young readers. For example, *What Happens After I Die?: Jewish Views of Life After Death* (Union of American Hebrew Congregations, 1990), also by Rifat Sonsino and Daniel B. Syme, presents textual, medieval, mystical, and modern views of Jewish responses to the greatest mystery of all. Also of interest is *The Book of Miracles: A Young Person's Guide to Jewish Spirituality*, by Lawrence Kushner (Union of American Hebrew Congregations, 1987), a sensitive introduction to the sacred and mysterious nature of life influenced by Jewish concepts.

Talmud

While Talmud cannot be overlooked in considering the essence of Jewish thought, even introductory works on Talmud are probably too much for American students unless they are in day schools. However, *When a Jew Seeks Wisdom: The Sayings of the Fathers*, by Seymour Rossel (Behrman House, 1975), a text for thirteen-year-olds and up, imparts the moral values of *Pirke Avot* in a pertinent way and in an absorbing format. *Learn Talmud*, by Jacob Neusner (Behrman House, 1979), is a textbook appropriate for those with at least some background; and *Who's Who in the Talmud*, by Alfred J. Kolatch (Jonathan David, 1981), is a simple reference aid, containing a dictionary of terms related to Talmud and brief biographic entries on Talmudic commentators. *Back to the Sources: Reading the Classic Jewish Texts*, edited by Barry W. Holtz (Summit Books, 1986) is a "later" book giving an introductory overview of Talmud and other basic works and suggesting supplementary reading. Other books dealing with this topic are listed elsewhere in this volume.

Jewish Observance

Judaism is transmitted in many ways: cognitively, through knowledge and study; experientially or emotionally, by sharing pleasurable moments surrounding rituals of traditional observance; and ethically, inculcating a value system rooted in Jewish thought and practice. Bridging the gap between information and observation, noted scholar Louis Jacobs produced *The Book of Jewish Practice*, (Behrman House, 1987) as a companion volume to his *The Book of Jewish Belief* (Behrman House, 1984), a two-volume set for now and later. The earlier large-format paperback explores all the basic precepts of Judaism from belief in God through ethics, the literature, Halakhah (Jewish law), philosophy, Israel, and the Hereafter. The 1987 work on practice moves thought to action, describing customs and ceremonies surrounding life-cycle events and holidays along with many additional insights into ethics and prayer.

As an ongoing guide, Rabbi Hayim Halevy Donin's *To Be A Jew: A Guide to Jewish Observance in Contemporary Life* (Basic Books, 1972) won't entertain thirteen-year-olds but most Orthodox and Conservative rabbis consider it a basic resource for understanding traditional observances and the ideas that have supported them through the ages.

Many young people are not ready for such intellectual consideration of the nature of Judaism. Instead, they can be given books that develop *menschlikeit* (moral character) by encouraging acts of Jewish *tzedakah* (charity) and social justice. Or books can promote in them a sense of community by teaching them how to celebrate the holidays that bind us historically and religiously together. One perennial source for novices *or* those experienced in Jewish practice is a "do-it-yourself kit" of Judaism, *The Jewish Catalog*, compiled and edited by Richard Siegel, Michael Strassfeld, and Sharon Strassfeld (Jewish Publication Society, 1973). Born of the same era and impulses that brought forth the *havurah* movement, *The Jewish Catalog* emphasizes personal and practical aspects of Jewish observance, rather than theoretical or philosophical. Although the bibliographies and resource lists are somewhat outdated, this is hands-on Judaism presented with the enthusiasm and idealism of the time that brought it forth. Each of the three volumes examines different aspects of Jewish life, and the set makes a fine gift.

Early adolescents reading at a less mature level could use *Celebrating Life: Jewish Rites of Passage* (Holiday House, 1984) by Malka Drucker, a thoughtfully arranged and illustrated explanation of the ceremonies involved in Jewish life-cycle events, which includes brief personal statements of the author's sentiments about her faith. Appropriate for readers eleven to fourteen, the approach is egalitarian and the book's usefulness is extended with an appendix, glossary, and index.

Observing through Prayer

Rabbi Hayim Halevy Donin produced another important resource, *To Pray As A Jew: A Guide to the Prayer Book and the Synagogue Service* (Basic Books, 1980), which covers every aspect of *davening* from behavior to the deepest significance of the words being said. *Service of the Heart: A Guide to the Jewish Prayer Book*, by Evelyn Garfiel (Northvale, N.J.: Jason Aronson, 1989), is a welcome reissue of a somewhat more basic guide to the *siddur*, a valuable resource for the years to come.

Seymour Rossel's text, *When a Jew Prays*, edited by Eugene Borowitz and H. Chanover (Behrman House, 1973), is well presented and appropriate for readers ten to thirteen.

Observing through Action

Most teens are stern judges of other people's behavior as they grope for guidelines toward shaping their own ethical code. *A Book of Jewish Ethical Concepts: Biblical and Postbiblical*, by Abraham P. Bloch (Ktav Publishing House, 1984), while definitely an adult book, will be accessible and meaningful to young readers because it is arranged by character traits and cites passages on such topics as anger, curiosity, envy, false impressions, confidence, insecurity, and other emotions teens know well. It offers reassurance that Judaism is a realistic faith, supporting us despite our imperfections while providing guidance toward improvement.

A personal approach to *tzedakah* is put forth by poet Danny Siegel, who believes that each of us can, and should, help mend the world. His works, *Gym Shoes and Irises* (Spring Valley, N.Y.: Town House Press, 1987), *Munbaz II and Other Mitzvah Heroes* (Town House Press, 1988), and more recently *Mitzvahs* (Town House Press, 1990), all offer essays on various topics relating to *tzedakah*. The second title offers profiles of exceptional, primarily unknown people deeply involved in doing good for others; the last displays the power of *mizvot* through still more stories, sources, and examples—personal, individual, and organizational.

The Sages Speak: Rabbinic Wisdom and Jewish Values, by William B. Silverman (Northvale, N.J.: Jason Aronson, 1989), weaves together words and stories of the Talmud, Midrash, and Hasidism to address imeless issues of how we can best demonstrate Jewish values in our daily lives.

Francine Klagsbrun's *Voices of Wisdom: Jewish Ideals and Ethics for Everyday*

The mitzvah of caring. (Courtesy of Dorot, Inc., a not-for-profit community agency serving the home-bound and homeless elderly of New York City)

Living (David R. Godine, 1989), an excellent gift, focuses on the concerns and controversies of modern life while making available centuries of Jewish view-points, arguments, and philosophies. Rabbinic parables, folktales, biblical cita-tions and epigrams deal with family, community, self, and other topics; brief introductions elaborate on specifically Jewish implications.

Observing through Celebration

Abraham Joshua Heschel has written that Judaism may be characterized as the art of significant forms in time, as an *architecture* of time, most of its observances depending on a certain hour of the day or season of the year. Certainly most Jews first approach observance and identity through the festivals. It follows that every young person will benefit from books that make holiday rituals personal, comprehensible, and comfortable to perform.

A valuable bookshelf book, quite philosophical and thoughtful, is *The Jewish Way: Living the Holidays* (Summit Books, 1988), by Rabbi Irving Greenberg, whose passionate commitment to Judaism is conveyed in its pages. For the questioning teen, this is an important work by a fine teacher, though probably most appropriate for the advanced child or one with considerable Jewish education but emerging doubts.

An especially appropriate *bat mitzvah* gift for a young woman raised in a traditional manner is *How to Run a Traditional Jewish Household,* by Blu Greenberg (Northvale, N.J.: Jason Aronson, 1989). A warm and engaging modern Orthodox woman's view of all the minutiae of Jewish everyday life, special life-cycle events, and the holidays, the work includes straightforward discussion of the changing role of women in Orthodox Jewish life.

The Philip Goodman "Jewish Holidays" anthologies (Jewish Publication Society, 1949–76) on the various holidays are standard works, useful and varied in content. A more contemporary look is found in Dalia Hardof Renberg's *The Complete Family Guide to Jewish Holidays* (Adama Books, 1985). Illustrated with photographs and line drawings, it includes diagrams for *sukkah* building and crafts, recipes, side-bar columns with supplementary information, an index, and even a Hebrew alphabet in print and script.

Other attractive and useful books on Jewish holidays are *Celebration—The Book of Jewish Festivals,* edited by Naomi Black (Jonathan David, 1989), and *The Jewish Holidays: A Guide and Commentary,* by Michael Strassfeld (Harper & Row, 1985). The first, noteworthy for its beautiful layout and color plates, combines explanatory text, stories, poetry, music, recipes, and crafts to provide an impressive *bar* or *bat mitzvah* gift book. There are no blessings to aid observance, however, and no index to promote use as a reference.

Strassfeld, an editor of *The Jewish Catalog,* is more thorough in *The Jewish Holidays.* Chapters divided by specific holidays or time periods cover history, ritual, suggestions for contemporary observances, and discussions of key themes or issues raised by the holiday. Remarks by contemporary commentators serve as *derash* or supplemental interpretations, expanding the author's comments with varied impressions and thoughts. A schedule of Torah readings, blessings for all occasions (only in Hebrew), a glossary of terms, and a calendar of Jewish festival dates through the year 2000 are included. A book for browsing now, for serious use in the future.

For more immediate use and easy reading, authors Miriam Chaikin and Malka Drucker have each written several thorough and appealing books on individual holidays for readers ten and up. Chaikin's titles (published by Clarion Books) are *Light Another Candle: The Story and Meaning of Hanukkah* (1987); *Make Noise, Make Merry: The Story and Meaning of Purim* (1986); *Shake a Palm Branch: The Story and Meaning of Sukkot* (1986); and *Sound the Shofar: The Story and Meaning of Rosh HaShanah and Yom Kippur* (1986). She also wrote *The Seventh Day: The Story of the Jewish Sabbath* (Schocken Books, 1983), illustrated by David Frampton's dramatic woodcuts.

Drucker's titles (published by aptly named Holiday House) include *Hanukkah: Eight Nights, Eight Lights* (1980); *Shabbat: A Peaceful Island* (1983), and *Sukkot: A Time to Rejoice* (1982). Her *Passover: A Season of Freedom* (1981) has gone out of print but may still be available in gift shops and certainly in Jewish or public libraries.

The History of Our People

The history of the Jewish people is a sweeping panorama of ups and downs, of moral victory and political defeat, of religious power and physical powerlessness. Part of the challenge of introducing young people to Jewish history is to avoid presenting it as one catastrophe after another. Adolescents want to be winners; even the most compassionate and sensitive will be hesitant about identifying with perennial victims. There is more to Jewish history than Holocaust and the grandeur should be included with the heartbreak.

Novelist Howard Fast long ago wrote a very readable overview of Jewish history, *The Jews: Story of a People* (Dell, 1982), which remains an exciting and pleasurable way to introduce adolescents to a four-thousand-year epic. Whatever the work may lack in concentrated scholarship, it more than compensates for in teen appeal and passion. Another Fast work of historical significance is *My Glorious Brothers* (Hebrew Publishing Co., 1977), an engrossing novel about the Maccabees that brings alive the events and characters of the Maccabean revolt against Syria and Hellenism. Far less literary, but well researched and presented is a little-known novel, *Heroes of Hanukkah*, by Donald Lieberman (Ktav Publishing House, 1980), another fictionalized version but this one is easier reading, concentrating less on characterization and more on military strategy and excitement.

Heritage: Civilization and the Jews, by Abba Eban (Summit Books, 1986), produced in connection with a nine-part television series, is one man's view of Jewish history but provides a survey that teens could supplement by viewing the tapes if available. David Bamberger has adapted another of Abba Eban's histories, *My People* (Random House, 1969), into a two-volume textbook set, *My People: Abba Eban's History of the Jews* (Behrman House, 1978–79), which presents a clear account of Jewish history from ancient times to the date of publication. Watercolor drawings, photographs, and maps make it more attractive than the term "textbook" would imply.

Bernard Bamberger's *The Story of Judaism* (Schocken Books, 1964) is a standard introduction, updated, as is Leo Trepp's *History of the Jewish Experience: Eternal Faith, Eternal People* (Behrman House, 1973), a textbook originally titled *Eternal Faith, Eternal People: A Journey into Judaism, Old and New Worlds.*

The path of Jewish settlement and migration twists and turns, influenced by and influencing world history. Whether in Europe, the Middle East, or the Ottoman Empire, Jewish presence can be noted by works of fact, fiction, and biography. Most prevalent are works on European Jewry. For example, Milton Meltzer

Across the generations. (Photograph by Erich Hartmann. Courtesy of Dorot, Inc.)

used diaries, letters, documents, news stories, memoirs, and other primary sources to describe this vanished way of life in *World of Our Fathers* by Irving Howe (Schocken Books, 1989). However, the past few years have seen an increase in books on Sephardim and in fiction on Jews in other lands as American publishers discover authors in English-speaking countries like Australia and South Africa and translate more works from Israel and elsewhere.

American Jewry

In America, young Jews are assimilating rapidly now that the outside world no longer defines their Jewishness for them by excluding them from the mainstream. More than ever, it is essential that they be helped to understand their place in American life *as Jews* if they are to preserve Jewish identity. Questions arise: What is an American Jew? How American? How Jewish? And there are other questions: How have our people contributed to the growth and well-being of this country? Have we been accorded our place in the history books and if not, why not?

Questions touching on identity are deeply personal. No adolescent wants to be different without good reason, so these issues need to be pondered honestly and discussed openly with children as they mature. Since most of the books dealing with the Jewish experience in America are for adults and not young readers, it will take some effort to supply resources for teens studying history in school and wondering where the Jews fit in.

Prolific Milton Meltzer followed up *The Jewish Americans: A History in Their Own Words, 1650–1950* (Crowell, Jr. Books, 1982,) with *The Jews in America: A Picture Album* (Jewish Publication Society, 1985). The former presents brief, informative introductions and first-person accounts taken from letters, journals, diaries, autobiographies, speeches, and other documents to establish the Jewish presence in America as one of personalities as well as facts. The latter, a combination of a hundred black-and-white photographs with Meltzer's engrossing narrative, uses fewer direct quotes but its well-chosen and well-organized pictures make it equally absorbing.

In 1992, we celebrate five hundred years since Columbus's discovery, and many books will mark that occasion. Norman H. Finkelstein has written about a less-trumpeted aspect of that eventful year. *The Other 1492: Jewish Settlement in the New World* (Scribners, 1989), for readers ten to fourteen, tells about the expulsion of Sephardic Jews and the eventual migration of a small group, in 1654, to New Amsterdam where they became the New World's first Jews.

Many books exist about immigrants settling in New York and other points east, but Kenneth Libo and Irving Howe, authors of *How We Lived* (Jewish Publication Society, 1979), left the Lower East Side to acknowledge the Jewish role in the westward expansion of America. For kids who hanker for open spaces, *We Lived There Too: In Their Own Words & Pictures—Pioneer Jews and the Westward Movement of America 1630–1930* (St. Martin's/Marak, 1985), lively with first-person sources both humorous and touching, opens up the Wild West as an unexpected home for wandering Jews, whether Sephardic, central European, or eastern European.

Another look at the westward movement is *Pioneer Jews: A New Life in the Far West* by Californians Harriet and Fred Rochlin (Houghton Mifflin, 1986). Lively anecdotes and generous illustrations add to its readability now; a careful index and extensive bibliography add to its usefulness later.

A large gift book, Linda Gutstein's *History of the Jews in America* (Chartwell Books, 1988), gives an overview of Jewish life in America. Besides many black-and-white illustrations, three sections of fine color plates show places reflecting Jewish presence, the works of Jewish artists, and some of the many Jewish celebrities who helped shape American culture.

Biographies are an excellent way to show the contribution that Jews have made to American life. Dutton has been publishing Jewish biographies for readers twelve and up in recent years. Figures in American history are *I Lift My Lamp: Emma Lazarus and the Statue of Liberty*, by Nancy Smiler Levinson (Dutton, 1986), and *A Justice for All the People: Louis D. Brandeis*, by David C. Gross (Dutton, 1987).

A slim paperback, *Dakota Diaspora: Memoirs of a Jewish Homesteader*, by Sophie Trupin (University of Nebraska Press, 1988), offers a moving first-person memoir of an ordinary pioneer based on the author's poignant recollections of her European family's displacement from a bustling *shtetl* to a sod house in the cold, lonely, and desolate Dakotas. No Lower East Side nostalgia here; just the bewilderment, courage, and determination of a different kind of Jewish immigrant.

Another biography is of a Jew whose legacy to America shows up more visibly in a teen's daily life than any I could mention, whatever their important contributions to moral and political causes. In Elizabeth Van Steenwyk's *Levi Strauss: The Blue Jeans Man*, for ages ten to fourteen (Walker and Company, 1988), a Jewish peddler's trip west during the Gold Rush was destined to change the clothing habits of generations yet to be born and to establish an American institution, blue jeans. Levi Strauss also became one of the most generous and civic-minded men of his day, whose values wear as well as his pants and his name.

Holocaust

While the Holocaust is an important part of history, teens often resent the message that it forms the central shaping event of our identity. Reading about the events of this century can raise compassion and determination to fight against evil; however, care must be taken that the image of the Jew as passive victim does not backfire and turn adolescents, eager for self-determination, away from Judaism.

A Nightmare in History: The Holocaust 1933–1945, by Miriam Chaikin (Clarion Books, 1987), a well-written, well-organized study, is recommended by the publisher for readers ten and up but, even though chapters on the camps are not as powerful as those in the Rogasky book below, it seems more suited to twelve-year-olds up. A very good introductory section on the history of anti-Semitism, a moving chapter on the Warsaw Ghetto uprising, and an excellent book list are some of the features of this work by an author who, in 1985, won the Sydney Taylor Body-of-Work Award from the Association of Jewish Libraries.

Smoke and Ashes: The Story of the Holocaust, by Barbara Rogasky (Holiday House, 1988), is a powerful examination of the workings of the Holocaust. It looks without blinking at the Nazi leaders and their machinery, using carefully chosen quotations and meticulous background detail to bring the bureaucratic aspects of genocide into focus. This author's style is controlled but her very economy has impact. She speaks of the indifference and inaction of the Allies and wrestles with the fundamental problem of human evil in a chapter titled "Is the Holocaust Unique?" From the acts of heroic non-Jewish rescuers to the punishment meted out to war criminals, Rogasky recounts the events of the Holocaust and ends by showing evidence that the seeds of hate still lie buried in the warm earth of many countries around the world.

For immediacy and the shock of recognition, *We Remember the Holocaust*, by David Adler (Henry Holt, 1989), is a moving and personal work for readers twelve and over. Some memories are by those who were only eight or nine at the time; pictures of the speakers at the ages they were during the war are incredibly moving. Skillful in organization and eloquent in arguments against blind hatred, unthinking indifference, and inhumanity, Adler's work looks unblinkingly at cruelty and death, but continues beyond it to affirmation and life.

Older books of great importance to young people are *They Fought Back: The Story of the Jewish Resistance in Nazi Europe,* edited and translated by Yuri Suhl (Schocken Books, 1975), and *Blessed is the Match: The Story of Jewish Resistance,* by Marie Syrkin (Jewish Publication Society, 1977). In direct contradiction to those historians who claim little resistance on the part of the Jews, these collections present sometimes first-hand accounts of fighting back, from sabotage to armed revolt. Books like *Hannah Senesh—Her Life and Diary* (Schocken Books, 1973), with its image of the heroic poet who gave her life fighting for freedom, should allay teen distress or contempt over the concept of Jew as sheep.

When Jews could not fight back, they sometimes found help through the moral strength of those we have come to know as Righteous Gentiles. Miep, in *Diary of a Young Girl* by Anne Frank (Pocket Books, 1990), is such a one. In *Rescue: The Story of How Gentiles Saved Jews in the Holocaust* (Harper & Row, 1988), author Milton Meltzer presents the opposite side of the story that he told in a prize-winning earlier book, *Never to Forget: The Jews of the Holocaust* (Harper & Row, 1976), this time citing dozens of examples of human decency and courage.

Reference Aids in History

The Young Reader's Encyclopedia of Jewish History (Viking Kestrel, 1987), a basic reference work on history for readers twelve and up, can be a good starting point, and Nicholas de Lange's *Atlas of the Jewish World* (Facts on File, 1984) would be a valuable adjunct to reading in Jewish history. For a chronological approach, *The Jewish Time Line Encyclopedia: a Year-by-Year History from Creation to the Present,* by Mattis Kantor (Northvale, N.J.: Jason Aronson, 1989), traces major movements in Jewish history, opening each chapter with a chronology and list of major figures before proceeding to a year-by-year summary of events, major publications, deaths, and catastrophes (which, unfortunately, predominate). The secular year is also given.

For Jewish events in context, turn to *Encyclopedia of Jewish History: Events and Eras of the Jewish People* (Facts On File, 1986), in which essays, detailed text, and many small, colored pictures demonstrate the interaction of world developments and Jewish history.

The World of the Bible for Young Readers, by Yair Hoffman (Viking Kestrel,

1989), is an oversize work showing Jews and those amongst whom they lived from 2000 B.C.E. to the third century C.E. Insets, color photographs, maps, charts, and drawings add interest to this good gift book.

Women in Judaism

If young Jews in America have trouble defining themselves, that difficulty is often compounded for girls. In some congregations, girls are not called to Torah or counted in a *minyan*; in others, a girl will wear a *tallis* and take full part in Jewish observance. In some circles, they marry at eighteen and rear many children; in others, they are expected to have more degrees than offspring. The role of women in Judaism has been, and continues to be, a topic of debate, and should be of concern to young men as well as to young women.

A *bat mitzvah* gift which links women with this search for self and meaning is a large pictorial work, *The Invisible Thread: a Portrait of Jewish American Women* (Jewish Publication Society, 1989), with photographs by Lori Grinker and personal interviews by Diana Bletter. Bletter interviewed women of many ages and degrees of observance, all of whom—whether ambivalent or involved—sensed a connection, an "invisible thread," tying them to Judaism. Artist or sociologist, in New York or the Deep South, each is shown as trying, in whatever way suits her best, to achieve "tikkun olam," the repairing of the world.

Such Jewish women are not new to our history, but as Sondra Henry and Emily Taitz found, they are seldom familiar to us. Henry and Taitz first published *Written Out of History: A Hidden Legacy of Jewish Women Reealed Through Their Writings and Letters*, rev. ed. (Biblio Press, 1990) to define Jewish women, through their own words, as a vital force in the life of the Jewish people. Historical reports, court proceedings, and letters show women filling a multitude of valuable and sometimes surprising roles. The authors use textual study to raise issues of how much of women's role in Judaism is law and how much simply outworn custom.

In 1981, Blu Greenberg, Orthodox author, wife, and mother of five, wrote *On Women and Judaism: A View from Tradition* (Jewish Publication Society, 1983). This important "for later" book combined feminist thought with love of tradition, admitting the problems but stating unequivocally that there are "both precedent and process within the Jewish tradition for bringing women to a position of full equality."

America and I: Short Stories by American Jewish Women (Beacon Press, 1990) is edited and introduced by Joyce Antler and includes stories by twenty-three of the twentieth century's best women writers, all expressing a woman's view of the American Jewish experience.

Israel

In spite of political and military fireworks in the Middle East, Jewish students yearly make pilgrimage to Eretz Yisrael. For many families, the link to Israel provides a major source of Jewish identity. Books on the Promised Land are important, therefore, in encouraging Jewish awareness. Often the books given for *bar* or *bat mitzvah* are pictorial and examine only limited aspects of the country's complex cultural and political life; choose carefully if you hope to show the diversity of the Israeli people and the harsh realities of life in the Promised Land.

The People and the Past

As an introductory reference work, Harriet Sirof's *The Junior Encyclopedia of Israel* (Jonathan David, 1980), with its concise entries, generous cross-indexing, and over two hundred photos and illustrations gives a clear picture of Israel, new and old. An update would be useful, but with events as they are in the Middle East, it would probably be obsolete before it came off the press.

Reading biographies of Israeli figures is a wonderful way to learn about the events and the nature of Israel, and many are available. For example, Franklin Watts has a school-oriented Impact Biography Series which includes a biography of Golda Meir by Mollie Keller (1983), as well as biographies of Theodor Herzl (1987) and Anwar Sadat (1982.) These are all thorough and well illustrated.

Three biographies in the Dutton Jewish Biography Series deal with Palestine before it became Israel. *Eliezar Ben-Yehuda: The Father of the Hebrew Language*, by Malka Drucker (Dutton/Lodestar, 1987), is the story of the man who resurrected Hebrew as the people's language; *A Spy for Freedom: The Story of Sarah Aaronsohn* (Dutton/Lodestar, 1984), by Ida Cowen and Irene Gunther, tells an exciting true story of love and espionage in Palestine during the days of World War I; and *Daughter of My People: Henrietta Szold and Hadassah,* by Hazel Krantz (Dutton/Lodestar, 1987), presents an uncritical look at Szold, who for forty years gave unstintingly of herself to Hadassah, the medical needs of Palestine's poor, and the problems of Youth Aliyah refugees during the Nazi regime. Jewish Publication Society's new biography series introduces a central figure in Zionism in *Theodor Herzl: The Road to Israel* (Jewish Publication Society, 1988) by Miriam Gurko.

In a much more difficult work, Chaim Herzog, president of Israel, approaches Jewish history through the stories of exceptional men and women in *Heroes of Israel: Profiles of Jewish Courage* (Little, Brown, 1989). From Joshua, Deborah, and Judah Maccabee through Joseph Trumpeldor, Hannah Senesh, and Yonatan Netanyahu, killed at Entebbe, these figures are intended as examples for those fighting for Israel's freedom today.

A diversity of Jews from all over the world have come to Israel and their stories have been told in fact and fiction. The rebirth of Israel came to life for many people when they read *Exodus,* by Leon Uris (Bantam, 1983). The incredible history and significance of this corner of the world was uncovered in James Michener's *The Source* (Fawcett, 1988), which uses the device of an archaeological dig to lay bare century after century of change and challenge. Both offer exciting reading to teen adventure lovers.

A more recent novel for young adults is *The Return* (Atheneum, 1987), by Sonia Levitin, author of many fine children's books. Through careful research, Levitin has re-created the painful lives of Ethiopian Jews, despised by their countrymen as "falashas"—strangers—and driven by their outcast status and their devotion to Judaism to make the long and dangerous trek to Sudan and thence, they hope, to the Promised Land. Levitin's own family fled from Berlin during the Nazi regime, so it is likely her first-hand knowledge of persecution and escape helped engender the true sense of courage, loss, hope, and compassion that come through in this fine book.

The Beauty of the Land

A particularly beautiful illustrated work is *Israel* (Harper & Row, 1988), translated by Philip Simpson from the original Hebrew text by noted author A. B. Yehoshua. Frederic Brenner's marvelous photographs needed no translation.

Faces and places will stay in the reader's memory, and Yehoshua's fine essays are honest and thought-provoking.

Another striking photographic work which offers an equally informational and absorbing text is *To the Promised Land: The Birth of Israel,* by Uri Dan (Doubleday, 1988). Published to commemorate the fortieth anniversary of the Land, this exciting and detailed depiction of the struggle that saw Israel become an independent nation includes many pictures never published before.

Front Page Israel (Salem, N.H.: Ayer) transmits, as the subtitle says, *"Major Events 1932–1978 as reflected in the front pages of The Jerusalem Post."* Giving insight into the events in Europe as seen from Palestine, this is an absorbing work for anyone, twelve to adult, interested in seeing the history of World War II from the vantage point of Eretz Israel.

A different but deeply moving work on Israel was the final work of Gail Rubin, a young American photographer killed on a beach in Israel by terrorists in 1978. *Psalmist with a Camera: Photographs of a Biblical Safari,* published posthumously (Abbeville, 1979), clearly demonstrates Rubin's love for the beauty she found in Israel during her nine years there. Facing each extraordinary photograph is a biblical reference to the flora or fauna depicted and a brief comment by the author. No other work better demonstrates the beauty of the "land of milk and honey" our ancestors entered so many thousands of years ago.

General Reference Works

Many works suitable for a *bar or bat mitzvah* to use now for casual reference and later for more serious research are covered in other chapters of this book and will, therefore, be noted only briefly here or not at all.

Definitely a "now" book, however, is David C. Gross's *The Jewish People's Almanac* (Hippocrene, 1988), described as "an unconventional comprehensive compendium of little-known, fascinating facts and information both upbeat and offbeat." Another such compilation is *The Jewish Directory & Almanac* (New York: Pacific Press, 1987), edited by Ivan L. Tillem. Recently published is Joseph Telushkin's *Jewish Literacy* (Morrow, 1991), which summarizes the "basics" of Jewish history, religion, and culture in short, readable entries.

A source of information arranged by topic and presented in question-and-answer format is Alfred J. Kolatch's *The Jewish Book of Why* (Jonathan David, 1981) and its sequel, *The Second Jewish Book of Why* (Jonathan David, 1985). The first deals exhaustively with customs, ceremonies, and holidays; the second is more philosophical and sociological in nature, exploring questions about Jewish identity, relationships with non-Jews, marriage, theology, women's roles, and some ethical dilemmas resulting from developments in modern medicine and technology. Notes lend authority to the answers, and indices make the information far more accessible in this nice gift set.

Geoffrey Wigoder's *The Encyclopedia of Judaism* (Macmillan, 1989), a reissue of a standard one-volume reference work, would be a valuable asset to any Jewish home, especially one without the multivolume *Encyclopaedia Judaica*, on which Wigoder was editor in chief. It contains over 1,000 articles and 300 pictures intended to reflect the entire spectrum of contemporary Judaism.

Another work bearing Wigoder's distinguished name is *The Encyclopedia of the Jewish Religion* (Adama Books, 1986), co-edited by R. J. Zwi Werblowsky, which attempts to focus on religious and halakhic terms and concepts, interpreters and arbiters, rather then encompassing the broad range of Jewish culture and history as do most general encyclopedias. Though the nature of Judaism blurs these lines somewhat, this remains a valuable resource for lay readers of all ages.

The Junior Jewish Encyclopedia, 10th ed., edited by Naomi Ben-Asher and Hayim Leaf (Shengold, 1984), is a reasonably priced, clearly written reference for younger readers and would be a good "now" gift.

The Treasury of Jewish Humor, edited by Nathan Ausubel (Evans, 1988), and *The Treasury of Jewish Quotations*, edited by Joseph L. Baron (Jason Aronson, 1985), are classic references frequently given as gifts. *Leo Rosten's Treasury of Jewish Quotations* has been reprinted (Jason Aronson, 1988) and young readers may enjoy Rosten's humorous asides on the joys and torments of language and his vignettes on some of the figures he quotes. A long glossary will help the reader navigate unfamiliar waters.

What You Thought You Knew about Judaism: 341 Common Misconceptions about Jewish Life, by a Canadian Orthodox rabbi, Reuven P. Bulka (Jason Aronson, 1989), is a fascinating compendium of misinformation gently corrected. Though Rabbi Bulka's is a traditional viewpoint and not all his truths will be universally accepted or acted upon, his work provides a gold mine of enlightenment and becomes valuable as a reference work by virtue of its detailed topical index.

Jewish Contributions to Civilization

This is an age hungry for positive role models. Most Jewish heroic figures are not glitzy enough to attract our youth, however, bemused as they are by the hype of media stars, rock concerts, and peep show journalism. It will take a conscious effort to provide books that set forth Jewish values, reflected in lives of worthwhile accomplishment.

A valuable reference work, *The Blackwell Companion to Jewish Culture*, edited by Glenda Abramson (Cambridge, Mass.: Blackwell Reference, 1989), offers brief biographical sketches of figures who have contributed to the arts, literature, language, philosophy, and the social sciences, with criteria for their inclusion being some conscious Jewish awareness, as perceived by the editors. That this issue of Jewishness remains fuzzily defined can be surmised from the title of Molly Cone's *The Mystery of Being Jewish* (Union of American Hebrew Congregations, 1989), in which she ponders "Who is a Jew?" by considering the lives and accomplishments of modern Jews from physicist Rosalyn Yalow to multifaceted Woody Allen.

Great Jews in Music, by Darryl Lyman (Jonathan David, 1986), is a single-volume guide containing over one hundred informative biographical studies and hundreds of additional brief sketches describing the careers and personal lives of selected artists from cantorial celebrities to modern performers. Personalities are included if they were either born of a Jewish mother or converted to Judaism. As in the Cone work above and most such books, this one has some unusual inclusions and exclusions but nevertheless provides good information on its subject for the reader twelve and up.

Jewish humor has a bite and *taam* (taste) all its own. A something-funny-for-everyone book is *The Big Book of Jewish Humor*, edited and annotated by William Novak and Moshe Waldoks (Perennial Library, 1990). Culled from standup comics, novelists, satirists, and journalists, this big book takes on the meaning of life, Jewishness and Goyishness, the Promised Lands of America and Israel, the difficulties of making a living, and even Bible and Theology, providing ample *mishigas* (silliness) without abandoning good taste. Is nothing sacred? Not here. Teens will love it.

A gift offering for the young sports enthusiast is Robert Slater's *Great Jews in*

Sports (Jonathan David, 1983), a complete, concise, and accessible roundup of Jewish athletes from around the world. Another, more recent sports book is *The Jewish Athletes Hall of Fame*, by Buddy Robert S. Silverman (Shapolsky, 1989), which covers only Jewish American sports figures, including owners, managers, and coaches along with the athletes themselves. Though not as well written or wide-ranging as the Slater, it concentrates on Jewish presence in *American* sports and should be warmly received.

The first Jewish player in baseball's Hall of Fame has told his story in *Hank Greenberg: The Story of My Life*, edited and with an introduction by Ira Berkow (Times Books, 1989). A sports figure whose Judaism was *not* incidental, Greenberg tells of the situations he encountered during his career (1933–1947), including prejudice, fights, and the 1934 American League pennant race game scheduled for Yom Kippur.

Darryl Lyman has two additional collections which present problems similar to those in his work on Jewish musicians when it comes to defining Jewishness. *The Jewish Comedy Catalog* (Jonathan David, 1989) has biographical coverage of almost a hundred Jewish comics, from Milton Berle through Woody Allen to Roseanne Barr (!). Some less savory aspects of personal lives may be found among the jokes and photographs and, with rare exception, no point is made of any positive interaction with Judaism; however, the brief historical introduction emphasizes the distinctive nature of a Jewish approach to comedy by even problematic Jews.

Lyman's *Great Jews on Stage and Screen* (Jonathan David, 1987) includes theatrical, movie, and television personalities among its many biographies and thumbnail sketches.

Literature and Folklore

Collections of tales and folklore abound with more published each year. Jason Aronson, Inc., is a publisher particularly devoted to this form: three of this company's titles worth noting are Ellen Frankel's *The Classic Tales: 4,000 Years of Jewish Lore* (1989), Annette and Eugene Labovitz's *Time for My Soul: A Treasury of Jewish Stories for our Holy Days* (1987), and Peninnah Schram's *Jewish Stories One Generation Tells Another* (1987). Other excellent collections are those selected and retold by Howard Schwartz: *Miriam's Tambourine: Jewish Folktales*

From Around the World (Oxford University Press, 1986) and *Elijah's Violin and Other Jewish Fairy Tales* (Harper & Row, 1985). Both are handsomely packaged, give sources for the tales, and have been graced with work by good illustrators, the first by Lloyd Bloom and the fairy tales by Linda Heller.

For teens, folklore can offer a way into the oral tradition of the Jewish people. Folktales capture our deepest fears, hopes, and aspirations, offer mystery and wonder, and introduce heroes such as Elijah the Prophet with his wonderful disguises and miraculous deeds. Elijah, in fact, is the subject of so many tales that professional storyteller Peninnah Schram based her latest collection of tales entirely on him. *Tales of Elijah the Prophet* (Northvale, NJ: Jason Aronson, 1991) contains stories of all complexions, an introductory chapter about Elijah's role in Jewish life and writings, as well as notes on sources and folk motifs, a glossary, bibliography, and index. Howard Schwartz's latest work, done in collaboration with Barbara Rush, *The Diamond Tree: Jewish Tales from Around the World* (Harper-Collins, 1991) is written for younger readers. The stories, each identified by country of origin and enhanced by brief notes at the back, also boast of wonderful illustrations by the award-winning artist Uri Shulevitz and can bridge the gap from the pre-adolescent to the octogenarian.

Most of us never outgrow the urge to hear a story. The dramatic resurgence of interest in storytelling and folk literature in recent years builds on a long Jewish history of learning through the telling of tales. It is an avenue worth exploring far more thoroughly than this brief discussion suggests.

Conclusion

For most American youth today, Judaism has become a voluntary commitment, involving a personal decision that can have tremendous impact on shaping adult life and character. This long-reaching decision should not be made unthinkingly, with prejudice or without knowledge.

Books of Jewish content and import, while offering no guarantees, can provide roadmaps that direct embarking travelers along the way toward true Jewish identification. Jewish books given to teens may be read cursorily at first, only to be treasured in adulthood and then passed on to a new generation of adolescents yet to come.

INDEX

About the Contributors

Barry W. Holtz is codirector of the Melton Research Center at the Jewish Theological Seminary of America and associate professor in the seminary's Department of Jewish Education. He is the author of *Finding Our Way: Jewish Texts and the Lives We Lead Today* (Schocken Books), and is the editor of *Back to the Sources: Reading the Classic Jewish Texts* (Summit Books).

Lawrence Square Kushner has served as the rabbi of Congregation Beth El of the Sudbury River Valley, in Sudbury, Massachusetts, for the past twenty years. He teaches at the Hebrew Union College–Jewish Institute of Religion in New York City and serves as the rabbinic chairman of Reform Judaism's Commission on Religious Living. He is the author of *The Book of Letters: A Mystical Hebrew Alef-Bait; Honey from the Rock: Visions of Jewish Mystical Renewal; The River of Light: Judaism, Spirituality, Consciousness;* and *The Book of Miracles: A Young Person's Guide to Jewish Spiritual Awareness.* His most recent book is *God Was in This Place and I, i Did Not Know: Finding My Self, Spirituality, and Ultimate Meaning* (Jewish Lights Press).

Everett Fox is associate professor of Judaica and director of the Program in Jewish Studies at Clark University in Worcester, Massachusetts. He is the author of a biblical translation with commentary, *Genesis and Exodus* (Schocken Books).

Eliezer Diamond is assistant professor of Talmud and Rabbinics at the Jewish Theological Seminary of America, and is former director of the Drisha Fellowship Program, an advanced Jewish Studies program for women. He has taught at Yeshiva University's Stern College and at the Reconstructionist Rabbinical College.

Ivan G. Marcus is professor of history and provost at the Jewish Theological Seminary of America. Author of *Piety and Society: The Jewish Pietists of Medieval Germany* (Leiden: E. J. Brill, 1981), he writes on the history of Jewish culture, education, and Jewish-Christian relations, especially in medieval Europe. He is working on an anthropological history of a Jewish child's initiation rite into formal schooling and is editing and translating the medieval Jewish classic *Sefer Hasidim* (Book of the Pietists).

Michael Stanislawski is the Nathan J. Miller Professor of Jewish History at Columbia University. He is the author of *Tsar Nicholas I and the Jews: The Transformation of Jewish Society in Russia, 1825–1855* (Jewish Publication Society); *For Whom Do I Toil?: Judah Leib Gordon and the Crisis of Russian Jewry;* and *Psalms for the Tsar.*

Jonathan D. Sarna is the Joseph H. Beller Braun Professor of American Jewish History at Brandeis University. He previously taught at Hebrew Union College–Jewish Institute of Religion in Cincinnati and directed its Center for the Study of the American Jewish Experience. Among his books are *Jacksonian Jew: The Two Worlds of Mordecai Noah* (Holmes & Meier); *People Walk on Their Heads: Moses Weinberger's Jews and Judaism in New York* (Holmes & Meier); *The American Jewish Experience* (Holmes & Meier); and *JPS: The Americanization of Jewish Culture, 1888–1988* (Jewish Publication Society).

Deborah E. Lipstadt is an adjunct professor of religion and Jewish Studies at Occidental College and the director of research of the Skirball Institute on American Values, an arm of the American Jewish Committee. She is currently writing a book on the Holocaust revisionists, those who deny that the Holocaust happened. She is the author of *Beyond Belief: The American Press and the Coming of the Holocaust, 1933–1945* (Free Press).

David Twersky is the Washington bureau chief and associate editor of the *Forward,* a national Jewish newspaper. He lived in Israel from 1974 to 1986 and has written for the *New York Times, Newsday, Partisan Review, London Review of Books, Tikkun, Dissent, The Nation, Jerusalem Post,* and other publications.

Elliot K. Ginsburg is associate professor of Judaic Studies in the Department of Near Eastern Studies and the Judaic Studies Program at the University of Michigan. From 1982 to 1991 he taught in the Department of Religion and the Judaic and Near Eastern Studies Program at Oberlin College. He has written some fifteen articles and reviews on the Jewish mystical tradition and is the author of *The Sabbath in the Classical Kabbalah* (SUNY Press), a translation of, and critical commentary to, a mystical treatise on Sabbath celebration.

Michael Paley is the director of the Earl Hall Center for Religious Life at Columbia University. He was formerly Jewish Chaplain at Dartmouth College. He is a founder of the Conference on Judaism in Rural New England and of Community

Impact, a volunteer network. He was the founding director of the Edgar M. Bronfman Youth Fellowships in Israel.

Jacob J. Staub is the dean of the Reconstructionist Rabbinical College. He has served as the editor of the *Reconstructionist* magazine (1983–1989) and has chaired the Academy for Jewish Philosophy (1988–1990). He is the author of *The Creation of the World According to Gersonides* (Scholars Press) and the co-author with Rebecca T. Alpert of *Exploring Judaism: A Reconstructionist Approach* (Reconstructionist Press).

Sue Levi Elwell is the founding coordinator of the Los Angeles Jewish Feminist Center of the American Jewish Congress. She is the author of *The Jewish Women's Studies Guide* (University Press of America) and co-author of *Jewish Women: A Mini-Course for Jewish Schools* (Denver: Alternatives in Religious Education, 1986). Rabbi Elwell teaches women's studies at UCLA and serves a congregation in the Los Angeles area.

Alan Mintz is the Braun Professor of Modern Hebrew Literature at Brandeis University. He is the author most recently of *Banished from their Father's Table: Loss of Faith and Hebrew Autobiography* (Indiana University Press) and co-founder and co-editor of *PROOFTEXTS: A Journal of Jewish Literary History*.

David G. Roskies is professor of Jewish literature at the Jewish Theological Seminary of America. He is the co-founder and co-editor of *PROOFTEXTS: A Journal of Jewish Literary History* and is author of two books on Jewish literary responses to catastrophe, *Against the Apocalypse: Responses to Catastrophe in Modern Jewish Culture* (Harvard University Press) and *The Literature of Destruction* (Jewish Publication Society). His volume *The Dybbuk and Other Writings by S. Ansky* will appear in the Library of Yiddish Classics series published by Schocken Books.

Mark Shechner is professor of English at the State University of New York in Buffalo. He is the author of *After the Revolution: Studies in the Contemporary Jewish Imagination: Conversion of the Jews: Selected Essays;* and the chapter on Jewish writers in the *Harvard Guide to Contemporary American Writing*.

Rita Berman Frischer, director of library services at Sinai Temple in Los Angeles, is a reviewer and writer for the Los Angeles *Jewish Journal* and other publications. A frequent judge on children's book award committees, she has lectured on literature for young readers at the University of Judaism, Hebrew Union College, and many other institutions and groups.